THE ARDEN SHAKESPEARE

THIRD SERIES

General Editors: Richard Proudfoot, Ann Thompson,
David Scott Kastan and H.R. Woudhuysen

MUCH ADO
ABOUT NOTHING

THE ARDEN SHAKESPEARE

ALL'S WELL THAT ENDS WELL	edited by G.K. Hunter*
ANTONY AND CLEOPATRA	edited by John Wilders
AS YOU LIKE IT	edited by Juliet Dusinberre
THE COMEDY OF ERRORS	edited by R.A. Foakes*
CORIOLANUS	edited by Philip Brockbank*
CYMBELINE	edited by J.M. Nosworthy*
DOUBLE FALSEHOOD	edited by Brean Hammond
HAMLET	edited by Ann Thompson and Neil Taylor
JULIUS CAESAR	edited by David Daniell
KING HENRY IV Part 1	edited by David Scott Kastan
KING HENRY IV Part 2	edited by A.R. Humphreys*
KING HENRY V	edited by T.W. Craik
KING HENRY VI Part 1	edited by Edward Burns
KING HENRY VI Part 2	edited by Ronald Knowles
KING HENRY VI Part 3	edited by John D. Cox and Eric Rasmussen
KING HENRY VIII	edited by Gordon McMullan
KING JOHN	edited by E.A.J. Honigmann*
KING LEAR	edited by R.A. Foakes
KING RICHARD II	edited by Charles Forker
KING RICHARD III	edited by James R. Siemon
LOVE'S LABOUR'S LOST	edited by H.R. Woudhuysen
MACBETH	edited by Kenneth Muir*
MEASURE FOR MEASURE	edited by J.W. Lever*
THE MERCHANT OF VENICE	edited by John Drakakis
THE MERRY WIVES OF WINDSOR	edited by Giorgio Melchiori
A MIDSUMMER NIGHT'S DREAM	edited by Harold F. Brooks*
MUCH ADO ABOUT NOTHING	edited by Claire McEachern
OTHELLO	edited by E.A.J. Honigmann
PERICLES	edited by Suzanne Gossett
SHAKESPEARE'S POEMS	edited by Katherine Duncan-Jones and H.R. Woudhuysen
ROMEO AND JULIET	edited by Brian Gibbons*
SHAKESPEARE'S SONNETS	edited by Katherine Duncan-Jones
THE TAMING OF THE SHREW	edited by Barbara Hodgdon
THE TEMPEST	edited by Virginia Mason Vaughan and Alden T. Vaughan
TIMON OF ATHENS	edited by Anthony B. Dawson and Gretchen E. Minton
TITUS ANDRONICUS	edited by Jonathan Bate
TROILUS AND CRESSIDA	edited by David Bevington
TWELFTH NIGHT	edited by Keir Elam
THE TWO GENTLEMEN OF VERONA	edited by William C. Carroll
THE TWO NOBLE KINSMEN	edited by Lois Potter
THE WINTER'S TALE	edited by John Pitcher

* Second series

MUCH ADO ABOUT NOTHING

Edited by
CLAIRE McEACHERN

Bloomsbury Arden Shakespeare
An imprint of Bloomsbury Publishing Plc

BLOOMSBURY
LONDON · NEW DELHI · NEW YORK · SYDNEY

Bloomsbury Arden Shakespeare
An imprint of Bloomsbury Publishing Plc

Imprint previously known as Arden Shakespeare

50 Bedford Square	1385 Broadway
London	New York
WC1B 3DP	NY 10018
UK	USA

www.bloomsbury.com

BLOOMSBURY, THE ARDEN SHAKESPEARE and
the Diana logo are trademarks of Bloomsbury Publishing Plc

This edition of *Much Ado About Nothing* first published 2006 by
Thomson Learning Ltd
Reprinted by Bloomsbury Arden Shakespeare 2009, 2011, 2012,
2013, 2014 (twice)

Editorial matter © Bloomsbury Publishing 2007

The general editors of the Arden Shakespeare have been
W. J. Craig and R. H. Case (first series 1899–1944)
Una Ellis-Fermor, Harold F. Brooks, Harold Jenkins and
Brian Morris (second series 1946–82)
Present general editors (third series)
Richard Proudfoot, Ann Thompson, David Scott Kastan
and H. R. Woudhuysen

British Library Cataloguing-in-Publication Data
A catalogue record for this book is available from the British Library.

ISBN: HB: 978-1-9034-3682-0
PB: 978-1-9034-3683-7

Library of Congress Cataloging-in-Publication Data
A catalog record for this book is available from the Library of Congress.

Series: The Arden Shakespeare Third Series

Printed and bound in India

The Editor

Claire McEachern is Professor of English Literature at the University of California, Los Angeles. She has edited *The Cambridge Companion to Shakespearean Tragedy* (2003), and co-edited (with Debora Shuger) *Religion and Culture in the English Renaissance* (1997), as well as five volumes of the Pelican Shakespeare (*1 and 2 Henry IV, Henry V, King John* and *All's Well That Ends Well*). Her other previous publications include *The Poetics of English Nationhood 1590–1612* (1996).

For Warner Mandeville (4.1.267–8)

CONTENTS

LIST OF
ILLUSTRATIONS

GENERAL EDITORS' PREFACE

The Arden Shakespeare is now over one hundred years old. The earliest volume in the first series, Edward Dowden's *Hamlet*, was published in 1899. Since then the Arden Shakespeare has become internationally recognized and respected. It is now widely acknowledged as the pre-eminent Shakespeare series, valued by scholars, students, actors and 'the great variety of readers' alike for its readable and reliable texts, its full annotation and its richly informative introductions.

We have aimed in the third Arden edition to maintain the quality and general character of its predecessors, preserving the commitment to presenting the play as it has been shaped in history. While each individual volume will necessarily have its own emphasis in the light of the unique possibilities and problems posed by the play, the series as a whole, like the earlier Ardens, insists upon the highest standards of scholarship and upon attractive and accessible presentation.

Newly edited from the original quarto and folio editions, the texts are presented in fully modernized form, with a textual apparatus that records all substantial divergences from those early printings. The notes and introductions focus on the conditions and possibilities of meaning that editors, critics and performers (on stage and screen) have discovered in the play. While building upon the rich history of scholarly and theatrical activity that has long shaped our understanding of the texts of Shakespeare's plays, this third series of the Arden Shakespeare is made necessary and possible by a new generation's encounter with Shakespeare, engaging with the plays and their complex relation to the culture in which they were – and continue to be – produced.

THE TEXT

On each page of the play itself, readers will find a passage of text followed by commentary and, finally, textual notes. Act and scene divisions (seldom present in the early editions and often the product of eighteenth-century or later scholarship) have been retained for ease of reference, but have been given less prominence than in the previous series. Editorial indications of location of the action have been removed to the textual notes or commentary.

In the text itself, unfamiliar typographic conventions have been avoided in order to minimize obstacles to the reader. Elided forms in the early texts are spelt out in full in verse lines wherever they indicate a usual current modern pronunciation that requires no special indication and wherever they occur in prose (except when they indicate non-standard pronunciation). In verse speeches, marks of elision are retained where they are necessary guides to the scansion and pronunciation of the line. Final -ed in past tense and participial forms of verbs is always printed as -ed without accent, never as -'d, but wherever the required pronunciation diverges from modern usage a note in the commentary draws attention to the fact. Where the final -ed should be given syllabic value contrary to modern usage, e.g.

> Doth Silvia know that I am banished?
> (*TGV* 3.1.219)

the note will take the form

> 219 **banished** banishèd

Conventional lineation of divided verse lines shared by two or more speakers has been reconsidered and sometimes rearranged. Except for the familiar *Exit* and *Exeunt*, Latin forms in stage directions and speech prefixes have been translated into English and the original Latin forms recorded in the textual notes.

COMMENTARY AND TEXTUAL NOTES

Notes in the commentary, for which a major source will be the *Oxford English Dictionary*, offer glossarial and other explication of verbal difficulties; they may also include discussion of points of theatrical interpretation and, in relevant cases, substantial extracts from Shakespeare's source material. Editors will not usually offer glossarial notes for words adequately defined in the latest edition of *The Concise Oxford Dictionary* or *Merriam-Webster's Collegiate Dictionary*, but in cases of doubt they will include notes. Attention, however, will be drawn to places where more than one likely interpretation can be proposed and to significant verbal and syntactic complexity. Notes preceded by * discuss editorial emendations or variant readings from the early edition(s) on which the text is based.

Headnotes to acts or scenes discuss, where appropriate, questions of scene location, Shakespeare's handling of his source materials, and major difficulties of staging. The list of roles (so headed to emphasize the play's status as a text for performance) is also considered in commentary notes. These may include comment on plausible patterns of casting with the resources of an Elizabethan or Jacobean acting company, and also on any variation in the description of roles in their speech prefixes in the early editions.

The textual notes are designed to let readers know when the edited text diverges from the early edition(s) on which it is based. Wherever this happens the note will record the rejected reading of the early edition(s), in original spelling, and the source of the reading adopted in this edition. Other forms from the early edition(s) recorded in these notes will include some spellings of particular interest or significance and original forms of translated stage directions. Where two early editions are involved, for instance with *Othello*, the notes will also record all important differences between them. The textual notes take a form that has been in use since the nineteenth century. This comprises, first: line reference, reading adopted in the text and closing square bracket; then: abbreviated reference, in italic, to the earliest edition to adopt the accepted reading, italic semicolon and noteworthy alternative reading(s), each with abbreviated italic reference to its source. Conventions used in these textual notes include the following. The solidus / is used, in notes quoting verse or discussing verse lining, to indicate line endings. Distinctive spellings of the basic text (Q or F) follow the square bracket without indication of source and are enclosed in italic brackets. Names enclosed in italic brackets indicate originators of conjectural emendations when these did not originate in an edition of the text, or when the named edition records a conjecture not accepted into its text. Stage directions (SDs) are referred to by the number of the line within or immediately after which they are placed. Line numbers with a decimal point relate to entry SDs and to SDs more than one line long, with the number after the point indicating the line within the SD: e.g. 78.4 refers to the fourth line of the SD following line 78. Lines of SDs at the start of a scene are numbered 0.1, 0.2, etc. Where only a line number and SD precede the square bracket, e.g. 128 SD], the note relates to the whole of a SD within or immediately following the line. Speech prefixes (SPs) follow similar conventions, 203 SP] referring to the speaker's name for line 203. Where a SP reference takes the form, for example, 38+ SP, it relates to all subsequent speeches assigned to that speaker in the scene in question.

Where, as with *King Henry V*, one of the early editions is a so-called 'bad quarto' (that is, a text either heavily adapted, or reconstructed from memory, or both), the divergences from the present edition are too great to be recorded in full in the notes. In these cases the editions will include a reduced photographic facsimile of the 'bad quarto' in an appendix.

INTRODUCTION

Both the introduction and the commentary are designed to present the plays as texts for performance, and make appropriate reference to stage, film and television versions, as well as introducing the reader to the range of critical approaches to the plays. They discuss the history of the reception of the texts within the theatre and in scholarship and beyond, investigating the interdependancy of the literary text and the surrounding 'cultural text' both at the time of the original production of Shakespeare's works and during their long and rich afterlife.

PREFACE

Much Ado About Nothing is a play in part about the informing pressures of community, pressures both constraining and enabling. While I knew that upon undertaking this work I would be engaging with several centuries' worth of editors and editions, and was prepared to be duly humbled, I was less aware of how much I would rely on colleagues yet breathing, and thus how genuinely, and generously, collaborative a process this kind of work can be. My greatest debt is to the Arden general editor Richard Proudfoot, whose careful eye, astonishing breadth and depth of knowledge, and unfailing tact had me convinced that *Much Ado* must be his favourite play as well (except that I suspect all other Arden editors feel the same about his relationship to theirs). Never has so much information been dispensed with such forbearance. I am also indebted to the two other members of the general editorial trinity. David Scott Kastan has been, as ever, the person to whom I can safely address all the really stupid questions; for this, for the invitation to edit, and for his unflagging friendship over the past twenty years I salute him. Ann Thompson offered me detailed guidance at the early stages of the project, and I hope she is pleased with the result. I was also fortunate to have my UCLA colleague Reg Foakes as my associate general editor; this edition was strengthened by his trademark scepticism and my work buoyed by his shared affection for the play. These people have read this work as if it were their own, and saved me from many an error, though probably not, alas, all.

My colleagues in the UCLA English Department have been indispensable sources of obscure references and tidbits for the commentary, as well as tolerant of my urge to explain to them all of their own work as it relates to *Much Ado*. Lowell Gallagher, Debora Shuger and Rob Watson have been most patient. The sage A.R. Braunmuller saved me many a trek to the library; Jayne Lewis read the Introduction in its entirety, and got the jokes. My chair Tom Wortham was incredibly accommodating in matters of scheduling. I am grateful to the university for research funding, which made it possible to hire two terrific research assistants in Claire Banchich and Christina Fitzgerald.

It was characteristic of the genial fates that oversaw the production of this book that Shakespeare Santa Cruz, at the University of California at Santa Cruz, chose to stage *Much Ado* in the summer of 1998. Artistic Director Paul Whitworth gamely invited me to serve as dramaturg despite my never having before seen the inside of a rehearsal room, and I can't wait to go back someday for another play. Professors Audrey Stanley and Michael Warren taught me much about the relationships between text and performance. Director Rick Seer of the University of San Diego more than graciously suffered my presence. I learned a great deal from him and all of his actors, Ursula Meyer and Jamie Newcomb in particular.

Another California institution that made the work of this edition pleasurable as well as possible is the Huntington Library. The staffs of the Reading Room, Reader and Reprographic Services were unfailingly helpful and generous with their time and expertise. I am especially indebted to Director of Research Robert C. Ritchie, who over the years that this work has been in progress has offered material support, workspace and lecture opportunities that furthered its progress immeasurably. On the other coast, the Folger Library was equally helpful when it came to a study of their promptbooks, and Barbara Mowat and Paul Werstine, twin engines of the Folger editions, helped launch this edition with a digitized copy of the Quarto, and shared works in progress with me. In Britain, the collections and staffs of the Shakespeare Centre Library, the Shakespeare Institute Library, the library of Cambridge University and the British Library were indispensable resources.

The expertise of the team at Thomson puts all other publishing houses to shame. Jessica Hodge was a constant and patient source of encouragement in all the years when this work was under gestation. Margaret Bartley has overseen its completion admirably, and Jane Armstrong has coordinated its production with good humour and good advice. Giulia Vincenzi and Philippa Gallagher were terrific when it came to hunting photographs and their photographers. The practical support of Fiona Freel was indispensable. My greatest debt is to my copy-editor, Hannah Hyam, without whose painstaking attention, care and good sense this book simply would not exist. As the final stages of this book's production coincided with a complicated pregnancy followed by a lively infant, all these women are to be especially commended for their flexibility and patience in working with a sleep-challenged editor.

Other people helped me by sharing unpublished work, discussing individual points, accompanying me to productions of the play, sharing notes on productions they had witnessed, and by offering support and encouragement. David Bevington, Juliet Fleming, Penny Gay, Phyllis Gorfain, Victoria Hayne, Jonathan Hope, Gordon McMullan, Pamela Mason, Barbara Ramsey and Jim Shapiro are among them, as are my parents and siblings.

Between the beginning and the completion of this work I acquired a family; I am grateful to my daughters Helena and Marielle for napping when the edition needed it most, and to my stepson Justice, who tells his teachers that his stepmother cleans the house for a living. This book is dedicated to my husband Chip Mandeville, who would challenge any number of Claudios if I needed him to.

Claire McEachern
Los Angeles, California

INTRODUCTION

Much Ado About Nothing is best known for the 'merry war' between one of its two couples, and an oxymoron could also describe this comedy's identity as a whole. Shakespeare offers a play of light and dark, of romantic union wrested from fear and malice, and of social harmony soothing the savagery of psychic violence. *Much Ado* claims one of Shakespeare's most delightful heroines, his most dancing word-play, and the endearing spectacle of intellectual and social self-importances bested by the desire to love and be loved in return. It is undoubtedly the most socially and psychologically realistic of his comedies, in its portrait of the foibles and generosities of communal life. Shakespeare represents a world governed, even poisoned, by male rivalry, in which conventions of gender and status shape emotional attachments, in which men and women fear each other, and in which only the most accidental of providences can save an innocent woman from the effects of slander, and a man from death by combat. The battle of the sexes it portrays, for all its lighthearted wit, risks real consequences and casualties.

This dual identity appears in *Much Ado*'s double life in the theatre and in scholarship. The play has two pairs of lovers, with two different, though perhaps equally rocky, paths to the altar. One pair have been the darlings of the theatre, the other, a target of scholarly scrutiny. *Much Ado* has thrived on the stage ever since its inception. This popularity has chiefly been credited to the combatants in the 'merry war', Benedick and Beatrice, whose sparring and eventual capitulation to each other has kept people laughing and weeping for centuries. Scholarship, on the other hand, has tended to concentrate on the darker elements, and hence on the Hero and Claudio plot. Thus, on the page the play

1

has largely come in for a censorious treatment, either (in the past) for its violation of the decorums of comedy and character alike, or (more recently) for its portrait of patriarchy, the success of whose artistic realization is overshadowed by critical distaste for the object portrayed. Advocates of the play's power to delight hear in Shakespeare's title a throwaway catch phrase, his lighthearted, shrugging comment on the ultimate triviality of human resistances to going the marital way of the world; the more sceptical ear registers, as the Elizabethan pun would have (*nothing* was slang for the female genitalia, and was pronounced the same as 'noting', which could mean 'noticing' or 'knowing'), the adverse power of communal opinion over individual identity, and the lethal seriousness of the matter of female chastity to the male imagination.

An edition needs to do justice to both the theatrical and the scholarly strands of the play. Yet editing is, by the nature of the medium, more pitched to the latter. It is difficult to reproduce the experience of the stage in print, though attempts are made throughout this Introduction and the commentary to provide instances of staging choices. But the stage is best experienced from a centre seat in the orchestra section, especially if it's a comedy, since nothing ruins a joke more than trying to explain it, particularly with footnotes. Effervescence does not improve with explication. Copious guidance on historical materials, or the intellectual traditions behind Shakespeare's choices, can often estrange, as can attention to conventions of genre, word–play and semantic resonances perhaps ringing in Shakespeare's ears but not necessarily available to the modern or even early modern theatre-goer. This edition treats the play as a literary text, not a script; actors and directors must make choices, but editors get to multiply them, albeit within parameters set by history and cultural moment. The risk of such an assignment (especially in this edition, attentive, as is the play, to the struggles between the sexes) is being charged, like many feminists, with having no sense of humour, let alone a sense of theatre. On the other hand, actors and directors (if not always theatre-goers) must also begin by reading the text.

Ultimately, the position of this edition (for editions, too, have positions, even though the pretence of the convention is neutrality) is that the two sides of this play – its light and its dark, sometimes understood as the theatrical and the scholarly – require each other. If Benedick and Beatrice please, it is not in spite of the universe in which they find themselves, but because the triumph of their union is wrought through and against near-tragedy. We treasure them in part because of what they hold at bay. If the ultimate pairing of Claudio and Hero challenges our expectations of comic deserts, it is because Shakespeare offers another vision of the human power to change and to choose. The play's distinctive mixture of delight and pathos depends upon this symbiosis.

Another premise of this edition, and one that governs the organization of this Introduction, has to do with the matter of temporal location (for editions, too, are of their moment, which is why editors are always producing yet more of them). This premise is that *Much Ado About Nothing* is also produced in and of time, built in and of its original culture, and a contributor to the subsequent ones in which it has been experienced. I thus begin with an extended discussion of what are traditionally considered Shakespeare's sources, but also other literary contexts not so usually considered sources – from cuckold jokes to conduct books – which inform the ideas and identities of this play. Some of these, as is conventional in source study, precede the 1598 date of this play; some of them follow it. Some contexts are cited by the play; some indicate the larger discursive universe to which the play, in turn, contributes. This, the longest section of the Introduction, is followed by a discussion of the play's structure and style, its relation to comic convention and its place in Shakespeare's corpus. Then come two reviews of the play's reception history in two different arenas: one, of staging possibilities over the course of the play's theatrical life to date, and the other, a brief critical résumé of the ways in which the play has been read and understood. The penultimate section focuses on the original texts and the choices made in generating the text of this edition.

BUILDING A PLAY: SOURCES AND CONTEXTS

The usual definition of a Shakespearean source is the work to which a play's plot is indebted. In *Much Ado About Nothing* Shakespeare portrays the unions of two couples. Only one of these pairs, however – Hero and Claudio – has what is conventionally considered a literary source, in the sense of a storyline already available elsewhere at the time of the play's composition. Traditional thinking about this play's debt to source material has thus tended to identify the Beatrice and Benedick material, as well as the Watch, as Shakespeare's original inventions, grafted on as comic relief to the oft-told backbone story of the slandered woman and her deceived betrothed. This vision of the play's relation to its sources locates the divergent natures of the two different love plots in their respective origins: Hero and Claudio's pairing, based on pre-existing narratives, represents 'conventional' romance, whereas the unprecedented Beatrice and Benedick plot represents something more unusual in both style and substance, a product of Shakespeare's genius, his comment on convention itself. This discrimination usually comes with the reminder that the Hero–Claudio plot is the 'main' plot, and the other, despite its tendency to upstage it, the mere subplot. On the other hand, revisions of this account of origins and originalities point out that, despite the apparent autonomy of the Beatrice and Benedick plot from the story of the slandered woman, both plots, in fact, turn on staged scenes and on fabricated accounts of love (of Don Pedro for Hero, Hero for Borachio, or Benedick for Beatrice, and she for him). Thus in this light the Benedick and Beatrice plot also derives from the calumny material. This remains nonetheless a plot-derived account of literary indebtedness, with Shakespeare doubling the offerings of his source (much as *The Comedy of Errors* multiplies Plautus' one set of twins) in order to multiply comic possibilities.

The usual suspects: Ariosto and Bandello

The plot-centred notion of a source gets us far with this play. The tale of the unjustly slandered woman was indeed a popular one in Renaissance literature (see Bullough). It appeared in many genres – tragedy, farce, romance and homily – and served as a vehicle for various meditations: on evidence, on love, on the powers of the senses, the rashness of the passions and the madcap complications of marital intrigue. Sexual slander was also a real concern of sixteenth-century courts (see Sharpe; Kaplan, *Culture*). The story's most ancient analogue was the fifth-century Greek romance of Chariton, *Chaereas and Kallirrhoe*, although more recent renditions lay behind Shakespeare's. Of these there were at least seventeen versions (both narrative and dramatic) extant at the time of the composition of *Much Ado*. The fifth Canto of Ludovico Ariosto's *Orlando Furioso* was perhaps the most prominent instance, itself probably based on the fifteenth-century Spanish *Tirant lo Blanco* by Juan Martorell.

Ariosto sets the story in question, an episode in his larger romance, in Scotland, and recounts it from the perspective of the lady's maid Dalinda (analogous to the figure of Shakespeare's Margaret), who relates her own misguided part in the proceedings. Dalinda is a lover of the knight Polynesso, Duke of Alban. He in turn wishes to marry her mistress Genevra, daughter of the Scottish king, 'Because of her great state and hie condition', although he promises to love Dalinda still: 'notwithstanding wife and all the rest, / I should be sure that he would love me best' (Book 5, 13.3, 14.7–8; Bullough, 85). He persuades Dalinda to make his suit to her mistress on his behalf, and when it is spurned – Genevra unwaveringly loves the Italian knight Ariodante – Polynesso wishes to revenge himself upon her. Polynesso asks Dalinda to make love to him in her mistress's clothing and hairstyle, under the pretext that it will serve as a therapeutic exorcism of his love for Genevra ('Thus I may passe my fancies foolish fit'), but really of course to deceive Ariodante (26.1; 88). Dalinda agrees, not knowing the true audience of her actions, and eager to resecure Polynesso's undivided attentions no matter how peculiar the means.

Ariodante, when confronted with Polynesso's claim to having enjoyed Genevra's 'yvorie corps' (38.2; 91), stoutly defends his lady. However, while fearful for his life from one he intuits is 'this false Duke' (43.4; 92), he nonetheless goes to the appointed viewing place accompanied by his brother, Lurcanio. Ariodante witnesses Polynesso ascend to Genevra's room, and 'straight beleev'd against his owne behoofe, / Seeing her cloth[e]s that he had seene her face' (50.3–4; 94). Lurcanio dissuades Ariodante from suicide, and the latter departs the Scottish court and is soon reputed drowned. The brother subsequently accuses Genevra of unchastity and culpability for Ariodante's death. Though Genevra's father, the King of Scotland, attempts to get to the bottom of the matter by interviewing her maids (an action which prompts Dalinda to warn Polynesso), he is nonetheless bound by Scottish law to sentence his daughter to death, unless a champion appears who can kill her accuser in a trial by combat, and thus prove her innocence. Polynesso packs off Dalinda to one of his castles (or so she thinks), with instructions to his men to murder her en route, a plight from which she is rescued by the knight Rinaldo, the principal hero of Ariosto's romance, now journeying through Scotland. She tells Rinaldo her tale, and he speeds to the court of Saint Andrews in time to prevent the combat between Lurcanio and an unknown knight, who, it turns out, is Ariodante in disguise. The lover had thought better of drowning himself, and decided to fight for his lady's honour even though he believed her guilty and the combat was against his own brother. All is revealed; Rinaldo slays Polynesso, the lovers are united, and Dalinda heads for a nunnery.

Ariosto's tale produced many spin-offs. It was first translated into English by Peter Beverly in 1566, and his *History of Ariodanto and Genevra* seizes upon the story as a frame on which to hang much poetry on the varieties and miseries of lovesickness. George Whetstone's *Rock of Regard* rendered it in 1576 (his hero is Rinaldo, his heroine Giletta, and the villain, also a rival lover, Frizaldo). A verse translation by Sir John Harington, *Orlando Furioso in English Heroical Verse* (1591), was more loyal to Ariosto. By this time the story had acquired an exemplary force, and Harington's moral is multiple: for example, the virtue in Genevra's preference of a humble knight to a duke, 'how wicked men often bewray their owne misdeeds . . . how God ever defends the innocent . . . how wickednesse ruines it selfe' (Bullough, 105). Edmund Spenser also found the story of homiletic utility, and in Book 2 canto 4 of *The Faerie Queene* (1590) he uses it to illustrate the dangers of intemperate action. Phedon, the lover figure, is tricked by his so-called friend Philemon into thinking his lady Claribell false to him 'with a groome of base degree' (24.3). Philemon's motives are vague: 'either enuying my toward good, / Or of himselfe to treason ill dispos'd' (22.2–3); nonetheless, he tells the maid Pryene that her beauty is worthier than her station, and persuades her to wear her mistress's 'most gorgeous geare' at an assignation (26.8). Phedon witnesses their embrace and, 'chawing vengeance all the way' (29.2), slays Claribell, only to rue his actions when Pyrene confesses the ruse (he then poisons Phedon and pursues Pyrene with a knife). When Guyon, knight of Temperance, finds him, he is being tortured by Furor and his mother Occasion, and serves up his tale as a warning against lack of moderation. Spenser's is the only version of the story in which the heroine dies.

The story also provided matter for drama, although the tenor of the plays is more farcical and less didactic than the poetic accounts (narrative accounts being better equipped than drama to provide opportunity for homily). The root here is the Italian *Il Fedele*, by Luigi Pasaqualigo (1576). Fedele loves Vittoria, who, although married to Cornelio, loves a man named Fortunio. Fedele discloses the latter information to the cuckolded Cornelio, and arranges for him to see a servant (in love with Vittoria's maid) enter the house to court an alleged Vittoria. The incensed Cornelio plans to poison his wife, but she by a trick escapes her fate. The play was translated into English by Anthony Munday, as *Fedele and Fortunio, the Two Italian Gentlemen* (1585), although this account is less racy than the Italian: 'Victoria is no promiscuous married woman but a maid uncertain in her choice between two suitors, and, after a number of equivocations, the story ends in no fewer than four happy marriages.'[1] Other dramatic versions included the Cambridge Latin production of *Victoria* (1580–3), by Abraham Fraunce, a court performance of *Ariodante and Genevra* in 1583 by the boys of Merchant Taylors probably based on Beverly, and a piece by Leicester's men in 1574/5 called *Panecia*.[2] The Pasaqualigo-derived versions, however, while providing ample evidence that the matter was apt for dramatic treatment, differ from *Much Ado* in that the latter's heroine is clearly chaste, Shakespeare's play deliberately courts tragedy, and his comedy lies elsewhere than in the spectacle of the duped husband (although the latter's spectre perhaps registers in the play's many cuckold jokes).

A nearer relative of Shakespeare's play is the prose novella 22 of Matteo Bandello's *La Prima Parte de le Novelle* (1554). This tale was translated into French, with the standard homiletic and rhetorical flourishes, by François de Belleforest in his *Histoires Tragiques* in 1569. Bandello's story, like Shakespeare's, is set in Messina, where the knightly and very wealthy Sir Timbreo de Cardona is a courtier of King Piero of Aragon, the latter having taken possession of the island in the wake of a Sicilian rebellion against the occupying French (there is virtually no mention of King Piero, however). During the courtly victory celebrations, Sir Timbreo falls in love with one Fenicia, daughter of an impoverished but ancient family. Her father is Messer Lionato de' Lionati. While Sir Timbreo's intentions are not initially honourable, he is forced by Fenicia's chaste conduct to offer her marriage, despite

---

1 Giorgio Melchiori (ed.), *The Merry Wives of Windsor*, Arden Shakespeare (2000), 17.
2 Bullough, 68. The name 'Panecia' betrays a link with the Bandello tale, as an imaginable error for Phanecia (= Fenicia). There was also a play by Jacob Ayrer, written between 1593 and 1605, titled *Die Schoene Phaenicia*.

the great difference in their social positions, 'for she never replied to any of the letters and messages he sent her except to affirm that she intended to keep her maidenhood inviolate for the man who would be given her as a husband' (Bullough, 113). The alliance is received happily by the entire town, chiefly on account of the universal regard in which Messer Lionato is held, 'since [he] was a gentleman rightly loved as one who sought to hurt nobody but to help all as much as he could' (114).

The only person disappointed by the match is one Sir Girondo Olerio Valenziano, who also loves Fenicia. Sir Girondo is also a proven soldier and ornament of the court, and comrade to Sir Timbreo (though curiously not in his confidence on the amorous score). Stricken by lovesickness and disappointment at the news of Fenicia's betrothal, Sir Girondo 'allowed himself to be carried away into doing an action blameworthy in anyone, let alone in a knight and gentleman such as he was' (114). He plots to destroy the match so as to gain Fenicia's hand for himself, and confides his desire to another courtier 'whom [he] had for confidant and helper in his crime . . . a fellow of little upbringing, more pleased with evil than with good' (115). This henchman goes to Sir Timbreo, relates the tale of Fenicia's duplicity, and makes an appointment to witness it. The hour arrived, Sir Girondo suborns one of his servingmen (having 'perfumed him with the sweetest of scents', 116) to enter, by ladder, a wing of Messer Lionato's house. The three pass by the hiding place of Sir Timbreo, where the fragrant servingman (to further increase plausibility) audibly cautions the others to take care of the ladder's placement, 'for the last time we were here my lady Fenicia told me that you had leaned it there with too much noise' (117). The man then climbs onto the balcony and purposefully enters the house 'as if he had a mistress within' (117). On the morrow the disappointed Sir Timbreo discreetly sends word by messenger to Messer Lionato that he will not, after all, have his daughter, and 'that you should find another son-in-law . . . because he has seen with his own eyes something in Fenicia that he would never have credited' (118). He instructs

Fenicia to 'find yourself another husband, just as you have already found yourself another lover . . . Sir Timbreo does not intend to have anything more to do with you, since you will make anyone who marries you a Lord of Corneto' (118). Messer Lionato, however, doughtily tells the messenger he is not surprised:

> I always feared, from the first moment when you spoke to me of this marriage, that Sir Timbreo would not stand firm to his request, for I knew then as I do now that I am only a poor gentleman and not his equal. Yet surely if he repented of his promise to make her his wife it would have been sufficient for him to declare that he did not want her, and not to have laid against her this injurious accusation of whoredom. It is indeed true that all things are possible, but I know how my daughter has been reared and what her habits are.

(118)

The story resolves itself in the best fashion of Italian novellas. The ever-virtuous Fenicia, from her sickbed, and surrounded by sympathetic friends and relatives, claims that Sir Timbreo's reversal was a providential means of preserving her from the arrogance which might have followed upon such a grand match. She then falls into a coma, is believed dead, is awakened as she is laid out for burial by her mother, and is dispatched by her ever-resourceful father to his brother's house in the country, 'so that after Fenicia had grown up and changed her appearance, as is usual with age, he might marry her off in two or three years under another name' (122). Her funeral proceeds as scheduled, provoking a universal sympathy, for 'all the citizens firmly believed that Don Timbreo had invented the lie about her' (122). The latter, meanwhile, surrounded by such adverse public opinion, 'began to feel great sorrow and a heartstirring such as he would never have thought possible' (122). Weighing the sum of the evidence (the remoteness of her bedroom from the entered balcony, her bedfellow sister, the location of her parents' bedchamber), it occurs to him that there might well have been other reasons for what he witnessed: 'maybe the man who had entered the house might have been doing so for another woman than Fenicia, or even to commit a theft' (123).

However, the greatest impact of Fenicia's funeral is upon Sir Girondo, who has become virtually suicidal not only for the loss of his beloved but for his dishonour in having been a cause of such harm. His contrition provides for the discovery of the deception. Consequently, a week after the funeral he confesses his sins to Sir Timbreo, and before her supposed tomb offers him both his poniard and his bared breast. Not to be outdone in chivalry, Sir Timbreo cites his own over-credulity as equally culpable, and the two men decide to clear Fenicia's name (Sir Timbreo only scolds Sir Girondo for not having disclosed his love to him, claiming that he would have 'preferred our friendship to my desire', 124). The repentant duo repair to Messer Lionato, who secures Sir Timbreo's promise to wed a woman of the latter's choosing. A year later Sir Timbreo willingly weds the much-improved Fenicia, who, like the phoenix after whom she is named, has been reborn through her trial. Sir Timbreo discovers her true identity before the marriage, but only after he recounts his love for the dead Fenicia. Sir Girondo weds her sister.[1]

Shakespeare's transformations of his sources: the creation of a social world

Ariosto and Bandello have been singled out as the most likely influences upon Shakespeare's play, the former for the particular means of the deception, and the latter for its obvious links of setting and names (Messer Lionato of Messina, King Piero of Aragon, etc.). The social universe of Bandello's novella is certainly the more akin to Shakespeare's Messina. Rather than court intrigue or the accidental landscapes of romance, he chooses to set his story in the gossipy confines of a leisured household in

---

1   For a fuller treatment of the differences of play and source, see McEachern, 'Fathering'.

a small town, places best suited to creating the sense of social proximity in which rumours are born and transmitted, in which the notable are much noted, mostly by each other. This sense of a provincial (if aristocratic) identity extends to the incongruously home-grown quality of Dogberry and his men (who, with their ostentatiously English names, may lend a comforting and plebeian familiarity to Messinese society, Messina being as remote as the moon to the majority of Shakespeare's audience). This sense of social proximity also accounts for the Watch's knowledge of and attention to their neighbour's doings ('I pray you watch about Signor Leonato's door, for the wedding being there tomorrow, there is a great coil tonight', 3.3.89–91). Shakespeare's portrait of communal and quotidian life – also conveyed by such details as the passing mention of Claudio's uncle (1.1.17), Benedick's trip to the barber (3.2.41–3), Margaret's account of the Duchess of Milan's wedding gown 'that they praise so' (3.4.15) – builds upon Bandello's implicit sense of the busy and close-knit Messinese society that rallies around the family of Messer Lionato and pressures Sir Timbreo to re-examine his convictions (though in Shakespeare's play the Friar's plan is a deliberate – if ineffective – implementation of this effect: '[Hero], dying, as it must be so maintained, / Upon the instant that she was accused, / Shall be lamented, pitied and excused / Of every hearer . . . When [Claudio] shall hear she died upon his words, / Th'idea of her life shall sweetly creep / Into his study of imagination', 4.1.214–16, 223–5). At the same time, the play's social universe, with its visiting dignitaries and fashionable speech, is not exclusively a provincial one. The leisured and literate universe of Baldassare Castiglione's *Il libro del cortegiano* (1528) provides another source of the play's social climate (as well as the typology of a courtly world in which beautiful people pass the time with elegant conversation and literary games).

Shakespeare's debt to Ariosto is a different one. If the exotic vistas, noble questants and providential accidents of romance are gone, to be replaced by the hothouse intimacies of small-town life

(Rinaldo has become a householder with two gowns), Shakespeare retains Ariosto's chivalric register in the forms of Benedick's challenge to Claudio, as well as in Leonato's and Antonio's similar moves to defend Hero's honour.

Perhaps the strongest link of Shakespeare's play to the Ariostan version of the tale lies not so much in plot as in social custom, in his concern with the romance's attention to social distinctions. This is embedded in Shakespeare's response to the role of the maid Dalinda. She provides Shakespeare, in her tale of dressing in her mistress's clothes, with the sartorial means of the deception. Shakespeare then elaborates the social circumstances that condition Dalinda's own curiously abject role in Genevra's slander into an entire sociological climate in which rank and name are both subtle but crucial factors in determining the slander of Hero.

The maid

There is in Ariosto a clear sense of the social requirements of marital union. Dalinda's station is far below that of the Duke Polynesso, even if we read her as a lady-in-waiting rather than a mere maid; in any case, she acknowledges the greater allure of her mistress's social position:

> Not all of love, but partly of ambition,
> He beares in hand his minde is onely bent,
> Because of her great state and hie condition,
> To have her for his wife is his intent:
> He nothing doubteth of the kings permission,
> Had he obtained *Genevras* free assent.
> Ne was it hard for him to take in hand,
> That was the second person in the land.
> (13.1–8; Bullough, 85)

The deception itself is heavily invested in the signs of clothing that mark Genevra's social identity: 'The gowne I ware' (recounts Dalinda) 'was white, and richly set / With aglets, pearle, and lace of golde wel garnished . . . Not thus content, the vaile aloft I set,

13

/ Which only Princes weare' (47.1–2, 5–6; 93). This impressive costume alone is sufficient to deceive Ariodante, who 'straight beleev'd against his owne behoofe, / Seeing her cloth[e]s that he had seene her face' (50.3–4; 94).

In Shakespeare's play, this emphasis on clothes and station provides the means and the rationale of Margaret's participation in the charade. Shakespeare sketches a character who like Dalinda is aware of her own relative lack of social status amongst the company: 'Why, shall I always keep below stairs?' she asks Benedick, flirting with him (5.2.9–10). She prides herself on her wit ('Doth not my wit become me rarely?', 3.4.63–4) in an environment where verbal prowess serves as a marker of social elegance, and her claim to having seen the dress of the Duchess of Milan adds to a similar social authority. The deception at the window, in which Margaret wears Hero's garments, and, in Borachio's words, 'leans me out at her mistress' chamber window, bids me a thousand times goodnight' (3.3.140–1), suggests that from Margaret's point of view the pair are engaged in an erotic game involving the impersonation of their social betters. Borachio has prepared his audience to see Hero making sport of her suit to Claudio by calling her lover Borachio by Claudio's name: 'hear me call Margaret "Hero", hear Margaret term me "Claudio"' (2.2.39–40). Margaret is innocent of her ultimate role in Hero's slander – Leonato says 'Margaret was in some fault for this, / Although against her will' (5.4.4–5), and Borachio claims she 'knew not what she did when she spoke to me' (5.1.291). But she is not innocent of social ambition, or at least a certain wistfulness about her inferior social station, enough so that we are asked to imagine that the game of mocking her betters is a plausible and pleasurable one for her to play.

'How many gentlemen?'

Margaret's charade in which she pretends to be Hero receiving a man into her bedchamber provides the particular mechanism of slander in this play, but Shakespeare locates her action in a larger social world shaped by concerns of status and place. The role of

rank is present from the opening lines of the play: 'How many gentlemen have you lost in this action?' asks Leonato, and receives the
reassuring reply: 'But few of any sort, and none of name' (1.1.5–7)
– in other words, nobody of note. Much of this attention to status
revolves around the presence of the Prince, the highest placed
member of this society whose disarming gestures of *noblesse oblige*
only accentuate his social, superiority ('Please it your grace lead
on?' 'Your hand, Leonato; we will go together', 1.1.152–3). It is a
concern present in Leonato's enthusiasm for what he believes is a
match of his daughter with the Prince; acknowledged in Beatrice's
own refusal of Don Pedro's hand – 'No, my lord, unless I might
have another for working days. Your grace is too costly to wear
every day' (2.1.301–3); and in Don John's cruel request to Claudio
to discourage the rumoured union of Hero and his brother – 'she
is no equal for his birth' (2.1.150).

Don Pedro thus represents the apex of a social pyramid
constructed out of relations of dependency and desire. (This is
in striking contrast to Bandello's version, where the analogous
figure receives only passing mention.) Some of these hierarchies
are intellectual, but mostly they are matters of caste, so that the
beautiful people can also lay claim to a beautiful language, and
the less glamorous seek to better themselves through speaking
elegantly. Shakespeare populates Messina with persons of social
prominence and those who attend upon them. Don Pedro has his
followers in Claudio and Benedick; Don John his, in Conrade and
Borachio; Hero and Beatrice are attended by Ursula and Margaret.
Antonio defers to Leonato, Verges to Dogberry, children to parents, soldiers to their leaders, the Watch to the constable. The lines
of power are subtle, sometimes suspended, but ultimately firm.
(Ursula and Margaret, for instance, are 'gentlewomen', take part
in the dance in 2.1 and in Beatrice's gulling, but are also required
to run errands. Some productions cast them as ladies-in-waiting;
others, as ladies' maids.) The nub of the play's brush with tragedy
is located in these social dynamics. While the Watch promptly
discover the truth about Hero's slander in advance of the wedding,

Dogberry's need first to impress upon Leonato his own importance, which he does by denigrating Verges, exhausts the harried
Governor's short supply of patience and ultimately prevents the
news from coming out in time to prevent suffering.

To say that Shakespeare gets all this from the fifth canto of
Orlando Furioso is to over-privilege the latter and underestimate
Shakespeare's accomplishment; what he does is to elaborate a
suggestion of caste into an entire and nuanced social universe in
which the distinctions between ranks are both insisted upon and
overlooked (the social differences of Ariosto's chivalric and royal
universe are, in fact, clearer and thus less treacherous). Hero, for
instance, may not be Don Pedro's social equal but the fiction of
his suit to Hero provokes no adverse comment and he proposes
himself as a match for Beatrice.

In fact, the chief difference of *Much Ado* from its sources lies
in Shakespeare's alteration of a fact of social status. It is crucial
to Shakespeare's version that Hero's suitor, unlike Sir Timbreo,
is not greatly above Leonato in rank, and perhaps not at all in
fortune, if Claudio's enquiry about Hero's inheritance is to be
credited (although such a question would have been routine and
not necessarily over-mercenary). Unlike Ariodante, he is not
significantly below her either. Claudio is also explicitly young –
'Lord Lack-beard' (5.1.187); 'young Florentine' (1.1.10); 'sir boy'
(5.1.83) – and however distinguished in battle, clearly dependent
upon Don Pedro's patronage and approval. Thus the explanation
of the lover's snobbery which allows Messer Leonato de' Lionati
to rebut Sir Timbreo's allegations with the confidence that he
knows 'how [his daughter] hath been reared and what her habits
are' is not available to Shakespeare's father character.

The difference results in a different figure of a father as well
as a lover, and opens up an entirely new dimension of psychological depth and loss for this father: 'mine, and mine I loved,
and mine I praised, / And mine that I was proud on – mine so
much / That I myself was to myself not mine / Valuing of her'
(4.1.136–9). Shakespeare's father character, in both the extremity

of his loss and the bravado of his recovery, is quite different from the confident and expedient Messer Lionato. Shakespeare seems interested in authority figures generally, adding Antonio in addition to Dogberry, expanding the role of Don Pedro, and inventing the Friar, resourceful where Leonato is not. And if Shakespeare's alteration of Bandello's status relations between the lovers gives scope for parental pain, the chivalric posture, perhaps inspired by Ariosto, allows Leonato to recoup a kind of disinterested avuncular posture sorely lacking in him by the end of the church scene. In his challenge to Claudio, he thus differs not only from Messer Lionato, confident in his daughter's virtue, but from Ariosto's King of Scotland, constrained by his own law into a kind of impotence vis-à-vis his daughter's defence. Unlike the paternal blocking figure of comic convention, Leonato displays a great emotional range; measured by the extravagance and quantity of the poetry alone, he far more than Claudio might conceivably be seen as the protagonist of the play's semi-tragic plot.[1] Othello's Brabantio, dead of a broken heart at his daughter's defection, is his tragic counterpart. Eighteenth-century pictorial representations of 4.1 demonstrate this centrality (see Figs 8, 9 and 10).

The villain

The subtle pressures of social hierarchy and rivalry also account for the unique nature of Shakespeare's villain. Don John is the bastard brother of Don Pedro. He is referred to as a prince, but he is perhaps not as much a prince as his brother, and when the play opens he has been recently vanquished in a fraternal battle. His illegitimacy is not made explicit in the play until 4.1 (though it is present in the Quarto speech prefixes and stage directions). However, Don John's melancholy and enviousness, perhaps betokened in the original productions by black costume, may have emblematized the circumstances of his birth for a Renaissance audience, and served implicitly to explain his disgruntlement (so

---

1 Leonato speaks 24 per cent of the play's verse; Claudio, 16.

17

that the revelation in 4.1 of his illegitimate birth would have come as a confirmation of a suspicion already afoot). Like *King Lear*'s Edmund, Don John's ethical nature seems predetermined by the political and economic circumstances of his birth. That the villain of a play concerned with sexual fidelity is an actual bastard seemingly rationalizes its emphasis on the importance of social legitimacy by producing evidence of the unpleasant consequences of violating it. Cuckoldry leads to (and stems from) villainy, or so is the implicit moral of the anxiety. Shakespeare's wrong-side-of-the-blanket villain is not exactly base-born, in the etymological sense of *vilein*, but he is a kind of walking impersonation of the way in which illegitimate sexual activity can produce social malcontents.

Whether or not Don John's illegitimacy is literally worn on his sleeve, his role in the story of slander is a unique one. In all previous versions of the story excepting Spenser's, the slander stems from a jealous rival for the heroine's hand. The convention of friends divided by the love of an often changeable woman is a cliché of Renaissance literature, and generates much rhetoric on the fickleness of fortune, women and friendship. (John Lyly's *Euphues: The Anatomy of Wit* (1578) is another example, and many of the play's comments on female infidelity echo those of that text.) Given the conventions within which Shakespeare is working, then, the villain of the play would ordinarily be Claudio's 'new sworn brother' Benedick (1.1.68), or even Don Pedro (whom indeed Claudio suspects of appropriating Hero), not Don John – or at least Don John ought to be enamoured of Hero as well. (This theory is sometimes advanced by productions seeking to explain his actions by means of longing glances towards her.)

Don John's malignity, however, is motiveless or at least mixed – he is jealous of Claudio's position with his brother, perhaps disgruntled about his subjugation in the recent war (in which Claudio subdued him), or perhaps just a 'plain-dealing villain' (1.3.29–30), a machiavel whose desire to spoil the pleasures of others comes with the character type (George Bernard Shaw

called him 'a true natural villain, that is to say, a malevolent person
. . . having no motive in this world except sheer love of evil', 157).
Yet Shakespeare softens his portrait of him as well as indicting
him: for while in the sources the jealous rival (even the otherwise
noble Sir Girondo) is wholly responsible for concocting his own
plan, one in which subordinates of few scruples are mere agents,
in *Much Ado* it is Borachio, identified as a drunkard by his name,
who hatches the details to mobilize Don John's unformed desire
to thwart Claudio's suit. The diffusion of criminal responsibility
between the two perhaps serves to dilute the sense of villainy so
that it does not overwhelm the capacity of comedy to contain or
forestall it. Evil in this play is muted by having been built by com-
mittee, and is thus a mirror image of the clumsy but ultimately
providential collaborations of Dogberry and his men.

The lover

The place where Shakespeare most decisively departs from his
predecessors is in the creation of his lover. Claudio is far more of a
cad than his counterparts. Ariosto's Ariodante is positively saintly,
defending his mistress against his brother's challenge despite
thinking her guilty. Sir Timbreo, once 'his despite was now in
great part cooled and reason began to open his eyes', begins to
himself work out the possibility that he was mistaken (Bullough,
123). Unlike Sir Timbreo, who is close enough to the window to
smell the alleged suitor, Claudio must form his judgement from
'afar off in the orchard', on a 'dark night' (3.3.144–5, 150), though,
on the other hand, unlike Dalinda, Margaret is not veiled. For Sir
Timbreo the seduction scene alone is sufficient to convince, while
for Claudio the 'oaths' of Don John and Borachio's further testimony are crucial. And whereas Sir Timbreo's rejection of Fenicia
is carried out by messenger, *after* he witnesses the window scene,
Claudio responds to the mere allegation of Hero's infidelity with
a ready plan of public vengeance: 'If I see anything tonight why
I should not marry her, tomorrow in the congregation where I
should wed, there will I shame her' (3.2.111–13).

The difference in these suitors' choices must partly have to do with the difference between a play and a prose account, and the dramatic opportunities of a scene of public rejection. But it is an unavoidable observation that Shakespeare deliberately provides us with a less than appealing suitor. Shakespeare may draw his heroine's name from the story of two loyal lovers, but the suitor in question resembles 'Leander the good swimmer' (5.2.30–1) – in Benedick's ironic term for the drowned swain – more in failure rather than steadfastness. Claudio's shortcomings in the trust department are also in keeping with his earlier lack of confidence in the loyalty of friends, when he suspects that Don Pedro has appropriated Hero for himself. His behaviour after the report of Hero's death is no less disappointing (the Friar's plan for instituting remorse seems not to have fully succeeded), which is consistent with the realism of this rendition. Shakespeare goes out of his way to give us a suitor who is morally faint of heart and faith, at a disadvantage in the lists of love and friendship.

This has rendered Claudio vulnerable to critical scorn, as 'a miserable specimen' (Ridley, 106), or 'the least amiable lover in Shakespeare' (Harbage, 192); another commentator claims that love never did have 'interest in his liver': 'The verb describing the young man's feeling is significantly "like" not "love" . . . What Claudio is really interested in is a good and suitable marriage' (Prouty, 42, 43). Defences of his behaviour, on the other hand, cite the conventional nature of his love: it is time for him to marry; Hero is an appropriate choice; Claudio has the support of his patron. J.R. Mulryne grants him a quasi-tragic status: 'Claudio lacks confidence in himself and is readily given to suspecting others . . . He is easy prey for Don John precisely because of a deeply ingrained mistrust of his own feelings; he cannot exclude the possibility of his being quite wrong about his most intimate beliefs' (Mulryne, 40). Other commentators point out that while the grounds of such a match may not be romantically thrilling, they are unobjectionable by the terms of the day. At the same time, as Sheldon Zitner aptly observes, 'the ensuing marriage of Claudio and Hero is not quite as everyone would like it. Nor can we condescend to Elizabethan audiences by assuming it was wholly as they liked it' (Oxf[1], 1). Benedick and Beatrice's courtship surely criticizes the younger pair's, and vice versa (much as in *The Taming of the Shrew*, where Shakespeare sketches a similar contrast between Petruchio and Kate and Lucio and Bianca).

These defences remind us, however, that while it would be inaccurate to interpret Claudio as contemptible, he is nevertheless somewhat of a disappointment. He is, above all, young: anxious for the approval of his elders and convention, unsure of himself, eager to do the right thing both in marrying and in extricating himself from a bad bargain.

The unpromising nature of Claudio as a hero deserving of comic happiness, as well as the enigma of his final union to a veiled woman, have suggested to Jonathan Bate another analogue for Shakespeare's play which might help to condition his status as a lover. This is Euripides' *Alcestis*, named after its heroine. She volunteers to die in place of her husband Admetus, whose hospitality to the gods has earned him in the event of his death the reprieve of a substitute (Alcestis is the only family member who volunteers for the mission). Hercules discovers her sacrifice, fetches her from the underworld and returns her to her husband in the veiled guise of a new wife. Admetus, however, has pledged not to remarry, and he protests at the gift. The occasion gives Admetus an opportunity to voice his own guilt at allowing his wife to die on his behalf: 'if Hero is an Alcestis, Claudio is an Admetus who repents of and learns from earlier unfair conduct . . . the mock death must make Claudio see Hero's virtues, must make him into a nobler lover' (Bate, 'Dying', 83). Unlike Sir Timbreo, but like Admetus, Claudio must accept his second bride without seeing her face, a stipulation that reverses the terms of his initial error (in which he identified a woman by outward signs rather than inner conviction), and forces him to have faith where once he lacked it. Hero's mock funeral, in turn, recalls and prefigures other of Shakespeare's mock deaths, such as Juliet's or Helena's or Hermione's, in which heroines undergo a trial passage to the underworld. Euripides' *Alcestis* is also structurally similar to *Much Ado* in its use of comic scenes (those of Hercules' drunken festivities during the heroine's funeral) to counterpoint the apparent tragedy and hint at the comic ending to come.

Claudio also bears comparison with other of Shakespeare's lacklustre suitors, in particular Bertram of *All's Well That Ends Well* and Proteus of *The Two Gentleman of Verona*, even Posthumus of *Cymbeline*, and his namesake Claudio of *Measure for Measure*. The type of the less than ideal protagonist who is nonetheless included in the redemptions of comedy may have been relatively unobjectionable to a Reformation audience not only familiar with the convention of the arranged marriage but unsurprised by the unregenerate quality of mankind in general.

Beyond the plot

The changes so far detailed concern for the most part matters of character, of Shakespeare's expansion of the psychological scope of his source materials chiefly by means of the manipulation of details of status. Don Pedro, for example, is transformed from a mere mention in Bandello to a type of *deus ex machina*, one of the 'only love-gods' (2.1.357), as well as a potentially melancholic figure isolated by his very privilege, 'too costly', in Beatrice's terms, to be worn in the workaday world of bourgeois marriage (2.1.302). He is in the party, but not of it, participating in disguise as a suitor, but not ultimately one of the final festive company: 'Prince, thou art sad – get thee a wife' (5.4.120). We still however are working within an understanding of source as referring to the origins of plot, and thus have yet to address the existence of Benedick, Beatrice or the Watch. If we are to account for these other elements, we need to move to a broader understanding of the cultural resources and generic exigencies that go into shaping an author's decisions. The intention is not to discount Shakespeare's originality, but better to illuminate the nature of his invention by comparison with shared cultural and dramatic assumptions that serve as foils to his own compositional choices.

Denouement

Certainly the presence of the Watch can be in part attributed to the representational requirements of drama. Unlike a novella or a poem, a play (unless it is *The Winter's Tale*) usually cannot wait a year (or even Bandello's week) for the remorse of the villain to effect a denouement. In Shakespeare, indeed, it is not clear whether the villain does repent – although Borachio is contrite, Don John flees, and Claudio's own acknowledgement of culpability is potentially graceless and unlikely to provoke much in the way of reparation without further prompting. Furthermore, this play's peculiar emotional tenor, of a comedy whose rewards are hard won, depends upon the pleasurable frustrations of a villainy only slowly apprehended. Hence the utility of the Watch as the agent of revelation: their inadvertent discovery of the deception nearly as soon as it has occurred helps to build a sense of comic providence, while the subsequent failure of Dogberry to communicate this information in a timely fashion helps to make possible the broadening of the play's emotional register (to include pain) that distinguishes this particular comic resolution. A subplot of Pasaqualigo's *Il Fedele*, and Munday's *Fedele and Fortunio*, involves an interception by the police, and Lyly's *Endymion* (1591) includes a similarly simple-minded watch.

The inept quality of the police force in *Much Ado* may indeed owe more to the realities of Elizabethan policing than to any other source. For instance, the contradictions, and difficulties, of ordinary citizens policing their betters in a hierarchical society – 'If you meet the prince in the night you may stay him . . . marry, not without the prince be willing' (3.3.73–4, 77–8) – will be satirized in Thomas Dekker's *Gull's Hornbook* (1609) (see Fig. 1). Dekker scorns the indolence and inefficacy of urban watches, easily smelled out by their excessive onion-eating ('to

1 An early modern watchman, with his bill and lantern, from Thomas
   Dekker's *Gull's Hornbook* (1609)

keep them in sleeping') and their preferential treatment of the
gentry ('the watch will wink at you, only for the love they bear
to arms and knighthood', 63). Dogberry's crew shares these
assumptions about their responsibilities: 'We will rather sleep
than talk; we know what belongs to a watch' (3.3.37–8). The
impulse to let a sleeping watch lie may in fact have been a strategic choice of a society with no standing army or police force,
and suspicious, as one historian puts it, of 'the over-efficiency
of even good enforcement systems' (Spinrad, 161). Thus while

2   Title-page of Will Kemp's *Nine Days Wonder* (1600). Kemp was notorious for the athleticism of his jig, and jigs often followed the ending of a play.

the semi-competent watch may be a familiar dramatic device and social reality, Shakespeare weaves it into the play's social texture, with its concerns with rank and status. Although, as A.P. Rossiter comments, 'As a real official Dogberry would be a terror. Conceited ignorance and vast self-importance in local government officers is – and was, in the time of Elizabeth – as good a joke in fiction as a very bad joke in fact' (Rossiter, 53).

In addition, the improvisational and extemporal abilities of the actor Will Kemp, who may have originally played Dogberry (if we take the Quarto speech prefixes as evidence), may have suggested to Shakespeare a role that would accommodate and even satirize the desire to upstage his fellows. Dogberry's own desire for the spotlight (he is both eager and outraged to be 'writ down an ass', 4.2.88) stems from a desire for social importance and apes the clown's stage charisma and notoriety (see Fig. 2).

Among Shakespeare's resources, then, if not 'sources' per se, we must also include the personnel of his company, their talents and reputations, and the need to make use of them.

Dialogue and debate forms

Another obvious requirement of drama is the need to transmit information through dialogue; hence the need for the play's many pairs: Leonato talks to Antonio, Beatrice to Hero, Claudio to Benedick, Don John to his followers Conrade and Borachio, Dogberry to Verges. Since information often unfolds through a process of debate, these pairs are often composed of foils: the demure miss and the sprightly spinster, the young cub and the cynical trencher-man, melancholy villain and deferential follower, despairing father and his consoling brother, all of which support the larger dialogic contrast of the two pairs of lovers. The use of such foils is arguably a device of any drama, indebted to the drama's roots in the scholastic convention of *in utramque partem* debate, in which contenders voiced opposing sides of an argument in order to demonstrate their rhetorical prowess (Altman). The prevalence of the dialogue convention in Renaissance prose fiction and rhetorical manuals – Castiglione's *Cortegiano*, Stefano Guazzo's *La civil conversazione* (1574), Lyly's *Anatomy of Wit* (1578) and *Euphues and His England* (1580) – bespeaks its availability for dramatic representation. Yet *Much Ado*, with its emphasis on wit, is particularly devoted to rhetorical contest, and these texts are especially pertinent. Many of Benedick's comments on the fair sex derive from Lyly, and Castiglione offers a model of intellectual contest and compatibility between the sexes, especially in his portrait of the exchanges between Lord Gaspare Pallavicino and Lady Emilia, the one a professed misogynist and the other a defender of her sex (Scott, 476). *Much Ado*'s stylistic register, from repartee to courtly exchange, is also indebted to debate forms. From Lyly's text comes the coinage for the very style in which the men of

Much Ado often converse, 'euphuism' being the form of verbal exchange which consists in complicated syntactic parallelisms, chiasmus or inversions, and balanced structures, and above all in a competitive turning and returning of one's own terms and those of others (see 'Style', pp. 62–3 below).

However, euphuism is not a merely stylistic feature of this play, for its forms provide the currency by which the men create community. Male banter is a kind of verbal version of the secret handshake, cementing bonds and denoting hierarchy in much the same manner as the exchange of women. One of the reasons Beatrice is perceived to be 'an excellent wife for Benedick' (2.1.324) is that she talks so much like the men in the play (in the play's original staging, Beatrice's verbal masculinity would have been underscored by the fact of a boy actor playing the role). Euphuism is thus not just a source of the play's prose patterns but a medium of its gender roles, and dialogue is not merely a formal necessity of drama but a marker of social identity. The existence of dialogue manuals itself bespeaks a market of people who want to learn to exchange witticisms (Dogberry no doubt owns one, or would if he could read, whereas Beatrice is offended at the notion that her wit derives from a jest-book).

In Shakespeare's use of dialogue structures and styles we can see another instance of his use of forms in order to create a social world. Sexual slander requires a universe of rank and rivalry shaped by alliances between men, themselves shaped, among other ways, by the traffic both in words and in women (so that the semantic looseness emphasized by verbal badinage contributes to the imputed looseness of women). Thus in investigating Shakespeare's construction of gender identity we find other materials that might be considered as contributing to the intellectual conditions of possibility of this play. These materials include not only the formal patterns of dialogue and debate conventions, but contexts such as conduct books, theological and medical discourses, and the popular humour of cuckold jokes.

Sexual stereotypes

The debate model also helps, for instance, to contextualize Shakespeare's creation of Benedick and Beatrice, in that the types of the misogynist and the shrew that they can invoke belong to a prominent tradition of a rhetorical debate literature which specifically exercised itself on the question of woman's worth.[1] Thus while this pair are 'unconventional' in their shared suspicion of romantic love considered as a matter of 'soft and delicate desires' (1.1.284), their portraits nonetheless recall (although they are by no means reduced to) another set of conventions. As Linda Woodbridge has demonstrated, the debate on the question of woman's worth dates from the time of medieval universities, and received new momentum with the arrival of print culture: 'Humanism gave it its characteristic Renaissance form, most evident in its rhetoric, its humanist arguments, and its addition of classical materials to the characteristic set of *exempla*' (Woodbridge, 15). In woman's favour were cited models of chastity, thrift and heroism; against her lay charges of sexual promiscuity, and weakness of reason and body (among other faults). Authors weighed in on both sides of the question in order to demonstrate their rhetorical gifts, sometimes in different publications and sometimes in the very same work (e.g. Nicolas Breton, author of both *Cornucopiae* (1612) and *The Praise of Virtuous Ladies* (1606), or C. Pyrrye, *The Praise and Dispraise of Women* (1569)). No less a celebrant of profane love than John Donne was also responsible for a youthful exercise on the question of 'Why Hath the Common Opinion Afforded Women Souls?' (Donne, *Problems*, sigs G2^v–3^r). Benedick's own sudden reversal from a man who swears 'till [love] have made an oyster of me he shall never make me such a fool' (2.3.24–5) to

---

1   Woodbridge locates Benedick in the tradition of the 'stage misogynist', a company of soldiers that includes Troilus, Sextus in Thomas Heywood's *The Rape of Lucrece* (1608), Gondarino in Francis Beaumont and John Fletcher's *The Woman-Hater* (1607), Caratack in their *Bonduca* (1613), Acutus in *Every Woman in Her Humour* (anon., 1609), Posthumus in *Cymbeline*, Enobarbus in *Antony and Cleopatra*, Bosola in John Webster's *The Duchess of Malfi* (1612/13), Iago and Hamlet (Woodbridge, 279).

an advocate of 'No, the world must be peopled' (2.3.233) mimics the agility of authors whose goal was to show themselves equally dextrous in arguing both sides of a case. The scholastic range of Benedick's reference also perhaps reflects his hailing from Padua, 'nursery of arts' (*TS* 1.1.2).

As this edition's commentary documents, several of Benedick's tirades against women (e.g. in 2.3) resemble the conventions and details of the formal attack on women, particularly the invective of Demosthenes, which was reprised in *Of Marriage and Wiving: An excellent, pleasant, and philosophical controversy between the two Tassi* (1599) (where the Tasso brothers took up different sides of the question):

> *Demosthenes*, writing vnto the Tyrant *Corynthus* his friend, who had requested him to set downe his censure, what qualities one should seeke to finde in a woman that he ment to marry withall, returned him this answere: First, shee must be rich, that thou maist have wherewithall to live in shewe and carrie a port: next, she must be nobly borne, that thou maist be honoured through her bloud: then she must be yong, that she may content thee: then faire, that thou need not to hunt after other game; and lastly, honest and vertuous, that thou maiest not take the paines to provide a spie to watch her.[1]

This list demonstrates the conventional quality of Benedick's portrait of the ideal woman in 2.3. Shakespeare's account differs, of course, in the deft stylistic drollery with which it is presented: Benedick begins his meditation by disavowing love ('love . . . shall never make me such a fool', 2.3.25), but cannot resist contemplating what a possible mate might look like. He seemingly concludes his description with another protestation of disdain – 'till all graces be in one woman, one woman shall not come in my grace' (27–8) – but then starts up again, as if he cannot resist

---

1   Tasso, sig. B2ᵛ. Ercole Tasso was contra, Torquato pro.

Matrimonium :

3   A man bearing the servile yoke, punishing stocks and effeminizing skirt of
matrimony. The fruit on his shoulder is the quince, symbol of fertility. From
Henry Peacham's *Minerva Britannia* (1598)

the speculation. Shakespeare thus broaches the stereotype of the
misogynist, but he animates it in the personality of one who seems
to protest too much, a character who seems to need the convention
as a defence against his own impulse to the contrary.

In describing a woman who is fair, wise, rich, virtuous, mild,
noble and of good discourse, Benedick contemplates a kind of
Renaissance fantasy girl, one who is all things to one man. She
is not one who appears very often in the more practical-minded
literatures of the day devoted to the process of mate selection
(see pp. 38–41 – most caution against ambition in the choice of a
wife). Even Benedick himself acknowledges the unlikelihood of

Vis Amoris.

4 The emblem illustrating *Vis Amoris*, from Henry Peacham's *Minerva Britannia* (1598). Hercules, as the text reads, 'hath throwne his Clubbe away, / And weares a Mantle, for his Lions skinne / Thus better liking for to passe the day, / With Omphale, and with her maides to spinne . . . Loues affection, did disgrace and shame / His virtues partes' (1–10). *Much Ado*'s many references to the emasculated Hercules recall this iconography.

his fantasy coming to fulfilment. More common was the notation of the failure to fulfil the ideal, and man's subservience to female domination brought on by the marriage yoke (see Figs 3 and 4). A chief obstacle to masculine happiness in marriage was a wife's failure to submit herself to being yoked, either verbally or sexually or both. Most of the Renaissance writings against women share the assumption about the link between verbal dexterity and sexual licence, and thus emphasize the threat of female loquaciousness to the security of patrilineal identity: 'A slow softe Tongue betokens Modestie, / But, quicke and loud signes of Inconstancy. / Words, more than swords, the inward Heart doe wound / And glib'd-tongu'd Women seldome chaste are found' (*Blazon*, sig. G1ᵛ). An ideal Renaissance woman was one seen but not heard, one who, in every sense, doesn't give anything away. We can sense in such statements the tenacity of medieval Christianity's idea of women as the heirs of Eve, that disobedient and fleshly creature who is punished for her disobedience with the arduous task of painfully peopling the world ('sure, my lord, my mother cried', 2.1.308). While the play ultimately repudiates many of these notions of female identity – Benedick readily decides to love his intellectual and verbal equal – they do inform both its jokes about the male distrust of women and the psychological grounds of the slander plot. Indeed, while Benedick has no share in the slander of Hero, he is the voice of the play's most misogynist commentary: 'That a woman conceived me, I thank her; that she brought me up, I likewise give her most humble thanks; but that I will have a recheat winded in my forehead, or hang my bugle in an invisible baldrick, all women shall pardon me' (1.1.223–7).

The idea of woman as subordinate to man was a stereotype with biological as well as theological and political dimensions: even as women were thought inferior to men in reason and intellect, so they were considered a somewhat more primitive life-form, whose blood, according to Galenic physiology, was colder, and whose metabolism more sluggish in nature than a man's.[1] In the humoral vocabulary which describes the Renaissance physique, the body is ruled by the four humours of blood, phlegm, choler and bile, and women were considered more phlegmatic than men. When Beatrice tells Benedick that

---

1 One anatomical theory of the period held that the ovaries and the uterus were an inverted penis and testicles that had not been conceived at a temperature high enough to expel them, right side out, of the foetus. See Thomas Lacqueur, *Making Sex: Body and Gender from the Greeks to Freud* (Cambridge, Mass., 1990).

32

she too loves none, and 'I thank God and my cold blood, I am of your humour for that' (1.1.123–4) (note that she vows not to love until a 'hot January', 1.1.89), she calls attention to her phlegmatic and thus essentially feminine nature.

Disdain

Beatrice, for her part, recalls in her alleged shrewishness the bane of much misogynistic writing, although the extent to which she fulfils descriptions of her as a 'harpy' (2.1.248), 'infernal Ate' (2.1.234) or 'my Lady Tongue' (2.1.252) has varied with the times and turns of productions (the eighteenth century tended to no-holds-barred shrew, whereas the nineteenth preferred the heart over the head). But this emphasis on Shakespeare's invocations of the Renaissance conventions of male suspicion of women should not obscure the fact that *Much Ado* portrays the resistance to marriage as characteristic of women as well as men. The characters of both Beatrice and Benedick draw on the convention of the 'disdainer of love' who comes to recant and even regret his or her former protestations of disinclination. Claudio swears off love at least twice. Spenser's *The Faerie Queene* includes both male and female versions: Prince Arthur, whose vow to eschew the distracting company of women is undermined by his erotic dream of a woman of no less persuasions than the Faerie Queene herself; and the arrogant Mirabella, 'borne free, not bound to any wight, / And so would euer liue, and loue her owne delight' (*FQ*, 6.7.30.8–9). Like Arthur, she is eventually humbled, though her comeuppance is significantly more abrading,[1] as she is brought before Cupid's court and sentenced to save as many loves as she had once scorned (twenty-two); her jailers on the journey are the tyrannous Disdain and the scourging Scorn, a pair which Hero describes as also riding 'sparkling' in the eyes of Beatrice (3.1.51)

1　Much as Beatrice's is, compared with Benedick's: the latter is won by flattery and appeals to his chivalry; the former, by a scourging account of the harsh (rather than playful) nature of her wit.

(though presumably directing their wrath towards her suitors rather than towards Beatrice herself). Beatrice is also stung in the masque scene by the allegation that she is 'disdainful' ('Well, this was Signor Benedick that said so', 2.1.118–19).

The 'scorner of love' who finds him or herself forced to recant was a familiar literary figure; the most prominent instance prior to Shakespeare lies in the first book of Chaucer's *Troilus and Criseyde*, where Troilus is punished as a heretic to love by falling for Criseyde. Among Shakespeare's works, *Love's Labour's Lost*, *Troilus and Cressida* and *The Two Gentlemen of Verona* provide male examples of the figure. Shakespeare's heroines almost to a woman display the ability to cast a cold eye upon the male of the species before themselves putting on the destined livery. Castiglione provides another precedent of disdain (or at least disinclination) being transformed by common opinion to the contrary: 'I have also seen a woman fall passionately in love with someone for whom to begin with she felt not the slightest affection, and this only from hearing that many persons believed the two were in love with each other.'[1] Beatrice, by contrast, believes 'better than reportingly' (3.1.116), and her reversal is prompted by her overhearing an account not only of Benedick's love but of her own allegedly uncharitable behaviour; however, the precedent does point to the imaginative currency of the love-conversion experience.

Modifications of type

These kinds of indebtedness demonstrate not just how Beatrice and Benedick derive from Renaissance assumptions about gender identity, but how the play also challenges these assumptions. However much they may invoke such discourses, Benedick and

---

1 Castiglione, *The Courtier*, 269. The passage goes on to remark on the force of communal report: 'this, I think, was because she took what everyone thought as sufficient proof that the man concerned was worthy of her love, and it almost seemed that what was common opinion served to bring from her lover messages that were truer and more credible than his own letters or words, or any go-between, could have communicated'.

Beatrice are not merely stereotypes; indeed, the fun of this play is the way in which they shake off these conventions of misogynist and shrew, and reveal them in the process as inadequate descriptions of human conduct. Benedick's reversal is as delightful as it is predictable, and Beatrice's bark lacks the bite of a more confirmed shrew such as Katerina. The charges of her shrewishness levied by her uncle and Antonio never really stick – as Leonato knows, 'There's little of the melancholy element in her' (2.1.316–17) – and part of what stings so about her gulling is the shock of Hero's exaggerated characterization of her as incapable of love: 'Stand I condemned for pride and scorn so much?' (3.1.108). Benedick's own allegations about her speech have more to do with the enviable speed and agility of her tongue rather than its mere logorrhoea. Bested as he often is by her wit, he is not a dispassionate judge.

As in the case of Benedick's acerbic bachelorhood, Beatrice's shrewishness is hardly a confirmed state, but rather a type which Shakespeare suggests only to bounce off, or back away from, in another demonstration of the play's concern with the frequent distance between who people imagine themselves to be and who they actually are. The sense throughout is that these two are using the conventions as a form of disguise or protective camouflage, or as a defence against the greater conventionality of being lovelorn; depending on the production, they throw them off either willingly or reluctantly, but throw them off they do. (Even if for yet another convention: Benedick, for instance, goes from being the most articulate source of the play's misogyny to a chivalric defender of woman's honour – a conversion from one norm of male behaviour to another. And Beatrice prompts this reversal by an acknowledgement of her own irretrievably female identity: 'O that I were a man . . . I cannot be a man with wishing, therefore I will die a woman with grieving', 4.1.315, 320–1.) Overall these gender stereotypes come across as rather archly staged roles; we can sense Shakespeare's nod to the conventional postures, but also his mockery of them.

The characterization of Beatrice in particular presents a striking departure from established Renaissance norms of gender identity. Despite the occasional dissenting voice (one nineteenth-century critic held her to be 'an odious woman' (Campbell, xlvi)), she is generally the most beloved of Shakespearean heroines, for her very vitality, generosity of spirit and wit, and the graceful but firm insistence with which she claims intellectual equality with men. Benedick's own characterizations of her as a 'harpy', 'infernal Ate' or 'my Lady Tongue' – all terms for a shrew – are comical in part because they are so far from the mark, as well as so obviously the slurs of one who has been bested by a woman who 'speaks poniards' (2.1.227). Her playful resistance to the thought of subjugation in marriage – 'Would it not grieve a woman to be overmastered with a piece of valiant dust? To make an account of her life to a clod of wayward marl?' (2.1.53–5) – smacks less of the shrew than of an intelligence truly indignant at the constraints social conventions impose upon selfhood (and a wit delighted with its own elaborative powers). The homicidal ferocity of her devotion to her cousin – 'Kill Claudio' (4.1.288) – is arresting but also cathartic, as is her thrilling cry against the unjustness of a world that so easily traduces a woman: 'What, bear her in hand until they come to take hands, and then with public accusation, uncovered slander, unmitigated rancour? . . . Talk with a man out at a window! A proper saying!' (4.1.302–4, 307–8). For all her intellectual pride, she is the first to admit that vanity is worth nothing when it is the cause of social divisiveness: 'Contempt, farewell; and maiden pride, adieu; / No glory lives behind the back of such' (3.1.109–10). Her wit works to produce pleasure and joy, with nothing truly grudging about it.

What is perhaps most surprising about Beatrice's relation to convention is that her flirtation with verbal prowess never seems to compromise her sexual reputation; it rather only argues for her intellectual parity with Benedick. This is significantly unlike the assumptions of much Renaissance misogynistic writing, where the link between verbal and sexual freedom is repeatedly underscored.

Though Beatrice is called 'too curst' (2.1.18) by Antonio, and Leonato warns her 'thou wilt never get thee a husband, if thou be so shrewd of thy tongue' (2.1.16–17), and Benedick wishes 'my horse had the speed of [her] tongue, and so good a continuer' (1.1.135–6), her verbal powers never call her chastity into question, and they are more than anything a source of delight. (In fact, her speech is not characterized by excess or amplification – that would be Benedick – so much as by the darting, spare quip.) The point is explicitly made (perhaps in order to reassure?) that she is 'an excellent sweet lady, and, out of all suspicion, she is virtuous' (2.3.157–8).

Other characters in the play do imagine Beatrice in racy situations ('A maid and stuffed!', 3.4.59). When the men gull Benedick, they relate a racy joke about Beatrice writing in her nightgown, herself horrified at having found 'Benedick' and 'Beatrice' 'between the sheet' (2.3.137–8). The sheets here are paper, but the joke lies in the pun informed by the connection of women, words and sex that propels so much of the conventional writings against women. Further corroboration of Beatrice's unladylike affection for words comes in the play's closing revelation that she, like Benedick, has been writing sonnets, and in her quip in the first scene that if Benedick were in her books – i.e. her good graces – 'I would burn my study' (1.1.75). Hero says about Beatrice that 'I never yet saw man – / How wise, how noble, young, how rarely featured – / But she would spell him backward' (3.1.59–61); what she means is that Beatrice manages to convert any male virtue into a fault, but the phrase 'spell . . . backward' gives a sense of Beatrice's power to pervert meanings through her facility with words, and her Diana-like ability to metamorphose both meanings and men.

Yet despite these assumed links between loose words and loose women, so prevalent in the culture at large, the fact remains that the eloquent Beatrice's virtue is never in doubt. There is some acknowledgement in Lyly that women should be well spoken when occasion requires it, and heroines who are both articulate and nonetheless virtuous are common in Shakespeare. Thus when her uncle says that Beatrice apprehends 'passing shrewdly' in her estimate of marriage, we should hear it in the sense of perceptive, or sharp, rather than cross or lewd – as she replies, 'I have a good eye, uncle; I can see a church by daylight' (2.1.72–3). To see clearly is an important and rare feature in this play, and it is 'my Lady Tongue' (2.1.252) who persuades a man to believe in her cousin's honour. In a plot whose stumbling block is the fear of cuckoldry, it is the quiet ones, like Hero, that you have to watch out for.[1]

Chaste, silent and obedient

In seeking to explain this apparent paradox it may help to turn to other materials which, while they are not usually considered 'sources' of this play, do help to illuminate the cultural forces against and with which Shakespeare shaped his own characters and situations. Of particular interest is a class of writings concerned with the organization and regulation of the early modern family (see L. Wright). These 'conduct books' share many of the assumptions of the debate literature when it comes to the disputed nature of womankind, but unlike that tradition, do so without irony, in deadly earnest, and not primarily in the service of rhetorical performance.

The conduct-book tradition derived from the impetus of Protestant reformers eager to define marriage as an institution crucial to spiritual well-being (and hence necessary for priests); it was a genre also helped along by the increasing sense of the family as an economic unit, and the importance of a proper wife to its prosperity. Thus marriage in such texts begins to be defined not merely as a way to avoid the damnation attendant upon unregulated lust, or as a means of peopling the world, but as a source of companionship both intellectual and spiritual. Briefs for this new kind of marriage were written by and for men, but they introduced a woman different from her medieval sisters. Eve

---

1 Bianca in *The Taming of the Shrew* is another superficially demure but troublesome figure (though more intentionally so than Hero).

was rewritten as a solution to the problem of Adam's loneliness in paradise; according to the reformer Heinrich Bullinger, Eve was taken 'out of the syde of man and not from the erth, lest any man shulde think that he had gotten his wyfe out of the myre . . . the wyfe is the husbandes flesh and bone . . . even out of thy syde, as one that is set next unto man, to be his helpe & companyon' (Bullinger, sig. A4^v). Citations of the Galatians verse 'there is neither Iew nor Grecian: there is neither bond nor free: there is neither male nor female' (3.28) helped to support this view of female spiritual fitness (if not parity). Bullinger is careful to stipulate that if woman was to be set alongside man, 'yet was she not made of the head' (sig. A4^v); other writers pointed out that if a rib was not exactly dirt, it did derive from the flesh, and hence was in need of male control. St Paul underscored this hierarchy: 'the head of every man is Christ and the head of the woman is the man' (1 Corinthians, 11); 'Wives, submit yourselves to your husbands' (Ephesians, 5). Spousal companionship in this culture is officially thus perhaps less a marriage of true minds than a (re)absorption of female into male. But we can also see that Shakespeare's offering of a Benedick and Beatrice-type intellectual pairing ('if they were but a week married, they would talk themselves mad', 2.1.325–6) animates the notion of intellectual and spiritual compatibility. When Benedick asks Beatrice 'Think you in your soul the Count Claudio hath wronged Hero?' he is speaking to a Protestant woman: 'Yea, as sure as I have a thought or a soul' (4.1.325–7).

However, Beatrice is an uncommon figure, 'odd and from all fashions' (3.1.72). It is the dilemma of Hero as a victim of slander and impersonation that these texts illuminate most clearly. The centrality of companionship to marriage meant that the process of choosing a suitable wife – one meant to help you get ahead as well as into heaven – began to loom large in the male imagination. Women were by both nature and culture inscrutable, and hence a whole industry of what we would call self-help books, or, less kindly, consumer guides, began to appear. Texts with titles such as *How a Man May Choose a Good Wife from a Bad* (1602), *A Discourse of Marriage and Wiving* (1615), or *A Looking Glass for Married Folks* (1610) reminded prospective early modern bridegrooms how important the choice of a spouse was to one's domestic peace, prosperity and spiritual salvation – as well as how difficult it was.[1] The ideal wife was one designed to suit male needs for emotional, economic and reproductive profit: she should be devout, thrifty, even-tempered, hard working, and above all chaste.

The very existence of such guides suggests, however, that the ideal is easier described than found; their recommendations for proceeding suggest that the reason for the difficulty lies not only in the scarcity of good women but also in the limitations of the technologies available to discover them. How could a woman's nature and character be known? These guides are thus semiotic in nature, designed to enable the prospective suitor to discover a virtuous spouse by interpreting the marks of her speech, appearance and reputation. Yet the difficulty of finding a good woman lay not only in the ways in which bad women might impersonate the good; one author warned that 'thys undertaking is a matter of some difficulty, for good wiues are many times so like vnto bad that they are hardly discerned betwixt' (Niccholes, sig. B4ᵛ). More troubling still was that even though a bridegroom needed to look for signs of virtue, the very existence of legible signs ironically rendered a woman suspect. For a good woman was by definition inconspicuous, but hence at times potentially inscrutable.

For example, the standard advice in such manuals was to observe signs of behaviour, such as 'a sober and mild aspect, courteous behaviour, decent carriage, of a fixed eye, constant look, and unaffected gate, the contrary being oftentimes signs of ill portent and consequence' (Niccholes, sig. C1ʳ). Redheads were to be avoided, as well as women who were either too beautiful ('many times both to herself and to them that beholde her beautie is a prouocation to much euil') or too far above one in social station (liable to upset the gender hierarchy) (R.C., sig. K1ᵛ–2ʳ). But

1 Heywood, *Man*; Niccholes; Snawsel.

the difficulty in choosing a helpmeet on these grounds was that
the viewer was always haunted by a sense that such signs might
be dissembled, or be inadequate as denotative guides, especially
as a meretricious sign is likely to be a warning one. A frequent
dilemma is that a good woman can be known by her speech, but
a truly good woman will be silent. Similarly, while 'the lookes'
are an index of 'godliness in the face', the truly godly face will
be veiled, 'to shewe how a modeste countenance and womanly
shamefastnesse doe command a chaste wife; it is observed, that
the word Nuptiae, doth declare the manner of her marriage. For
it importeth a couering, because Virgins which should be married,
when they come to their husbands for modestie and shamefastness
did couer their faces' (R.C., sig. G4^r).

This paradox would bedevil John Milton, who nearly half a century after *Much Ado*'s composition writes in his divorce tracts that
'who knows not that the bashful muteness of a virgin may oftimes
hide all the unliveliness and natural sloth which is really unfit for
conversation?'[1] We can hear here the bewilderment of a man confronted by the contradiction between the cultural ideal of a woman
who kept her signs to a minimum and his own definition of marriage as a 'happy conversation' (if not a couple talking themselves
mad). Milton's plaintiveness here prefigures that of Henry Higgins
in *My Fair Lady* ('Why can't a woman be more like a man?') but it
also owes something to notions of companionate marriage and the
incipient challenge it posed to and for traditional definitions of the
ideal female identity as chaste, silent and obedient.

Hero

These difficulties in interpreting a woman's façade, the sense that
she may be 'but the sign and semblance of her honour' (4.1.31),
perhaps account for Hero's vulnerability, and the ease with which

---

1   Milton, *The Doctrine and Discipline of Divorce* (1643), in Milton, *Poems and Prose*,
    708. 'Conversation' at this time meant, in addition to verbal exchange, cohabitation
    or society (*OED* 2) as well as sexual intercourse or intimacy (*OED* 3).

it is possible to slander her demure person. There is so little of her to go on. What there is is contradictory: she is silent in the presence of men, and pert in that of women – the discrepancy instances Shakespeare's psychological realism, surely, but also lends to her elusiveness. Both she and Claudio are very young, a 'forward March chick' (1.3.52) and a 'lamb' (1.1.15), and Hero is more often spoken about than a speaker herself. Ironically, however, and perhaps consequently, much of the play's thematic preoccupation with misinformation and misrepresentation – the 'noting' of its title – takes Hero as its object. She is rumoured to be Don Pedro's choice; she is rumoured to be unchaste; she is rumoured to be dead; she is masked, she is buried, she is veiled. The actual slander occurs by means of the manipulation of her clothing, in Spenser's version, the 'gorgeous geare' of Claribel (*FQ*, 2.4.26.8). (The play's leitmotif on the unreliable nature of fashion's significations is also voiced by Borachio in his disquisition on that 'deformed thief' (3.3.126ff.), and the Watchman's corroborative comments.) But the seeds of the slander are present in Claudio's initial choice of her, when he feels the need to ask both Benedick and Don Pedro for their warrants of her modesty, beauty and fortune – their own 'noting' of her. As his sense of Hero's attractiveness relies on the corroboration of his companions' second opinions of Hero's character, so it is vulnerable to the idea that others could desire her, and perhaps she them. (This dynamic of competitive desire is also invoked in the gulling of Benedick, where, to induce his interest, Don Pedro confesses to an attraction to Beatrice: 'I would she had bestowed this dotage on me. I would have doffed all other respects and made her half myself', 2.3.165–7). Claudio approaches Hero from the outside in, as it were, by judging the marks of her demeanour and reputation; given that in mixed company at least Hero is appropriately demure (unlike her forthright cousin), the task of deciphering her inner nature is one that requires the assistance of friends. But it remains a difficult one.

The enigmatic nature of Hero's appearance is made most clear at the moment of Claudio's rejection of her. He asserts that her blush, the conventional mark of female virtue, is a sign of shame, not embarrassment: 'guiltiness, not modesty' (4.1.40).[1] Her father agrees with this estimate: 'Could she here deny / The story that is printed in her blood?' (4.1.121–2). The Friar on the other hand has a different interpretation of Hero's visage: 'I have marked / A thousand blushing apparitions / To start into her face, a thousand innocent shames / In angel whiteness beat away those blushes' (4.1.158–61). Was a blush a sign of innocence, or experience?[2] Either reading demonstrates the way in which knowledge of Hero's ethical identity relies on judgements about an appearance that is at once intrinsically ambiguous and imitable.[3] Hence while the docile Hero, the 'good daughter', is the enigmatic victim of others' manipulation of her representation, it is Beatrice, so clearly identified as the weaker sex by virtue of her unruly tongue, who paradoxically is transparently virtuous, 'out of all suspicion' (2.3.157).

Cuckolds

Much of this play's emotional process involves the need for discovery and disclosure – of Don John's villainy, of Benedick and Beatrice's mutual affections, of Hero's virtue and face, and so on. But if the revelation of a woman's true identity is necessary to marital security, the discovery of a man's is potentially horrifying (partly because the two are so interdependent). The dilemma of the conspicuous – what is visible and what is not – is also part of a popular tradition of cuckold humour that informs much of the play's comedy. While there are no actual cuckolds in Shakespeare's plays, Samuel Johnson wrote in some dismay, in a note on *Merry Wives* 3.5.140–1, that 'There is no image which our

---

1 Compare with Isabella's enigmatic blush in *MM* 1.4.16–17.
2 See 4.1.32n., and McEachern, 'Blush'.
3 The story of Susannah and the elders, in which the virtuous Susannah is slandered by two judges who attempt to blackmail her into sexual commerce by threatening her with a blot on her reputation, is another popular Renaissance instance of a woman being imprisoned by the very qualities she is trying to preserve; see Kaplan, 'Slander'; and e.g. Robert Greene, *Mirror of Modesty* (1584), 7ff.

author appears so fond of as that of a cuckold's horns. Scarcely a light character is introduced that does not endeavour to produce merriment by some allusion to horned husbands' (*Johnson on Shakespeare*, 186). *Much Ado* is riddled with these jokes, as the characters make sport with the horn on their very way to the altar. Cuckoldry is not merely the matter of a running joke, but a theme that touches on the obstacle to love itself. Its prevalence warrants some explanation, especially given that what Johnson found an excrescence is more often, to modern readers, obsolescence.

The idea that a deceived husband would grow horns which would reveal him to his community as a dupe of his wife and her lover is ancient and cross-cultural, although its ubiquity in Tudor–Stuart literature bespeaks a particular fascination for this moment. In addition to fuelling many a drama, the theme was the subject of many ballads and pamphlets, with titles such as *Cornucopiae* (Breton). There was even a place in London known as Cuckold's Haven, three miles east of St Paul's, and marked by a wooden pole sporting animal horns (see Bruster).

The word 'cuckold' comes from the word for cuckoo, the bird known to lay its eggs in another bird's nest in order that its chicks should be nurtured. The origins of the notion of horns are obscure, however; the *Oxford English Dictionary* points out that in German the word for cuckold comes from the word for capon, and is derived from the 'practice formerly prevalent of planting or engrafting the spurs of a castrated cock on the root of the excised comb, where they grew and became horns' (horn 7a). Another account explains that horns owe their origin to the practices of the Greek emperor Andronicus, who had horns placed on the houses of his conquests, in order to signify the compensatory grant of hunting privileges to their husbands.[1] The most renowned source

---

1 *Brewer*. As Bruster records, this is similar to one account of the origins of Cuckold's Haven, which was attributed to the land grant of King John to the miller of Charlton, who caught the king kissing his wife; the miller was required to secure his title by walking once a year (on St Luke's day, patron saint of endurance) to the point marking his boundary with a pair of buck's horns affixed to his head.

5   Diana and Actaeon, from Henry Peacham's *Minerva Britannia* (1598). Diana,
     goddess of the moon, sports the crescent horn which would become the
     bovine property of the cuckold.

of the notion is Ovid's *Metamorphoses*, and its story of Diana and
Actaeon (3.138–249). Actaeon, a notable hunter, is punished for
his inadvertent glimpse of the chaste goddess of the hunt in her
bath by being transformed by her into an antlered stag; he is then
pursued and killed by his own hounds (see Fig. 5, and cf. *TN*
1.1.21–3).

Ovid's version is helpful for explaining cuckolds in that it
associates horns with female power over men, although it is also
somewhat confusing in that Diana acts to protect her chastity
rather than to relieve herself of it. (Of course, from an orthodox
point of view any female sovereignty over sexuality is an instance
of unruly behaviour, and chastity is property to be deployed in
the service of male alliance, so even an aggressively chaste Diana

bears no small resemblance to an unfaithful wife, in that she seeks to control her own sexual access.) There are other differences as well: the plaintive vulnerability of Actaeon is a far cry from the jolly comedy of the cuckold, who is usually a figure less of pathos than of sport. Actaeon is punished for an excess of vision, rather than a lack of it. And despite the use of the term 'Actaeon' to describe cuckolds, most Renaissance representations of cuckolds (with the exceptions of Falstaff, and the hunting chorus of *As You Like It*) involved not antlers but the bovine horn, as *Much Ado*'s jokes about 'the savage bull' (1.1.242–3, 5.4.43) and the 'curst cow' (2.1.20–1) underscore (cattle, like cuckolds, were servile beasts of burden and endurance). This horn bears a resemblance to the crescent moon sported by Diana herself, so that the cuckold, feminized by his wife's usurpation of sexual initiative, literally bears the emblem of female mutability.

The status of the cuckold's horn as both ludic and lucid is borne out by the uses of bovine horn in the period, as horn was known for its light-bearing and light-shedding properties; polished, it served as material for windows and lanterns (lant-horns) as well as hornbooks (alphabet primers in which the page bearing the letters was overlaid with a protective and transparent piece of horn). Crucially, this property of transparency only applies to bovine horn, not antler, which is opaque.[1] Horns are thus associated with visibility; they make the concupiscent conspicuous (see Fig. 6).

---

1 Rabelais supplements this material register by the mythic in Book 3 of *Gargantua and Pantagruel*, in which the quest of Panurge to find an answer to the question of whether, should he marry, he will be cuckolded, includes a dream vision (of his wife planting horns on his head), which he is advised to interpret according to whether the dream comes to him through the Gates of Ivory or the Gates of Horn. Whereas the former are misshapen and impenetrable, 'exactly the way you can't possibly see through ivory', the latter can be trusted, 'because [horn] is so diaphanous, so shining, and you can see them perfectly' (*Gargantua*, 2.68). The reference is to Book 19 of the *Odyssey* (probably the earliest site of the commonplace), where the chaste Penelope contemplates cuckolding Odysseus, and wonders aloud to a visiting stranger about a dream in which an eagle kills a flock of geese. When the (disguised) Odysseus assures her that it surely means that her husband will return and rout the suitors, she demurs that the authority of dreams depends on their gate: 'The dreams that pass through the gates of polished horn / are fraught with truth, for the dreamer who can see them' (19.637–8).

6 A seventeenth-century woodcut accompanying the ballad 'A Married Man's Miserie', which depicts the conspicuous plight of the cuckold. The figure on the right is winding a recheat (see 1.1.225). The cuckold wears the bovine horns (similar to those of his satyr-like rival) and seems to reside at the sign of the antler.

These features help to explain some of the function of the cuckold humour in this play, and reveal Shakespeare's preoccupation with the need for it not to be merely a matter of a recurrent locker-room gag. For while Shakespeare devotes many of the plot's twists and turns to questions of the enigmatic, also at work is the horror of the conspicuous, of having one's most intimate nature revealed in a society where social camouflage is of such supreme importance.

For Benedick the fear of such horns lies in their power to make a man visible; his fears of cuckoldry take the form of a fear of becoming a spectacle: 'pluck off the bull's horns and set them in my forehead; and let me be vilely painted, and in such great letters as they write "Here is good horse to hire", let them signify under my sign, "Here you may see Benedick, the married man"' (1.1.245–9); 'pick out mine eyes with a ballad-maker's pen and hang me up at the door of a brothel-house for the sign of blind Cupid' (1.1.234–6). This fear of becoming conspicuous is compounded by the status of the bovine horn as an instrument of sound as well as of sight, the vehicle of the 'recheat winded in my forehead' (1.1.225–6) (cf. Fig. 6). The dread of cuckoldry is a dread of becoming visible, the observed of all observers, of having your inmost domestic business revealed to the world. Thus a cuckold is emasculated, not merely by having his place taken by another, but in being rendered vulnerable to representation. The cuckold, who has failed to see his wife's behaviour, becomes a sign for others to see. What is funny about a cuckold is that not only can he not see his wife's faithlessness, he cannot see his own horns (hence Benedick's recourse to the figure of Cupid outside the brothel, emblematic not only of love's fated blindness, or that caused by venereal disease, but of that due to the failure of a husband's ability to see). Indeed a cuckold who is cognizant of his wife's behaviour is not technically termed a cuckold but a 'wittol', a word formed by splicing the word 'wit' onto the second syllable of cuckold.[1] He is in on the joke.

One of the comic attractions of the cuckold, and what differentiates him from the tragic Actaeon, is that it allows those around him to be in the know – to be, as it were, wits. He is funny because he provides a spectacle of ignorance that allows omniscience on the part of his audience. Cuckoldry thus personifies the structure of dramatic irony, that phenomenon by which a certain group of people (including us) is privy to information not available to others (certain characters). In its most comfortable, silliest form, this is knowledge at the expense of a dupe, and productive of the

---

1   Middleton's Allwit, in *A Chaste Maid in Cheapside* (1613), is such an instance.

pleasures of complicity (*Merry Wives*); in a less comfortable form, we get *Othello*, or *The Winter's Tale*, in which we are tortured by what we know but cannot share.

Much Ado veers between these two kinds of knowledge, the comic and the tragic. The spectacle of Beatrice and Benedick deluded is funny, that of Claudio and Leonato just the opposite. This is a play known for its wit; to have wit is to be in the know. It is the superior wit of both Benedick and Beatrice that marks them out as tempting victims for a kind of structural cuckolding, a desire to turn them into the butts of others' wits, and so rob them of their preening immunity to the bestial foolery of love, to dupe them into 'a mountain of affection th'one with th'other' (2.1.338–9) on false pretences, a transformation which will, or so it is hoped, rob them of their wit: 'The sport will be when they hold one an opinion of another's dotage, and no such matter . . . which will be merely a dumb-show' (2.3.208–11). The hope is that these two who pride themselves on their intellectual distance from human foibles will become, in love, a spectacle for others, unwitting of the deception practised upon them.

Thus the cuckold provides Shakespeare not merely with a species of joke, but with a design of comedy. The play is built around the question of who knows what, and when. It is formed by a series of movements of confusion and disclosure. The knowledges at stake include: the question of Hero's true suitor, mistaken by Leonato and Antonio, then Claudio and Benedick; the content and effects of the gulling plots; the discovery of the Watch, in which we are comforted by the knowledge of villainy apprehended (and frustrated, Othello-like, at its failure to be disseminated); Hero's mock 'death', and the forging of a bond between Beatrice and Benedick (by which they become, in effect, wittols, or complaisant in their own deception). In each situation some character or characters are at an epistemological disadvantage, and so provide the sport of others and ourselves. The conversion of characters into effective 'cuckolds' not only provides for the figural attention to the play's imagery of metamorphosis, but prepares for the greater emotional transformations of sceptics into lovers. Much of a production's closing tenor is determined by whether Beatrice and Benedick remain 'cuckolds' – that is, not fully cognizant of the origin or impetus of their mutual attraction – or become 'wittols': having some ownership of their own feelings. For one unusually cynical critic, for instance, they are merely victims of a 'social conspiracy': 'They are tricked into marriage against their hearts; without the pressure that moves them to professions of love, they would have remained unmarried . . . they constantly tantalize us with the possibility of an identity quite different from that of Claudio and Hero, an identity deliberately fashioned to resist the constant pressure of society. But that pressure finally prevails' (Greenblatt, 1386). An alternative vision might find the two in full possession of their own emotions, having united over and beyond the ways in which their community has prompted them. Either way, Shakespeare asks us to ponder the complicated relations of self- and social knowledges.

STRUCTURE AND STYLE

A distinguishing feature of *Much Ado About Nothing*'s architecture is the structure not merely of discrepant awareness, but of discrepant tones: it generates multiple emotional movements – towards sadness, towards happiness – sometimes contrapuntally, sometimes simultaneously.[1] This variety sometimes occurs in the form of a disjunction that reassures, as in the awareness of comic providence at work even as tragic events unfold (granted, for instance, in the apprehension of the garrulous Borachio prior to the scene in which we know Claudio has vowed to denounce Hero). Or, as Barbara Everett has written of 5.3 (the monument scene), 'the fact that [Hero] isn't dead, and that we know she isn't,

---

1   See B. Evans for the notion of discrepant awareness.

and that her family, too, know that she isn't, turns this grieving ceremony at the tomb into something like the masked dances which characterize this sophisticated comedy: an art, a game, a pretence' (Everett, 'Unsociable', 72). At other times the mixture can produce apprehension, such as when our trust in an ultimate comic direction must suffer impatience at the inability of providential action to prevent malign forces from having a certain sway. The Watch moves in inefficient if not mysterious ways.

This mixture of tones can also produce moments in which the comic and the tragic are so fused that one is not sure whether laughter or tears is the appropriate response, such as in Beatrice's command to Benedick to 'Kill Claudio' (4.1.288), or in the pathos of Leonato's own challenge to Claudio in 5.1, in which he seems to forget that Hero is not really dead (though of course, from a father's perspective, she might as well be). *Much Ado* is not classified as a tragicomedy (perhaps it is rather, à la Polonius, a comitragedy?) for it can and probably should wear its tragic potential lightly, but I would argue that it is unique among Shakespeare's comedies in its temporary proximity to the edge of the cliff (off which both Othello and Leontes will fall). Like Beatrice, who knows that at her birth 'sure . . . my mother cried; but then there was a star danced' (2.1.308–9), this play acknowledges the ways in which human joys and sorrows can often travel together.

'The course of true love'

Harmony clouded by discord is a defining aspect of comedy. While Aristotle cannot help us explicitly here, his model of the narrative sequence of tragedy – a fall from high to low – is echoed and reversed by definitions such as that of William Webbe, in *A Discourse of English Poetry* (1586). Webbe writes that comedy provides an inverse image of the tragic transit from felicity to misfortune: 'The Comedies, on the other side, were directed to a contrary ende, which, beginning doubtfully, drewe to some trouble or turmoyle, and by some lucky chaunce alwayes ended to the joy and appeasement of all parties' (Webbe, 39).[1] This is an essentially medieval, which is to say a Christian, apprehension of the function of comedy's providential conversions of trouble into joy (such that comic harmonies model and prefigure an eternal felicity). Classical models were also pertinent to Shakespeare's comic process; their plots presented the manoeuvrings of a young man towards a young woman, and the confrontation between the erotic ambitions of youth and social obstacles thereto (usually fathers, or discrepancies in social rank, or both – or, as Lysander puts it, 'differen[ce] in blood / . . . misgraffed in respect of years / . . . Or else it stood upon the choice of friends / . . . Or . . . / War, death, or sickness did lay siege to it', *MND* 1.1.135–42). But even this formula, as Frye pointed out, includes a relationship to tragedy:

> Even in New Comedy the dramatist tries to bring his action as close to a tragic overthrow of the hero as he can get it, and reverses this movement as suddenly as possible . . . Thus the resolution of New Comedy seems to be a realistic foreshortening of the death–and–resurrection pattern, in which the struggle and rebirth of a divine hero has shrunk into a marriage, the freeing of a slave, and the triumph of a young man over an older one.
>
> (Frye, 169)

Shakespeare's modifications of this model are many (for example, the questing hero of classical comedy is more often a hardworking heroine in boy's clothing, so that gender identity rather than social rank must be corrected). It has also been argued that Shakespearean comedy is equally indebted to native folkloric

---

1 The majority of Renaissance definitions of comedy were satiric or homiletic, e.g. Philip Sidney: 'Comedie is an imitation of the common errors of our life, which [the poet] representeth in the most ridiculous and scornful sort that may be; so that it is impossible that any beholder can be content to be such a one' (although Sidney also considers comedy a source of delight) (Sidney, *Defence*, 44); George Puttenham: '[comedies] tended altogither to the good amendment of man by discipline and example' (Puttenham, 47); or Thomas Lodge: 'their matter was more plessant [than tragedies] for they were such as did reprehend' (Lodge, 37).

rituals of social regeneration, although *Much Ado* is in a minority among his comedies in its lack of even a metaphorical green world (a world that the 1993 Kenneth Branagh film did, however, provide). Messina is resolutely its sociable self – although the inversions of gulling, masquerade, slander and false death, and the hallucinatory social universe created by the resolutely social practices of eavesdropping and rumour could be argued to produce a climate akin to that of the forests of Arden and Athens.[1] However, Shakespeare's greatest elaboration upon his comic models lies in his transformations of the blocking mechanism, and *Much Ado* occupies a pivotal role in its evolution.

Shakespeare begins most of his comedies with a problem in need of a solution; they differ in regard to what kind of problem, how seriously we are meant to take it, and what collateral damage it does before it can be put right. In his early plays the obstacles are more akin to those of the classical models: uncooperative fathers (*Taming of the Shrew*, *Midsummer Night's Dream*), or social obstacles needing to be finessed by a discovery of hidden identity (*Comedy of Errors*). The convention of comedy requires us to have confidence that these are puzzles that will be duly solved in due time. In the comedies of the later 1590s, however, we begin to meet more intractable obstacles, which have to do with the psychological rather than social barriers to desire's satisfaction. As in the comedies which cluster near *Much Ado* – *Merchant of Venice*, with its threat of death, or *Twelfth Night*, with its elegiac melancholy and wilfulness – the troubles of *Much Ado* come not from a meddling father or a problem of social rank but from within the self.

In fact, the play begins without a problem of the conventional sort; there is no social or paternal objection to the match of Hero and Claudio; if anything, all parties concerned are eager, even automatic, in their approval. Even in the case of a match for the

---

1   Barber, who also notes an affinity between the verbal skirmishes of Benedick and Beatrice and the 'customs of Easter Smacks and Hocktide abuse between the sexes' (7).

unparented Beatrice it is clear that neither station nor parental permission is wanting to render her marriageable (and Benedick admits she is beautiful). So according to comic convention, the problem is rather that there is no problem; hence we are poised to anticipate one. When it comes, it comes from inside the lovers, not without; while the origins of Don John's villainy may be obscure (so to speak), his disruption of the course of true love works by playing upon overt elements of male psychology which appear in the play as commonplaces ('I think this is your daughter.' 'Her mother hath many times told me so', 1.1.98–100). In this respect the impediments to love in both pairs originate in the same source: male suspicion of female sexual inconstancy and its corollary, rival male predation. Don John's first attempt to 'cross' Claudio relies on nothing more than a lie about Don Pedro's own preference for Hero, so that by the end of Act 2 we have already experienced a miniature comedy, of error and its discovery, in which the obstacle derives from fears about male rivalry and female perfidy: 'Friendship is constant in all other things, / Save in the office and affairs of love . . . for Beauty is a witch / Against whose charms faith melteth into blood' (2.1.160–1, 164–5).

Benedick's reluctance to wed seems to stem from the same distrust of women that Claudio demonstrates (and the elder soldier's attitude perhaps serves as the model for the younger). While it is true that Beatrice's reluctance must be included in this catalogue of psychic obstacles, and while she does make the standard joke about marital infidelity ('to a cow too curst he sends none', 2.1.21), there is evidence that we are to construe her aversion to marriage, like Claudio's, as a response to Benedick's own ('Indeed . . . he lent it [his heart] me awhile, and I gave him use for it, a double heart for his single one. Marry, once before he won it of me with false dice; therefore your grace may well say I have lost it', 2.1.255–8). In Shakespeare's location of the barrier to sexual harmony within the human heart, *Much Ado* is, despite its gaiety, kin to the 'problem plays', with their dispiriting vision of the unequivocally fallen nature of human beings.

Another feature of *Much Ado*'s comic trouble is the way in which Shakespeare delays both its gestation and resolution. He mounts it in a staggered fashion, and once afoot, it is long brewing and difficult, perhaps impossible, to shrug off (the play may end with characters who have overcome their distrust of women enough to proceed to the altar, but they are still making jokes about cuckolds). No doubt this is partly because the mood is one of relief and celebration. After 2.1, with the resolution of the mini-comedy in Claudio and Hero's betrothal, Don John reapplies himself to his task, but we know as of 2.2 that an entire week must elapse before Borachio's incriminating masquerade will take place, as Leonato has fixed that term for the preparations of the wedding, and the plot is laid for the eve thereof. The interim is a halcyon time that does not, in Don Pedro's phrase, 'go dully by us' (2.1.336). Hence *Much Ado* can be played as the frothiest of Shakespeare's comedies. Its central acts are filled with the gullings in 2.3 and 3.1, and the contemplation of the 'limed birds' in 3.2 and 3.4. While Don John is presumably lurking (and a production may choose to underscore this in various ways), it is easy to forget this amidst the general gaiety of prenuptial high jinks. The conversions of Benedick and Beatrice give a sense that psychic obstacles to love are yielding, and provide another comedy in miniature, so that by the end of 3.1 we have them nearly aligned with each other even as Hero and Claudio were at the end of 2.1.

Don John reappears and approaches Claudio and Don Pedro with news of Hero's transgression at the end of 3.2, but, reinforcing the sense of quiescence, the Watch expeditiously apprehend Borachio in the very next scene. Like the gullings of Benedick and Beatrice, this apprehension is almost too easy (indeed, the loves of Benedick and Beatrice will be forged again at a higher heat). The ease signals that the trouble is not over yet. Hero's heart is unaccountably heavy in 3.4, and with 3.5 (Leonato brushing off the tedious Dogberry and Verges) arrives that familiar component of tragedy, haste, which rushes us into the church scene, where the plot of Don John nearly achieves its intended effects: 'to misuse the prince, to vex Claudio, to undo Hero and kill Leonato' (2.2.25–6).

The staggered arrival of trouble lies partly in Shakespeare's countervailing of its advances with the antidotes of a different momentum: Don John dupes Claudio in 2.1, and then Don Pedro corrects the error; Borachio recounts his dastardly deeds only to be immediately apprehended. But the difficulty of the villains in getting traction lies also in our own desire to forget their existence (while the comic obstacle here can be described as lurking and creeping – and Don John's malevolence is in some sense all the more threatening for being unexplained – it can also be imagined as effervescently transcended or held at bay by 'festival terms').

Shakespeare's use of time contributes to this effect. The play can be apprehended in three movements. The first (through 2.1) comprises some 760 lines (nearly one-third of the total), and represents the actions of one afternoon and evening. The second movement, just described, occupies another 870 lines, and represents a week; the remaining 1,000 lines depict the preparations for the wedding, its interrupted course, Beatrice and Benedick's troth-plight, Benedick's challenge to Claudio, the revelation of truth, the monument scene, and the re-betrothal scene, all of which occur in a twenty-four-hour period. In other words, the first and last thirds of the play each represent the events of a day, and the middle section a week, so that the latter operates like a kind of hammock of time, in which all seems well. However, the first and last movements are compacted and busy; the middle, indolent (this overall structure is replicated in the construction of scenes, so that long ensemble moments – the opening (1.1), the dance (2.1), the church scene (4.1) and the challenges (5.1) are interleaved with series of shorter, two- or three-person scenes[1]).

---

1   This is somewhat of a false distinction, in that the longer scenes do not involve the entire ensemble at all times, but are composed of a series of smaller conversational groupings which while occupying continuous time and space do serve to keep the action dynamic and shifting. See Jenkins.

Thus, whereas many comedies spend their entire length embroiled in a crescendo of compounded confusion, *Much Ado* maintains a seeming innocence for two-thirds of its length. Or rather, while its participants are embroiled in the psychic obstacles which provide the comic oyster with its grit, they do not *know* they are embroiled until 4.1. While it is true that the finer details of this treatment of time may go unnoticed in performance, the general effect is of difficulty held at bay for a rather long period, followed by a protracted flurry of resolution, rather than, as with much comedy, a problem foregrounded from the beginning and compounded to a pitch of comic imbroglio, then solved in a single revelatory denouement.

Once the denunciation occurs, Shakespeare modulates the tone of the play significantly, and it becomes explicitly rather than implicitly tragic. In a masterly stroke, he moves in 4.1 from the formal verse drama of the church scene, in which emotions are wrought to a high pitch, to the relatively diffident – yet no less emotionally staggering – prose cadences of Beatrice and Benedick's professions of love. Benedick and Beatrice exchange confessions of love, but they do so, as Beatrice acknowledges, in sorrow and because of it: 'It were as possible for me to say I loved nothing so well as you. But believe me not – and yet I lie not. I confess nothing, nor I deny nothing. I am sorry for my cousin' (4.1.269–72). Leonato's grief at the perverse course of events exceeds comfort in 5.1, and Benedick's challenge quite spoils the (now uncouth) attempt of the Prince and Claudio to return to the teasing banter of 3.2. The audience of course views all of these sadnesses from the privileged knowledge that help is on the way, but in the meantime we also witness real suffering and the birth of real seriousness of feeling. Beatrice's desire to kill Claudio, and the Friar's plan for Hero – a mock death perhaps, followed by incarceration in a convent – both reveal a potential for irrevocable pain and danger. If the young pair are not exactly reborn in their ending, they both certainly escape forms of death, so even this third movement contains a third comedy, of joint resurrection, in miniature.

When the ending finally comes, all is well, but emotions are nonetheless raw (as in the sparring between Benedick and Claudio: 'some such strange bull leaped your father's cow / And got a calf in that same noble feat / Much like to you, for you have just his bleat', 5.4.49–51). Thus while *Much Ado*, like any comedy, performs a ritual of social renewal, this also includes the renewal of less than desirable aspects of the human creature. Hence, perhaps, the recurrence of the cuckold humour in virtually the final line – 'Prince, thou art sad – get thee a wife, get thee a wife! There is no staff more reverend than one tipped with horn' (5.4.120–2). The ending thus in a recursive fashion circles to reprise several earlier actions – the wedding, the masque, the merry war and the cuckold banter – and the reiteration gives a sense of the persistent quality of the play's problems.

Considered as a linear narrative, then, the structure of this play works by means of alternating scenes of hope and trouble. In one scale are male distrust of women, rivalry between men, and the sliding vices of social climbing; in the other, the fierce loyalty of Beatrice to her cousin, Benedick's willingness to take her word over his fellow soldiers', the Friar's hope and resourcefulness and the providential efficacy of the Watch and its captain. Also, perhaps, Claudio's willingness to trust in a veiled woman. One can consider the mixed emotional palette as producing a comedy whose harmonies are haunted by darker forces, or, more genially, as a supremely balanced, even temperate portrait of human experience comprising both positive potentials and flaws.

Two plots?

One thing which makes this play difficult to discuss in terms of structure is that one is not sure whether to treat its design diachronically or synchronically: that is, we could treat it either as a series of actions unfolding in time, designed to raise and condition our expectations sequentially – as we experience them when we first read or see the play – or as plots and situations that exist in parallel and antithetical relations (which are more usually recollected in scholarly tranquillity). The latter apprehension of *Much Ado* as an organic structure (rather than a narrative sequence) also yields the sense of its layered action, and Shakespeare's construction of psychic textures and truths that are melded of both hope and despair. Even as the plot reprises certain actions, so Shakespeare interweaves ostensibly separate but mutually illuminating strands of action, so that we are drawn into a sustained comparison of different characters as part of an ongoing enquiry into what constitutes a human being. It is an enquiry that extends from externals such as rank, role, speech, manners and dress, to more interior concerns such as self-knowledge, humanity towards others and openness to change. (It may be no coincidence that the word 'man' and its cognates occur more frequently, by a substantial margin, in *Much Ado* than in any other work of Shakespeare's.[1])

Traditional thinking about this play's structure has concentrated on the notions of main plot and subplot, one of a near-tragic tone, the other of a comic. This sense of the play as bifurcated is compounded by the realization that most of the first, or 'comic' half, leading up to the church scene of 4.1, is in prose, and the remainder of the play, dealing with more sombre matters, is in verse (the actress Maggie Steed, who played Beatrice, refers to this as a 'broken backed' structure (Steed, 42)). This unflattering sense of the play's discontinuity has been countered by other visions that emphasize the continuity and intersection of the two romances by means of various features of its design, including thematic parallels between the two plots. Some of these parallels are representations of behaviour. The most obvious is that signalled in its title, that of 'noting', the way in which social creatures perceive each other. This practice occurs in all of the 'discrete' plots and social groupings, and is staged in several scenes. Borachio overhears Don Pedro and Claudio in 1.1, as does Antonio's servant; Don John sours the betrothal by means of a

---

1   The runners up are *As You Like It*, then *Twelfth Night*; I owe the point and its statistics to RP.

masquerade staged for Claudio's benefit; Hero gulls her cousin by devising 'honest slanders' (3.1.84); Benedick and Beatrice are both prompted to love by overhearing themselves and their admirers described; the Watch overhear Borachio's relation of his perfidy. The play is full of instances in which characters perceive each other indirectly, and hence often erroneously. The effect is that Messina seems a world of many social proximities, where it is easy to come by information and misinformation about oneself and others. The prevalence of noting gives a sense of a community closely, claustrophobically knit together.

A similar pattern of repetition and echoing occurs in episodes that call attention to social rank. Leonato's solicitude towards the Prince (1.1) is echoed in Dogberry's fawning upon Leonato (3.5). Margaret imitates her mistress in masquerade, and then flirts with Benedick about her social aspirations: 'Will you then write me a sonnet in praise of my beauty?' (5.2.4–5). Both Beatrice and Don John call attention to Don Pedro's high status, and the Watch are assured that 'If you meet the prince in the night you may stay him . . . marry, not without the prince be willing' (3.3.73–4, 77–8). The repeated noting of social place helps to create the texture of a social world homogenous in its assumptions. The repetition of similar motifs in different keys helps give the sense of a community bound at all levels by a consensual sense of its boundaries. This sense of the world is also created through Shakespeare's attention to incidental social details: the passing mentions of Claudio's uncle and Antonio's son, Margaret's chatty report on the Duchess of Milan's gown, Benedick's visit to the barber, the passing notations of time and place – all of these conjure a universe vivid, even solid, in its quotidian particulars. These details are not essential to the plot (to the extent that some of them have prompted debate about Shakespeare's compositional method), but they create a sense of a busy social world, of offstage lives and possibilities, and (in keeping with the play's themes) a sense of the audience's overhearing or witnessing a portion of a universe complete only in another dimension.

Another feature common to several of the play's strands is the amusing spectacle of a self-regard that fails to fully describe the self in question. The alacrity with which the confirmed bachelor Benedick resolves to be in love and the earnestness with which Lady Disdain vows to tame her maiden pride are two such instances, in which a character's self-professed reputation is no match for the more insistent desire to love and be loved. To these we must add the pomposity of Dogberry, whose exorbitant sense of self-importance quite outpaces the regard in which he is held by others. A more poignant version of these self-misconceptions is provided in Leonato, a father whose affectionate avuncularity gives way to a radical emotional investment in his daughter with infanticidal overtones.

Not just actions but situations are reiterated. One gulling scene follows another, and the challenge of Benedick to Claudio comes on the heels of Leonato's (and Antonio's). The love song of 2.3 ('Sigh no more, ladies') is echoed in the tomb ritual's song in 5.3 ('Pardon, goddess of the night'); the masquerade of 2.1 is reversed by the veiled women of 5.4; Hero receives the proposal of a disguised suitor in 2.1, and Claudio must accept a veiled bride in 5.4. The impersonation of Hero occurs at night; so does her mock burial. With each of these repetitions we sense the congruence of situations, as well as their individual particularity. The gulling of Benedick, for instance, works by flattering him, whereas Beatrice's gullers undertake a kind of scourging of her faults. Leonato's challenge is full of pathos; Benedick's of grim sincerity. The reiterations generate a series of foil effects, which give a sense of the commonality and the idiosyncrasy of persons – a nuanced portrait of a community. *Much Ado* bears comparison in this architectural respect with the *Henry IV* plays, which Shakespeare had recently completed, and in which he also works along these mirroring lines, so that rebellion in the tavern echoes rebellion in the state, the robbery of purses prefiguring the suppression of Percies. So too, parts of *Much Ado* echo and haunt each other, prefigure and invert their counterparts.

The construction of variation within symmetry, and symmetry within variation, is also the property of the 'dual' plot. The play opens with two pairs ostensibly belonging to antithetical romantic traditions: Hero and Claudio represent the marriage of partners suitable in age, wealth and station, and who conduct their courtship in the terms of stylized romance: 'Lady, as you are mine, I am yours. I give away myself for you, and dote upon the exchange' (2.1.282–4). The more ornery couple, 'too wise to woo peaceably' (5.2.67), seem compatible only in their wit, their shared contempt for romance – 'I had rather hear my dog bark at a crow, than a man swear he loves me' (1.1.125–6) – and, of course, their obsession with each other. But as the play moves on, both couples are tested, and modify the extremity of their positions. Claudio acts most unchivalrously, and Beatrice is forced to seek a champion. One couple gains experience, and emotional texture; the other has recourse to convention. Both unions take the form of an initial approach followed by a severance, followed by a rapprochement, so that marriage comes about as a result of experience and loss as well as desire and momentum. The play begins with Benedick and Beatrice estranged; the crisis between Claudio and Hero helps to unite the former pair, even as it drives Claudio and Hero apart. The figure of a dance comes to mind here, as Shakespeare poses the two pairs as foils and then tempers their differences. The overall effect, as in the emotional tenor, is of balance, symmetry and temperance, shadows in light, and light breaking through shadows.

Style

Relations of similarity and variety also characterize this play's language. In *Much Ado* Shakespeare explores the powers and the pleasures of speaking well. The dialogue is formal, mannered and elegant, but also enlivened by the well-turned phrase, the quick retort, and the punch-line, governed by the tension between the decorous and the daring. The contrast between these two forms is in part what pleases: the way in which the energies of witty badinage can be sparked from the elegant cadences of a more formal and mannered conversation, and vice versa. Conversation is both a dance and a form of combat. Words are swapped, tossed and stolen. Some speakers are more nimble than others, but all aspire. The best in this kind endow a mannered language with a sense of the impromptu and the improvisational, while others study their forms in a hope of mastering their patterns. Above all we have the sense of being in the presence of a kind of everyday eloquence, all the more enviable because seemingly effortless. Additionally, in its very linguistic textures the play explores the larger thematic questions of the pleasures of artifice and the corresponding paranoia about semantic stability.

Prose and the prosaic

Shakespeare demonstrates in *Much Ado* a rare devotion to prose structures; nearly 70 per cent of the play's lines are prose, of which Benedick, with 399 of 2,485 lines, possesses the lion's share.[1] Only *Merry Wives*, at nearly 90 per cent, has a higher proportion (*Twelfth Night* and *As You Like It* following behind), and *Much Ado* makes prose the choice of principal characters as well as of the more usual suspects such as the Watch (and critics dedicated to the main plot/subplot distinction have cited these allocations in support of their position). This prose comes in several styles, and before examining its kinds we might consider a few critical assumptions about Elizabethan dramatic prose.

Even Shakespearean prose, for all its glories, tends to be treated somewhat as a poor relation in critical evaluations. One of the first things schoolchildren are taught about Shakespeare is that verse typically belongs to the aristocratic main characters, and prose to the motley speakers of the non-noble subplots, as if social station was a prerequisite for verbal ornament, and learning the prerogative of the line break. We are reminded that prose is most often the

---

1   The figures belong to Vickers, 433, table 1, and T. King, 193.

property of madmen and the lower orders: 'the normal mode of speech in the [Elizabethan] play was verse, and the introduction of prose signified the failure of a character to conform with the prevailing mode of his world' (M. Crane, 3). True in some degree as such statements are, they carry with them the implicit assumption of prose as a debased and undisciplined, or even unlearned and unadorned, medium, as if the absence of the governing regularity and pressure of a verse line opens the door to all manner of social ills. In its favour, on the other hand, prose can be considered (at least by modern students) more 'natural' and colloquial, and more true to how people really talk (although actors do cite the similarity of the iambic rhythm and a heartbeat): 'prose, the form of common speech, introduces an atmosphere of realism; and prose speakers in Shakespeare constantly recall the existence of a world which, although not the 'real world' of the audience, is nevertheless somehow physically nearer than the poetic world' (M. Crane, 100). In this light, prose exists merely to get the job done with a minimum of flourish.

Such assumptions have some utility in approaching the style of *Much Ado*. The prose in the play is indeed often easy and direct, even utilitarian: 'I learn in this letter that Don Pedro of Aragon comes this night to Messina' (1.1.1–2); 'Was not Count John here at supper?' (2.1.1); 'In my chamber window lies a book. Bring it hither to me in the orchard' (2.3.3–4). Socially subordinate characters can be very prosaic, on occasion: 'I like the new tire within excellently, if the hair were a thought browner. And your gown's a most rare fashion, i'faith. I saw the Duchess of Milan's gown that they praise so . . . By my troth, 's but a night-gown in respect of yours . . .' (3.4.12–18). Verse is reserved for moments of high formality (or moments which aspire thereto), such as Claudio's wooing and rejection of Hero, and Leonato's lethal disappointment in his daughter. In general the prose cadences of this play contribute to its portrait of a world replete in everyday detail.

However, such a distinction is also misleading. Some of Shakespeare's most virtuoso speakers often conduct themselves in prose: Falstaff and Hal ('the most comparative, rascalliest, sweet young prince', *1H4* 1.2.77–8), to cite two most immediately antecedent to *Much Ado*; Hamlet comes soon after. *Much Ado*'s prose is not exclusively plebeian, and, on the contrary, the efforts of social climbing and striving are conducted through attempts to master its distinctive, and decidedly elitist, patterns. While in the hands of the more eloquent these forms can seem unpremeditated and effortless, they are not unornamented or unlearned, or without artifice. Far from it.

Euphuism

Much Ado's prose style is influenced by and comments upon (although it rises above) the category of Renaissance literary style known as 'euphuism', after the writings of the dramatic and prose fiction writer John Lyly, in particular his prose works *Euphues: An Anatomy of Wit* (1578) and *Euphues and His England* (1580). These texts both feature a young man named Euphues ('Wellborn') who engages his friends in protracted discourses on the nature of friendship, love, women, and other subjects of philosophical merit. It is a style characterized by techniques of amplification such as parallelism and antithesis, chiasmus, strings of rhetorical questions, structural symmetries and turns of logic, and full of internal poetic effects generated by alliteration, syllabic echoing, the repetition of verbal roots, rhyme, puns, phrases patterned on sound and syntax, and myriad rhetorical figures identifiable only to the connoisseur. Crowning these aural effects were displays of humanist learning: epigrams, aphorisms, proverbs, classical allusions and examples, fables, and information from natural and un-natural history. In other words, this is a prose as complicated, and as figurally rich, as any verse.

While the term 'euphuism' credits Lyly with this style, he was less the originator than the popularizer of a mode that had been a hallmark of Renaissance humanism. This was a prose modelled after Ciceronian oratory in its copiousness and ornament; its balances and symmetries were meant to connote not merely rhetorical poise but ethical temperance.[1] At the same time, like all Renaissance rhetoric, euphuism is eloquence in the service of persuasion, or 'moving' (in Sidney's term), intended to shape the response of its recipient. As such it is indebted to the tradition of *in utramque partem* debate; authors employ its argumentative line in order to persuade or dissuade a presumed antithesis, and the syntactical register is itself replete with antithesis, balance and reversals. Its figures and methods were circulated in handbooks of rhetoric, such as *The Civil Conversation of M. Steven Guazzo* (1581), as well as promulgated by the mimetic methods of Renaissance schooling. This prose was written by 'wits', whose personae conveyed an ease, balance, temperance, agility and all-round suaveness (their number included John Donne, Thomas Nashe, Thomas Lodge and Ben Jonson); it achieved a vogue in the years 1590–1612.[2] The intellectual poise and apparent disinterestedness of Benedick and Beatrice model this pose as well.

It is not, at first glance, a prose style particularly suited to drama; in Lyly's prose the processes of amplification produce monologues that, however enlivened at the level of the clause, are daunting (and mind-numbing) in their stamina. An example apropos to the sexual mistrust that pervades *Much Ado* is provided by the disappointed Euphues, in his warning against love in the vein of Ovid's *Amores*:

> This is therefore to admonish all young Impes and nouices in loue, not to blow the coales of fancie wyth desire, but to quench them with disdayne. When love tickleth thee decline it lest it stiffle thee, rather fast than surfette, rather starue than striue to exceede. Though the beginning of loue bringeth delyght, the ende bringeth

1   See W. Crane: '[wit] connoted . . . a flow of ideas and words ample for the development of any topic at length, along with quick comprehension of thought and readiness in answering' (9).
2   As well as a backlash, in the anti-Ciceronian rhetoric of Justus Lipsius, Francis Bacon and others. See Croll.

destruction. For as the first draught of wine doth comfort the stomacke, the second inflame the lyuer, the thirde fume into the heade, so the first sippe of loue is pleasaunt, the seconde perilous, the thirde pestilent. If thou perceiue thy selfe to be entised with their wanton glaunces, or allured with their wicked guyles, eyther enchaunted with their beautie or enamoured with their brauerie, enter with thy selfe into this meditation. What shall I gayne if I obtayne my purpose? nay rather what shall I loose in winning my pleasure? If my Lady yeelde to be my louer is it not lykely she will bee an others lemman?

(Lyly, Anatomy, 248)

This is a mere portion of a passage that has been underway, and continues, for hundreds of lines. Indeed, part of the point is the authorial staying power to sustain the subject while generating interest and texture with marks of ingenuity and invention. The writer must aspire to an encyclopaedic range of reference and reiteration, whilst managing to stay on topic, balancing digressive expansion against thematic pertinence. This is a style that Benedick might call 'so good a continuer' (1.1.136).

Some of *Much Ado*'s set pieces are akin to this not only in style but also in subject, such as Benedick's monologue against love in the beginning of 2.3 ('I do much wonder that one man, seeing how much another man is a fool when he dedicates his behaviours to love, will, after he hath laughed at such shallow follies in others, become the argument of his own scorn by falling in love . . . ', 2.3.8ff.). This, the longest prose speech in *Much Ado* (27 lines), is rivalled only by the speech at the end of the same scene in which Benedick recants his position. In performance it is usually highly entertaining, chiefly because of the sense of argument that propels it; even as he scorns Claudio, Benedick is slowly persuading himself. This sense of suasion derives from Shakespeare's focus on the meditative and dialogue-like features of Lyly's prose, as he builds on and improves upon its patterns of call and response, internal echoes and retorts, rhetorical questions and answers, reversals and symmetries. (If Lyly's marathon style seems untheatrically static, it does contain within it the dialogic structures that make it surprisingly adaptable to drama, albeit in much smaller doses. Lyly himself exploited these.)

Yet the Shakespeare passage is infinitely more flexible than the Lyly, and more agile in sketching the drollery of a personality in debate with itself. It is true that Benedick unfurls parallel balanced structures: three sentences in succession list the contrasts between the 'before' and 'after' versions of Claudio, with respect to his musical tastes, clothing and speech ('I have known when . . . and now . . . '; 'I have known when . . . and now . . . '; 'He was wont . . . and now . . . ', 2.3.12–19). But where Lyly's prose would be just beginning to warm up, Benedick stops and shifts the enquiry to himself, and the mesmeric repetitive queries give way to a blunter, more flat-footed idiom: 'I cannot tell; I think not' (22). Then, just when it seems that Benedick has resolved the matter with the seal of logic ('till he have made an oyster of me he shall never make me such a fool', 24–5), he starts up yet again with musing on the features of women: 'One woman is fair . . . ' (25). He concludes again, with a chiastic flourish: 'But till all graces be in one woman, one woman shall not come in my grace' (27–8). But then he begins *again*, this time even more specifically: 'Rich she shall be . . . ' (28–9). The 'continuer' features of the style are harnessed here to paint a mind irresistibly returning to a closed subject with a moth's attraction to a flame, so that the length of Benedick's argument simultaneously sustains and undermines his conviction. At the beginning of the speech Benedick is perplexed by the notion of a soldier in love, but by the end he is contemplating the colour of her hair, so that the audience begins to anticipate (if it hasn't already concluded) that Benedick himself might 'become the argument of his own scorn by falling in love' (11–12). Shakespeare's prose conjures a mind divided despite itself.

The agonistic aspect of euphuism's verbal one-upmanship is evident most clearly in dialogue rather than soliloquy, such as the first exchange between Beatrice and Benedick (also a disavowal of love):

BENEDICK What, my dear Lady Disdain! Are you yet
    living?

BEATRICE Is it possible Disdain should die, while she
    hath such meet food to feed it as Signor Benedick?   115
    Courtesy itself must convert to Disdain if you come in
    her presence.

BENEDICK Then is Courtesy a turncoat. But it is certain I
    am loved of all ladies, only you excepted; and I would
    I could find in my heart that I had not a hard heart, for   120
    truly I love none.

BEATRICE A dear happiness to women – they would else
    have been troubled with a pernicious suitor. I thank
    God and my cold blood, I am of your humour for that:
    I had rather hear my dog bark at a crow, than a man   125
    swear he loves me.

BENEDICK God keep your ladyship still in that mind,
    so some gentleman or other shall scape a predestinate
    scratched face.

BEATRICE Scratching could not make it worse, an 'twere   130
    such a face as yours were.

BENEDICK Well, you are a rare parrot-teacher.

BEATRICE A bird of my tongue is better than a beast of
    yours.

BENEDICK I would my horse had the speed of your   135
    tongue, and so good a continuer. But keep your way,
    o'God's name; I have done.

BEATRICE You always end with a jade's trick; I know you
    of old.

(1.1.112–39)

This exchange is always greeted with delight in the theatre; it contains the first shots across the respective bows. As Brian

Vickers comments, 'repartee is more than a linguistic device here: to Beatrice and Benedick it is a way of life, a mutual witty antagonism which has evidently long continued and seems destined to go on' (Vickers, 176). Here, instead of a speaker punning upon his own terms, the contest of antagonists personifies and animates the push-and-pull features of euphuism's internal debate. Words of one speaker are taken and turned by the other, returned inverted or askew, transported, and otherwise perverted. Puns are crucial. Shakespeare moves here beyond the polished, patterned verse of plays like *Love's Labour's Lost* towards a more improvisational and realistic repartee, which, while it may commence as elegant twists and turns, degenerates into little more than name-calling, as both speakers strain to sustain the rally.

It is no coincidence that the passages in *Much Ado* that display the most virtuoso instances of euphuism are those either where a debate is underway, or a character is engaged in argument with himself, or where high feeling – either rage or contempt – propels the language. Indignation and invective, contempt and disdain are the motive forces of this style. Don John's speech on his melancholy in 1.3 ('I had rather be a canker in a hedge than a rose in his grace', 25ff.), and Beatrice's excoriation of Claudio in 4.1 ('Count Comfit', 314), are two moments where Shakespeare fuels the persuasive features of the style with the implosive pressures of disdain.

Verbal handshakes

The combative aspect of euphuism – whether it appears as persuasion or invective – derives in part from its roots in debate forms, but also from the social function of the style as it is rendered in Lyly's works. Euphuism is the currency of social alliance and competition, the means by which Lyly's characters (and the real-life wits they inspired) signal their associations and their rivalries. It is as much sociolect as aesthetic, an identity which Shakespeare's practice in *Much Ado* makes clear. The language is the means by which members of this group signal their membership in the group, and their relations to each other, relations of both rank and gender (while euphuism is a primarily male discourse here, Beatrice's usage marks her out as both fashionable and an 'excellent wife for Benedick', 2.1.324). Speakers are distinguished by their relative proficiency in its patterns, a proficiency that is linked in part to social position. It is a dialect that signals the relations of a courtly class of persons, and is the means by which they display their membership in this class, and also the means by which others display their aspirations to the fashionable company.

The most slavish speakers of the idiom, for instance, include the Messenger and Balthasar, those subordinate male figures attending upon, and imitating, their betters. Don Pedro's nameless messenger, harbinger of the troop's arrival at Leonato's dwelling, signals the arrival of the courtly gentlemen in his description of Claudio: 'He hath borne himself beyond the promise of his age, doing in the figure of a lamb the feats of a lion; he hath indeed better bettered expectation than you must expect of me to tell you how' (1.1.13–16). This speech is met with Leonato's rather laconic comment on Claudio's uncle; the Messenger tries again in a description of his embassy: 'there appears much joy in him, even so much that joy could not show itself modest enough without a badge of bitterness' (20–2). Again, Leonato (bemused?) translates this ornate speech into the vernacular: 'Did he break out into tears?' (23), but then he too meets the challenge, matching the Messenger's *polyptoton* (repetition of the same word root in different forms), and raising it with an *antimetabole* (the inversion of word or clause order within a sentence): 'A kind overflow of kindness; there are no faces truer than those that are so washed. How much better it is to weep at joy than to joy at weeping!' (25–7). By the time the troop arrives, Leonato himself is at full throttle: 'Never came trouble to my house in the likeness of your grace, for, trouble being gone, comfort should remain; but when you depart from me, sorrow abides, and happiness takes his leave' (94–7).

Don Pedro and Leonato as the two most important political figures in the play use this language as a form of mutual acknowledgement (hence perhaps Leonato's reluctance to match the Messenger's style). Their speech is courtly, decorous and balanced, trading and complementing each other's terms with the measured elegance of a formal dance. Don John, on the other hand, disdains this language in the first scene in order to signal his reluctant membership in this fellowship: 'I am not of many words' (150). (Later, however, with Conrade, he shows himself quite voluble in these very cadences, and 'the closeness of the patterning concentrates his ruthlessness still more' (Vickers, 178).)

The dilatory, even flowery, habits of euphuism render it vulnerable to cutting in modern productions; indeed, even this play's own characters can find an over-dedicated speaker tiresome. Dogberry is the prime exhibit here, but to his tediousness we can add Balthasar's – whose thematic punning on his 'notes' invites Don Pedro's impatience in 2.3: 'Why, these are very crotchets that he speaks' (2.3.54). Margaret's attempt to subject Beatrice to her own treatment in 3.4 receives a similar response. As with Balthasar, the efforts of the lower-status figure invite the contempt of the higher: 'O God help me, God help me, how long have you professed apprehension?' 'Ever since you left it. Doth not my wit become me rarely?' (3.4.61–4). Even as Margaret dresses herself in her mistress's clothes, she seeks to speak her betters' language, and even as Beatrice matches and betters Benedick by means of repartee, Margaret vies with her social superior by means of verbal one-upmanship.

It is chiefly the socially subordinate characters who have become over-literal (or would that be over-figural?) in their upwardly mobile emulation of the fashionable stylistic patterns. For more prized than a slavish imitation are the improvisational renditions of euphuism's best speakers. Beatrice and Benedick reign supreme here. What distinguishes them from the more formal or tedious speakers of the idiom – much as Shakespeare himself transcends Lyly – is their ability to animate its forms, chiefly by means of aggressive appropriations and inversions of the meanings of the speech of others.[1] If Don Pedro and Leonato exchange decorously calibrated compliments, Beatrice and Benedick take off the gloves. The two chief weapons in their arsenal are amplification and the turning of terms. Benedick excels at the former and Beatrice at the latter, which means that Benedick entertains chiefly by means of the longer speech (e.g. 2.1.219–39), whereas Beatrice tends to get the better of him in repartee (occasions which, in turn, give rise to Benedick's diatribes). Both characters convey a vibrant sense of verbal energy, whether in Benedick's talent for heaping image upon image or in Beatrice's dancing puns. This energy carries a sexual charge (not merely because of its production of *double entendres*, reproved by nineteenth-century critics as unbecoming to them both); it is the energy of flirtation, the dance of attraction and elusiveness that constitutes the mating ritual of these two wits. The semantic fluidity they both exploit in making words dance for them, the ability to 'fright' a word 'out of his right sense' (5.2.52–3), dramatizes at a linguistic level the larger thematic questions in the play, the way in which signs are unstable, unpredictable and subject to manipulation, whether in play or in perversion.[2] This aspect of language also provides for one of the play's funniest moments, when the newly amorous Benedick, confronted with the as yet unconverted Beatrice, tries to parse her harsh words in his favour: 'Ha! "Against my will I am sent to bid you come in to dinner" – there's a double meaning in that' (2.3.248–9).

---

1 Indeed, there are places where Benedick cites Lylyean formulations almost scornfully, as if they were clichés, such as his phrasing of his disdain for Claudio's choice of Hero as herself undistinguished: 'too low for a high praise, too brown for a fair praise' (1.1.163–4); cf. 'I know not how I should commend your beauty, because it is somewhat too brown, nor your stature, being somewhat too low' (Lyly, *Euphues*, 261).

2 Lynne Magnusson argues that not only does the play recognize language 'as productive of mistakes and misapprehensions' but also its characters 'deploy a complex range of prevention and repair mechanisms to compensate' for this aspect (Magnusson, 158).

While euphuism is a distinctive feature of this play's prose style, it is not an exclusive one, and it would be a mistake to describe the style as steeped in euphuism, nor is word-play as a hallmark exclusive to that idiom. Like his use of gender stereotypes, Shakespeare's stylistic debts are more a matter of allusive citation, of the deft mining of a resource, or the pointed and strategic deployment of a pattern. Above all, one senses the way in which his writing animates its resources.

'The even road of a blank verse'

Prose is the dominant form of this play's language, but verse also plays a part in marking character and situation. Much of it (16 per cent) belongs to Claudio: his announcement to Don Pedro of his affection for Hero, his first speech of disappointment when misled about Don Pedro's intentions towards her, and his rejection of her in the church scene all occur in a rather serviceable, primarily end-stopped line. Hero too, though not of many words herself, speaks most of them in verse, in the gulling of Beatrice (13 per cent of the total). The other prime verse speakers are Leonato (24 per cent), in the wake of Claudio's rejection, and the Friar, with his long practical and philosophical speech in 4.1 (9 per cent). Most of the verse arrives with the wedding scene and its aftermath, although a notable exception is the moment when Beatrice comes forward after the gulling scene to acknowledge her conversion into a lover, in the form of a truncated sonnet.

As this moment suggests, verse serves as a marker of the conventional romance (so much so that Benedick, new-styled as a lover, finds himself struggling to write poetry, and we find in the final scene that both members of the couple have authored sonnets). It is also the marker of high formality: the masked dance, the tomb scene, or the final encounter of Claudio with a veiled bride. Other abstractions of the self are also registered in verse: the Friar's meditation on the retrospective effects of loss, and Leonato's complaints of his injuries in 4.1 and 5.1. Indeed, Shakespeare gives to Leonato the verse most adventurous in construction, and most psychologically expressive, in that it displays a syntactic responsiveness and dynamism, as well as a richness of imagery. Tellingly, this is the language of pain, belonging to the play's most tragic moments, moments whose protagonist, at least as is measured by poetic intensity, is Leonato. Compared with the figural business of the prose, the verse is rather unathletic in its imagery, but given that verse here appears at moments of emotional intensity its function seems to be to provide a measured dignity of expression rather than a sense of inventive elaboration. Its figures seem to arise as a consequence of emotional pressure rather than calculation.

Image patterns

The dominant 'donor-field'[1] of *Much Ado*'s metaphors belongs to the beasts: Claudio is a 'figure of a lamb' doing the 'feats of a lion' (1.1.14–15), a 'poor hurt fowl' (2.1.185), a calf (5.4.50); Hero is a 'forward March chick' (1.3.52) and accused of having the lust of 'pampered animals' (4.1.59); Don John is 'trusted with a muzzle' (1.3.30) and decrees not to 'sing in my cage' (1.3.31–2); Margaret has a 'greyhound's mouth' (5.2.11) and her tongue keeps pace at 'Not a false gallop' (3.4.86). The 'two bears' (3.2.70) Beatrice and Benedick are the most often transfigured: he is a 'jade' (1.1.138), a 'savage bull' (1.1.242–3, 5.4.43), an 'oyster' (2.3.24), a 'kid-fox' (2.3.40) and a fish (2.3.110). Beatrice is a 'harpy' (2.1.248), a 'lap-wing' (3.1.24), a 'haggard' (3.1.36), also a fish (3.1.29), and speaks of taming her own 'wild heart' to Benedick's hand as if it were a bird (3.1.112). Dogberry, of course, is an ass (4.2.75). The effect of this menagerie is to underscore the carnal nature of humans in love, to depict them as the prey of Cupid's hunting and trapping, as well as to give a sense of the Ovidian stature of the metamorphosis performed by love. This range of reference is underscored by the play's second greatest figural resource, the classical: 'infernal Ate' (2.1.234); 'Hercules' (2.1.231–2, 337; 3.3.131–2; 4.1.319);

---

1   The term belongs to Thompson & Thompson.

'My visor is Philemon's roof' (2.1.85); 'You seem to me as Dian in her orb, / . . . But you are more intemperate . . . / Than Venus' (4.1.56–9); 'the wheels of Phoebus' (5.3.26). This latter register both complements and offsets the bestial litany, providing a veneer of learned civility over the sex: 'lusty Jove / When he would play the noble beast in love' (5.4.46–7).

Another prominent strain of imagery is that belonging to that 'deformed thief' fashion.[1] Shakespeare frames Borachio's extended discourse on fashion in 3.3 (that on the unreliable indices of fashion's representations, the discrepancy, for instance, between the size of a codpiece and that of its contents) with a series of similar images: Don Pedro hopes to 'fashion' (2.1.340) a match between Beatrice and Benedick; Benedick 'wears his faith but as the fashion of his hat: it ever changes with the next block' (1.1.70–2); Beatrice is an 'infernal Ate in good apparel' (2.1.234), who thinks a beardless husband fit only to be 'Dress[ed] . . . in my apparel and [made] . . . my waiting-gentlewoman' (2.1.29–30). Don John says that the word 'disloyal' is 'too good to paint out [Hero's] wickedness' (3.2.98–9); Benedick's transformation into a lover is signalled by the 'fancy that he hath to strange disguises' (3.2.30); and Hero's wedding is prefaced by a scene which details the complicated artifice of an Elizabethan bridal regalia, with its false hair, layered gowns and perfumed millinery. Shakespeare emphasizes with such incidents fashion's fickleness and power to obscure the truth of identity.

Songs

Another subset of the play's stylistic modes is that of its explicitly musical measures. *Much Ado* is a play replete with the melodious conventions of aristocratic courtship: masked balls, serenades before chamber windows, lute warbling and sonnet writing. The intrigue begins with a stately dance in 2.1, and is resolved with one in 5.4, the latter intended to 'lighten' not only 'our wives' heels' (117) but also the foregoing gloom. In between occur a

---

1   A preoccupation of *Hamlet* and *All's Well* as well. See Ormerod.

number of musical interludes: Balthasar's song 'Sigh no more' (2.3.60ff.); Margaret's injunction to 'Clap's into "Light o'love"' (3.4.40); Benedick's attempt at 'God of love' (5.2.26–9); and the song of contrition at Hero's alleged tomb, begging 'Pardon, goddess of the night' (5.3.12ff.). Early performances (at Blackfriars theatre) may have punctuated intervals in the action with yet more music, and most plays were followed by a jig, perhaps once upon a time performed by the fleet-of-foot Will Kemp, who played Dogberry. Beatrice may skip a few steps of Scotch jig, measure or the cinque-pace to accompany her discourse on marriage in 2.1 (64–70). The play is punctuated and structured by song, perhaps not surprisingly, given its many meditations on the harmonies and dissonances of human connection.

Much of this music is more disconcerting than decorative in the content of its lyrics. A song whose refrain is 'Men were deceivers ever' (2.3.61) in a play replete with cuckold jokes provides a rare acknowledgement of the way in which men too can violate love's faith; as W.H. Auden wrote, 'the serenade convention is turned upside down in Balthasar's song, and its effect is to suggest that we shouldn't take sad lovers too seriously . . . If one imagines the sentiments of the song being an expression of character, the only character they suit is Beatrice' (Auden, 115).[1] Margaret's invocation of 'Light o'love' is another such grace note recommending a carefree attitude to love's trials. Indeed, the one relatively 'sincere' attempt at a romantic song comes from Benedick, in his attempted warbling of the plaintive and popular (even hackneyed) Elizabethan song 'God of love', but he is the first to admit that the tune sits ill in a throat more used to other registers. In this company, the 'song of woe' sung by the mourners at Hero's tomb strikes a rare sombre note, but the gravity of that, too, is undercut by our knowledge that the virgin knight in question is not really dead. In this light, the references to yawning graves, the heavy rhyme of 'moan' and 'groan',

---

1 Kenneth Branagh's film took Auden's hint and had Emma Thompson as Beatrice read it at the start of the film.

risk sounding overdone. The music throughout the play thus stands a degree askance to its action, in a way that provides an ironic commentary, respite from, or alternative perspective on that action. The individual settings of a given performance will, of course, shape the degree of distance invoked here. Of the three songs sung in the play, a probable original setting exists only for 'God of Love', sung to the dance tune of 'Turkeylony' (after the Italian 'Tordiglione'), which was initially printed in 1562 by the actor William Elderton, and much imitated.

STAGING *MUCH ADO*

Much Ado About Nothing is rife with representations of theatre, not merely, as in some of Shakespeare's works, as a metaphor for human experience, but as an actual practice of the play's characters. Some of this registers as the habit of certain characters of imagining themselves, or being imagined by others, as playing established roles: for instance Benedick's tendency to 'speak after [his] custom, as being a professed tyrant to their sex' (1.1.160–1); Don John's sense of himself as a confirmed melancholic; or Beatrice's reflexive perversity in describing men: 'How wise, how noble, young, how rarely featured – / . . . she would spell him backward' (3.1.60–1). But in addition to this sense of theatrical identity, as that of a reputation to be upheld, the play instances explicit performances, involving costumes, scripts, and even blocking, intended to persuade their audiences of a given understanding about themselves or another. While critics have noted the importance of eavesdropping to the play – an instance of an auditor, such as Borachio, or Antonio's servant, inadvertently overhearing an exchange – many scenes are also deliberately staged by characters for the consumption of an unwitting onstage audience, the difference from conventional theatre being that the audience in question – Benedick, Beatrice – is under the impression that he or she is eavesdropping, rather than attending an explicitly fictional performance; as Benedick avouches,

'I should think this a gull, but that the white-bearded fellow speaks it' (2.3.119–20). These scenes most obviously include the two intended to capture Benedick and Beatrice's affections, but also the dance masquerade by which Don Pedro secures Hero for Claudio, the performance of Borachio and Margaret at Hero's window, and the plotted humiliation of Hero at the wedding by a Claudio who casts himself in advance of the event in the part of a scorned bridegroom: 'If I see anything tonight why I should not marry her, tomorrow in the congregation where I should wed, there will I shame her' (3.2.111–13). The ritual at the tomb, the masked dance and the final tableau of four veiled women present other species of theatre.

This is, then, a play for which Shakespeare writes characters who repeatedly stage actions in order to shape the response of an audience, and a play that thematizes the role of theatre in shaping human identity.[1] *Much Ado* thus dramatizes the practice of using theatre to create a deliberate effect – namely, to induce or to dissuade love.[2]

The effect of a given production of *Much Ado* itself is of course harder to specify, although we could say, safely (if blandly), that amusement, and hence a certain pleasure, are the desired goals (if only to secure an audience's continued custom). In its reliable ability to deliver such amusement, *Much Ado* has been a mainstay of the Anglo-American Shakespearean repertory. The title-page of the Quarto indicates that it has 'been sundry times publickly acted', although the first documented evidence is of a court production in 1613. It was the seventh most popular of Shakespeare's plays staged by the late eighteenth century, and between 1879 and 1964 it was staged thirty-five times at Stratford-upon-Avon (roughly every three years) (Hogan, vol. 2, 717). It is a staple of American summer Shakespeare festivals, particularly in the wake

---

1 Nova Myhill indicates this aspect of the play (Myhill).
2 As Jean Howard discusses, early modern anti-theatrical voices cited the production of illicit erotic identity as an undesirable function of the public theatre (Howard).

of the 1993 Branagh film, and at the beginning of the twenty-first century the sixth most popular performance among Shakespeare's plays at the two leading Shakespeare venues of Britain and North America.[1] What constitutes its appeal has changed, however, with the moment, place and culture of production. But as in the playlets performed by its characters, its general effect comprises many local choices.

In many respects *Much Ado*'s production history follows the general contours of Shakespearean stage history: it was rewritten in the Restoration, revived in the eighteenth century, popularized by David Garrick, bowdlerized in the nineteenth century, and made spectacular by Victorian production values. Berlioz wrote an opera loosely based upon it, and Wagner's *Das Liebesverbot* treats William Davenant's *The Law Against Lovers* (1662), itself in part a reworking of the play. The early twentieth century saw a return to minimalist Elizabethan staging practices, but also film treatments that expanded the possibilities of realistic stagings (for instance location shootings in real villas). John Cox has amply narrated these changes, and points out that the two recurrent features of this play's staging include the fortunes of its portrayal of a strong heroine, and the temptations of the courtly milieu for designers (Cox, *Shakespeare*). This account will not rehearse the chronological stage history of the play per se, but will rather take up questions of staging, certain answers provided in the history of productions and their implications for the play's effect.

Tonal choices

In the case of *Much Ado*'s production history, the presiding question has usually been one of how 'light' or 'dark' a production is: to what degree is the war between the sexes (comedy's usual topic) a 'merry' one, or a conflict with real casualties to minds and hearts? How corrosive a portrait does a production paint of male

---

1 The Royal Shakespeare Theatre and the Stratford Shakespeare Festival in Ontario, Canada. See Taylor, 'Proximities'.

suspicion of and anxiety about women, and the social universe in which it is permitted to prosper? Is the event of Hero's slander easily repaired, shrugged off like one of the play's many witticisms, or does the play depict a more sombre picture of damaged and damaging relations between the sexes? To what degree, in other words, can the play be rendered a 'happy' comedy, a portrait of regenerative energies triumphing over obstacles to sexual and social union – or are its harmonious conclusions in dance and reunion precarious and provisionally engineered? Another way of putting this question has been to ask to what extent the play belongs to Benedick and Beatrice – an instance of a man able to break ranks with his own sex in order to cast his faith with a woman's word ('Think you in your soul the Count Claudio hath wronged Hero?', 4.1.326–7). Or is the joyfulness of their coupling clouded by its location in a universe in which a known villain's word trumps a woman's honour? (These questions rephrase that of the subplot/mainplot debate in a different guise, although the association of 'darker' elements with the Hero and Claudio plots fails to acknowledge the degree to which Benedick is the most eloquent speaker of the play's slanders against the fair sex.) Perhaps the simplest formulation of this choice, in post-modern terms, is how ruthlessly 'patriarchal' a world emerges in production, in which patriarchy is principally understood as a system of male alliance and rivalry conducted through the exchange of and competition for women.

Terminologies aside, the degree and inflection of patriarchy is not merely a concern that arises with modern political sensibilities. For instance, nineteenth-century productions tended to cut much of the play's bawdy and cuckold humour, a habit that displays in itself a patriarchal gesture. The goal was presumably to purify the play of material offensive to the tender sensibilities of a middle-class audience, or unbecoming to actresses in search of a new gentility and respectability for their profession. Bell's Shakespeare edition, for instance, notes that Beatrice's comment to Don Pedro about Benedick – 'So I would not he should [put me down], my lord, lest I should prove the mother of fools' (2.1.261–2) – 'rather trespasses on virgin diffidence; archness and real modesty are no ways incompatible; therefore it is a pity the author should have suffered this pleasant lady to even peep over the line of decency . . . In this and in her next speech, she is again too knowing' (Bell, 2.236). The cuts also had the effect of rendering the male characters of the play more idealized than they appear in the Quarto text – again, all to the good, at least for George Steevens, editing *Much Ado* in the late eighteenth century: 'It is to be lamented, indeed, that [Benedick's wit] is disgraced by unnecessary profaneness; for the goodness of his heart is hardly sufficient to atone for the license of his tongue' (Steevens, 2.163). The practice of editing such language out of production had the side-effect of rendering much of this humour unfamiliar, with the consequence that it continues to be cut from more recent productions in a period less squeamish about sexual material.

For similarly sentimentalizing and sanitizing reasons, most nineteenth-century productions changed Benedick's farewell to Beatrice in the concluding lines of 4.1 from a relatively brisk envoi to a more protracted, and potentially cloying, dialogue originally inserted by J.P. Kemble in 1788. The Quarto text reads:

> *Bened.* Enough, I am engagde, I will challenge him,
> I will kisse your hand, and so I leaue you: by this hand,
> Claudio shal render me a deere account: as you heare of
> me, so think of me: goe comforte your coosin, I must say
> she is dead, and so fare-well.

The rewritten lines read:

> *Ben.* Enough I am engag'd, I will challenge him.
> *Beat.* Will you?
> *Ben.* Upon my soul I will. I'll kiss your hand, and so
> leave you. By this hand, Claudio shall render me a
> dear account.

Beat. You'll be sure to challenge him.
Ben. By those bright eyes, I will.
Beat. My dear friend, kiss my hand again.
Ben. As you hear of me so think of me. Go, comfort
    your cousin – I must say she is dead and so farewell.
Beat. Benedick, kill him, kill him if you can.
Ben. As sure as he is alive, I will.[1]

Despite her repeated insistence on Claudio's death, Beatrice becomes here, paradoxically, more querulous, less adamant, and hence more conventionally 'feminine'; Benedick, by contrast, emerges as more gallantly reassuring to his damsel in distress, rather than grim or troubled by the charge he has accepted. Cox notes:

> Kemble's ending built the scene to a climactic curtain line, significant in the eighteenth- and nineteenth-century theatre where each scene was a discrete unit marked by the fall of the curtain. However, Kemble's dialogue made the developing relationship between Beatrice and Benedick seem less provisional at this point than in the quarto text, and tended to sentimentalise the passage.
>
> (Cox, *Shakespeare*, 197)

Here, practical concerns of the theatre have an impact on the depictions of gender and romantic union. Ellen Terry, the great actress of Beatrice in the late nineteenth century, objected to what she termed 'the buffoonery' of this business in Henry Irving's 1884–5 production: 'I had been compelled to give way about a traditional "gag" in the church scene . . . I protested, and implored Henry not to do it. He said that it was necessary: otherwise the "curtain" would be received in dead silence' (Terry, 127). The preference here was for applause rather than sobering reflection, a choice not necessarily pressing for a Renaissance staging in

---

1   J.P. Kemble, Partbook for Beatrice, marked in Kemble's hand (Shattuck, S5).

which neither the structure of acts nor the technology of curtains applied.

As this example shows, a given production's inflections of the play can involve quite broad measures, and for reasons of stagecraft as well as thematic considerations. However, a production need not go so far as rewriting the dialogue, as the factors influencing its tones are many and minute, and can be as subtle as a gesture, such as the abstention of Judi Dench's Beatrice from the final dance of John Barton's 1976 production of the play (she was left awkwardly holding Benedick's sword, while he joined in the dance, a choice which complicated the symmetries and sexual harmonies that a dance might reinforce) (Cox, *Shakespeare*, 235). Like a musical score, a script is only fully realized through the instruments of voice and gesture. Such details of nuance are not always recoverable from reviews or prompt copies. Yet it is important to underscore, especially for the reader of a play, that every production aggressively rewrites as well as inflects the text, whether through cutting, sequencing, the timing of entrances and exits, or the addition of business and dumb-shows not scripted in the original (see Fig. 7). For instance, cuts and amplifications change with historical moment, political context and cultural taste. If nineteenth-century productions cut the bawdy (and much else, in order to accommodate changes of elaborate scenery), more recent productions keen to delineate a swift-moving plot have jettisoned the play's euphuistic language, and, with it, the verbal medium of male bonding. The eighteenth century was not fond of puns; the nineteenth, of sexual banter; the twentieth, of complicated rhetorical exhibitions (comic productions tend to favour plot over poetry, whereas tragedy's poetry is more often indulged). Each period, each production – each performance – offers an individual moment in the play's history.

Social representations

Much of a production's tonal range depends on its depiction of the world of male privilege. Choices must be made about big

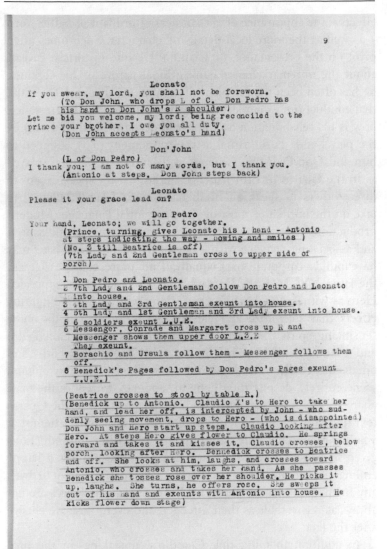

Leonato
If you swear, my lord, you shall not be forsworn.
(To Don John, who drops L of C. Don Pedro has
his hand on Don John's R shoulder)
Let me bid you welcome, my lord; being reconciled to the
prince your brother, I owe you all duty.
(Don John accepts Leonato's hand)

Don' John

(L of Don Pedro)
I thank you; I am not of many words, but I thank you.
(Antonio at steps. Don John steps back)

Leonato
Please it your grace lead on?

Don Pedro
Your hand, Leonato; we will go together.
(Prince, turning, gives Leonato his L hand - Antonio
at steps indicating the way - bowing and smiles)
(No. 3 till Beatrice is off)
(7th Lady and 2nd Gentleman cross to upper side of
porch)

1 Don Pedro and Leonato.
2 7th Lady and 2nd Gentleman follow Don Pedro and Leonato
    into house.
3 4th Lady and 3rd Gentleman exeunt into house.
4 5th lady and 1st Gentleman and 3rd Lady exeunt into house.
5 6 soldiers exeunt L.U.E.
6 Messenger, Conrade and Margaret cross up R and
    Messenger shows them upper door L.3.E
    They exeunt.
7 Borachio and Ursula follow them - Messenger follows them
    off.
8 Benedick's Pages followed by Don Pedro's Pages exeunt
    L.U.E.)

(Beatrice crosses to stool by table R.)
(Benedick up to Antonio. Claudio X's to Hero to take her
hand, and lead her off, is intercepted by John - who suddenly seeing movement, drops to Hero - (who is disappointed)
Don John and Hero start up steps. Claudio looking after
Hero. At steps Hero gives flower to Claudio. He springs
forward and takes it and kisses it. Claudio crosses, below
porch, looking after Hero. Bennedick crosses to Beatrice
and off. She looks at him, laughs, and crosses toward
Antonio, who crosses and takes her hand. As she passes
Benedick she tosses rose over her shoulder. He picks it
up, laughs. She turns, he offers rose. She sweeps it
out of his hand and exeunts with Antonio into house. He
kicks flower down stage)

7   1.1 (146–53), from a promptbook of a 1904–5 touring American production
    by E.H. Southern and Julia Marlowe which spells out details of stage actions.
    Note the business between Don John, Claudio and Hero, meant to motivate
    Don John's plot against the two lovers.

effects – the appearance of the soldiers as brilliant or battle-worn – as well as the more local details of character. Such tones often pivot on the presentation of Claudio. Despite historicist caveats about the unremarkable or conventional nature of his conduct, he has often been the recipient of treatments that seek to excuse that conduct (for example, being cast as very young). For instance, how is his rehabilitation as a non-cad accomplished (if at all) by the play's end? Is the ritual at the monument (5.3), assigned to him and Don Pedro by Leonato as a kind of reparation, played as in the Quarto text (in which Claudio doesn't speak except to direct others to speak on his behalf), or is Claudio allowed to take on the burden of most of the penitential language? Modern productions eager to bolster this character's sympathetic aspect, and associating penance with a personal voice (Elizabethans may have found a corporate grief equally, if not more, contrite), choose the latter, and, as in the Branagh film, include a semi-concealed Hero as witness to Claudio's grief, along with music and lighting effects that solemnize and elevate the moment. (In the same sensitizing spirit, they have also cut the banter of Don Pedro and Claudio with Benedick in 5.1.) Yet most eighteenth- and nineteenth-century productions, interestingly, cut the epitaph scene entirely, despite their general tendency to render the male characters as more gallant in their behaviour than in the Quarto text (perhaps the scenic requirements of a verisimilar attempt at a family monument were daunting, and impeding, in productions given to lavish staging and yet eager to move towards a happy ending in under four hours; or perhaps they preferred not to dwell any further on Claudio's error). Motives for such choices are not always as recoverable as their effects – and even those are elusive after the fact.

In addition to mitigating Claudio's 'mistaking' in the final fifth of the play, a production can soften or intensify his culpability in the acts leading up to it, for instance by means of casting and acting choices. Claudio can be played as particularly young, impressionable and vulnerable, torn between Hero and hero-worship (of Benedick and his contempt for marriage). His unsavoury decision to 'shame' Hero 'in the congregation where I should wed' (3.2.112–13) can be delivered as either reluctant or ready. Declan Donnellan's 1998 Cheek by Jowl production presented Claudio as 'sexually awkward . . . however much Bohdan Poraj's . . . Claudio professes to love Hero, he loves his cohorts more: in one of Donnellan's several comic coups, when Hero accepts his offer of marriage, Claudio runs not into her arms, but Don Pedro's instead' (Logan).

Perhaps most influential on the portrayal of Claudio has been the decision whether or not to stage the balcony scene described by Borachio: 'she leans me out at her mistress' chamber window, bids me a thousand times goodnight . . . Claudio and my master, planted and placed and possessed by my master Don John, saw afar off in the orchard this amiable encounter' (3.3.140–5). This scene is not staged in Shakespeare's text. However, some productions do choose to represent it, a decision that, if it results in a convincing action, can help make Claudio's reaction plausible, or (more usually) if too transparent, can undermine sympathy for him.[1] Fidelity to the Quarto text leaves the audience reliant only on what is suggested to our imaginations by Borachio's drunken account. A similar instance of directorial supplementation often occurs in the placement of Hero as a visible witness to the epitaph scene – such as 'a sudden shocking glimpse of the wanly immured Hero' – a blocking decision that seeks to address the problem of *her* feelings about Claudio's penance.[2]

---

1 Gary Taylor recounts another such intervention in the 1998 production at the Stratford Festival, Ontario, directed by Richard Monette, who 'moved "Fear no more the heat of the sun" from *Cymbeline* 4.2, into 2.1, giving Jennifer Gould's Hero a chance to sing and therefore a prolonged moment of center stage attention . . . the song then reappeared just before the intermission, in an interpolated scene outside Hero's bedroom window: Don Pedro and Claudio never saw Hero, but the sound of Margaret's voice singing a song we all associated with Hero made their mistake immediately understandable. This addition not only clarified the plot; it also unfortunately exculpated the men' (Taylor, 'Proximities', 340).

2 Michael Billington, review of Gregory Doran's 2002 RSC production, *Guardian*, 5 May 2002.

Another intervention has occurred in the fate of 1.2, the scene where Antonio relates to Leonato his servant's inaccurate report of Don Pedro's plan to woo Hero; Garrick's 1777 production rewrote the scene to correct the error: 'It was agreed upon, that the prince / should in a dance, woo Hero, as for himself; and / having obtained her, give her to Count Claudio' (Cox, *Shakespeare*, 104). Many other eighteenth- and nineteenth-century productions adopted this 'correction', thus removing one instance of mistaken information; others relocated the scene to the beginning of 2.1 (the dance scene), so that Don John's malevolent plan follows immediately upon the exchange between Don Pedro and Claudio. The change renders villainy less casual, in a world where information is more mediated.

The treatment of the character of Claudio is just one example of how a production shapes its general portrait of its world through local choices. Other means of doing so include how the other male characters, and the bonds between them, are rendered. For example, how does Leonato react to Claudio's repudiation of Hero in the church scene (4.1)? Eighteenth-century depictions of Hero's swoon in this scene demonstrate an increasing focus upon Leonato's experience: in the frontispiece to Nicholas Rowe's edition (Fig. 8), he is indistinguishable; in the William Hamilton painting (Fig. 9), he is foregrounded in the lower left corner, and more prominent than Claudio; in the etching by Edward Francis Burney (Fig. 10), he is central and virtually Lear-like in his distraught domination over the fallen form of his daughter. Is his subsequent rejection of Hero vicious or pained – i.e. is his long speech of betrayal and rejection (120–43) cut, or perhaps accompanied by physical violence towards the actress playing Hero? Cox relates that nineteenth-century Leonatos were dignified and idealized by abridgement of their words, whereas 'Tony Church (RST 1971), on the other hand, reacted with "Victorian paternal outrage"' (Cox, *Shakespeare*, 182) – ironically, the Victorian actors habitually rendered fatherhood more benevolently.

8 Hero swoons after Claudio's repudiation in the church scene (4.1), the
   frontispiece to Nicholas Rowe's edition of 1709, with an undifferentiated
   Leonato

9 Hero swoons after Claudio's repudiation in the church scene (4.1), engraving by Jean Pierre Simon of the painting by William Hamilton (1790), with Leonato foregrounded at the left

10 Hero swoons after Claudio's repudiation in the church scene (4.1), engraving by Edward Francis Burney (1791), with a distraught Leonato in central place

Similarly, is Leonato's challenge to Claudio in 5.1 played as a comedy, of two old geezers rushing for their rusted swords à la Capulet (perhaps with an Antonio literally deaf to Leonato's cries of 'Brother'), or with dignity and pathos? (In the 2002 Gregory Doran RST production, set in Mussolini's 1936 Sicily, 'Hero's aged uncle suddenly draws a nasty little knife to threaten Claudio' (Hemming).) Are Benedick's cuckold jokes, or diatribes against 'my Lady Tongue', delivered teasingly or tinged with malice – for instance, does Beatrice enter during his speech in 2.1 in which he compares her to 'infernal Ate', and thus herself hear his excoriation of her (and if so, is Benedick aware of her presence)? Is the exchange between Don Pedro and Benedick in 5.1 (with Don Pedro's return to bawdy jokes about Beatrice) kept or cut (frequently the latter)? A notable strength of Franco Zeffirelli's 1967 BBC television production is that the socially superior sneering of Don Pedro and Claudio at this point was not cut, in keeping with a general impression of how far both fall short of any kind of courtly ideal.

How much is made of the military context of the play? Is it presented as a pretext for dashing uniforms or does it provide a continuing framework of male alliance based on aggression towards each other and towards women, 'a bastion of laddishness', in one reviewer's words, describing Donnellan's 1998 Cheek by Jowl production? Or, as another reviewer described it, 'This *Much Ado* is about men behaving badly', in which Don Pedro is 'clearly the sort of chap for whom towel-flicking in the locker-room is not just hearty fun'.[1] For instance, do the men appear in uniform, and when do they change into civilian costume, if at all? Do all of them do so? John Gielgud writes of his attempt to distinguish Benedick by means of costume from the elegant atmosphere urged by the staging:

---

1 John Peter, *Sunday Times*, 14 June 1998; Benedict Nightingale, *The Times*, 8 June 1998. This production attempted to counter the weight of male privilege by turning uncle Antonio into aunt Ursula.

I kept trying to make Benedick into more of a soldier. At first [the designer] encouraged me to be a dandy, wearing comic hats [which] used to get laughs the moment I came on in them . . . I gradually discarded them, and wore leather doublets and thigh boots and became less of a courtier. I tried to inject a good deal more bluffness and strength into the part. Benedick ought to be an uncouth soldier, a tough misanthrope, who wears a beard and probably smells to high heaven.

(Gielgud, 135–6)

Michael Billington noted in a *Guardian* review of the 1976 Barton production that in his colonial setting 'what Barton makes more clear than I ever remember is that, in this world of privileged impishness, Don John's pointless destructiveness is simply an extension of the prevailing officers' mess ethical code'.[1]

Also significant is the play's portrayal of the role of social caste in the relations between men, given the ways in which this play binds sexual rivalry to social rivalry. Is Leonato a grand governor of Messina, secure in his position with respect to Don Pedro (and thus one who can plausibly entertain the initial, erroneous, idea of his daughter's alliance with the Prince)? Or is he a more provincial sort, a genial gentleman farmer (as in Branagh's 1993 film) eager to ally himself with the Prince despite the truth of Don John's claim that Hero is 'no equal for his birth' (2.1.150)? Does Dogberry provide a hyperbolic or an eccentric instance of this concern with rank? For example, is his officious attempt in 3.5 to impress Leonato with his own importance at the expense of Verges presented as an idiosyncratic foible or an extreme symptom of the same social system that has Leonato so eager to forge an alliance with the Prince or his protégé? Many nineteenth-century productions cut this scene altogether. Barton's production, set in British India, cast Dogberry and the Watch as turbaned Sikhs, and the other characters as

---

1   *Guardian*, 10 April 1976.

British military, thus adding a racial and colonialist dimension to Dogberry's pomposity and malapropisms (see Fig. 11).

Other productions have set the play in Italy but depicted the Watch as English provincials (in keeping with the hints of region suggested by their names, Oatcake and Seacoal). This latter choice can render the Watch as stalwart John Bulls doggedly in pursuit of justice amidst their decadent Latin betters. As one commentator put it,

> the very figure of Dogberry is reassuring – evil cannot be rampant in a city which he and his 'most quiet watchmen' sufficiently protect . . . It is part of the irony, grave but not yet bitter, which underlies the play, that in this community of brilliantly accomplished men and women, it is not by dint of wit but through the blind channels of accident and unreason that the discovery makes its way.
>
> (Gollancz, 142)

The tradition of depicting Dogberry as corpulent also has ramifications for our sense of his pomposity and efficacy (see Fig. 12); the nineteenth-century critic Henry Giles opined that

> Dogberry is, I am persuaded, of an ample size – no small man speaks with his sedate gravity. There is a steadiness of bearing in him which you never observe in men of deficient length, breadth, or rotundity. No man of the lean and dwarfish species can assume the tranquil self-consequence of a Dogberry.
>
> (cited in Furness, 353)

The Elizabethan Dogberry, on the other hand, was originally played (if we go by the Quarto's speech prefixes) by the athletic clown Will Kemp, whose notoriety – 'one . . . that hath spent his life in mad jigs and merry jests' (Wiles, 24) – may have contributed to his presence and popularity (and mostly likely would have seen him leading the jig which traditionally followed the close of

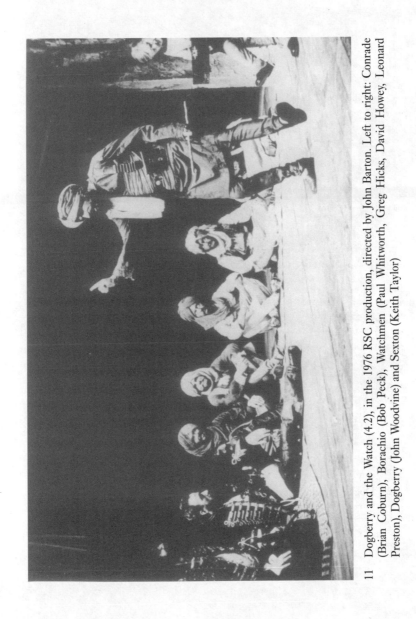

11 Dogberry and the Watch (4.2), in the 1976 RSC production, directed by John Barton. Left to right: Conrade (Brian Coburn), Borachio (Bob Peck), Watchmen (Paul Whitworth, Greg Hicks, David Howey, Leonard Preston), Dogberry (John Woodvine) and Sexton (Keith Taylor)

12 Dogberry addresses the Watch in 3.3, engraving by Henry Meadows (1845)

a play) (see Fig. 2).[1] Kemp, if the actor of Falstaff, was no stranger to padding.

Not just the heroes but the villain are shaped by directorial choice. Is Don John himself portrayed as motiveless in his malignity, or is he given some pretext, such as an unrequited attraction to Hero (indicated by means of longing glances or some other nonverbal business), or a clear designation as the sore loser in the recent war with Don Pedro, a view reinforced by 1.3.30–1? (Recall that he is not identified as a bastard until 4.1, and while his envy and melancholy would have been legible to a Renaissance audience as signs of his bastardy, they do not function so for a modern audience, even if bastardy itself served for us as a sufficient cause of his discontents.) In the 1999 East Los Angeles Classic Theatre production, directed by Tony Plane, 'a betrothal between the Mexican Hero and Anglo Claudio strikes a chord of racial hatred within the cruel Don John – designating a specific reason for his treachery that one rarely finds in the play' (Provenzano). A 1995 production at the Old Globe in San Diego was directed by Jack O'Brien as a comedy 'through and through. Even the baddest villain, Don John, gets inventive bits of visual gags that pay off at terrific rates . . . tall, scowling, harbors an unnatural fear for a flower pot that no matter what he does he cannot avoid knocking over'.[2] Conversely, Helena Kaut-Howson's Royal Exchange production in Manchester in 1997 had Don John 'addressing the unfortunate Conrade as he shaves . . . holding his minion's head under water for a frighteningly long time and . . . pressing the open blade of a cut-throat razor against Conrade's tongue' (Lindop). In the 1996 Royal Shakespeare Company production directed by Michael Boyd, an inebriated Borachio actually urinated on the (raked!) stage, a choice that sought to underscore the villainous with the uncouth, and at the risk of total alienation of the

---

1 Wiles argues that Kemp's public persona was that of a plain common man eschewing pretension, in which case Dogberry would have been in some tension with Kemp's other identity.
2 *Los Angeles Times*, 21 January 1995.

audience. The tendency of many modern productions is to emphasize the brutality of the world of male privilege at the expense of the play's delight in union, a tendency which can unbalance the play; as Peter Holland has written of Bill Alexander's 1990 RSC production,

> the exploration of [Susan Fleetwood's] Beatrice, so firmly structured into the play, was endlessly compromised by the production's self-congratulatory and comforting return to a fascination with the difficulties of masculinity. Such treatment of gender looks ostensibly modern, in being prepared to critique the male world at all, but it is a regression and an evasion of the challenge to masculinity that could be achieved by a sustained re-examination of the spaces left by patriarchy.
>
> (Holland, 36)

Choice of place and time

Some of the decisions that inflect a production are quite specific matters of gesture or tone of delivery. Others are made through more general choices of setting and design. Productions have rendered Messina as a courtly and idealized world, full of a beautiful and brilliant leisured class of people, with corresponding time on their hands for intrigue and games (much like their literary precursors, the inhabitants of Castiglione's urbane universe). This staging works well both in Renaissance guise and for later periods suggestive of leisure (Regency, Edwardian), although high-Renaissance Italianate settings have been a favourite choice for the play's portrait of an elegant and indolent social world.

Other productions have delivered it as a more gritty and grubby provincial outpost, full of provincials eager to entertain the troops; another choice is the rural idyll, unsophisticated and innocent by contrast with the intruding military universe. A 1988 production at the Shakespeare Santa Cruz Festival set Messina in the American frontier west; their 1998 staging, directed by Richard Seer, chose a post-First World War provincial Sicily, all hanging laundry in sun-baked streets (also a choice of Doran's 2002 RSC production). Robert Smallwood compares the opening tableaux of two different 1988 productions, one of 'bored wealth . . . a society rich, decadent, and selfish' (Di Trevis's modern-dress production at Stratford, in which Don Pedro's party descended from a noisy hovering helicopter for the 1.1 entry); one of 'co-operation and mutuality . . . contented interdependence' (Judi Dench's direction of the Renaissance Theatre Company): 'one director wished the disintegrating events of the play to be unsurprising, almost what such a society deserved; the other made them seem a shocking intrusion into harmony, eliciting from us a response of pain and pity' (Smallwood, 192). Such effects depend of course on the audience's reaction to wealth as something either to spurn or to identify with.

Both of these productions were instances of what is called 'Directors' Shakespeare', late twentieth-century mountings of the play influenced by academic understandings, which sought to present a strong interpretative angle, almost an argument, about it, often making thematic points by decisions about staging and scenery. So the striking mirrored floor of Terry Hands's 1982–5 RSC production conveyed both brilliance and the sense of a world of confusingly inverted images; in the 1996 main-stage version of Michael Boyd's Stratford production, the large onstage picture frame made the point about how our knowledge of each other is conditioned by its framing representations.

Such decisions often also reflect changing theatre fashions as well as the immediate constraints of theatre architecture, budget and personnel. Shakespeare's theatre used little scenery, and eighteenth-century stagings used stock scenery, whereas Victorian productions were notoriously sumptuous exercises in pictorial realism, entailing substantial cuts to the text in order to allow for scene-shifting; running time could still approach four hours (Charles Kean 1858; Irving's Lyceum 1884–5; Beerbohm Tree 1905). On the other hand, our own age achieves a comparable running time by playing so slowly that even heavily cut texts can seem interminable. Shaw described Herbert Beerbohm Tree's lavish 1905 production as having 'all the lovely things Shakespeare dispensed with . . . in bounteous plenty. Fair ladies, Sicilian seascapes, Italian gardens, summer nights and dawns (compressed into five minutes), Renascential splendours, dancing, singing, masquerading, architecture'.[1] Such extravagances produced a backlash of sorts, and early twentieth-century productions moved towards a simpler, more gestural style, influenced by the stagings of William Poel, Harley Granville-Barker and Edward Gordon Craig, who sought to 'recover' Elizabethan stage practices. The full-blown cathedral scenery of the Irving production, complete with rood screen, pillars, altar, etc., became in the 1903–4 Craig production a matter of a simple curtain and sophisticated lighting effects:

> The only illumination in this dimly lit 'church' came from an imaginary stained-glass window above the proscenium arch that cast a great pool of light on the floor below . . . The characters were only lit when they entered the acting area which was the pool of coloured light; outside it, they became silhouettes like the columns.
>
> (Cox, *Shakespeare*, 50)

The change was indebted to new technological possibilities as well as to shifts in taste (see Fig. 13).

Such choices are also historically, politically and above all practically determined: casting Benedick and Beatrice as middle aged, and potentially more world weary than their younger counterparts, may have been an option unavailable to the all-male Elizabethan theatre company, where Beatrice's pertness was also that of the boy actor. William Davenant's 1662 rewriting of the play, *The Law Against Lovers* (in which the Benedick and Beatrice plot is grafted onto a retooled *Measure for Measure*), increases the quotient of salacious banter between Beatrice and Benedick (now a Restoration libertine). The adaptation may have been fuelled by a

---

1 *Saturday Review*, 11 February 1905.

13   Edward Gordon Craig's preliminary sketch for the church scene (4.1) in his
     production of 1903–4

desire to compound the racy novelty of women playing the female roles, of which the revised play had four prominent ones plus two bit parts. Davenant was granted a theatrical monopoly (the other went to Thomas Killigrew) in the Restoration, and *Much Ado* was one of nine Shakespeare plays to which he had the rights (Killigrew claimed the rest). As Victoria Hayne writes, the decision to reduce his repertoire by conflating *Much Ado* and *Measure for Measure* seems odd, except when we consider Davenant's need to generate roles for his new company of female actors; one of the roles, that of Beatrice's sister Viola, seems gratuitous:

> her primary function is to dance, equipped with castanets, and to sing two songs, including a quartet with Beatrice, Benedick, and Lucio entitled 'Our Ruler Has Got the Vertigo of State' . . . [yet] Pepys regarded her performance as the highlight of the evening.
>
> (Hayne)

Cultural moment

The changing force of theatrical taste is demonstrated most clearly through the interpretation of Beatrice throughout the centuries. Much as productions are judged to range between light and dark, portrayals of Beatrice range between the shrewish and the more pliably tender-hearted. Her command to 'Kill Claudio' (4.1.288), for instance, has been received as either the unladylike vengeance of a virago, or the fierce loyalty of a woman moved by sisterly feeling for her cousin (Cox, 'Stage'). Whether this moment gets a laugh (and whether that laugh is a nervous one) can indicate the degree to which a production attempts to move into a serious vein – or is allowed to do so by its audience. The prefatory remarks to the Kemble text noted that 'her generous indignation at the slander cast upon Hero tends very happily to heighten our admiration of her character, which has previously appeared somewhat open to suspicion of insensibility and shrewishness' (Kemble). In the 2004 Globe production, on the other hand, directed by Tamara Harvey and

played by an all-female cast, the line was 'said snappily to guffaws
... in a production ... gently feminist in mood ("as you are a man"
is said with an equal measure of disdain and pity)' (Mahoney).
That the play presents us with an outspoken yet upright
female argues that such a figure was conceivable in 1599 (even
if played by a boy and dressing like an Ate in good apparel).
However, stage tradition throughout the centuries has qualified
the anomaly of her initial appearance, often in the direction of
muting any unladylike tendencies. Restoration performances
found the verbal agility of Beatrice attractive; James Miller's
1737 *Universal Passion*, another rewriting of the play (splicing it
with Molière's *La Princesse d'Elide*), recast Hero and Claudio as
another pair of witty lovers, thus 'doubling the possibilities for
witty raillery' (Cox, *Shakespeare*, 10). (The clergyman Miller's
play was, however, largely sanitized of salacious dialogue.)
Shakespeare's original text returned to the stage in 1721 and
1737 (at Lincoln's Inn Fields and Covent Garden, respectively),
on the latter occasion as part of the response to lobbying by the
Shakespeare Ladies' Club, described by Michael Dobson as 'an
informal pressure group which lobbied theatre managements
to revive more Shakespeare, insisting that his patriotic and
uplifting drama should drive both the libertine excesses of
Restoration comedy and the invading irrationality of Italian
opera from the corrupted contemporary stage' (Dobson, 63).
Dobson notes that 'As Shakespeare's status as a British hero
rose, so the practice of rewriting his plays came to be seen
as positively treasonous' (64). With Garrick's 1748 rendition,
Beatrice (played by Hannah Pritchard) continued to be valued
for her verbal sportiveness: 'Every scene between them was
a continual struggle for superiority; nor could the audience
determine which was the victor' (Davies, 146). As Cox writes,
the main interest in this period was focused on 'the social status
which the actress's manners gave to Beatrice'; her verbal elegance
thus largely functioning to denote her social position rather than
indicate unladylike outspokenness (Cox, *Shakespeare*, 14).

During the nineteenth century, however, the emphasis shifted from Beatrice's mind to her heart. Helena Faucit played the role for forty-three years, from 1836 (when she was 19, to the 61-year-old Charles Kemble's Benedick) to 1879 (the latter at the opening of the Shakespeare Memorial Theatre in Stratford-upon-Avon). The tenor of her performances can perhaps be judged from her reflections upon the role. Beatrice posed somewhat of a challenge to her understanding of 'the part women have played, and are meant to play, in bringing sweetness and comfort, and help and moral strength, into man's troubled and perplexing life'; 'I cannot write [of Beatrice] with the same full heart, or with the same glow of sympathy, with which I wrote of Rosalind.' Nonetheless, she allows that 'a young, beautiful, graceful woman, flashing out brilliant sayings, charged with no real malice, but with just enough of a sting in them to pique the self-esteem of those at whom they are aimed, must always, I fancy, have a peculiar fascination for men of spirit' (Faucit, 300). A review of her performance corroborates her modulated pitch:

> When Beatrice was left in the Chapel with Benedick, Miss Faucit rose to the greatest height of her acting; her alternations of grief for Hero, of indignation at the treatment which her cousin had received, her eagerness to have Claudio killed, and her wish that she were a man . . . were rendered with great force, but did not exceed the display of a true womanly spirit.

Or, as another estimate put it, 'high spirits run away with the tongue but not with the manners, this is the key-note struck by Miss Faucit'.[1]

While some nineteenth-century actresses continued to emphasize Beatrice's asperity, the general tendency was in the direction of 'true womanly spirit', a tradition epitomized at the century's

---

1   *Manchester Guardian*, 11 April 1866, cited in Furness, 388; *Manchester Examiner and Times*, 11 February 1866, in Furness, 389 (reviews of Charles Dillon production, Broadway Theatre, Manchester, 1866).

14   Ellen Terry as a kinder, gentler Beatrice in Henry Irving's Lyceum production, 1884–5

end by the actress Ellen Terry (see Fig. 14), who managed to temper the termagant by means of performances most frequently described by the terms 'sunny', 'boisterous' and 'merry' (as opposed to 'caustic', 'contemptuous' or 'tart') (Cox, *Shakespeare*, 35–43 *passim*). Here, ebullience provided a context for Beatrice's verbal combativeness that took the sting out of the zingers:

> enchanting in her tenderness, full of an admirable vivacity, never once playing the shrew, and though her words were sharp as steel, they seemed always sheathed in velvet and to convey the idea that she loved Benedick; she softened the wordy blow that she struck him and turned it to nought by the tender light of her eyes, or by a manner deviously arch and winsome, which in itself was ever half-caressing.[1]

With the twentieth century, and the advent of a popular political feminism, one would have thought that the spikier aspects of Beatrice's character would have become more plausible, but the sentimentalizing nineteenth-century tradition held on strong until mid-century. Then, after the Second World War, actresses of the part such as Katharine Hepburn, Peggy Ashcroft, Maggie Smith and Janet Suzman began to inject a bit more spirit into their renditions; Emma Thompson's Beatrice, in the 1993 Branagh film, 'seemed representative of twentieth-century feminism in its mature phase: not edgily assertive . . . but assured of her powers as a woman, and confident from the beginning of her ascendancy in the "merry war"' (Cox, *Shakespeare*, 83). Nonetheless, the production cut 180 lines of banter between Beatrice and Benedick, so whatever assurance Thompson conveyed had to be managed without them.

If Beatrices range between women of feeling and women of wit, Benedicks too have parameters: these are most often the gruff and the urbane, or the soldier and the courtier, or Garrick's vivacious humorist, or Charles Kemble's elegant courtier (see Fig. 15). Recent productions have cast him as somewhat dissolute. Nicholas Le Provost, in the Doran RSC 2002 version, 'is a

1 L. Clarke Davis, *Philadelphia Inquirer*, 19 March 1884.

15 Charles Kemble as Benedick, drawing by J.H. Lynch, published by
Engelmann, London (1828)

lank-haired, unshaven old louche for whom even the plink and fizz of soluble aspirin proves too vexatious the morning after the night before' (Marmion).[1] The nature of the union between the two characters is another measure of a production's pitch: does the prospect of love occur as a surprise to them, or is it afoot from the beginning? How do the actors choose to deal with the text's suggestions that there has been some romantic history between them? 'You always end with a jade's trick' Beatrice tells Benedick, 'I know you of old' (1.1.138–9). How do they deliver their final exchange in 5.4 ('BENEDICK They swore that you were almost sick for me. / BEATRICE They swore that you were well-nigh dead for me', 80–1)? Is this a dead-earnest reprise of an earlier pique, or is it delivered with a knowing eye to their audience, and a recognition of their own collaboration in their gullings? Finally, how egalitarian a match is their union finally rendered? Most editions and productions since Lewis Theobald's edition have assigned the line at 5.4.97, 'Peace! I will stop your mouth', to Benedick, rather than to Leonato (as in the Quarto, and this edition), and accompany his command with a direction to kiss her; what happens if this line is delivered by a Leonato intervening in the renewed combat, and handing Beatrice to Benedick, who then kisses her (or, if one is going to emend in the absence of bibliographical evidence for likely error, why not change 'mouth' to 'mouths'?). It may remain a gesture of male authority, but there is a difference whether it comes from an incipient husband or an uncle and guardian (especially an uncle whose own paternal authority has been qualified by his behaviour in 4.1).

Afterlives

My emphasis here on Beatrice and Benedick is also that of the tradition of stage reviews, and the tendency of productions in the

---

1 In the 1998 Cheek by Jowl production, it was Saskia Reeves's Beatrice who over-indulged: 'a spiky, sparky young spinster who bums drags from her uncle's cigar and gets drunk at her cousin Hero's engagement party' (Charles Spencer, *Daily Telegraph*, 8 June 1998).

direction of lighthearted comic warfare rather than a distressing indictment of male privilege (the reasonable assumption being that audiences expecting the latter do not go to comedies). The play's identification with its nominal subplot is on record from its earliest stage history, as Benedick and Beatrice became a trope both for the play and for the portrait of sexual attraction – of kindred yet combative minds – that they depict. The title-page of the Quarto notes that it was 'sundrie times publickely / acted by the right honourable, the Lord / Chamberlaine his seruants', but by the second recorded mention the couple have moved downstage. The Lord Chamberlain's accounts of 20 May 1613 record payment to John Heminge for 'presenting [at Whitehall] before the Princess highnes the Lady Elizabeth and the Prince Pallatyne Elector fowerteene severall playes', including 'Benedicte and Betteris' (Chambers, 2.343). This staging occasion presumably found the play suitably festive for a wedding celebration. So too Charles I's copy of the Second Folio notes 'Benedik and Betrice' next to the title. For Robert Burton, in his *Anatomy of Melancholy* (1628), the pair had become a shorthand or type for those lovers 'which at the first sight cannot fancy or affect each other, but are harsh and ready to disagree, offended with each other's carriage, like Benedick and Beatrice in the comedy, and in whom they find many faults' (for Burton, it was an antipathy most readily resolved by proximity: 'by this living together in a house, conference, kissing, colling, and such like allurements, begin at last to dote insensibly one upon another') (Burton, 3.107). Leonard Digges's dedicatory poem to the Second Folio in 1640 groups the pair with the Eastcheap gang as guaranteed crowd-pleasers: 'Let but *Falstaffe* come, / *Hal*, *Poines*, the rest you scarce shall have a roome / All is so pester'd: let but *Beatrice* / And *Benedick* be seene, loe in a trice, the Cockpit Galleries, Boxes, all are full.'[1]

---

1 Preface to the 1640 edition of Shakespeare's poems, printed in Chambers, 2.233. Other indices of the play's cultural currency were its citation in Thomas Heywood's *Fair Maid of the Exchange* (1607): 'I could not indure the carrier of her wit' (4.3.50, cf. 2.1.251–2); 'I am horribly in love with her' (4.3.57, cf. 2.3.226–7); ''tis most tolerable and not to be endured' (4.3.157–8, cf. 3.3.35–6).

And like Falstaff, whose presence warranted him a play of his own in *Merry Wives*, the popularity of these inevitably allied antagonists is confirmed by their own 'excerptability', not only in Restoration adaptations such as Davenant's and Miller's, but in the sparkling literary imitations of Restoration wit comedy, of Jane Austen's sparring Elizabeth Bennett and Mr Darcy, or the cinema's tart Katharine Hepburn and suave Spencer Tracy. Berlioz's opera of 1861, titled *Béatrice et Bénédict*, converted the figures of Claudio and Hero into merely the instigators of the former match,

> and the vocabulary that admirers of [Beatrice and Benedick] exhaust in describing them – sprightly, vivid, animated, vital, vivacious, and so on – is perfectly appropriate to describe the effects Berlioz achieves with the jazzy syncopations, veering melodic lines, trills and arpeggios, dotted and cross-rhythms, and lilting triplet figures.
>
> (Schmidgall, 275–6)

If the repulsion and eventual attraction of kindred spirits wasn't a convention before Shakespeare's play (and *The Taming of the Shrew*), it certainly became so in its wake. Other stage conventions bequeathed, or at least popularized, by this play, include the distracted father of the bride, and the witty or bookish woman (Beatrice's sisters include not just Elizabeth Bennett, but Jane Eyre and *Little Women*'s Jo March). The contrasting use of two romantic plots as foils to each other is another lasting legacy. As recently as 2001, for instance, Mira Nair's film *Monsoon Wedding* pits the arranged bourgeois marriage against the more untoward union of two servants.

Origins

While modern audiences are used to imagining the play's staging in verisimilar terms (and a high-Renaissance Italianate setting has always proved tempting to designers with big budgets), the Elizabethan stage on which the play originally appeared (perhaps the Curtain, north of the city of London, but the Globe is also a possibility) required a different kind of imagination. While specific details are inevitably speculative, this stage probably would have been a thrust stage, about forty feet across, surrounded by a standing-room pit and tiered galleries. At the rear of the stage would have been the 'tiring-house', a space with two or three curtained openings, and perhaps a gallery above; above the stage (though not covering it entirely) may have been an overhanging roof, supported by downstage pillars. The outdoor Renaissance theatre space was not dedicated to realistic staging; there was no representational scenery per se (although there may have been properties, such as an arbour, or a monument, both of which are in Henslowe's list of properties for the Rose playhouse). Shakespeare wrote his play for this kind of stage. It would have been a fast-paced production. The rapid Elizabethan delivery would have fuelled the bantering quality of the language, and the unlocalized nature of its settings works well with the shifting continuity of Shakespeare's scenes.

For instance, the editorial controversy over whether Don Pedro and Claudio's conversation, an exchange which seems to take place wherever the play opens – somewhere in the vicinity of Leonato's house – but is overheard by a man of Antonio's in 'a thick-pleached alley in mine orchard' (1.2.8–9), and then also by Borachio while being 'entertained for a perfumer, as I was smoking a musty room' (1.3.54–5), has posed problems for productions dedicated to realistic scenery (unless we imagine it as a conversation continued out of our earshot in successive locations). The Elizabethan stage, however, does not require that the scenery change with the language – rather, the language creates the scenery. Borachio's 'arras' (1.3.57) could be one of the tiring-house curtains or its gallery; the 'penthouse' of 3.3 (100) the tiring-house roof. But such concrete locations are not essential; the governing distinction of this play's settings in the early acts is that of indoors and outdoors, and an architecture of the social proximity conducive to overheard conversations. In

111

The Spanish Tragedy:

Or,

HIERONIMO is mad againe.

Containing the lamentable end of *Don Horatio*,
and *Belimperia*; With the pittifull Death
of HIERONIMO.

Newly Corrected, Amended, and Enlarged with new
Additions, as it hath of late been diuers
times Acted.

LONDON,
Printed by *Augustine Mathewes*, and are to bee fold by
Iohn Grismand, at his Shop in Pauls Alley, at the Signe
of the Gunne, 1 6 2 3.

16   Title-page of Thomas Kyd's *The Spanish Tragedy* (1623), showing a stage-
property arbour

Acts 4 and 5 a church, a jail and a monument are indicated by the language, as are the distinctions of night and day.

Such flexibility is particularly useful in the gulling scenes; both Benedick and Beatrice are said to conceal themselves in a honeysuckle arbour (see Fig. 16). The chief criteria of the humour of these scenes, particularly that involving Benedick, depend on their listeners being visible to the audience, but thinking themselves invisible to their gullers. However, the scene can be often far funnier, and more dynamic, the less it is particularized by actual props (see Figs 17 and 18). Also, since the gulling scenes follow each other, the actress playing Beatrice is often hard put not to repeat the same gags as Benedick, a risk compounded by actual furniture (and perhaps contrary to the rather different emotional tenor of the later gulling scene). Many productions hence cut 3.1 heavily, and 'load it with comic business' (usually involving water, e.g. garden hoses, duck ponds, and wet laundry, in order to account for Beatrice's head cold in 3.4) (Cox, *Shakespeare*, 145), despite the fact that there is something inherently more sobering about Beatrice's gulling, with its charges of cruelty and perversity, and her epiphany (with her first launch into verse) is less droll than Benedick's. In general, the less verisimilar the staging, the more imaginative flexibility exists for both an actor and an audience. Barton's 1976 production kept Judi Dench's Beatrice immobile and shrouded behind a screen (see Fig. 19); in 1998, Shakespeare Santa Cruz's Ursula Meyer made what she could of the cover provided by a redwood tree and the parasols of her fellows. The 1990 Bill Alexander RSC staging 'exercised a sexually discriminatory policy that gave Benedick a cypress tree to climb up and fall out of in 2.3 but left Beatrice in 3.1 propped up against the proscenium arch looking unsure whether she was effectively invisible or not' (Holland, 35). Incidentally, this latter scene was the most illustrated of the play during the nineteenth century (Altick; and see Fig. 20).

In casting the play a director can range from a minimum casting, with as much doubling as the play permits (see Appendix), to

17 A relatively minimalist staging of Benedick's gulling scene (2.3) in Terry
    Hands's 1983 RSC production, with Derek Jacobi as Benedick (standing),
    and left to right Don Pedro (Derek Godfrey), Claudio (Robert O'Mahoney)
    and Leonato (Edward Jewesbury)

18 A more realistic staging of Benedick's gulling scene (2.3), with a property arbour akin to that pictured in Fig. 16. John Gielgud as Benedick, in his production at the Shakespeare Memorial Theatre, 1950, with left to right Leonato (Andrew Cruickshank), Don Pedro (Leon Quartermaine) and Claudio (Eric Lander)

a plethora of extra non-speaking attendants suggestive of luxury and high society. The original staging would have required at least twelve adult actors for fifteen male speaking parts (not including the Watch). All female parts were played by boy actors, of which four are required. These sixteen actors speak 97 per cent of the lines.[1] The actors playing Hero and Margaret can be cast as physically similar, for example in height (or not – either way conditions our understanding of Claudio's susceptibility to 'mistaking'). We know from the text that Hero is, in Benedick's phrases, 'Leonato's

---

1   The statistic is T.J. King's (T. King, 86). See also Weil.

19 3.1 in John Barton's 1976 production, with Ursula (Marilyn Taylerson, left) and Hero (Cherie Lunghi); Judi Dench's Beatrice is behind the curtain, with a collection of servants watching from above

20 3.1 in the engraving by James Heath of W. Peters's painting for Boydell's Shakespeare Gallery (1791); in the nineteenth century, the most frequently illustrated scene of the play

short daughter' (1.1.200–1), 'too low for a high praise, too brown for a fair praise and too little for a great praise' (1.1.163–5), in other words, that she was short and maybe portrayed as a brunette (although 'brown' could refer to complexion as well as to hair colour), probably played by a boy actor younger and less accomplished than the actor required for Beatrice (at 262 lines, the fifth largest part, after the four principal men, Benedick, Leonato, Don Pedro and Claudio). The other casting information provided by the Quarto text is that the parts of Dogberry and Verges were perhaps written for and played by the comic actors Will Kemp and Richard Cowley.

The innovation of modern technologies and tastes notwithstanding, productions based on such original choices remain remarkably viable. Perhaps the only constant requirement among these choices is the necessity that the play be given a period and a setting in which male honour is dependent on female identity, and sexual chastity is a matter of life and death. This has tended to dictate settings in moments prior to the sexual revolution of the late twentieth-century West, although a reliance on stereotypes of Latin machismo has pushed it as far as the decades immediately before the First World War, and Mira Nair's 2001 film *Monsoon Wedding* gracefully transposes many of the play's themes and structures to modern bourgeois India. For Elizabethans, too, Latin countries represented passionate tendencies; as Benedetto Varchi put it in 1615,

> people in hot climates are more jealouse, eyther because they are much giuen and enclined to Loue naturally, or else that they hold it a great disparagement and scandal, to have their Wiues or their Mistresses taynted with the foul blot of unchastitie; which thing those that are of contrarie regions, and such as liue under the North Pole, take not so deepe at the heart.
>
> (*Blazon*, sig. E3ᵛ)

At the same time, it must be a culture in which the relative independence of Beatrice is possible, anomalous but not unintelligible. She has, for instance, been played as a wartime nurse, a Wallis Simpsonesque socialite, and an aspiring painter. Hence the preference for setting the play in moments of transition in sexual politics (which, opportunely, most moments seem to be).

CRITICISM

The unusual emotional palette of *Much Ado* was a main topic of commentary from very early on in the play's critical history. In 1709 Charles Gildon in his 'Remarks' included with Rowe's edition observed that 'this play we must call a comedy, tho' some of the incidents and discourses are more in a tragic strain; and that of the accusation of Hero is too shocking for either Tragedy or Comedy' (Gildon, cited in Furness, 347). This estimate was still current in 1873: 'Here is no stuff for a comedy. A girl slandered and ill-treated to an unutterable extent is not an object to awaken merriment. And it is degrading that she should finally, without hesitation, marry her slanderer.'[1] Such estimates of the play's violation of comic decorum continue, although they seem to have had little effect on the play's popularity on the stage, no doubt due to the theatrical dominance of the Beatrice and Benedick material, which has carried the rest of the play in its wake.

Of chief interest to Gildon and many who followed him is what was understood to be Shakespeare's realistic representation of character, such that aesthetic stumbling blocks (the problematic nature of this comedy) were often apprehended as ethical ones (the dubiousness of certain moral portraits): 'he always draws men and women so perfectly, that when we read, we can scarce persuade ourselves but that the discourse is real and no fiction' (Gildon, cited in Furness, 348). With the nineteenth century (and the habit of novel reading) comes a strong attention to the

1   Roderich Benedix, *Die Shakespearomanie* (1873), cited in Furness, 377.

construction of character, judged according to its psychological verisimilitude and historical plausibility. For William Hazlitt in 1817, for instance,

> Dogberry and Verges in this play are inimitable specimens of quaint blundering and misprisions of meaning; and are a standing record of that formal gravity of pretension and total want of common understanding, which Shakespeare no doubt copied from real life, and which in the course of two hundred years appear to have ascended from the lowest to the highest offices in the state.
>
> (Hazlitt, 303)

Hazlitt's attention to Dogberry and Verges is unusual (although see also Aubrey; H. Evans; Allen), in that most commentators in his century focused their gaze upon Benedick and Beatrice: their comportment, their language, and the probability and suitability of their tempers as measured by both current and Elizabethan mores. In spite of their power on the stage, they were often found lacking in the decorum department: 'If Benedick and Beatrice had possessed perfect good manners, or just notions of honour and delicacy, so as to have refused to become eavesdroppers, the action of the play must have stood still.'[1] Even as the play's version of comedy was sometimes considered ungainly, so, often, were its jokes and its portrayal of personality. More than one response attributes what was seen as the indelicacy of the play's humour to another form of realism, deriving from Shakespeare's submission to his own age's crude sensibility:

> Beatrice's wit, let it be frankly avowed, is uncommonly Elizabethan. It would have been called 'chaff' if our rude forefathers had known the word in that sense . . . This kind of merry combat would be thought blunt by a groom and a scullion . . . The wit combat must be judged historically.[2]

---

1   Mrs Inchbald, *British Theatre* (1822), cited in Furness, 348.
2   Andrew Lang, *Harper's Magazine*, September 1891, cited in Furness, 362.

George Bernard Shaw located what he felt was the play's uncouth sense of humour (redeemed only by the music of the language) in Shakespeare's own artistic immaturity:

> The main pretension in *Much Ado* is that Benedick and Beatrice are exquisitely witty and amusing persons. They are, of course, nothing of the sort. Benedick's pleasant-ries might pass at a sing-song in a public house parlor, but a gentleman rash enough to venture on them in even the very mildest £52 a year suburban imitation of polite society today would assuredly never be invited again . . . It took the Bard a long time to grow out of the provincial conceit that made him so fond of exhibiting his accomplishments as a master of gallant badinage.
>
> (Shaw, 141)

To the sense of Shakespeare's violation of comic protocol, then, was added the sense of his violation of polite manners. Shaw's deliberate and typically antibardolatrous overstatement no doubt misses the point that Benedick and Beatrice are amateurs, whose wit deliberately varies in achievement, but his caricature nonetheless relies on the equation of formal and ethical decorums.

At the same time, many of these nineteenth-century estimates were influenced by the current stagings of the play, dominated by their successful Benedicks and Beatrices. Responses rapidly came to concentrate on the figure of Beatrice as a trope for the play's mixed palette. For instance, Mrs Jameson, in her *Characteristics of Women* (1833), writes:

> Shakespeare has exhibited in Beatrice a spirited and faithful portrait of the fine lady of his own time . . . In Beatrice, high intellect and high animal spirits meet, and excite each other like fire and air. In her wit, (which is brilliant without being imaginative,) there is a touch of insolence, not unfrequent in women when the wit predominates over reflection and imagination. In her temper, too, there is slight infusion

of the termagant; and her satirical humour plays with such an unrespective levity over all subjects alike, that it required a profound knowledge of women to bring such a character within the pale of our sympathy. But Beatrice, though wilful, is not wayward; she is volatile, not unfeeling . . . we are yet more completely won by her generous enthusiastic attachment to her cousin.

(Jameson, 1.128)

Here, again, is the sense of Shakespeare's psychological realism, filtered through contemporary mores about appropriate female behaviour. Beatrice's wit is only fully redeemed and balanced by her loyalty to Hero. Not surprisingly, Benedick and his wit tend to come off in such accounts as far more palatable, 'because the independence and gay indifference of temper, the laughing defiance of love and marriage, the satirical freedom of expression . . . are more becoming to the masculine than the feminine character' (Jameson, 1.128). Beatrice appears rather as a more risky (if ultimately temperate) blend of traits.

In general, as went Beatrice, so went the play. Not everyone was convinced of Shakespeare's power to err on the side of good taste. In 1838 Thomas Campbell called Beatrice 'an odious woman', a sentiment not without its supporters over the centuries:

Mrs. Jameson concludes with hoping that Beatrice will live happy with Benedick, but I have no such hope . . . I once knew such a pair: the lady was a perfect Beatrice; she railed hypocritically at wedlock before marriage, and with bitter sincerity after it. She and her Benedick now live apart, but with entire reciprocity of sentiments, each devoutly wishing that the other may soon pass into a better world.

(Campbell, xlvi)

Not surprisingly, the relatively silent Hero comes off much better in this kind of response. Nineteenth-century codes of gender propriety were not one-sided, however, and Claudio comes in for his fair share of censure, as giving gentlemen a bad name: 'arrogant, faint-hearted, liable to hasty change of mood, and in anger capable of heartless cruelty, he repeatedly brings into question his qualification to be the hero of the Play, the fortunate lover'; 'aesthetically impossible'; 'the most hateful young cub'.[1] It was not until the twentieth century, with the critical pressure to move towards investigating historical contexts, that such opinions began to be countered by insistence on the conventionality and historical aptness of Claudio's actions (Neill; Page).

Opinions of *Much Ado*'s characters – their probability, likeability and propriety – dominate much of the first two centuries of response. Concerns with other elements did appear, in the rare formalist diagnosis ('one of Shakespeare's few essays at what may be called genteel comedy' (Coleridge, 2.135)), or attempts to locate the play within Shakespeare's corpus, 'its reach backward and forward' (Furnivall, lv). But if Shakespeare's characters were considered psychologically probable, his plot was deemed less so, although, interestingly, the failings of genre were often linked to the failings of moral character: what was unpleasant about Claudio, for instance, is tied to what is ungainly about the play's status as comedy (Claudio's inclusion in a comic ending). Conversely, defenders of the overall artistry of the play tended to defend the ethical nature of its characters as well:

> For power of composition, for faultless balance and blameless rectitude of design, there is unquestionably no creation of his hand that will bear comparison with *Much Ado About Nothing* . . . As for Beatrice, she is as perfect a lady, though of a far different age and breeding, as Celimène or Millamant, and decidedly more perfect woman than could properly or permissibly have trod the stage of Congreve or Molière . . . But Alceste would have taken her to his own.
>
> (Swinburne, 152)

---

1   F. Kreyssug, *Vorlesungen ueber Shakespeare* (1862), cited in Furness, 374; Heinrich Bulthaupt, *Dramaturgie der Classiker* (1884), in Furness, 378; Andrew Lang, *Harper's Magazine*, September 1891, in Furness, 361; Faucit, in Furness, 361.

This 1880 account by A.C. Swinburne no doubt bears the influence of the actress Ellen Terry's gracious and graceful Beatrice, and in his reading the play, far from being a botched version of comic and drawing room decorums alike, approaches a classical ideal of both dramatic proportion and female self-sacrifice.

Some of Shakespeare's works turn on enigmas that repeatedly fuel critical approaches (Why does Hamlet delay? Is Henry V nasty or nice?), so that different critical generations return time and again to the same question, trying to answer it with the tools and vocabulary of the particular moment. If *Much Ado*'s critical history offers such a touchstone, it is in fact this question of the play's tonal and generic mixture. In the formalist era, for instance, this sometimes showed up in criticism as the question of *Much Ado*'s stylistic 'unity' (usually answered in the negative), or of its formal coherence (one plot or two?), or of its relationship to its multiple sources.[1] Historically *Much Ado* has been judged a rather motley effort, though agreeable in parts; it is the rare reader who perceives Shakespeare's mixture as, in fact, the point. To wit: 'Shakespeare . . . generate[s] a novelistic sense of the real, of a world where people live together to a degree that is socially and psychologically convincing, and new in the poet's work . . . by *embracing* contradictions everywhere' (Everett, 'Unsociable', 73; see also Craik).

In more recent times, questions of aesthetic unity have become less fashionable, as have questions of character and morals, but attempts to find coherence in the play's construction have persisted, only moving from the formal to the thematic register. Shakespeare comes across in such accounts as concerned throughout the play with some governing preoccupation that works to unify otherwise discordant elements: for instance, with knowledge,[2] or fashion,[3] or slander,[4] or social status,[5] or self-regard,[6] or the power of

1 See, for instance, D. Cook; Mueller; Osbourne; Prouty; Traugott.
2 Berry; Fergusson; Henze; Lewalski, 'Love'; Myhill; Rossiter.
3 J. Evans; Friedman, 'Man'; Ormerod.
4 Cerasano; Sexton.
5 Kreiger; M. Taylor.
6 Rose.

language,[1] or the role of wit.[2] The standard dialectical move of such analyses is to note the play's formal and ethical disparities, but then to overcome them by pointing to the overriding currency of the theme in question.

This play, like most of Shakespeare's works, has run the twentieth-century critical gauntlet that stretches from formalism[3] through psychoanalytic,[4] feminist, and materialist and new historicist criticisms.[5] Not surprisingly, feminist criticism has struck the richest vein, as the play's portrait of patriarchy outrages and encourages in equal measure. Thus the nineteenth-century study of the morality of character became the study of the morality of a political system. Interestingly, as a result of these recent attentions to power structures, the Hero and Claudio plot, for so long upstaged (quite literally) by Beatrice and Benedick, has begun to achieve a new prominence. Beatrice and Benedick, by contrast, have begun to return to their ornamental status, perhaps because they are harder to assimilate to a grim view of power's deforming effects upon personhood, and the figure of Beatrice challenges rigid notions of patriarchy's comprehensive or coercive force. No doubt the pendulum will keep on swinging.

TEXT

First impressions

Much Ado About Nothing exists in one authoritative early text, the Quarto of 1600 ('quarto' refers to the format of a book made of sheets folded twice, to provide four leaves, or eight pages). The first official mention of this text occurs on 4 August 1600, in an entry in the Stationers' Register (the record of the Stationers' Company, in which a member paid a fee to enter the name of a

---

1   Dawson; Dobranski; Drakakis; Hunt; Jorgensen; Magnusson; Straznicky.
2   W. King; McCollum.
3   There are, surprisingly, given the role of language in the play, few analyses of the style per se. See Barish; Vickers, 171–249.
4   C. Cook; Girard.
5   Berger; Howard; McEachern, 'Fathering'; Neely, 24–57; Williams.

book to which he wished to establish a claim). The entry reads as follows:

> as yo^w like yt: / a booke Henry the ffift: / a booke Euery man in his humo^r.: / a booke The Com[m]edie of muche A doo about nothinge. / a booke to be staied
>
> (Greg, 1.15)

This list follows a series of entries of plays registered in 1600 as belonging to the Lord Chamberlain's Men, Shakespeare's company, the leading one in London at the time. The meaning of the phrase 'to be staied' is unclear; it was perhaps an attempt to protect these texts from unauthorized publication.[1] It was somewhat unusual for an acting company to publish its texts, for it was more lucrative to disseminate them in performances to which admission was paid, rather than in exchange for the one-time fee – about forty shillings – that a publisher would give for the rights; eighteen of Shakespeare's plays, for instance, did not appear in print until the publication of the First Folio in 1623 (a folio is a book made from sheets folded once to produce two leaves and four pages). But in 1599–1600 a batch of play manuscripts belonging to the Lord Chamberlain's Men (plays were typically the property of the company, not the author, who sold them to the players along with his rights) was sold and published in authorized editions, including *Romeo and Juliet* (Q2), *A Midsummer Night's Dream*, *The Merchant of Venice*, *2 Henry IV*, *A Warning for Fair Women* (anon.), and Ben Jonson's *Every Man Out of His Humour*. It has been conjectured that the sale of these plays was occasioned by the move into the Globe theatre in 1599–1600, which would have required capital and publicity, or that the Privy Council's limitation, on 22 June 1600, of the number of London theatres to two, and restriction of their performances to twice a week, imposed a similar fundraising exigency.[2]

---

1 *As You Like It* did not see print until the 1623 Folio, Jonson's *Every Man in His Humour* appeared in 1601, and *Henry V* was published in an inferior text in 1600.
2 Taylor, 'Introduction', 86; *Acts*, 395–8; Blayney, 386; Erne, 115–28, offers another view.

The next record of *Much Ado*'s existence occurs nineteen days later, on 23 August, when the Register records:

> **Andrewe Wyse Willm Aspley** Entred for their copies
> vnder the / hand[e]s of the wardens. Twoo book[e]s.
> the one called: Muche a Doo / about nothinge. Thother
> the second p[ar]te of the history of kinge henry / the
> iiijth wth the humo^{r}s of Sr Iohn ffallstaff': Wrytten by mr
> Shakespere / xij^d
>
> (Greg, vol. 1, 274)

Later that year both quartos duly appeared, printed for the publishers Wise and Aspley by Valentine Simmes, who also printed several other Shakespeare quartos around this time (the title-page for *Much Ado* reuses type set for the quarto of *2 Henry IV*). The title-page reads:

> [Ornament] Much adoe about / Nothing. / *As it hath been
> sundrie times publikely* / acted by the right honourable, the
> Lord / Chamberlaine his seruants. / *Written by William
> Shakespeare.* / [Ornament] / LONDON / Printed by
> V. S. for Andrew Wise, and / William Aspley. / 1600.

Here, then, is our first and, as it turns out, most authoritative text: identified as a record of a play whose calling card was its performance on more than one occasion by the most prominent playing company in London. (The name of the author was likely, as listed, to be a selling point of only secondary or recent importance, and indeed the entry of 23 August is the first time Shakespeare's name appears in the Register, though plays had been printed with his name since 1598 (Arber, 2.170).)

We can conclude from other sources that the play was a relatively fresh item, in addition to being presented as a popular and prestigious one. *Much Ado* is not mentioned in the survey of notable works of English writers, entitled *Palladis Tamia*, compiled by Francis Meres and registered in 1598, which means either that Meres overlooked it or that it postdates the composition of his (otherwise quite up-to-date) list.[1] As for a terminal date of composition, we know from the Quarto speech prefixes referring to the clown Will Kemp (designated to play Dogberry) that the play must have been performed (or been intended to be performed) prior to early 1599, when Kemp left the Chamberlain's company to embark on his marathon jig to Norwich. Perhaps a more intuitively conclusive if less objective measure is provided by stylistic patterns, which locate *Much Ado* in a prosy phase, on the heels of *1* and *2 Henry IV* (1596–8) and in the vicinity of *Merry Wives* (1597–1600).[2] And while the sequencing of Shakespeare's works is a notoriously tendentious exercise, it could be argued that *Much Ado*'s sophistication of comic structure (in which circumstantial blocking mechanisms have become psychological ones) indicates that its theme and character anticipate the problem comedies of the early 1600s. The earliest conjectured date of composition is thus the middle to latter part of 1598, with a closing limit of the early months of 1599.

Making a book

The representations of the title-page notwithstanding, truth in advertising has been in dispute as long as salesmanship has existed. The text of the Quarto does not in fact derive from a performance 'sundrie times publikely acted'. It was instead printed from Shakespeare's 'foul papers' – or early complete draft of a play – which had not as yet 'undergone such polishing as might have been necessary before it could be held to represent a satisfactory performance' (Wells, 'Foul-paper', 1). We know this because of certain marks of composition (e.g. a characteristic lightness

---

1   Meres rated the up-and-coming Shakespeare's plays as 'the most excellent in both kinds [i.e. comedy and tragedy] for the stage . . . his *Gentlemen of Verona*, his *Errors*, his *Love Labours lost*, his *Love labours wonne*, his *Midsummers night dream*, and his *Merchant of Venice*' (Chambers, 2.194); scholars once surmised that *Love labours wonne* was an alternative title for *Much Ado*, but this was disproved by evidence that in 1603, by which time the *Much Ado* Quarto was identified as such on the title-page, a bookseller named Christopher Hunt listed the former play as being in stock. See Baldwin, 31.
2   The dates are taken from Bevington.

of punctuation), a certain sketchiness of stage directions, as well as certain inconsistencies of dialogue and speech prefixes (e.g. characters designated variously both by function and by given name). For instance, characters are named in entry directions who not only never speak in the scene in question but never appear in the play at all. This kind of evidence stands as witness to Shakespeare's compositional process, a kind of picture of his mind in action, making it up as he goes along, changing his mind as the story line emerged, and not necessarily backtracking to render his document internally consistent.

Had the Quarto been a record of a 'satisfactory performance' akin to others that we possess, it probably would have travelled the following route: Shakespeare's draft would have been recopied for a promptbook, which would then have been licensed by the Master of the Revels for theatre performance. (The licence would have rendered this text a valuable piece of company property, and hence unlikely to be passed along to a printer.) This 'prompt copy' would then have been annotated for performance by a bookkeeper (the person who cued entrances and prompted forgotten lines), who presumably would have regularized the text with respect to stage directions (although this is to assume that the company's practice was to record details which may have been tacitly understood, or nailed down only verbally, by actors). In some instances such bookkeepers noted the names of individual actors, especially in minor roles, a practice that at one point was the basis for the theory that the Quarto SPs of '*Kemp*' and '*Cowley*' for Dogberry and Verges meant that the Quarto was indeed derived from the promptbook. (This notion has since been dismissed as implausible, and the names attributed to Shakespeare's own use of the names of the actors he had in mind for the parts.[1]) The 1623 Folio version of the play is a reprint of Q based on a copy of Q (no longer extant) lightly annotated by reference to the company's

---

1 See Wilson, 67–8. The Quarto displays the variety of the ways in which Shakespeare thought of his characters as he scribbled his way through: by function (*Const.*, *Dog.*, *Ke.*); type (*Bastard, Don John, Old, Antonio*); and title (*Don Pedro, Prince*).

promptbook. The name of '*Iacke Wilson*' in the entry SD at 2.3 is that of a singer cast in the role of Balthasar and must be presumed to be derived from a theatrical document.[1] The ample evidence for direct reprinting of F from Q rules out the alternative possibility of the promptbook having itself served as printer's copy for F. Differences of the Folio are noted in the textual collation.

In addition, the text of the Quarto lacks such bookkeeperly detail as has sometimes been held characteristic of promptbooks, revealing instead various features consistent with the alternative of its having been printed from an informal and incompletely revised authorial draft of the play. Bibliographers imagine the genesis of Q in these terms: Shakespeare's draft, once having been copied for a promptbook, became available, and was considered serviceable, for a printer's use (as copying was costly and laborious, this would have been an economical use of this superseded but good-enough document). At the printer's workshop, it would have been set into type by hand. In the case of *Much Ado*, it was (somewhat unusually) set by a single typesetter, Simmes's 'Compositor A'. Identification of this workman involves his participation in setting other playtexts, from which it appears that, among his various working habits, leaving the unabbreviated forms of SPs unpunctuated is distinctive. Compositor A would have set his text into type choosing one of two methods of page formatting. If he did so by 'formes' (a forme was a block of type printing one side of an entire printed sheet), he would have set at one time the four pages contained on a single side of the sheet to be printed, that is, pages 8, 1, 4 and 5 on one side, and 2, 7, 6 and 3 on the other. Setting by formes required the advance estimation (or 'casting off') of copy to instruct the compositor exactly what section of the text to set for each page, a process that could sometimes result

---

1 Other differences of the Folio from the Quarto include its division into five acts (though scenes are not indicated after '*Actus primus, Scena prima*'); SD changes seeming to reflect playhouse practice; commonsense SD changes not necessarily involving playhouse origin; erroneous SD changes; omission, or addition, of dozens of words, and omission of five short passages (at 1.1.290–1; 3.2.31–4; 4.1.18; 4.2.19–22; and 5.4.33 (see textual notes)); many minor textual variations.

in crowded pages (or the contrary) if miscalculations occurred. The crowded final sig. L1^r of *Much Ado* in the forme-set Folio, for instance, betrays such an error; as casting off is more difficult to do with prose than verse, verse might then be strategically set as prose in order to make up the required space, and *Much Ado* is a prose-heavy play. (Other space-saving stratagems could include the abbreviation of names in SPs, the omission of lines, or the condensation of SDs.) Despite the calculations required, however, setting by formes is a relatively efficient method of typesetting, as one entire side of a sheet can then go to press and be printed while the compositor sets the remaining four pages. It would have been unusual to set a play quarto (presumably not a large or exceptionally lucrative print run) according to the other, less time-saving method, namely, 'seriatim', in consecutive order, so that a forme will be complete and ready to print only when seven of the eight pages (in quarto) or three of the four (in folio) are set in type. The scholar John Hazel Smith argued further on the basis of typographical evidence (the apparent pattern of roman and italic type usage for the letter 'B', required by this B-heavy play) that Q was indeed set by formes.[1] The crowded Q page G1^r, with thirty-nine instead of thirty-seven lines of text, seems to be an instance of compensating for casting-off errors (another explanation could be that the proofreader discovered that the compositor, by eye-skip or other mishap, had left two or three lines out in his initial setting – this is less likely, of course, with cast-off copy, where the number of lines per page is the basis of the calculation and such an error would presumably come to light at the end of the page).

Charlton Hinman, whose detective work is discussed in his introduction to the Q facsimile, argues however that despite such persuasive analysis, the pattern of type usage in *Much Ado* (as well as the preponderance of prose) in fact points 'for the most part' to

---

1 Smith, 'Quarto'. Smith argued that the heavy demand for italic B 'was met by regularly removing the italic Bs from the newly wrought-off type pages for use in the composition of the immediately following sheet' (Hinman, xiii).

a seriatim setting (e.g. distinctive type recurs in alternate sheets in a pattern indicative of consecutive composition). Hence he argues that the peculiarities of Q's text must be the result of something other than casting-off errors – obscurities in the copy itself, perhaps (Hinman, xv). Correction of hand-printed books took place immediately after a forme of type went to press, when a proof sheet was run off. However, the printing of the uncorrected forme continued while the proof was read and marked up, with the consequence that the corrections, made at press during a pause in printing, do not appear in every copy of the pages in question. In general, stop-press correction was carried out early in the printing of the forme, so that many more corrected than uncorrected copies of a given forme were printed. Corrected and uncorrected states of several formes have been identified among the seventeen surviving copies of Q, distributed at random among those copies. The corrections made to *Much Ado* in this manner are of minor errors of typesetting and unfortunately have no bearing on the play's few verbal cruces.[1]

So, while the odds are that the Quarto text of *Much Ado* may depart in minor ways from its 'foul papers' copy, this is in all likelihood mainly at the level of insignificant detail. Hinman concludes that Compositor A's work is 'not obviously corrupt, even when it does not follow its original' (Hinman, xvii). And, it is important to re-emphasize, these foul papers were themselves merely an initial-to-intermediate step on the way to a hypothetical promptbook (which in turn may not have been as ideally tidy and consistent as scholars have liked to imagine, and which, in any case, is not the same as a text, such as that of this edition – or Q or the First Folio – prepared for the imaginative experience of reading rather than the embodied practices of the theatre).

This edition, like any previous edition, has thus sought to modify and modernize the original text so as to make the play

---

1   See the full record of variants given by Hinman in his introduction to the Shakespeare Quarto Facsimile of *Much Ado* (a record later emended at F2v.4, where '*Leonati*' is a misprint for '*Leonato*').

legible to the mind's eye. The pages reproduced here (Fig. 21) give some sense of the work that takes place in producing today's text. Speech prefixes have been regularized, and entrance and exit directions made consistent with the required personnel. Some more substantive changes apply to the language (though not many, as the Quarto is generally quite free of such confusion). Some concern matters of punctuation. The Quarto text is lightly punctuated – potential full stops, for instance, are at a minimum, and colons occur instead. This allows for some flexibility in determining meanings, and such instances have been indicated in the textual notes.

The majority of alterations concern logistical matters of personnel and action. For instance, Quarto SDs have been clarified when necessary, with additions enclosed in square brackets. What is presented here is not the text of the original performance. It is not the text of any performance, and indeed it is intended to be open ended rather than restrictive (not to be confused with indecisive) in suggesting possibilities for stage action, despite the editorial temptation to block the play – a temptation made inevitable if not irresistible by the fact that this reader, like any other, builds in the course of her experience of the play expectations about how its characters might or might not behave. An edition truly scrupulous about these matters would perhaps provide multiple-choice SDs; however, there are enough notes on these pages as it is, the number of choices is unwieldy if not infinite, and my assumption is that other readers will have their own opinions about how characters might or might not behave, and will undoubtedly exercise them.

Who's in, who's out

In practice, this means that most clarifications of the Quarto's irregularities are fairly obvious ones: who is on stage in a particular scene, when they arrive, when they need to leave. The dialogue itself will give the reader clear answers to many such questions (which is probably why the writer didn't overload his

Much adoe

eate his heart in the market place.

Bened. Heare me Beatrice.

Beat. Talke with a man out at a window, a proper faying.

Bened. Nay but Beatrice.

Beat. Sweete Hero, fhe is wrongd, fhe is flaundred, fhee is vndone.

Bened. Beat?

Beat. Princes and Counties! furely a princely teftimonie, a goodly Counte, Counte Comfect, a fweete Gallant furely, O that I were a man for his fake! or that I had any friend woulde be a man for my fake! But manhoode is melted into curfies, valour into complement, and men are only turnd into tongue, and trim ones too : he is now as valiant as Hercules, that only tels a lie, and fweares it : I cannot be a man with wifhing, therfore I will die a woman with grieuing.

Bened. Tarry good Beatrice, by this hand I loue thee.

Beatrice Vfe it for my loue fome other way than fwearing by it.

Bened. Thinke you in your foule the Count Claudio hath wrongd Hero?

Beatrice Yea, as fure as I haue a thought, or a foule.

Bened. Enough, I am engagde, I will challenge him, I will kiffe your hand, and fo I leaue you : by this hand, Claudio fhal render me a deere account : as you heare of me, fo think of me : goe comforte your coofin, I muft fay fhe is dead, and fo farewell.

Enter the Conftables, Borachio, and the Towne clearke in gownes.

Keeper Is our whole diffembly appeard?

Cowley O a ftoole and a cufhion for the Sexton.

Sexton Which be the malefactors?

Andrew Mary that am I, and my partner.

Cowley Nay thats certaine, we haue the exhibition to examine.

Sexton But which are the offenders? that are to be examined let them come before maifter conftable.

Kemp Yea mary, let them come before mee, what is your name,

---

21 *Much Ado About Nothing*, 1600 Quarto, sigs G3ᵛ–4ʳ (4.1.305–4.2.54). Note the variety of speech prefixes for Dogberry (*Keeper*, *Andrew*, *Kemp*, *Ke.*); the use of actors' names (*Cowley*, *Kemp*); the use of colons where a

about Nothing.

name,friend?

Bor. Borachio.

Ke. Pray write downe Borachio. Yours firra.

Con. I am a gentleman fir,and my name is Conrade.

Ke. Write downe maifter gentleman Conrade : maifters, do you ferue God?

Both Yea fir we hope.

Kem. Write downe, that they hope they ferue God : and write God firft,for God defend but God fhoulde goe before fuch villaines:maifters,it is prooued alreadie that you are little better than falfe knaues , and it will go neere to be thought fo fhortly, how anfwer you for your felues?

Con. Mary fir we fay,we are none.

Kemp A maruellous witty fellowe I affure you , but I will go about with him:come you hither firra, a word in your eare fir,I fay to you. it is thought you are falfe knaues.

Bor. Sir,I fay to you, we are none.

Kemp VVel,ftand afide, fore God they are both in a tale: haue you writ downe,that they are none?

Sexton Mafter conftable, you go not the way to examine, you muft call foorth the watch that are their accufers.

Kemp Yea mary , thats the efteft way, let the watch come forth : mafters, I charge you in the Princes name accufe thefe men.

Watch 1 This man faid fir,that don Iohn the Princes brother was a villaine.

Kemp Write downe,prince Iohn a villaine : why this is flat periurie,to call a Princes brother villaine.

Borachio Maifter Conftable.

Kemp Pray thee fellowe peace, I doe not like thy looke I promife thee.

Sexton VVhat heard you him fay elfe?

Witch 2 Mary that he had receiued a thoufand duckats of don Iohn, for accufing the Ladie Hero wrongfully.

Kemp Flat burglarie as euer was committed.

Conft. Yea by maffe that it is.

Sexton VVhat elfe fellow?

Watch

modern edition might use full stops; and the lightness of the punctuation generally.

script with stage directions): for instance, 'exit' for a character who says goodbye, or otherwise needs to be got offstage (e.g. 1.2.21, 2.3.7). Sometimes, however, characters are given an entry when they shouldn't have been (2.1.195); sometimes, an exit when they need to remain on stage (2.1.145). A slightly more complicated category involves those instances when a character says goodbye, but doesn't leave promptly, or makes a false exit (e.g. 3.3.85, not atypically involving Dogberry, who displays a frequent reluctance to quit the stage when prompted).[1] But none of these adjustments should be open to serious objection.

Other unremarkable editorial supplements relate to addressees or stage action, and are also evident from the dialogue: for example '[*Hero falls.*]' (4.1.109); '[*Hands Seacoal the lantern.*]' (3.3.24); '*Enter* Beatrice[, *who hides*].' (3.1.23). The one SD of this type in this edition most likely to raise eyebrows is that provided at 5.4.97, describing the stage action which accompanies the line: 'Peace! [*to Beatrice*] I will stop your mouth. [*Hands her to Benedick.*]'. This speech is given in Q (and F) to Leonato, but since Theobald's 1733 edition has been assigned to Benedick, with the accompanying supplemental direction '[*He kisses her.*]'. This edition returns the line to Leonato, and in restoring the line to its Quarto speaker my assumption is that Leonato, a directing presence throughout this scene, intervenes to impose himself upon the bickering couple ('Peace!') and then addresses himself to Beatrice, who has just spoken ('I will stop your mouth.'), signalling his intent to silence her merely by giving her to a husband. As a directive delivered

---

1   The Folger edition makes the not unattractive suggestion that Dogberry does indeed return yet again at the end of 3.3, in response to a watchman's 'Call up the right master Constable' (159) and by reading the uncorrected Quarto's SP '*Conr.*' as an error for *Con.*, or constable (Qc = *Con.*). My sense however is that unless we imagine Dogberry's offstage location to be extremely close to hand, the disruption to the general hubbub of the scene's closure required by the time necessary to summon Dogberry is not theatrically plausible in terms of pacing or character: 'Shakespeare has left remarkably little time for the proposed action to take place' (Wells, 'Crux', 85–6).

by a third party to a couple, it has the precedent of Beatrice's own command to Hero at 2.1.285–6 ('Speak, cousin, or, if you cannot, stop his mouth with a kiss and let not him speak neither.'). I confess I also feel that if Leonato speaks the line it provides for a more egalitarian accommodation between the lovers, one that seems in keeping with the tenor of their relationship throughout. This edition's SD here is thus more prescriptive than most in the same category (though, I'd argue, less so than Theobald's), and according to a principle of editorial abstemiousness that restricts itself to spelling out only actions indicated by the dialogue, I probably ought to refrain. But I thought the direction necessary to counterbalance the weight of editorial precedent being shifted aside here. (In defence of said abstemiousness, I have left it to the reader's imagination whether or not Benedick does kiss Beatrice, although I confess in mine he does, or perhaps she him.) Obviously, other actions may accompany the line; the important point here is its speaker.

A somewhat stickier category of entry SD involves uncertainty about when certain actors need to arrive on stage. For instance, Margaret and Ursula are members of the dance in 2.1, where they also speak, but they are never given an entrance in the scene. Rowe introduced them in the initial entry, but since they do not speak until the dance, it is also possible to have them enter, as they do here, with the revellers at 75. Arguments against the latter choice are that this somewhat violates the convention by which masked revellers entered a family party from without (as in *Romeo and Juliet*); arguments for it are that since the two women are given no lines until the dance, it might be awkward to have them enter with the immediate family (and social betters) at the beginning – although, as discussed below, Shakespeare seems to have no problem with occasionally bringing on extra actors just to give the impression of social bustle. The decision may depend on whether a production imagines the two women as ladies-in-waiting, or more like household servants – the former might well be part of the intimate family group, the latter might still be cleaning up after the supper, and thus enter with the general throng. Alternatives of this kind are discussed in the commentary throughout.

A similar case involves the entry of Leonato and Hero in the same scene, after the confusion over whom Hero is to marry has been cleared up. The Quarto locates their entry with Don Pedro at 2.1.192 (although it also erroneously includes Don John, Conrade and Borachio); the Folio (again, perhaps cued by the promptbook) has them enter with Beatrice and Claudio at 239. This choice is attractive since neither of them speaks until then, and it has been thought awkward to have them present during Benedick's discussion of the confusion over Hero's suitor, and Benedick's subsequent diatribe against Beatrice. As Zitner points out, 'this' in his phrase 'your grace had got the good will of this young lady' (198) is not necessarily demonstrative (Oxf[1]).[1] However, their entry with Beatrice somewhat dilutes the force of her entry with the sullen Claudio, and in my imagination Benedick is playing to a crowd, despite (or perhaps because of) the indelicacy involved in abusing Beatrice in earshot of her kin, or even that of discussing the disposition of Hero's hand in her earshot (tact is not his strong suit). In other words, either decision can be rationalized. I have adopted the Quarto direction; like the entry of Margaret and Ursula, the choice in a production will have certain atmospheric consequences, but in neither instance is much at stake.

So much for the relatively neutral choices. There are, however, a few places in the Quarto that require a somewhat more radical decision. For instance, in the entry directions to 1.1, Q lists '*Innogen his wife*', repeating '*his wife*' at the start of 2.1; she, along with '*a kinsman*' (also at 2.1.0), is known as a 'ghost' character, that is, one who enters but is not otherwise invoked or given anything to do or say. The 'kinsman' is perhaps the same man Leonato mentions in 1.2: 'where is my cousin your son? Hath he provided

---

1 Zitner, following a conjecture by Harold Jenkins, boldly has Leonato and Hero enter with Beatrice and Claudio at 2.1.275 but at separate doors.

this music?' (1–2); by 5.1.280, however, Antonio is childless, and Beatrice in 4.1 without a supportive kinsman to champion Hero. This figure's lack of substance is an instance of Shakespeare's working method of conjuring up a raft of personnel, and then streamlining as he goes along, finding (or not finding) things for them to do, sorting out the action and necessary bodies as the plot thickens and occasion requires. The Florentine Claudio's Messinese uncle, mentioned in passing in the dialogue of 1.1 (at 17) but never again, seems to materialize from a similar desire to create and populate a social universe. There are also instances of characters mentioned in entry directions who have nothing to say in the scene in question – for example Balthasar at 1.1.90.1, or the Sexton at 5.1.248.1. These are not as ghostly, in that they do speak elsewhere, and, as they seem not out of place in these scenes (Balthasar is a member of Don Pedro's company, the Sexton has just apprised Leonato of Borachio's trick), they have been left in their mute peace. Again, in this play about social foibles Shakespeare seems to generate a sense of society through a critical mass of actual bodies on stage and references to others elsewhere, a choice that can be followed or not according to the resources of a particular production (e.g. doubling constraints; see the Appendix).

Unlike the kinsman, however, mother Innogen is not explicitly written out of the play; such a figure is present in the Bandello tale, and recent arguments (in a thematic and political rather than theatrical vein) have been made for her silent presence (Friedman, 'Hush'd'; Baker), especially as she does not vanish after 1.1 but persists in the entry direction to 2.1.[1] She is referred to indirectly in 1.1: 'DON PEDRO . . . I think this is your daughter. / LEONATO Her mother hath many times told me so. / BENEDICK Were you in doubt, sir, that you asked her? / LEONATO Signor Benedick, no, for then were you a child' (98–102). This jocular little exchange might

---

1 Grounds for supposing either that Shakespeare might have written 2.1 first, or that he thought she might still be useful.

conceivably have been imagined by Shakespeare to be carried out in the presence of the woman in question (although it would be unseemly, given the relative formality of the occasion).[1] But there is no other mention of her in the play (even when we might expect one, as when Leonato disowns Hero in 4.1). Shakespeare moves quickly to the father–motherless daughter dyad, one dramatically and psychologically profitable elsewhere in his work (e.g. Lear, Prospero, Shylock). By 4.1, Leonato and Dame Nature alone are her parents (128–9), which adds to the sense of Hero's vulnerability and isolation in her lone parent's abandonment of her. It has traditionally been difficult for editors to imagine Innogen as a Hermione-like bystander to her daughter's trials; and it seems equally important that Beatrice give full and sole cry to a female and familial defence of Hero. (The mother in Bandello is also silent, but she does succour her daughter in her moment of trial. But nurturing mothers are scarce in Shakespeare's plays, to put it mildly, and a figure with the maternal instincts of Lady Capulet or Volumnia might have strained comic credibility too far.) Editors since Theobald have concurred that despite her persistence in the entry SDs Shakespeare ultimately found her more powerful in her absence than her presence, and so she has been retired from the fray.

Who gets to say what?

The choice to delete Innogen is clearly not one of a merely tidying-up nature, or at least it is one that also involves notions of character and context. Similar questions are also involved in addressing the Quarto's speech prefixes. For instance, in the dance in 2.1, Q initially partners Margaret with Benedick (*Bene.*) for three exchanges, and then switches the male partner to Balthasar

---

1   The exchange moved Shaw to comment: 'From his first joke, "were you in doubt, sir, that you asked her?" to his last, "There is no staff more reverend than one tipped with horn," he is not a wit, but a blackguard . . . [*MM*'s] Lucio is much more of a gentleman than Benedick, because he keeps his coarse sallies for coarse people' (Shaw, 141).

(*Balth.*) for the last two. The '*Bene.*' SPs spread from sig. B4ʳ (2) to B4ᵛ (1), while both '*Balth.*' SPs are on B4ᵛ. Edward Capell supported the change of partners with a SD '[*turning off in Quest of another*]', and there are grounds for some bantering relationship (reprised in 5.2) between Benedick and Margaret (although of course the male dancers are masked here).[1] From Theobald on, however, all five of the male partner's speeches have usually been given to Balthasar (the exception being J. Dover Wilson's Cambridge edition, which thought Borachio apropos, and argued that in the Quarto SD '*Balthaser, or dumb Iohn*', '*or*' was a misreading of '*B or*', for Borachio). Wells, however, thinks it 'more likely that "*or*" is a misreading of ampersand, or even of "*and*"', or even that the compositor misread all the SPs (all those Bs again) and that what we have, as elsewhere, is another instance of the 'foul-paper' traces of Shakespeare's rethinking of the action as he worked through his plot: first he conceived of a Benedick–Margaret exchange, then realized in the course of writing that a more powerful climax to the scene lay in partnering Benedick and Beatrice (Wells, 'Foul-paper', 12). This edition rests with this conclusion, though I'd argue that a Beatrice and Benedick pairing was always the intended destination – the only real problem is finding a partner for Margaret.

The speaking members of the Watch in 3.3. and 4.2 present another instance of the Quarto in need of some clarification in ways that entail notions of character. In 3.3, at their first appearance, Q begins by distinguishing between the first speaker ('*Watch* 1') and the man identified by him as George Seacoal ('*Watch* 2'). But after line 27 ('*Watch* 2 How if 'a will not stand?') the various voices of the band are all prefaced from sigs E3ᵛ to E4ᵛ with a mere '*Watch*', until the very end of the scene, at 157, from whence '*Watch* 1' and '*Watch* 2' alternate the last four Watch speeches (on sig. F1ʳ). There are, I would argue, at least three watchmen on stage:

1 See Mason; other partner-switchers include Malone, Collier, Stevenson, and most recently the Folger edition.

Watch 1, Hugh Oatcake and George Seacoal ('they can write and read', 12); there may be at least one other, from whom Watch 1 distinguishes them (unless he is merely eager to distinguish them from himself). As Wells argues of the undifferentiated lines, 'Each speech could be spoken by the same man, and he could be any one of the three who are certainly present. Equally, each speech could be spoken by a different actor, none of whom need have spoken before' (Wells, 'Foul-paper', 11). The lack of specificity among their SPs may have a typographical or compositorial origin, or be due to casualness on Shakespeare's part. A different explanation would be that Shakespeare left the speeches undifferentiated so as to provide for the flexibility required by a given performance (perhaps he had no idea how many bodies would be available once the play came to be staged). This edition follows as much as possible Q's omission to individuate these speeches, on the assumption that this allows for a certain choral flexibility of voices and in the confidence that a reader will not be unduly confused.

Two final SP issues need a word here, as they represent instances of this volume's departure from the usual editorial consensus. The first concerns 5.3, the scene at Leonato's family monument, where he has formerly instructed Claudio to 'Hang her an epitaph upon her tomb / And sing it to her bones' (5.1.274–5). In the Quarto, which I have followed, the text of the epitaph follows the SP of an anonymous and unprecedented figure of 'A Lord', who also speaks the couplet which follows the song: 'Now unto thy bones good night; / Yearly will I do this rite' (5.3.22–3). Claudio, according to Q, speaks twice during the actual ceremony, first to ask 'Is this the monument of Leonato?' (5.3.1), and then to direct: 'Now music sound, and sing your solemn hymn' (5.3.11). But all editions since Rowe have also assigned the epitaph and the couplet to Claudio, in view of Leonato's instructions. The voice of the Lord may be felt to dilute the force of Claudio's penance, and, according to Capell, the copy or the compositor may simply have failed to provide a speech prefix for Claudio in these places. While I cannot be accused of a wish to go lightly on my imagined Claudio, I would argue that the sheer anomaly of the unprecedented Lord suggests that he is meant to be there, doing what he does; and also, given the highly formal, public and ritual nature of this ceremony, it need not appear callous for a delegate to speak on Claudio's behalf and the collective behalf of the male community which slandered Hero (quite the opposite). It is also clear that contrary to Leonato's directive Claudio instructs others to sing and that the singer who was (and perhaps still is) Balthasar, unless he is doubling as the Lord, may be the likeliest singer here too. In Claudio's defence, following Q's SPs means that here (and only here) for the first time does Claudio initiate and control the action, becoming in effect director or stage manager of the scene; rather than discrediting his sincerity, these assignments lend him a new and needed authority and weight. It is for these reasons that I have remained with the Quarto.

Finally, I have also returned two speeches of 5.4 to their Quarto speaker, Leonato. The second, at line 97, is discussed above; the first appears at line 54, and accompanies the delivery of Hero to Claudio: 'This same is she, and I do give you her.' This line has since Theobald been assigned to Antonio, as Leonato has said earlier to him 'You must be father to your brother's daughter / And give her to young Claudio' (15–16). Theobald's assumption is that Shakespeare forgot he had written the earlier instruction; my sense is rather that Leonato is the one who forgets, steps in to take over from his brother, and begins again to direct the action, as he does at 56, 66, 118, and, as I've argued above, at 97 (we don't assume 56 is a mistake, so why 94?). Admittedly, these decisions are governed by a mental picture of a character, but that is always the case, and not, I think, something for which to apologize. All these original SPs represent workable, stageable choices, consistent with character and context, even if they are not as sentimentally attractive as other possible alternatives.

I risk labouring these choices as instances of this edition's general tendency (always difficult to describe, since editing is mostly a series of very local and often inconsistent choices) to have as much confidence in Q as possible. This is to discount neither its origin in a pre-theatrical text, nor the evidence it offers of Shakespeare's exercise of the authorial right to change his mind in the course of composition, nor, certainly, that productions and readers will reassign these matters as desired. Nor is it an attempt to abdicate editorial responsibility; the choice to follow Q is a choice like any other, and it has the virtue of not obscuring the identity of the original text. It is rather an attempt to give weight to Shakespeare's instincts (if we are right in supposing that Q gives evidence of them), in the understanding that a conscientious reader will take all such decisions with a grain of salt and an eye to the textual notes. *Much Ado* is a play deliberately designed by its author to stage the processes of misinformation, misapprehension and misdirection: for instance, there are at least two different accounts of who will propose to Hero and five different accounts of the event at her bedchamber window; and Don John is named as a bastard in the Quarto SPs and SDs, but, in a manner emblematic of the play's concern with confusion and disclosure, he is not so defined in the dialogue until the fourth act. This kind of architecture of misinformation compounds the editorial challenge of a base text which is clearly a work in progress, as one is forced to ponder whether inconsistencies are evidence of a playtext not yet fully realized, or, rather, of a playtext very fully realized. Given the degree to which Shakespeare is actively concerned in *Much Ado* with the vagaries of human communication, I believe one is well advised not to compound matters with an idea of an author more absent-minded than is strictly necessary. The assessment of what constitute theatrically unviable loose ends in an Elizabethan playscript is always going to require a large measure of caution, and of care not to impose standards of our own imagining onto it.

MUCH ADO
ABOUT NOTHING

LIST OF ROLES

THE SOLDIERS

DON PEDRO	*Prince of Aragon*	
DON JOHN	*illegitimate brother to Don Pedro*	
Signor BENEDICK	*a lord of Padua*	
Signor CLAUDIO	*a lord of Florence*	
BALTHASAR	*an attendant to Don Pedro*	5
CONRADE	} *companions to Don John*	
BORACHIO		
LORD		

THE HOUSEHOLD OF THE GOVERNOR OF MESSINA

LEONATO	*Governor of Messina*	
ANTONIO	*brother to Leonato*	10
HERO	*daughter to Leonato*	
BEATRICE	*niece to Leonato*	
MARGARET	} *waiting women to Hero*	
URSULA		
BOY		15

TOWNSPEOPLE OF MESSINA

FRIAR Francis		
DOGBERRY	*master constable*	
VERGES	*a headborough*	
Members of the WATCH		
George SEACOAL	} *members of the Watch*	20
Hugh Oatcake		
Francis Seacoal, *a* SEXTON		

OTHERS

MESSENGERS

Attendants, Musicians

LIST OF ROLES Rowe's was the first
edition (1709) to list the characters,
classifying them according to both
rank and gender.

1 DON PEDRO The *Prince of Aragon* hails
from a region in north-west Spain,
unlike his followers, who are Italian.
Messina, a port city of north-east
Sicily, was under Spanish rule in
Shakespeare's time. The Quarto entry
SDs often list him merely as *'Prince'*,
or *'Prince Pedro'*; these have been
emended to DON PEDRO throughout.

2 DON JOHN Don John's bastard status
is not voiced in the play until 4.1.188,
though he is designated in Q's SPs
as such, and bears telling character
traits typical of literary bastards (see
1.1.90.2n.) Unlike the villains of his
sources, Shakespeare's villain is not a
rival lover of Hero.

3 Signor BENEDICK Benedick's name
derives from *benedictus* or *benedict*, he
who is blessed, or a blessing; etymologically, it also refers to a good saying
or one of 'good speech' (*bene dicte*),
perhaps an apt name for one known for
verbal dexterity. Padua was a commune
of north-east Italy to the west of Venice,
renowned for its university – 'nursery
of arts', according to *TS* (1.1.2).

4 Signor CLAUDIO Claudio's youth is
mentioned several times in the text,
and he shares his name with other
of Shakespeare's young lovers, not-
ably *MM*'s unfortunate swain; the
name was derived from the Roman
Claudii, a family of despotic fame; in
Shakespeare's Bandello source, 'Sir
Timbreo de Cardona'. Florence was
known in Elizabethan England for its
trade and cultured and ostentatious
power.

5 BALTHASAR Shakespeare also uses the
name in *CE*, *MV* and *RJ*. The Folio
substitutes the name of *'Iacke Wilson'*
in the entry direction at 2.3.34.1–2;
though this was a common name, at
least two men have been identified as
possible candidates for the performances which may have provided the
copy-text for F (neither would have
been old enough for the original per-

formances, though some other Jack
Wilson may have served). The first is
John Wilson (1595–1674), who gradu-
ated as Doctor of Music at Oxford in
1644 and became Professor of Music
in 1656 (see Rimbault). Cam[1] identifies him with 'Mr. Wilson the singer',
who was a guest at Edward Alleyn's
28th wedding anniversary, 22 October
1620.

6 CONRADE by his own account (4.2.15),
a gentleman

7 BORACHIO The name derives from
the Spanish word for 'drunkard' (*bor-
racho*, from the term for a leather wine
bottle); cf. *'Bourrachon*: A tipler, quaf-
fer, tossepot, whip-canne; also little
Bourrachoe' (Cotgrave). See Thomas
Middleton, *The Spanish Gypsy* (1625),
1.1.2–8: *'Diego*: Art mad? / *Roderigo*:
Yes, not so much with wine . . . I am
no Borachio . . . mine eye mads me, not
my cups' (Middleton, 6.118).

8 LORD This person is identified in Q
only in the SPs in 5.3; it is unclear
whether he is associated with Leonato's
household or the soldierly contingent.

9 LEONATO The governor of the Sicilian
city of Messina would have been
a medium fish in a small pond. In
Shakespeare's Bandello source, 'Messer
Lionato de' Lionati' is of significantly
lesser rank than his daughter's suitor.
Benedick describes him at 2.3.120 as
the 'white-bearded fellow'.

10 ANTONIO is referred to in Q's SDs/
SPs as *'old man'/'Old'*, and (by 5.1)
'Brother' or *'Bro.'* He appears to live
either with or adjacent to his brother
Leonato (he refers to the garden where
much of the play's action takes place
as *mine orchard*, 1.2.8–9). While he is
described as having a son in 1.2, no
such person appears in the play.

11 HERO The name was notorious from
Christopher Marlowe's poem *Hero and
Leander* (1598), where it belongs to a
priestess of Venus who forsakes her
vestal duties for her lover. In George
Chapman's continuation of Marlowe's
unfinished poem, when Leander
drowns on Hero's behalf, she returns
the compliment; thus she is a figure

of a complicated sexual loyalty, and an overriding devotion. Her counterpart in Bandello is Fenicia (from 'phoenix', a bird noted for its capacities of resurrection). See also 4.1.79n.

12 BEATRICE from the Latin Beatrix, for 'one who blesses'; in Elizabethan pronunciation probably *Bettris* or *Betteris* (as metre requires)

13 MARGARET based on the gentlewoman Dalinda of Ludovico Ariosto's *Orlando Furioso* (1532), waiting lady to the princess Genevra, and lover of Polynesso; the latter, ambitious of Genevra's hand in marriage and desirous of separating her from her own beloved Ariodante, persuades Dalinda to dress in her mistress's clothes (on the pretence that he can then imagine himself Genevra's lover and exorcise his love for her), and arranges to have Ariodante view their assignation.

14 URSULA spelled Ursley (e.g. 3.1.4) and so pronounced

15 BOY appears only in 2.3

17 DOGBERRY from the decidedly English rustic botanical name for the fruit of the wild cornel or dogwood, a common shrub. Perhaps played in the Lord Chamberlain's Men by the hearty and nimble actor of clown roles Will Kemp, prior to his departure from

the company in 1599. See 3.3.0.1n. on *constable*, and p. 128.

18 VERGES (1) from the dialect form of verjuice, the sour juice of unripe grapes of the agresto vine (one upon which the ripe fruit and flowers appeared simultaneously), and perhaps a reference to the lean physiognomy of the actor Richard Cowley, who first played the role; (2) an oblique reference to the Court of the Verge (responsible for policing trespasses within 12 miles of the royal person); (3) a reference to the verge, the staff associated with the office of constable, upon which the latter would presumably lean. A headborough is a parish officer one rank below constable.

19 Members of the WATCH This neighbourhood citizen patrol is composed of at least four officers (see 3.3.0.2n.), two of whom are named in the play (see 20, 21n.).

20,21 George SEACOAL and Hugh Oatcake northern provincial British names

22 SEXTON Francis Seacoal, also called 'town clerk' (4.2.0.2). A sexton was a minor church official.

23 MESSENGERS There are three SPs for a messenger in the play, in 1.1, 3.5 and 5.4. They need not be the same person; the one who appears in 1.1 seems to be of the military party.

MUCH ADO ABOUT NOTHING

[1.1]   *Enter* LEONATO, Governor of Messina,
         HERO *his daughter and* BEATRICE *his niece,*
                    with a Messenger.

LEONATO   I learn in this letter that Don Pedro of Aragon
comes this night to Messina.

MESSENGER   He is very near by this. He was not three
leagues off when I left him.

LEONATO   How many gentlemen have you lost in this   5
action?

1.1 Act divisions originate with F
(from the Blackfriars' practice of
breaking continuous action into parts
punctuated by musical intervals); scene
divisions (apart from F's '*Actus Primus,
Scena prima*') were enumerated by
eighteenth-century editors. The early
texts do not designate locations; Pope
was the first to do so. A courtyard,
garden or entryway before Leonato's
dwelling is a typical production choice,
and Don Pedro's greeting – 'are you
come to meet your trouble?' (91–2)
– implies that Leonato encounters his
guests near the threshold of his home.
Antonio's reference to *mine orchard*
(1.2.8–9) as the site of the conversation
between Don Pedro and Claudio
which concludes this scene further
suggests that it is a verdant space, and
that its architecture may contain a
structure conducive to eavesdropping
(but see 1.3.54–9 for confusions on
this score). Productions often use this
opening scene to set the tone; choices

have included aristocratic splendour,
military milieu and rural idyll. See
pp. 98–100.

0.1 *LEONATO . . . **Messina** Q also lists
'*Innogen his wife*' after Leonato, in this
SD and at the entrance to 2.1, although
she is given no lines. Beginning with
Theobald in his 1733 edition, editorial tradition omits her. Theobald
surmised that Shakespeare 'in his first
plan designed such a character, which,
on a survey of it, he found would
be superfluous'. Some recent scholars
however have suggested she be a silent
presence in the play. See pp. 138–40.

1, 9 *Pedro Q has *Peter* instead of the
Spanish Pedro, or Bandello's Italian
Piero.

1–2 **Aragon . . . Messina** See List of
Roles, 1n.

3–4 **three leagues** a distance between 7
and 13 miles. The Messenger has rid-
den ahead of the troop to announce
their arrival.

6   **action** battle

1.1] *Actus primus, Scena prima.* F   0.1–2 Messina, HERO] *Theobald (Leonato, Hero); Messina, Innogen
his wife, Hero Q*   1, 9 Pedro] *Rowe;* Peter *Q*

MESSENGER   But few of any sort, and none of name.

LEONATO   A victory is twice itself when the achiever
brings home full numbers. I find here that Don Pedro
hath bestowed much honour on a young Florentine   10
called Claudio.

MESSENGER   Much deserved on his part, and equally
remembered by Don Pedro. He hath borne himself
beyond the promise of his age, doing in the figure of a
lamb the feats of a lion; he hath indeed better bettered   15
expectation than you must expect of me to tell you how.

LEONATO   He hath an uncle here in Messina will be very
much glad of it.

MESSENGER   I have already delivered him letters, and
there appears much joy in him, even so much that joy   20
could not show itself modest enough without a badge
of bitterness.

---

7   **sort** rank, reputation (see *MM* 4.4.18)
or possibly kind, since *name* designates
noble family. Cf. *H5* 4.8.74, where the
king asks 'What prisoners of good sort
are taken, uncle?' and later a recital of
English casualties by rank concludes
with 'None else of name, and of all
other men / But five-and-twenty'
(4.8.104–5). This is a verse line, although
perhaps an involuntary or accidental one;
or the Messenger could be attempting to
initiate a more formal register, which
Leonato declines to match.

8   **twice itself** double
    achiever victor

9   **full numbers** i.e. all the soldiers who
set out to the battle

10–11   **young . . . Claudio** Leonato's
comment could suggest that he is teasing his daughter with news of an
admirer. Claudio's youth is emphasized here, and in the Messenger's
reply.

12–13   **equally remembered** properly
acknowledged, duly rewarded

14–15   **in . . . lion** The Messenger speaks,
and Leonato replies, in the mannered

cadences of the 'euphuistic' style (noted
for inversions and balanced syntactic
structures; see pp. 65–70); such forms
of verbal exchange serve as a way for the
men in this play to create and recognize
alliance. These lines and others like them
are often cut in productions committed
to a less mannered stylization of characters, or in moving the plot along more
expeditiously.

15–16   **better bettered expectation**
more than merely fulfilled his promise

17   **an uncle** No further reference to
or appearance of this person occurs,
though his mention can give a sense
of a 'wider and more intimate back-
ground to the characters, and to create
in us the illusion of lives and homes
apart from the action of the stage'
(Ard[1]).

20–2   **that . . . bitterness** His happiness demanded some mark of sadness
so that it would not seem excessive; a
badge is 'a mark of service worn by
the retainers of a nobleman' (Wright)
(hence, a sign of subordination). For
adverbial use of *much* see Abbott, 51.

LEONATO   Did he break out into tears?

MESSENGER   In great measure.

LEONATO   A kind overflow of kindness; there are no faces   25
truer than those that are so washed. How much better
is it to weep at joy than to joy at weeping!

BEATRICE   I pray you, is Signor Mountanto returned
from the wars or no?

MESSENGER   I know none of that name, lady; there was   30
none such in the army of any sort.

LEONATO   What is he that you ask for, niece?

HERO   My cousin means Signor Benedick of Padua.

MESSENGER   O, he's returned, and as pleasant as ever he
was.   35

BEATRICE   He set up his bills here in Messina and

24 i.e. copiously, although the term *measure* also connotes a sense of (manly)
temperance
25 kind . . . kindness natural show of
family feeling; cf. *Ham* 1.2.65: 'A little
more than kin, and less than kind.'
25–6 no faces truer 'that is, none honester, none more sincere' (Johnson)
27 weep . . . weeping an inversion
typical of the euphuistic style. Cf.
Mac 1.4.33–5: 'My plenteous joys, /
Wanton in fulness, seek to hide themselves / In drops of sorrow.'
28 Signor Mountanto i.e. Signor
Upthrust, from *montanto* or *montant*,
a fencing term for an upward thrust,
as Capell first recognized, citing Ben
Jonson, *Every Man in His Humour*
(1598), 4.7.76–9: 'I would teach [them]
the special rules, as your punto, your
reverso, your stoccata, your imbroccatto,
your passada, your mountanto' (Jonson,
3.262). The term implies a type of
overweening fashionable fencing-room
combat (akin to witty banter), rather
than doughty soldiership, and perhaps

also a sense of the braggart soldier, as
well as a sexual innuendo (e.g. both the
thrust of a penis and the 'mounting'
of a partner). Cf. 2.1.338–9, and Don
Pedro's aim to bring Benedick and
Beatrice into a 'mountain of affection,
th'one with th'other.'
34 pleasant agreeable
36 bills handbills, or posters, to announce
what is in this case an archery contest; cf. Thomas Nashe, *Have with
You to Saffron Walden* (1596): 'setting
up bills, like a Bearward or Fencer,
what fights we shall have, and what
weapons she will meet me at' (Nashe,
3.121). Beatrice jokingly describes
Benedick as having challenged Cupid,
the blindfolded and winged god of
love (and child of Venus) notorious for
his wayward archery, which suggests
that Benedick had either sought to
enter the contest of love (i.e. become
a lover), or, on the contrary, sought to
fight against (or perhaps shoot at?) the
bird-like Love (since he later professes
himself an apostate to that religion).

28+ Signor] *(Signior)*   Mountanto] Montanto *Pope*

challenged Cupid at the flight; and my uncle's fool,
reading the challenge, subscribed for Cupid and
challenged him at the bird-bolt. I pray you, how many
hath he killed and eaten in these wars? But how many　　40
hath he killed? For indeed I promised to eat all of his
killing.

LEONATO　Faith, niece, you tax Signor Benedick too
much, but he'll be meet with you, I doubt it not.

MESSENGER　He hath done good service, lady, in these　　45
wars.

BEATRICE　You had musty victual, and he hath holp to

37　**flight** either a type of arrow, light and well feathered, suited for long-distance shooting, or, more likely, a long-distance shooting contest, of the most challenging kind, using such arrows. There may be also a pun on 'flyte'; a 'flyting' was a kind of Scottish insult contest (such as that which Beatrice and Benedick engage in at their first meeting).

my uncle's fool A fool was a type of house jester or entertainer, but Beatrice may be elliptically referring to herself, given her role in her uncle's household – much as she later terms Benedick the 'prince's jester, a very dull fool' (2.1.125). No such character appears in Leonato's household in the course of the play. Barbara Everett observes: 'certain speeches of Beatrice . . . do cohere into an attitude that utilises a "fool's" uncommitted wit and detached play of mind, together with a clown's grasp of earthy reality, yet committed in such a new way that they are given the effect of female veracity against a masculine romanticism or formality' (Everett, 'Much Ado', 326).

38　**subscribed for** signed up on Cupid's team, as his representative; took the part of; vouched or answered for

39　**bird-bolt** a short blunt arrow (as opposed to the *flight*), the child Cupid's weapon of choice ('Proceed, sweet Cupid, though hast thumped him with thy birdbolt under the left pap', *LLL* 4.3.22–43), or that of other less than proficient archers, as in John Marston's *What You Will* (1607): 'Some boundlesse ignorance should on sudden shoote / His grosse knobbed burbolt' (Induction, 39–40). Beatrice's (enigmatic) sense is either that the fool insisted on using the blunter and less swift weapon in order to mock Benedick's pretensions to be a ladies' man; or that the fool (as Beatrice?) clumsily transformed the nature of the contest from swift shooting to more fumbling childish attempts.

41–2　**promised . . . killing** a proverbial phrase (Dent, A192.2) deriding someone's swaggering ferocity, suggesting that he didn't kill any at all. Cf. *H5* 3.7.94: 'I think he will eat all he kills.'

43　**Faith** in faith; truly
　　tax accuse, censure

44　**be . . . you** pay you back; get even with you (perhaps with a pun on 'meat', as well as 'mate' or ' checkmate', all of which were pronounced similarly)

47　**holp** helped

---

39 bird-bolt] *Pope*[2] *(Theobald);* Burbolt *Q*　47 victual] *F (*victuall*);* vittaile *Q*

eat it. He is a very valiant trencher-man: he hath an
excellent stomach.

MESSENGER   And a good soldier too, lady.   50

BEATRICE   And a good soldier to a lady; but what is he to
a lord?

MESSENGER   A lord to a lord, a man to a man, stuffed with
all honourable virtues.

BEATRICE   It is so indeed, he is no less than a stuffed man;   55
but for the stuffing – well, we are all mortal.

LEONATO   You must not, sir, mistake my niece; there is a
kind of merry war betwixt Signor Benedick and her.
They never meet but there's a skirmish of wit between
them.   60

BEATRICE   Alas, he gets nothing by that. In our last
conflict, four of his five wits went halting off, and now

48 **trencher-man** hearty eater, glutton;
'trencher' from the French *trenchoir* =
wooden platter; although in the later
Middle Ages trenchers were made of
day-old bread, so perhaps a trencher-
man ate even his very plate.

49 **stomach** (1) digestive organ; (2)
appetite: see 2.3.246–7, 'You have no
stomach, signor?'; (3) courage

51 **soldier . . . lady** (1) i.e. compared to
a lady; (2) an aggressive (with sexual
suggestion) suitor; or, alternatively, (3)
a man who treats women like a soldier
rather than a suitor (cf. *H5* 5.2.148–
9: 'I speak to thee plain soldier'); (4)
braggart soldier (i.e. only a soldier
among ladies). Beatrice's turn on the
Messenger's terms signals her entry
into the verbal one-upmanship which
characterizes the exchanges of men in
this play, whereby terms and meanings
are appropriated and returned, transformed, to their speaker.

53 **A . . . to a man** i.e. he behaves with
an awareness of both social rank and
common decency

stuffed well provided or fortified with
(in a military sense); cf. *RJ* 3.5.181,
'Stuff'd, as they say, with honourable
parts', and *WT* 2.1.184–5, 'whom you
know / Of stuff'd sufficiency'.

55 **stuffed man** rich person; scarecrow
dummy; fat man (especially if he is
one of 'excellent stomach'), replen-
ished. See also 3.4.59, 'A maid and
stuffed!', where *stuffed* = pregnant
and/or sexually penetrated. Dent,
S945.1, citing T. Becon's *Principles
of Christian Religion* (1552), sig. A3ᵛ,
lists this phrase as both proverbial
and flattering: 'Your father is learned
and hath a brest stuffed with al godlye
virtues.'

59 **skirmish** battle; the metaphor indicates the rivalrous nature of the
euphuistic mode.

62 **five wits** sometimes synonymous with
the five senses – cf. Chaucer, *The
Parson's Tale*, 272 – but also, as here,
the mental capacities of wit, imagination, fantasy, judgement and memory.
Cf. *Son* 141.9–10: 'But my five wits,

48 eat] ease *F*   He is] he's *F*   trencher-man] *(trencher man), F*   56 stuffing – well] *Theobald;*
stuffing wel, *Q*   61 that. In] *F;* that, in *Q*

is the whole man governed with one, so that if he have
wit enough to keep himself warm, let him bear it for a
difference between himself and his horse, for it is all the   65
wealth that he hath left to be known a reasonable
creature. Who is his companion now? He hath every
month a new sworn brother.

MESSENGER   Is't possible?

BEATRICE   Very easily possible. He wears his faith but as   70
the fashion of his hat: it ever changes with the next
block.

MESSENGER   I see, lady, the gentleman is not in your
books.

BEATRICE   No; an he were, I would burn my study. But I   75

nor my five senses, can / Dissuade one
foolish heart from serving thee.'
halting limping (ignominiously);
Beatrice extends the military metaphor.
64 wit . . . warm proverbial: having sense
enough to come in out of inclement
weather (Dent, K10); cf. *TS* 2.1.260:
'PETRUCHIO Am I not wise? / KATH-
ERINA Yes, keep you warm.'
64–5 bear . . . horse keep it as a sign to
distinguish himself from his horse
65 difference a coat of arms designed
to differentiate branches of the same
family; cf. *Ham* 4.5.180–1: 'You must
wear your rue with a difference.'
66–7 to . . . creature in order to know
himself to be a rational human and not
a beast, reason being the quality that
distinguishes the two
68 new sworn brother newly pledged
comrade (in arms); 'sworn brother'
was a chivalric phrase (*fratres iurati*);
cf. *H5* 2.1.11–12: 'we'll be all three
sworn brothers to France'.
70 faith friendship (with his *sworn brother*)
71 fashion style. A charged word in the
play, with various meanings: as a verb, to
shape, to continue, to frame, transform,
counterfeit, pervert; as a noun, the
action of making, visible character-

istics, appearance, mode of behaviour,
prevailing custom, convention, a mode
of dress (*OED* fashion *v.* 1, 2a, 4, 4b; *sb.*
1, 2a, 6a, 8a, 9a, 10). See 1.1.92–3: 'The
fashion of the world is to avoid cost, and
you encounter it'; 3.3.114–37, *passim*.
72 block i.e. style; a block was a wooden
mould for shaping felt hats, changing
with the fashion of hat. Cf. Thomas
Dekker, *Seven Deadly Sins of London*
(1606): 'the blocke for his heade alters
faster then the Feltmaker can fitte
him' (Dekker, *Sins*, 2.60); perhaps
also contemptuously implies that
Benedick's friends are blockheads
(*OED* block *sb.* 15a).
74 books favour; proverbial (Dent, B534).
The phrase is of uncertain origin, possibly
from (1) record books of employers,
in which servants' names were listed;
(2) guest books; (3) books of a college
listing members; (4) heraldic registers,
cf. *TS* 2.1.223: 'A herald, Kate? O, put
me in thy books'; (5) account books of a
tradesman in which creditable customers
were listed. As is typical in such shifting
word-play, Beatrice transposes the
context to a collection of books.
75 an if (common throughout, e.g. 130,
180, 189, etc.)

66 left to] *Collier*; left, to *Q*   67 creature.] *F*; creature, *Q*   75 an] *(and)*; if *Pope*   study.] *F*; study, *Q*

pray you, who is his companion? Is there no young
squarer now that will make a voyage with him to the
devil?

MESSENGER   He is most in the company of the right noble
Claudio.   80

BEATRICE   O Lord, he will hang upon him like a disease!
He is sooner caught than the pestilence, and the taker
runs presently mad. God help the noble Claudio! If he
have caught the Benedick, it will cost him a thousand
pound ere 'a be cured.   85

MESSENGER   I will hold friends with you, lady.

BEATRICE   Do, good friend.

LEONATO   You will never run mad, niece.

BEATRICE   No, not till a hot January.

MESSENGER   Don Pedro is approached.   90

Enter DON PEDRO, CLAUDIO, BENEDICK, BALTHASAR
and [DON] JOHN *the bastard.*

76 **pray you** pray of you, beg of you
77 **squarer** swaggerer; trouble-maker (as
    one who 'squares' for a fist-fight)
82 **pestilence** plague
    taker victim
83 **presently** shortly, immediately
84 *****the Benedick** in Q, Benedict, its only
    instance of that spelling. Benedicts, or
    benets, were Catholic priests qualified
    to perform exorcisms, and madness
    was often thought to be caused by
    demonic possession, hence *caught the
    Benedict*. See also List of Roles 3n.
84–5 **cost . . . pound** i.e. friendship
    with Benedick is expensive (perhaps
    because of his appetite for fashion?)
85 **ere** before
    'a he
88 i.e. *you* are immune to catching the
    Benedick. The allegedly colder female
    humoral temperament was thought to

be less susceptible to love's passions;
see 119n.
90 **is approached** has arrived
90.1–2 Don Pedro's company has often
    entered with great ceremony in the
    theatre, and may on the Renaissance
    stage have been announced with a
    musical flourish.
90.2 *the bastard* Don John's illegitimate
    birth is not mentioned by another
    character until 4.1.188, although it
    could be reflected in his melancholy
    temperament and his estrangement, now
    reconciled (1.1.148), from his brother
    Don Pedro. Bastards were thought by
    nature, and nurture, to be covetous due
    to their lack of social legitimacy (and
    property); Francis Bacon writes in his
    essay *Of Envy* (1597) that 'Deformed
    persons, and eunuchs, and old men, and
    bastards, are envious. For he that cannot

84 Benedick] *F2*; Benedict *Q*   85 'a] he *F*; it *F2*   88 You will never] You'l ne're *F*   90.2 DON JOHN]
Rowe; Iohn *Q*

155

DON PEDRO   Good Signor Leonato, are you come to meet
your trouble? The fashion of the world is to avoid cost,
and you encounter it.

LEONATO   Never came trouble to my house in the likeness
of your grace, for, trouble being gone, comfort should   95
remain; but when you depart from me, sorrow abides,
and happiness takes his leave.

DON PEDRO   You embrace your charge too willingly. I
think this is your daughter.

LEONATO   Her mother hath many times told me so.   100

BENEDICK   Were you in doubt, sir, that you asked her?

LEONATO   Signor Benedick, no, for then were you a child.

DON PEDRO   You have it full, Benedick; we may guess by
this what you are, being a man. Truly, the lady fathers
herself. Be happy, lady, for you are like an honourable   105
father. [*Don Pedro and Leonato walk apart.*]

---

possibly mend his own case, will do
what he can to impair another's' (Bacon,
25). Cf. the behaviour of Edmund in
KL. It is apt that the villain of a play
so preoccupied with male anxiety over
cuckoldry and its social and emotional
consequences be a bastard. Shakespeare
departs from his sources in not making
his villain a rival lover.

92 **trouble** i.e. the effort and expense of
entertaining a guest
fashion way, custom
cost expense of guests
93 **encounter** come to meet
94 **likeness** appearance, person
98 **charge** expense; responsibility
100 the first of the play's many references to
the dubious sexual fidelity of women. Cf.
KL 2.2.320–4: 'REGAN I am glad to see
your highness. / LEAR . . . If thou shouldst
not be glad, / I would divorce me from

thy mother's tomb, / Sepulchring an
adultress.' Leonato's reference to his
wife's frequent verbal warrant ('many
times told me') contrasts with the visual
proof of Hero's physical resemblance
to her father (Leonato's double proof
differentiates him from Prospero, who
can only affirm 'Thy mother was a piece
of virtue, and /She said thou wast my
daughter', *Tem* 1.2.56–7).

102 **a child** i.e. incapable of fathering a
child upon my wife, implying not only
that Benedick is a womanizer, but that
he is the only one in the community
103 **full** fully answered, i.e. he's got you
there
104–5 **fathers herself** physically resembles her father, and thus needs no
other warrant of her paternity
105–6 **Be . . . father** i.e. it is Hero's good
fortune to resemble her father, whose

91+ SP DON PEDRO] *Capell (D. Pe.); Pedro Q;* PRINCE *Folg*[2]   are you] you are *F*   92 trouble?]
Collier; trouble: *Q*   101 sir] *om. F*   106 SD] *Ard*[2] (*Don . . . Leonato talk aside*); *Oxf*[1] (*speaks
privately with Leonato*)

BENEDICK   If Signor Leonato be her father, she would
not have his head on her shoulders for all Messina, as
like him as she is.

BEATRICE   I wonder that you will still be talking, Signor   110
Benedick; nobody marks you.

BENEDICK   What, my dear Lady Disdain! Are you yet
living?

BEATRICE   Is it possible Disdain should die, while she
hath such meet food to feed it as Signor Benedick?   115
Courtesy itself must convert to Disdain if you come in
her presence.

BENEDICK   Then is Courtesy a turncoat. But it is certain
I am loved of all ladies, only you excepted; and I would
I could find in my heart that I had not a hard heart, for   120
truly I love none.

BEATRICE   A dear happiness to women – they would else
have been troubled with a pernicious suitor. I thank
God and my cold blood, I am of your humour for that:

honour consists not only in his own
attributes but in his possession of a
chaste wife and legitimate offspring
(and also, as Benedick's subsequent
comment implies, a venerably aged
appearance)

107–8 **she ... shoulders** i.e. she wouldn't
want to resemble his white-bearded
appearance exactly

111 **marks** notices, is paying attention to
(except, of course, Beatrice)

112 **Lady Disdain** Benedick refers to
Beatrice as if she were a personifica-
tion in a morality play or an allegori-
cal debate, as she does herself with
Courtesy (116). The figure of the disdainful woman was a conventional one
(Prouty, 54); Spenser's Mirabella in
The Faerie Queene (1596) was condemned to wander the world, guarded by Disdain and Scorn, in order to

save 'so many loues, as she did lose'
(*FQ*, 6.7.37.9), and the indifference of
the Petrarchan mistress fuelled many
a sonnet-writer's powers of pleading
invention. Cf. 3.1.51–2, 'Disdain and
Scorn ride sparkling in her eyes, /
Misprising what they look on.'

115 **meet** appropriate, fit (with a pun on
'meat' and 'mate', as at 44)

116 **convert to** change into

119 **only you excepted** all except for
you

122 **dear happiness** stroke of good luck

124 **of your humour** i.e. of your mind
(medieval physiology designated four
humours – blood, phlegm, choler and
melancholy – thought to determine
health and temperament). If Beatrice
has *cold blood* she is phlegmatic, thus
apathetic or indifferent. Renaissance
medical thought considered women

I had rather hear my dog bark at a crow, than a man   125
    swear he loves me.
BENEDICK   God keep your ladyship still in that mind,
    so some gentleman or other shall scape a predestinate
    scratched face.
BEATRICE   Scratching could not make it worse, an 'twere   130
    such a face as yours were.
BENEDICK   Well, you are a rare parrot-teacher.
BEATRICE   A bird of my tongue is better than a beast of
    yours.
BENEDICK   I would my horse had the speed of your   135
    tongue, and so good a continuer. But keep your way,
    o'God's name; I have done.
BEATRICE   You always end with a jade's trick; I know you
    of old.

to be cooler of humour, and temperature, than men, and the phlegmatic
temperament the more impervious to
love: 'Now, as women are much more
moyste than men, so in like manner
we may discern in them, that fren-
zies and furiousness is not so familiar
with them as men, in regard they will
neuer runne mad for loue, or any other
worldly desire . . . whereas men from
time to time, make themselues as in a
publique theatre, the subject of very
tragicall follies' (Gibson, sig. B3ᵛ).
125 **dog . . . crow** presumably a frenzied
and aggravating noise, and one which
drives the crow away
128 **scape** escape
    predestinate for predestinated (i.e.
    inescapable, fore-ordained); some
    verbs with stems ending in -*d* or -*t*
    may form participles which may drop
    the final *d* (see Abbott, 342). Cf. 3.2.2,
    consummate.
132 **rare parrot-teacher** one who
    repeats endlessly so that a parrot will
    learn a phrase

133–4 i.e. better a talking bird than a
    mute beast
136 **so . . . continuer** a horse of great
    stamina; Beatrice (according to
    Benedick) talks at great length (a
    stereotypically unappealing trait in
    women in this period).
    keep your way i.e. carry on
137 **'o** in
    I have done i.e. I am done sparring
    with you
138 **jade's trick** A jade is a wayward
    horse, canny to devious ways of
    unseating a rider; the term was rarely
    applied to men. Beatrice, pursuing the
    equine metaphor, accuses Benedick
    of ducking out of the game of wits
    prematurely and underhandedly (i.e.
    by denying her the opportunity to
    reply).
138–9 **I . . . old** There is a suggestion
    here of a history between them of such
    premature abdications on Benedick's
    part; cf. 2.1.255–8: 'Indeed, my lord,
    he lent it me awhile, and I gave him use
    for it, a double heart for his single one.

130 an] *(and)*   132 parrot-teacher] *(parrat teacher), F2*   137 o'] *(a)*

DON PEDRO   That is the sum of all, Leonato. [*Addresses the*   140
company.] Signor Claudio and Signor Benedick, my
dear friend Leonato hath invited you all. I tell him we
shall stay here at the least a month, and he heartily
prays some occasion may detain us longer. I dare swear
he is no hypocrite, but prays from his heart.   145

LEONATO   If you swear, my lord, you shall not be forsworn.
[*to Don John*] Let me bid you welcome, my lord, being
reconciled to the prince your brother. I owe you all
duty.

DON JOHN   I thank you. I am not of many words, but I   150
thank you.

LEONATO [*to Don Pedro*]   Please it your grace lead on?

DON PEDRO   Your hand, Leonato; we will go together.

Exeunt all but Benedick and Claudio.

CLAUDIO   Benedick, didst thou note the daughter of
Signor Leonato?   155

Marry, once before he won it of me
with false dice; therefore your grace
may well say I have lost it.'
140 **sum of all** i.e. the full account
(presumably of the battle)
143 **a month** See pp. 56–7 for a discussion of the play's time scheme.
146–7 **you shall . . . forsworn** i.e. I
won't do anything to falsify your vow
147 **being** now that you are
150 **not . . . words** Reticence was a hallmark of the melancholic, a humoral
personality type also noted for being
'lean, dry, lank, the face beneath pale,
yellowish, swarthy . . . enuious and
jealous, apt to take occasions in the
worse part, and out of measure passionate. From these dispositions of

the heart and braine arise solitarinesse,
weeping, and . . . melancholie laughter . . . of pace slow, silent, negligent,
refusing the light and frequency of
men, delighted more in solitariness
and obscurity' (Bright, sig. H6ᵛ). On
the Renaissance stage Don John may
have been dressed in black, the colour
symbolic of melancholy.
152–3 **lead on . . . go together** As the
person of highest rank, Don Pedro
should precede the company into the
house; he courteously refuses to enter
before his host.
154 **note** (1) take special notice of (hence
Benedick's reply); (2) remark, the first
of many instances of this usage in the
play. See also 2.3.55n.

140 That] This *F*   all, Leonato.] *Collier²*; all: Leonato, *Q*   140–1 SD] *Ard² (Turning to the company.)*;
Oxf¹ (ending his talk with Leonato)   142 tell him] tell you *F3*   147 SD] *Hanmer subst.*   147–8 lord, . . .
brother.] Lord; . . . brother, *Hanmer*   152 SD] *Oxf*   153 SD *all but*] *Rowe*; Manent *Q*, Manet *F*

BENEDICK   I noted her not, but I looked on her.

CLAUDIO   Is she not a modest young lady?

BENEDICK   Do you question me as an honest man should
do, for my simple true judgement? Or would you have
me speak after my custom, as being a professed tyrant   160
to their sex?

CLAUDIO   No, I pray thee, speak in sober judgement.

BENEDICK   Why, i'faith methinks she's too low for a high
praise, too brown for a fair praise and too little for a
great praise. Only this commendation I can afford her: 165
that were she other than she is, she were unhandsome;
and being no other but as she is, I do not like her.

CLAUDIO   Thou thinkest I am in sport. I pray thee tell me
truly how thou lik'st her.

BENEDICK   Would you buy her that you inquire after her?   170

CLAUDIO   Can the world buy such a jewel?

---

160 **custom** habit
professed well-known
160–1 **tyrant to** slanderer of
163–5 **Why . . . praise** The implication is
that the actor or actress playing Hero
is to be short (low), slight and dark –
perhaps as opposed to Beatrice, of
whom the actress Helena Faucit said:
'if what Wordsworth says was ever true
of anyone, assuredly it was true of her,
that "Vital feelings of delight / Had
reared her to a stately height"' (Faucit,
297). 'Brown' was often contrasted with
a more conventional beauty, as in *TC*
1.2.90ff., or *H8* 3.2.294–6: 'I'll startle
you / Worse than the sacring-bell
when the brown wench / Lay kissing
in your arms, Lord Cardinal'; or the
first line of John Donne's poem 'The
Indifferent': 'I can love both fair and
brown'. Benedick's formulation recalls
the comments of John Lyly's Fidus to
Euphues, in *Euphues and His England*
(1580), concerning the virtues of witty
women: 'And this is the greatest thing,

to conceive readily and answer aptly
. . . A nobleman in Siena, disposed to
jest with a gentlewoman of mean birth
yet excellent qualities, between game
and earnest gan thus to salute her:
"I know not how I should commend
your beauty, because it is somewhat
too brown, nor your stature, being
somewhat too low, and of your wit I
cannot judge." "No," quoth she, "I
believe you. For none can judge of wit
but they that have it" . . . He perceiving
all outward faults to be recompensed
with inward favour, chose this virgin
for his wife' (Lyly, *Euphues*, 60).
165 **afford** provide
169 **how . . . her** Claudio's need for
corroboration of Hero's universal
desirability will turn out to be closely
coupled with fear of her faithlessness,
and replicates a concern of Lyly's hero
Euphues: 'If my lady yeeld to be my
lover is it not likely she will be another's leman?' (Lyly, *Anatomy*, 95). Cf.
287n.

BENEDICK   Yea, and a case to put it into. But speak you this with a sad brow? Or do you play the flouting jack, to tell us Cupid is a good hare-finder and Vulcan a rare carpenter? Come, in what key shall a man take you to   175 go in the song?

CLAUDIO   In mine eye, she is the sweetest lady that ever I looked on.

BENEDICK   I can see yet without spectacles, and I see no such matter. There's her cousin, an she were not   180 possessed with a fury, exceeds her as much in beauty as the first of May doth the last of December. But I hope you have no intent to turn husband – have you?

CLAUDIO   I would scarce trust myself, though I had sworn the contrary, if Hero would be my wife.   185

BENEDICK   Is't come to this? In faith, hath not the world one man but he will wear his cap with suspicion? Shall

172 **case** jewel case; clothing; Elizabethan slang for vagina ('because it sheathes a sword', Partridge)

173 **sad brow** i.e. in all seriousness
flouting jack irreverent rascal; 'jack' was a term of contempt. To flout was to scorn, and George Puttenham in his *Art of English Poesy* (1589) describes the 'broad floute or Antiphrasis' as 'when we deride by plaine and flat contradiction' (Puttenham, 201).

174–5 **Cupid . . . carpenter** To describe the blind archer Cupid as proficient in spotting hares for a hunt, or the blacksmith Vulcan (god of fire) as a carpenter (hence more likely to burn wood than to build with it), is akin to, or so Benedick implies, mocking Hero by ascribing to her qualities she does not possess. (Vulcan was, incidentally, a notorious cuckold, whose wife Venus consorted with Mars, god of war.)

176 **go** i.e. to join in, follow along

178 **I** This could also be heard as 'eye', a sense which Benedick's reply perhaps punningly seizes upon. Love was thought to enter through the portal of the eyes: 'which are the faithful spies and intelligencers of the soul, steals gently through those sences, and so passing insensibly through the veines to the Liuer, it there presently imprinteth an ardent desire of the object, which is either really louely, or appears to be so' (Ferrand, sig. E2ʳ).

179 **I . . . spectacles** Benedick's accurate vision compares to Beatrice's 'good eye', which can 'see a church by daylight' (2.1.72–3).

180 **cousin** Beatrice, niece of Leonato

181 **fury** passionate rage; avenging Greek goddess with snakes in her hair sent to torment or punish wrong

187 **wear . . . suspicion** the first of many jokes about the cuckold's horns, which presumably would be difficult

180 an] *(and)*

I never see a bachelor of threescore again? Go to,
i'faith. An thou wilt needs thrust thy neck into a yoke,
wear the print of it and sigh away Sundays. Look, Don   190
Pedro is returned to seek you.

Enter DON PEDRO.

DON PEDRO   What secret hath held you here that you
followed not to Leonato's?
BENEDICK   I would your grace would constrain me to tell.
DON PEDRO   I charge thee on thy allegiance.   195

to conceal inconspicuously under a
cap, and of course the wearing of
which might well draw attention.
Cf. William Painter's *The Palace of
Pleasure* (1569): 'All they that weare
hornes, be pardoned to weare their caps
vpon their heads' (Painter, 2.37). The
conspicuousness of horn was seconded
by its use as an instrument of sound
(cf. 225–6, 'have a recheat winded in
my forehead'); the horn's identity as a
material of notoriety was seconded by
its function as the translucent material
used in lanterns, as in *MND* 5.1.238:
'*This lantern doth the horned moon
present*'). See pp. 43–50.
188 **threescore** sixty
Go to go on, get away
189–90 **thrust . . . Sundays** The yoke,
the wooden bar used to join pairs of
oxen, was a symbol of marriage, and
Sunday, the day of restrictions on
public pastimes, was presumably less
amusing when spent as a husband
and father rather than as a bachelor;
one would then also have, as Wright
observes, 'most leisure to reflect on
your captive condition' (Furness).
The image of the yoke as a sign of

marital confinement was a common
one. Cf. Torquato and Ercole Tasso,
Of Marriage and Wiving (1599): 'He
that will not believe [that wives deprive
us of our own sweete naturall freedom]
is as bad as a pettie Hereticke . . . if
he but call to minde the picture of
matrimonie itself as the most wise
Egyptians drewe the same, one while
painting it as man that had both his
hands and his feete manacled together,
an other while representing it with
such a plain-fashioned yoke as you
tie horned Oxen in thrall, which
doubtlesse is a most manifest imprese
or signe of bondage, slaverie, and
continualle servile drudging' (Tassi,
sig. F4ʳ). (Oxen were cattle gelded only
after reaching maturity.)
190 **wear . . . it** be branded or stamped
(by the impression left by the yoke
upon the flesh); be made into a sign
191.1 *Q's stage direction (see t.n.) is
faulty, since Don John first hears of
the intended marriage from Borachio
in 1.3.
194 **constrain** compel, order; the remark
suggests that Claudio makes silencing
gestures.

189 i'faith.] *Capell* (i'faith;*)*; yfaith, *Q*   An] *(and)*   191.1] *Hanmer; Enter don Pedro, Iohn the
bastard. Q*   196 Claudio?] *Oxf¹;* Claudio, *Q*   203 'it] *Dyce;* it *Q*   204 so'] *this edn;* so *Q*   so!] so!'
Dyce*   213 spoke] speake *F*

BENEDICK   You hear, Count Claudio? I can be secret as
a dumb man; I would have you think so. But on my
allegiance – mark you this, on my allegiance – he is in
love. With who? Now, that is your grace's part. Mark
how short his answer is: with Hero, Leonato's short   200
daughter.

CLAUDIO   If this were so, so were it uttered.

BENEDICK   Like the old tale, my lord: 'it is not so, nor
'twas not so'; but indeed, God forbid it should be so!

CLAUDIO   If my passion change not shortly, God forbid it   205
should be otherwise.

DON PEDRO   Amen, if you love her, for the lady is very
well worthy.

CLAUDIO   You speak this to fetch me in, my lord.

DON PEDRO   By my troth, I speak my thought.   210

CLAUDIO   And in faith, my lord, I spoke mine.

BENEDICK   And by my two faiths and troths, my lord, I
spoke mine.

CLAUDIO   That I love her, I feel.

DON PEDRO   That she is worthy, I know.   215

BENEDICK   That I neither feel how she should be loved

---

197 **dumb man** mute
198 **allegiance** sworn loyalty to a prince
or lord
203 **old tale** Benedick refers to the
punch-line of a story (of the robber-
bridegroom genre) in which a woman
discovers her suitor to be involved in
some criminal activity and convicts
him before her family; he continually
denies the charge but finally incontro-
vertible evidence is produced, to which
the man in question replies with this
formula.
205 **shortly** perhaps with a pun on *short*
(i.e. with a reference to Hero's stature)
205–6 **God . . . otherwise** i.e. God forbid

I should not love her
207 **Amen** a response to Claudio's
prayer
208 **well worthy** worthy of love; honourable; wealthy
209 **fetch me in** lead me on (and presumably invite ridicule for such an
admission), trick me into confessing
210 **By my troth** i.e. on my word; *troth* =
truth, and is similar to *faith*, as in the
following line.
212 **by . . . troths** i.e. to both Claudio and
Don Pedro, which could, as Benedick
comically implies, refute each other
(if one cannot swear allegiance to two
persons simultaneously)

nor know how she should be worthy is the opinion that
fire cannot melt out of me; I will die in it at the stake.

DON PEDRO   Thou wast ever an obstinate heretic in the
despite of beauty.   220

CLAUDIO   And never could maintain his part but in the
force of his will.

BENEDICK   That a woman conceived me, I thank her; that
she brought me up, I likewise give her most humble
thanks; but that I will have a recheat winded in my   225
forehead, or hang my bugle in an invisible baldrick, all

218 **at the stake** Religious dissenters (cf.
heretic, 219) were burnt at the stake
in England in great numbers under
Mary Tudor, 40 years prior to this
play's Elizabethan staging, although
the penalty was applied to a few under
Elizabeth as well. Benedick's professed
inability to confess to Hero's lovability
despite his multiple troths and faiths
parodies the obduracy of Protestant
martyrs who refused to acknowledge
the miraculous transubstantiation of
blood and bread, the supremacy of the
Pope, and other articles of the Roman
Catholic faith.

220 **despite of** contempt or scorn of (the
true faith of beauty)

221–2 **never . . . will** could not persist in
his belief were it not for his obstinacy
(wilfulness was thought to be a moti-
vation of heresy); cf. Milton, *Of True
Religion* (1673): 'Heresie is in the will
and choice profestly against Scripture'
(Milton, *Religion*, 109). There may
also be a sexual innuendo (*part* =
penis; *will* = sexual desire).

225–6 **recheat . . . forehead** a hunting
call to summon hounds, blown on the
(cuckold's) horn which will grow on
Benedick's forehead if he marries. The
recheat calls attention to the horn hidden by the *invisible baldrick* (see 226n.);
horns and bugles were fashioned of

cattle horns or boar tusks. Jane Anger,
in *Her Protection for Women* (1589),
imagines horns to be the property of
the cuckolder rather than the cuckold,
and audible as well as visible: 'their sex
are so like to Bulls that it is no marvel
though the Gods do metamorphose
some of them to give warning to the
rest . . . for some of them will follow
the smock as Tom Bull will run after
the Town Cow. But lest they should
running slip and break their pates, the
Gods, provident of their welfare, set
a pair of tooters on their foreheads
to keep it from the ground' (Anger,
176). The Ovidian transformation of
Benedick into a bull joins a pattern of
similar imagery of metamorphoses in
this play: Dogberry's desire to be 'writ
down an ass' (4.2.88); Claudio's muta-
tion from a *lamb* to a *lion* and a *hurt
fowl* (1.1.15, 2.1.185); Hero into a *chick*
(1.3.52); Beatrice into a *lapwing*, a *haggard* (hawk) and a *curst cow* (3.1.24, 36;
2.1.20–1); and Benedick and Beatrice
alike as besieged animals (*kid-fox*, *two
bears*, 2.3.40, 3.2.70).

226 **hang . . . baldrick** i.e. entrust my
manhood to the unverifiable quantity
of female chastity; a bugle is a horn but
also a penis (the dual meaning suggests
the vulnerability of phallic power, the
ease with which a penis can become a

225 recheat] *Rowe²* (recheate); rechate *Q*

women shall pardon me. Because I will not do them the *maybe*
wrong to mistrust any, I will do myself the right to trust *got*
none. And the fine is – for the which I may go the finer *hurt?*
– I will live a bachelor. 230

DON PEDRO   I shall see thee, ere I die, look pale with love.

BENEDICK   With anger, with sickness, or with hunger, my
lord, not with love. Prove that ever I lose more blood
with love than I will get again with drinking, pick out
mine eyes with a ballad-maker's pen and hang me up at 235
the door of a brothel-house for the sign of blind Cupid.

DON PEDRO   Well, if ever thou dost fall from this faith,
thou wilt prove a notable argument.

horn by the displacement of a husband by another man). A baldrick is a belt or girdle slung across the body to hold a horn or sword; *invisible* suggests either its immateriality (i.e. the difficulty of securing, or proving, female fidelity), or its obscurity (in which case Benedick wishes not to need to hide his member – or his shameful cuckold's horn – in a secret place), or the ignorance in which a cuckold sometimes sports his horns (Kittredge). Invisibility can also denote insubstantiality; the word 'nothing' was slang for the 'hole' of the vagina (as in *Much Ado About . . .*) as opposed to the 'something' of the penis, and hence Benedick could also mean 'I don't want to have to hide my shameful cuckold's horn', or, more likely, 'You won't catch me putting my penis/horn in an untrustworthy hole.' See 2.3.55n.

229 **fine** conclusion
finer more richly dressed (because freed of the expense of a wife). Some productions costume Benedick as a dandy; others, as a soldier.

231 **pale with love** The pallor of love-melancholy was thought to be caused

by the combination of 'yellow choler and the waterish parts of the blood' (Ferrand, sig. G5ʳ).

233–4 **lose . . . love** The sighs of love were thought to draw blood danger-ously away from the heart and towards the extremities; cf. *MND* 3.2.97: 'With sighs of love, that costs the fresh blood dear'.

234 **get . . . drinking** a reference to the restorative effects of wine, which red-dens the complexion (hence rendering it more sanguine); proverbial: 'Good wine makes good blood' (Dent, W461)

235 **ballad-maker's pen** the writing implement dedicated to love songs and loved ones; cf. *AYL* 2.7.148–9: 'a woeful ballad / Made to his mistress' eyebrow'.

236 **sign . . . Cupid** Like taverns, houses of prostitution had signs denoting their trade and name. Benedick implies that the gruesome image of his blinded self (because Cupid is blind, and perhaps because venereal disease causes blind-ness) would be an appropriate advert-isement for such an establishment.

238 **notable argument** notorious sub-ject for discussion

236 brothel-house] *(brothel house)*, F

BENEDICK   If I do, hang me in a bottle like a cat and shoot
at me, and he that hits me, let him be clapped on the   240
shoulder and called Adam.

DON PEDRO   Well, as time shall try. 'In time the savage
bull doth bear the yoke.'

BENEDICK   The savage bull may, but if ever the sensible
Benedick bear it, pluck off the bull's horns and set   245
them in my forehead; and let me be vilely painted, and

---

239 **hang . . . cat** referring to the apparent
custom of suspending a cat (dead?
alive?) in a wicker basket (cf. *Oth*
2.3.141, 'twiggen bottle') as a target
for a shooting contest. Steevens–Reed[2]
cites as corroboration a pamphlet
Wars, or the Peace is Broken: 'arrowes
flew faster than they did at a catte
in a basket, when Prince Arthur, or
the Duke of Shoreditch, strucke up
the drumme in the field'. Benedick's
image sustains the theme of gruesome
punishments visited upon heretics and
apostates, as well as the links between
archery and love.

240–1 **clapped . . . Adam** congratulated
as the best archer. As Theobald
surmised, Adam is probably a reference
to the renowned northern outlaw
archer Adam Bell, who together with
Clym of the Clough and William of
Cloudesley comprised a legendary trio
of archers; see *English and Scottish
Ballads* (Child, 5.124).

242 **try** reveal, test; proverbial: 'Time
tries all things' (Dent, T336)

242–3 **In . . . yoke** proverbial (Dent,
T303). Shakespeare could have also
heard or read the phrase in Thomas
Kyd's *The Spanish Tragedy* (1592),
2.1.3: 'In time the sauage Bull
sustaines the yoke'; or in Thomas
Watson's *Ecatompathia* (1582), sonnet
47: 'In time the Bull is brought to
weare the yoake.' There are Italian

and classical antecedents for both, e.g.
Ovid, *Tristia*, 4.6.1, and *Ars Amatoria*,
1.471. A bull compelled to the yoke
was more than likely to be rendered an
ox (i.e. castrated) in the process (the
ox, along with the camel and the snail,
was an emblem of endurance).

245 **horns** The association of horns with
cuckoldry is ancient and cross-cultural,
but of obscure origin; the *OED* (*sb.*
I 7a) suggests that it derives from
the ancient practice of 'engrafting the
spurs of a castrated cock on the root
of the excised comb, where they grew
and became horns'. *Brewer* (1142) cites
the stag's battle for herd dominance;
when a stag is 'horned', he loses his
herd until he can return the favour
to another stag. The Ovidian myth
of Actaeon (*Met.*, 3.138–249), in
which the hunter views the chaste and
divine huntress Diana bathing, and
is consequently turned by her into
a stag and slain by his own hounds,
also provides an association of horn-
wearing with female power over
men; however, Diana, goddess of the
moon, sported the emblem of crescent
horns (sign of the moon as well as
of its mutability), which most closely
resemble the bovine horns (rather than
antlers) conferred upon most cuckolds.
See pp. 43–50.

246 **vilely painted** i.e. have his portrait
painted in a crude or degrading style

246 forehead;] forehead, *Q*   vilely] *(vildly)*

in such great letters as they write 'Here is good horse to hire', let them signify under my sign, 'Here you may see Benedick, the married man.'

CLAUDIO   If this should ever happen, thou wouldst be   250
horn-mad.

DON PEDRO   Nay, if Cupid have not spent all his quiver in
Venice, thou wilt quake for this shortly.

BENEDICK   I look for an earthquake too, then.

DON PEDRO   Well, you will temporize with the hours.   255
In the meantime, good Signor Benedick, repair to
Leonato's, commend me to him and tell him I will
not fail him at supper, for indeed he hath made great
preparation.

BENEDICK   I have almost matter enough in me for such   260
an embassage. And so, I commit you –

---

251 **horn-mad** (1) stark raving mad; (2) mad with jealousy; (3) angry as an enraged bull: pun on the cuckold's horns intended. Cf. *MW* 3.5.140–2: 'If I have horns to make one mad, let the proverb go with me: I'll be horn-mad'; *CE* 2.1.58–60: 'Why, mistress, sure my master is horn-mad / . . . I mean not cuckold-mad, / But sure he is stark mad'; Dent, H628.

252 **quiver** i.e. of arrows (with sexual suggestion of spending phallic power)

253 **Venice** renowned for its courtesans and prostitutes. The traveller Thomas Coryat, in his *Crudities* (1605), writes that 'The name of a Courtezan of Venice is famoused over all Christendom' (Coryat, 1.401).

quake According to Ferrand, symptoms of love-melancholy included 'loss of appetite, weeping, sobbing and sighing, frequent sighings, continuall complaints,

languishing countenance, feebleness of the knees' (Ferrand, sig. E2ʳ).

254 **earthquake** a rare event, thought to herald momentous changes. Benedick continues Don Pedro's pun on *quiver*.

255 **temporize . . . hours** become more temperate, or realistic in and with time (Latin *tempus* = time, so the phrase could mean 'delay the event'; *hours* could also pun on whores, with whom Venice was reputedly replete). Cf. *Cor* 4.6.16–17: 'All's well, and might have been much better if / He could have temporiz'd.'

256 **repair** go

257 **commend me** send my regards

258 **fail him** fail to be present

260 **I . . . me** i.e. I believe I possess adequate sense; cf. 2.1.303–4: 'I was born to speak all mirth and no matter.'

---

251 horn-mad] (horn madde), *Pope*   256 meantime] (meane time)   261 you –] *Theobald;* you. Q

CLAUDIO   'To the tuition of God. From my house' – if I
    had it –
DON PEDRO   'The sixth of July. Your loving friend,
    Benedick.'   265
BENEDICK   Nay, mock not, mock not. The body of your
    discourse is sometime guarded with fragments, and the
    guards are but slightly basted on neither. Ere you flout
    old ends any further, examine your conscience. And so
    I leave you.   *Exit.*

CLAUDIO
    My liege, your highness now may do me good.   271
DON PEDRO
    My love is thine to teach; teach it but how,
    And thou shalt see how apt it is to learn
    Any hard lesson that may do thee good.
CLAUDIO
    Hath Leonato any son, my lord?   275

262–5 **To . . . Benedick** In these tags the
men mock epistolary closing formulae.
The sixth of July was the quarter-day
when rents were due, and hence a likely day for letter-writing.
262 **tuition** protection
266–8 **The . . . neither** i.e. the substance
of your speech is often badly ornamented; the metaphor of Claudio's
language as a body decorated (*guarded*)
with ragtags of speech or clichés (*old
ends*) which are loosely sewn (*slightly basted*) onto the garment uses the
imagery of fashion itself to describe
the fashionable discourse of puns and
turns so prized by the men in this
play. Benedick implies that Claudio's
attempt at ornate speech is rather a
motley effort.
268 **flout** quote or recite with sarcastic
purpose (*OED v.* 1b)

269 **old ends** well-worn quotations,
clichés
270 SD Borachio and/or Antonio's servant may perhaps enter unseen before
the end of the scene, though they
need not.
271 **liege** lord
good a favour
271–2 **your . . . thine** Claudio uses the
formal second person pronoun; the
Prince the more intimate one.
272 **My . . . to teach** The love I bear you
is at your service, to be instructed as to
how to help you.
273 **apt** eager
it i.e. his love for Claudio
275 This question need not appear as
mercenary as it seems to a modern
audience; any Renaissance count worth
his salt would and should have been
curious about the financial standing

---

262 'To . . . house'] *this edn;* to . . . house *Q*   262–3 – if . . . it –] *Capell subst.;* if I had it *Q*   263
it –] *Theobald;* it *Q*   264–5 'The . . . Benedick.'] *this edn;* the . . . Benedicke. *Q*   269 conscience.]
Steevens–Reed² (conscience:); conscience, *Q*

168

DON PEDRO

    No child but Hero; she's his only heir.

    Dost thou affect her, Claudio?

CLAUDIO   O my lord,

    When you went onward on this ended action

    I looked upon her with a soldier's eye,

    That liked, but had a rougher task in hand   280

    Than to drive liking to the name of love.

    But now I am returned, and that war-thoughts

    Have left their places vacant, in their rooms

    Come thronging soft and delicate desires,

    All prompting me how fair young Hero is,   285

    Saying I liked her ere I went to wars.

DON PEDRO

    Thou wilt be like a lover presently

    And tire the hearer with a book of words.

    If thou dost love fair Hero, cherish it,

    And I will break with her and with her father,   290

    And thou shalt have her. Was't not to this end

of his contemplated intended. 'Young' Claudio can also be played as seeking to establish the adult or business-like nature of his interest. The question establishes for the audience the fraternal isolation of Hero, who has no male relative to avenge her honour when need be; Antonio's *son* (at 1.2.2) is, like Innogen of the SDs, a character who vanishes once he becomes an encumbrance to the plot (see 5.1.280).

277 **affect** love

278 **went onward on** set out on
    ended action completed military mission

280 **in hand** before me

281 **drive** convert

282 **that** now that

283 **left . . . vacant** deserted their posts
    rooms places

285 **young** The emphasis on Hero's youth accords with that on his own age at 1.1.10 and 5.1.180.

287 **like a lover** Garrulousness was considered a trait of lovers, 'which proceeds from the fulness of their Heart, for loue, sayes Plutarch, is naturally a great Babler . . . For that louers haue a strong desire to enduce all others to the belief of that whereof themselues are already persuaded . . . they would willingly haue these opinions of their beloued confirmed also by all other men's judgements' (Ferrand, sig. G5ʳ).
    presently instantly, in no time

290 **break** broach the question

291–2 **Was't . . . story** i.e. isn't this the reason you were setting out to weave so well-crafted a tale (*OED* twist *v.* 3b)

283 vacant,] *Capell;* vacant: *Q*   290–1 and . . . her] *om. F*

That thou began'st to twist so fine a story?

CLAUDIO

How sweetly you do minister to love,

That know love's grief by his complexion!

But lest my liking might too sudden seem,   295

I would have salved it with a longer treatise.

DON PEDRO

What need the bridge much broader than the flood?

The fairest grant is the necessity;

Look what will serve is fit. 'Tis once, thou lovest,

And I will fit thee with the remedy.   300

I know we shall have revelling tonight;

I will assume thy part in some disguise

And tell fair Hero I am Claudio;

And in her bosom I'll unclasp my heart

And take her hearing prisoner with the force   305

And strong encounter of my amorous tale.

Then after, to her father will I break,

And the conclusion is: she shall be thine.

In practice let us put it presently.   *Exeunt.*

293 **minister to** assist

294 **complexion** appearance (love was thought to induce pallor); four syllables

296 **salved it** elaborated upon it (so as to soften the brunt of its sudden appearance); *salve* literally means to anoint or soothe (as in an ointment for an injury, such as that which causes love's grief).

297 i.e. why elaborate any more than necessary?

298 Don Pedro seems to mean that Claudio's need for his aid is his best motive for giving it.

299 **Look what** whatever
once once and for all

304 **in her bosom** privately; in her heart

305–6 **take . . . tale** capture her with the forceful urgency of my love talk (Don Pedro employs a military idiom). Why Don Pedro feels that his masquerading as Claudio in order to woo Hero is an appropriate *remedy* (300) for Claudio's plight is not clear; the plan seems to speak to the Prince's penchant throughout to be one of 'the only love-gods' (2.1.357), as well as his tendency to imagine himself the lover of other men's women (2.3.165). The scheme represents the first instance of several in the play where a man takes (or is thought to take) Claudio's place with respect to Hero.

293 you do] doe you *F*

170

[1.2]   *Enter* LEONATO *and* [ANTONIO,] *an old man,*
         brother to Leonato[, meeting].

LEONATO   How now, brother, where is my cousin your
  son? Hath he provided this music?
ANTONIO   He is very busy about it. But brother, I can tell
  you strange news that you yet dreamt not of.
LEONATO   Are they good?   5
ANTONIO   As the event stamps them, but they have a good
  cover: they show well outward. The prince and Count
  Claudio, walking in a thick-pleached alley in mine
  orchard, were thus much overheard by a man of mine:
  the prince discovered to Claudio that he loved my niece   10
  your daughter, and meant to acknowledge it this night
  in a dance; and if he found her accordant, he meant to
  take the present time by the top and instantly break
  with you of it.
LEONATO   Hath the fellow any wit that told you this?   15

1.2 The location is in or near Leonato's
house. This scene has often been cut
or transposed to the beginning of 2.1
(Cox, *Shakespeare*, 110).
1 How now hello there; Leonato's
greeting suggests he and Antonio enter
separately.
1–2 my . . . son another relative who
appears only by report and disappears
in the course of the action (at 5.1.280
Antonio has no son); 'cousin' (and
'coz') was used of all close relations
beyond immediate family.
5 they *News* is usually plural in
Elizabethan usage.
6 *event stamps outcome will reveal
6–7 good cover auspicious external
appearance; Antonio uses the imagery

of books and book-binding.
8 thick-pleached alley a path lined by
closely woven intertwined branches
(and hence an optimal site for potential
eavesdropping)
9 man i.e. servant; presumably this
is the same conversation overheard
(more accurately) by Borachio as well.
10 discovered disclosed
11 your daughter The designation
is perhaps to distinguish her from
Beatrice.
12 accordant agreeable, willing
13 by the top by the topknot; proverbial:
'Take Time by the forelock, for she is
bald behind' (Dent, T311). Cf. *AW*
5.3.39.
13–14 break . . . it broach it with you

1.2] *Capell (SCENE II)*   0.1 ANTONIO] *Rowe*   0.2 *meeting*] *Cam*   3+ SP] *Rowe (Ant.); Old Q*
4 strange] *om. F*   6 event] euent *F2;* euents *Q*   7 outward.] *Pope;* outward, *Q*   8 thick-pleached]
(thicke pleached), Theobald mine] my *F*   9 much] *om. F*

ANTONIO   A good sharp fellow; I will send for him, and
    question him yourself.

LEONATO   No, no; we will hold it as a dream till it appear
    itself. But I will acquaint my daughter withal, that
    she may be the better prepared for an answer, if   20
    peradventure this be true. Go you and tell her of it.

                                                    [*Exit Antonio.*]

            [*Enter Attendants, and cross the stage.*]

    Cousins, you know what you have to do. O, I cry you
    mercy, friend: go you with me and I will use your skill.
    Good cousin, have a care this busy time!   *Exeunt.*

[1.3]   *Enter* DON JOHN *the bastard and*
                        CONRADE *his companion.*

CONRADE   What the goodyear, my lord! Why are you thus
    out of measure sad?

DON JOHN   There is no measure in the occasion that
    breeds, therefore the sadness is without limit.

18 **hold it as** consider it but
18–19 **appear itself** materializes
19 **withal** with what you have told me
21 Depending on his speed, Antonio may
    exit only at the general dispersal at
    line 24, as he does in some productions
    and editions. As Oxf¹ notes, 'the text
    requires only bustle here'.
22–23 **cry you mercy** beg your pardon
24 **have a care** be careful (may suggest a
    stage action of clumsiness for the actor
    to whom it is addressed)
1.3 The location is in or near Leonato's
    house.
1 **What the goodyear** a benign ex-

pletive, similar to 'What the devil',
possibly derived from the early modern
Dutch exclamation 'wat goedtjarr': 'as
I hope for a good year'
2 **out . . . sad** excessively melancholy,
    out of sorts
3 **measure in** moderation of; limit to
3–4 **occasion that breeds** source that
    causes his sadness. The term *breeds*
    may suggest that the irremediable
    cause of Don John's grief is his own
    bastardy; alternatively, it could refer to
    his melancholy or to the recent defeat
    at the hands of Claudio.

21 SD] *Boas*   21.1] *Capell (Enter several persons, bearing things for the banquet); Exit Antonio, Enter
Antonio's son with a Musician / Boas; Exit Antonio. Enter Antonio's son, with a Musician and Others. /
Kittredge; Several cross the Stage here / Theobald (after to do 22); Enter Attendants Oxf*   22 Cousins]
Cousin *Waters-Bennett*   1.3] *Capell (SCENE III)*   0.1 DON] *Rowe; sir Q*   1 goodyear] *(goodyeere),
Malone   lord!] Hanmer; lord, Q*   3+ SP] *Iohn Q*   4 breeds] breeds it *Theobald*

CONRADE   You should hear reason.   5

DON JOHN   And when I have heard it, what blessing
brings it?

CONRADE   If not a present remedy, at least a patient
sufferance.

DON JOHN   I wonder that thou – being as thou sayst   10
thou art, born under Saturn – goest about to apply a
moral medicine to a mortifying mischief. I cannot hide
what I am. I must be sad when I have cause, and smile
at no man's jests; eat when I have stomach, and wait
for no man's leisure; sleep when I am drowsy, and   15
tend on no man's business; laugh when I am merry,
and claw no man in his humour.

CONRADE   Yea, but you must not make the full show of
this till you may do it without controlment. You have
of late stood out against your brother, and he hath ta'en   20
you newly into his grace, where it is impossible you

5   **reason** The term suggests the exorbitance of Don John's sadness.
8   F's change of 'at least' to 'yet' is perhaps to accommodate its erroneous expansion of Q's 'brings' (6) to 'brin-/geth'.
9   **sufferance** forbearance, endurance; cf. 5.1.38, pain, suffering.
11   **born under Saturn** saturnine, morose – because born under that planet, described by Stephen Bateman in *Upon Bartholomew* (1582) as 'an euill willed Planet, colde and drie, a night Planet and heauie . . . and therefore a childe . . . that be conceiued & come forth vnder his Lordship, [shall] dye, or haue full euill qualyties' (Bateman, fol.129ᵛ, cited by Furness). According to Robert Burton in his *Anatomy of Melancholy* (1621), those born under Saturn were excessively melancholy (Burton, 1.2001); Andrew Gurr suggests that melancholics dressed emblematically in black on the Renaissance stage (Gurr, 182).
   goest about attempt
12   **moral . . . mischief** philosophical remedy to a mortal injury. Don John, like other men in the play, is an accomplished euphuistic speaker.
14   **stomach** appetite
14–15   **wait . . . leisure** do not wait until another man is free to eat with me
16   **tend on** attend to
17   **claw . . . humour** soothe, flatter, stroke, no man when he is moody (much as Conrade seeks to do with Don John)
19   **till . . . controlment** until you are free to act without risk of restraint
20   **stood out against** defied, fallen out with (Don Pedro's recent military battle was with Don John)
20–1   **ta'en . . . grace** recently forgiven you, taken you into his favour; *ta'en* is pronounced 'tane'.

7 brings] brin-/geth *F*   8 at least] yet *F*   12 moral] mortall *F2*   20 ta'en] *(tane)*

should take true root but by the fair weather that
you make yourself. It is needful that you frame the
season for your own harvest.

DON JOHN   I had rather be a canker in a hedge than a rose   25
in his grace, and it better fits my blood to be disdained
of all than to fashion a carriage to rob love from any. In
this, though I cannot be said to be a flattering honest
man, it must not be denied but I am a plain-dealing
villain. I am trusted with a muzzle and enfranchised   30
with a clog. Therefore I have decreed not to sing in
my cage. If I had my mouth I would bite; if I had my
liberty I would do my liking. In the meantime, let me
be that I am, and seek not to alter me.

CONRADE   Can you make no use of your discontent?   35
DON JOHN   I make all use of it, for I use it only. Who
comes here?

Enter BORACHIO.

22–3 **take . . . yourself** be firmly established except by behaving well
23–4 **frame . . . harvest** behave so as to
ensure that you prosper; manipulate (by a
pretence of agreeableness) circumstances
in order to pursue your own goals
25 **canker** wild or dog-rose (hence, like a
weed, uncultivated but hardy; an appropriate emblem for one whose social
position is of dubious legitimacy); cf.
1H4 1.3.174–5: 'To put down Richard,
that sweet lovely rose, / And plant this
thorn, this canker, Bolingbroke?'
26 **grace** with pun on grass
fits my blood suits my humour and
my (illegitimate) birth
27 **fashion a carriage** adopt a demeanour (as opposed to behaving without
pretence)

rob love gain favour on false pretences
28 **flattering honest** The oxymoron conveys his contempt of honesty.
29 **but** i.e. that
30–1 **trusted . . . clog** i.e. allowed into
favour only by virtue of harsh restrictions laid upon my behaviour. A clog
is a heavy block of wood attached
like a hobble to the leg or neck of a
man or animal in order to prevent
escape or straying. Don John imagines
himself as a dog, a horse and a bird in
succession.
32 **had my mouth** i.e. was unmuzzled
33 **my liking** what I please
35 **make . . . of** find no way to profit
from
36 **I use it only** it is my entire occu-
pation

22 true] *om. F*   29 plain-dealing] *(plain dealing), Rowe*   30 muzzle] *(mussell)*   33 meantime]
(mean time)   36–8] *Pope; Q lines only, / Borachio? /*   36 I make] I will make *F*   37.1] *Capell;
after 38 Q*

What news, Borachio?

BORACHIO   I came yonder from a great supper. The
prince your brother is royally entertained by Leonato,   40
and I can give you intelligence of an intended marriage.

DON JOHN   Will it serve for any model to build mischief
on? What is he for a fool that betroths himself to
unquietness?

BORACHIO   Marry, it is your brother's right hand.   45

DON JOHN   Who, the most exquisite Claudio?

BORACHIO   Even he.

DON JOHN   A proper squire! And who, and who? Which
way looks he?

BORACHIO   Marry, on Hero, the daughter and heir of   50
Leonato.

DON JOHN   A very forward March chick! How came you
to this?

BORACHIO   Being entertained for a perfumer, as I was

---

39 **great** lavish
41 **intelligence** news
42 **model** blueprint, ground-plan
43 **What . . . fool** what manner of fool is
he
44 **unquietness** discord; women were often
stigmatized as a source of unquietness.
45 **Marry** a common asseverative mild
oath (originally 'by the Virgin Mary')
46 **exquisite** dainty; perfect (cf. 4.1.314–15)
48 **proper** exemplary
squire youthful follower of a knight
(and knight-in-training), and also a
stock figure of an ideal lover, as in
Chaucer's General Prologue to *The
Canterbury Tales*: 'A lovere and a lusty
bacheler / With lokkes crulle as they
were laid in presse' (Chaucer, 80–1)
And who i.e. and on whom does he
look
50–1 Borachio's specification of Hero as

Leonato's heir could make explicit a
mercenary element in Claudio's motives,
although cf. 1.1.275n.
50 *on Q's 'one' is unlikely, as it suggests
that Hero is unknown to Don John and
Conrade as well as Borachio.
52 **forward March chick** upstart youth;
the phrase could equally apply to
Claudio (presumptuous *start-up*, 61), or
Hero (precocious, saucy, even immodest,
although there is no evidence of such a
character until the exchange with Don
Pedro in the dance in 2.1). A chick
born in March would be an early bird.
Some productions present a Don John
with his own interest in Hero; unlike
Shakespeare's sources, however, *MA*'s
villain is not a rival lover of Hero.
54 **entertained . . . perfumer** employed
to render a disused room sweet-smelling
by burning aromatic substances

---

45 brother's] *F*; bothers *Q*   48 squire!] squier, *Q*   who? Which] *Rowe²*; who, which *Q*   50 on] *F*;
one *Q*   52 March chick] *(*March-chicke*)*

smoking a musty room comes me the prince and   55
Claudio, hand in hand in sad conference. I whipped me
behind the arras, and there heard it agreed upon that
the prince should woo Hero for himself, and having
obtained her, give her to Count Claudio.

DON JOHN   Come, come, let us thither; this may prove   60
food to my displeasure. That young start-up hath all
the glory of my overthrow. If I can cross him any way,
I bless myself every way. You are both sure, and will
assist me?

CONRADE   To the death, my lord.   65

DON JOHN   Let us to the great supper; their cheer is the
greater that I am subdued. Would the cook were o'my
mind. Shall we go prove what's to be done?

BORACHIO   We'll wait upon your lordship.   *Exeunt.*

---

55 **comes me** come towards me
56 **hand in hand** The description could
  provide a SD for the actors in 1.1.
  sad serious
  me myself; *me* here (and at 55) is an
  obsolete form similar to the classical
  ethical dative, where 'me' functions
  to draw attention to the speaker, by
  making the remark sound colloquial.
  See Abbott, 220.
57 **arras** tapestry wall-hanging (named
  after the town in France where produced). Borachio's comment suggests
  that the conversation he overhears was
  not conducted in Antonio's orchard
  after all (though it is continuous with
  the opening setting of 1.1), or that it
  was pursued indoors, or that the arras
  is outdoors – or that Shakespeare is
  not overly concerned with such specif-
  ics. Getting things slightly wrong is a
  theme of the play.
58–9 **for . . . Claudio** Borachio either
  mishears Don Pedro's plan, or renders it
  in its most callous form by implying that
  Don Pedro will 'obtain' Hero and then
  transfer her to Claudio's ownership;

either way, he does communicate that
the ultimate intention is to acquire Hero
for Claudio, but his formulation points
out to Don John a way to harass Claudio
at 2.1.148–53, by convincing him that
Don Pedro woos indeed *for himself*.
60 **thither** i.e. to the party
61 **food** i.e. fuel
  start-up upstart
61–2 **hath . . . overthrow** has reaped
  all the benefits of my fall from (Don
  Pedro's) grace (presumably by taking
  Don John prisoner)
62 **cross** vex, make trouble for; however,
  taken in the sense of 'to make the sign
  of the cross', the term also allows the
  play on words with *bless*. Don John
  tends to turn his own terms without
  the aid of an interlocutor, perhaps a
  sign of his solipsism.
63 **bless** benefit
  sure firmly with me, loyal
67 **subdued** i.e. defeated
67–8 **o'my mind** i.e. possessed of pois-
  onous thoughts
68 **prove** investigate
69 **wait upon** attend upon (i.e. follow)

56 me] *om. F*   64 me?] *F*; me. *Q*   67 o'] *(a)*; of *F*   69 SD] *F*; exit. *Q*

[2.1]   *Enter* LEONATO, *his brother* [ANTONIO],
               HERO *his daughter and* BEATRICE *his niece.*

LEONATO   Was not Count John here at supper?
ANTONIO   I saw him not.
BEATRICE   How tartly that gentleman looks! I never can
   see him but I am heart-burned an hour after.
HERO   He is of a very melancholy disposition.   5
BEATRICE   He were an excellent man that were made just
   in the midway between him and Benedick: the one is
   too like an image and says nothing, and the other too
   like my lady's eldest son, evermore tattling.
LEONATO   Then half Signor Benedick's tongue in Count   10
   John's mouth, and half Count John's melancholy in
   Signor Benedick's face –
BEATRICE   With a good leg and a good foot, uncle, and
   money enough in his purse, such a man would win any
   woman in the world – if 'a could get her good will.   15

2.1 The location is in or near Leonato's
house, presumably in a space separate from the site of the *great supper*
(1.3.66) and the rest of the company,
who enter revelling at 75. Don Pedro's
comment to Leonato at the end of the
scene ('Go in with me', 357) suggests
that the dance takes place either outdoors or in a relatively public space.
The scene is usually set in night-time
(post-supper), which in Renaissance
staging would have been signified by
torches.
0.1–2 Rowe provides an entry here for
Margaret and Ursula, who need to
be onstage by the dance (75), where
this edition, after Capell, locates their

entrance. See 75.2–3n. and p. 137.
1 Leonato's question could suggest
   that as his party enters they cross
   paths with or glimpse the exit of Don
   John's.
3 **tartly** disagreeable, acid
   looks appears; regards one (perhaps
   a suggestion for Don John's stage
   action)
8 **image** statue; picture
9 **my ... son** i.e. a spoiled heir apparent,
   licensed to chatter
   evermore tattling a charge that
   Beatrice has had laid against her as
   well; see 1.1.135–6.
13 **good leg** nice limbs, graceful bow
15 **good will** favour

2.1] *Actus Secundus F; scene i. / Rowe*   0.1 ANTONIO] *Rowe*   0.2 HERO] *Theobald; his wife, Hero Q;*
Innogen, Hero / Rowe   niece.] *Oxf¹; neece, and a kinsman. Q; niece, Margaret and Ursula / Rowe*   2+
SP ANTONIO] *Rowe (Ant.); brother Q*   10+ Signor] *(signior)*   12 face –] *Rowe; face. Q; face –.*
F2   15 world –] *F (world,); world Q*   'a] *he F*

LEONATO   By my troth, niece, thou wilt never get thee a
husband, if thou be so shrewd of thy tongue.

ANTONIO   In faith, she's too curst.

BEATRICE   Too curst is more than curst. I shall lessen
God's sending that way; for it is said 'God sends a curst   20
cow short horns' – but to a cow too curst he sends none.

LEONATO   So, by being too curst, God will send you no
horns.

BEATRICE   Just, if he send me no husband. For the which
blessing I am at him upon my knees every morning and   25
evening. Lord, I could not endure a husband with a
beard on his face! I had rather lie in the woollen.

17 **shrewd** shrewish, sharp, critical; observ-
ant or penetrating (and unladylike in its
bawdy *double entendre*), as at 71
18 **curst** cantankerous, perverse; Antonio's
estimate of Beatrice's excessive
shrewishness would consign her to the
choleric category of shrew occupied
by *TS*'s Kate, although John Draper
points out that according to Don Pedro
'she has "a merry heart," was "born in
a merry hour," and truly by nature has
"little of the melancholy element in
her"': in short, she seems, like Benedick,
to be either sanguine by nature or
mildly choleric under the influence of
the sun: this marks her off from Kate
the Shrew as less violent and more
witty and amenable' (Draper, 265).
19 **Too** with pun on 'two'
20 **sending** something sent; gift, endow-
ment
that way in that respect
21 **short horns** i.e. providentially, the
least harmful ones, in the case of an
angry cow, but also, for a cuckold, the
least conspicuous ones
24 **Just** exactly
send . . . husband Beatrice's reply to
Leonato could imply either that she

couldn't then cuckold her husband, or
be herself cuckolded (horns were an
equal-opportunity side-effect of marital
infidelity, in which case the wife would
be called a cuckquean); see Painter's
Palace of Pleasure: 'Behold Ladyes
. . . this History which for example
I have willinglye recited to thintente
that when your husbands do make you
hornes as big as a Goate, you may
render unto him the monstrous heade
of a Stagge' (Painter, 2.37). As with the
cuts to the male banter of cuckoldry
in 1.1, Beatrice's lines have often been
censored in productions concerned to
present her in a ladylike manner.
25 **I . . . him** I address myself to him
26 **Lord** This could be delivered as the
invocation of a prayer.
27 **beard** Beards were a sign of virility
and maturity (cf. Benedick's contempt
for Claudio as 'Lord Lack-beard'
at 5.1.187); Beatrice's preference
contradicts contemporary opinions of
what Renaissance women want. Ferrand
(143) professes to the contrary that
'women cannot endure a man that hath
but little beard; not so much for that
they are commonly cold and impotent,

20–1 'God . . . horns'] *Capell subst.*; God . . . hornes *Q*

LEONATO   You may light on a husband that hath no beard.

BEATRICE   What should I do with him? Dress him in my
apparel and make him my waiting-gentlewoman? He   30
that hath a beard is more than a youth, and he that hath
no beard is less than a man; and he that is more than
a youth is not for me, and he that is less than a man, I
am not for him. Therefore I will even take sixpence in
earnest of the bearward and lead his apes into hell.   35

LEONATO   Well then, go you into hell?

BEATRICE   No, but to the gate, and there will the devil
meet me like an old cuckold with horns on his head,
and say, 'Get you to heaven, Beatrice, get you to heaven.
Here's no place for you maids!' So deliver I up my apes   40
and away to Saint Peter fore the heavens. He shows me

as that, so much resembling Eunuchs,
they are for the most part inclined to
baseness, cruelty, and deceitfulness'. In
effect, Beatrice rejects both men with
beards and men without. Benedick has
a beard, which he shaves before 3.2.
in the woollen i.e. in rough blankets
without sheets
28 **light on** find yourself with
29–30 **Dress . . . apparel** the fate of
Hercules in the house of Omphale,
who forced the captive Hercules to
wear women's clothes and spin wool
with her maids (Ovid, *Fasti*, 2.317ff.;
Heroides, 9.55ff.); cf. Benedick's fear at
231–3: 'She would have made Hercules
have turned spit, yea, and have cleft his
club to make the fire too' (see 231–3n.,
232n. on *turned spit*).
31 **more . . . youth** too old
32 **less . . . man** too young for marriage;
insufficiently virile
34–5 **in earnest of** as an advance payment from
35 **bearward** someone who keeps bears

(e.g. for bear-baiting) or trained apes.
Q's 'Berrord' could be modernized
as 'bearward' or 'bearherd', both
of which were in use in the period
(although 'bearward' was the more
common word); both are homophones
for the earlier *beard*. The aural link
provides Beatrice with her shift
to the notion of an animal herder
and from there she moves to the
proverbial idea (Dent, M37) that
spinsters were doomed to lead apes
in hell (presumably as punishment for
having disdained human reproduction
and concomitant childminding?). Cf.
George Peele, *The Arraignment of
Paris* (1584), 4.2.6: 'All that be Dian's
maids are vowed to halter apes in
hell.' Apes were considered mimics of
men.
40 **no place** i.e. because maids are presumably pure of sexual taint
41 ***Saint . . . heavens** Q's punctuation (see t.n.) has invited dispute as
to whether *fore the heavens* is either

28 on] vpon *F*   30 waiting-gentlewoman] *(waiting gentlewoman), Rowe*   35 bearward] *Knight;*
Berrord *Q;* bearherd *F3*   36 hell?] *Hanmer;* hell. *Q*   39–40 'Get . . . maids!'] *Capell subst.;* get . . .
maids, *Q*   41 Peter fore . . . heavens.] *Oxf;* Peter, for . . . heavens. *Pope subst.;* Peter: for . . . heauens, *Q*

where the bachelors sit, and there live we as merry as
the day is long.

ANTONIO [*to Hero*]   Well, niece, I trust you will be ruled
by your father.   45

BEATRICE   Yes, faith, it is my cousin's duty to make
curtsy, and say, 'Father, as it please you.' But yet for
all that, cousin, let him be a handsome fellow, or else
make another curtsy, and say, 'Father, as it please me.'

LEONATO   Well, niece, I hope to see you one day fitted   50
with a husband.

BEATRICE   Not till God make men of some other metal
than earth. Would it not grieve a woman to be over-
mastered with a piece of valiant dust? To make an
account of her life to a clod of wayward marl? No,   55

a mild oath, or a reference to Saint
Peter's location (before), or to the part
of the heavens to which Saint Peter
assigns Beatrice.
42 **bachelors** unmarried persons of
either sex
42–3 **merry . . . long** proverbial (Dent,
D57)
46–7 **make curtsy** i.e. demonstrate
respect (perhaps a suggestion for stage
action)
49 **Father . . . me** Beatrice's advice to
Hero anticipates the equally novel
wish of Helena in *AW* (1.1.151–2), to
'lose' her virginity 'to her own liking'.
50–1 **fitted with** The metaphor is a sartorial one, but contains a sexual innuendo as well.
52 **metal** also play on 'mettle' (substance
of character, as opposed to material
component); cf. Barnaby Rich, *The
Excellency of Good Women* (1613): 'But
the better to make tryall of women's
perfection in generall, let us examine
their first creation, wherein it is to be
noted the substance whereof they were

formed, which was of the purified
mettall of man' (Rich, sig. A4ʳ).
53–4 **over-mastered** An early modern
woman was supposed to acknowledge
a husband as her master; the marriage
service of the *Book of Common Prayer*
(1559) reads: 'Ye women submit yourselves unto your own husbands as
unto the Lord, for the husband is the
wife's head even as Christ is the head
of the Church' (*BCP*, 298). See also
259–60n.
54 **valiant dust** Cf. Genesis, 2.7: 'And
the Lord God also made the man of
the dust of the ground, and breathed
in his face the breath of life, and the
man was a liuing soule.' Beatrice's
oxymoron recalls the warning of the
Geneva Bible's marginal note: 'Hee
sheweth whereof mans body was created, to the intent that man should
not glorie in the excellencie of his own
nature.'
55 **wayward** errant (because fallen)
marl soil of lime and clay, sometimes
used for fertilizer

44 SD] *Rowe*   47, 49 curtsy] *(cursie)*   47 say, 'Father, as] *(say, father, as)*; say, as *F*   47–9 'Father
. . . me.'] *Theobald*; Father . . . me. *Q*   52 metal] *(mettal)*   54 an] *om. F*

uncle, I'll none. Adam's sons are my brethren, and
truly, I hold it a sin to match in my kindred.

LEONATO   Daughter, remember what I told you. If the
prince do solicit you in that kind, you know your
answer.   60

BEATRICE   The fault will be in the music, cousin, if you be
not wooed in good time. If the prince be too important,
tell him there is measure in everything, and so dance out
the answer. For hear me, Hero; wooing, wedding and
repenting is as a Scotch jig, a measure and a cinque-   65
pace. The first suit is hot and hasty, like a Scotch jig,
and full as fantastical; the wedding mannerly-modest as
a measure, full of state and ancientry; and then comes
Repentance, and with his bad legs falls into the cinque-

---

57 **kindred** relations too close for marriage; Elizabethan devotional texts
(such as catechisms, or the *Book of
Common Prayer*) often list degrees of
consanguinity within which marriage
is forbidden.

59 **in that kind** on that subject (of marriage); Leonato believes that the Prince
intends to woo Hero for himself.

62 **in good time** at the appropriate
moment; rhythmically
important hasty (importunate, cf. *KL*
4.3.26 and *AW* 3.7.21); overbearing,
too grand (as in Beatrice's comment
to the Prince at 302–3 that he is 'too
costly to wear everyday')

63 **measure** moderation; a stately dance
(see 68); temperate quality
measure in everything proverbial
(Dent, M806)

64 **the answer** a musical (and antiphonal)
response

65 **Scotch jig** an especially lively (even
lewd) dance in the round

65–6 **cinque-pace** a capering dance (gal-
liard) with a five-beat step followed by
a leap (hence difficult to perform); pronounced 'sink-a-pace', hence the pun,

and the incongruity, at 70). Thomas
Middleton also characterizes dances in
this fashion in *Women Beware Women*
(1627), 3.2.215–18: 'Plain men dance
the measures, the sinquapace the gay;
/ Cuckoldes dance the hornpipe, and
farmers dance the hay; / Your soldiers dance the round, and maidens
that grow big; / Your drunkards, the
canaries; your whore and bawd the jig'
(Middleton, 6.317).

66 **suit** courtship of a lover

67 **full as fantastical** every bit as extra-
vagant, passionate
mannerly-modest decorous

68 **state** pomp
ancientry tradition

69 **Repentance** Beatrice's personifica-
tion invokes the medieval morality
play's plot of human life, in which the
protagonist ideally finished by entering the grave repenting of his worldly sins (and hence accompanied by an
actor representing Repentance).
bad legs The literary device of person-
ification represented moral identities in
physiognomic terms, as in Spenser's
Faerie Queene, where Gluttony (for

---

62 important] importunate *Rowe*³   67 mannerly-modest] *(manerly modest), Theobald*

pace faster and faster, till he sink into his grave.   70
LEONATO   Cousin, you apprehend passing shrewdly.
BEATRICE   I have a good eye, uncle; I can see a church by
daylight.
LEONATO [*to Antonio*]   The revellers are entering, brother.
Make good room. [*Antonio steps aside, and masks.*]   75

Enter DON PEDRO, CLAUDIO, BENEDICK,
BALTHASAR[, *masked, with a Drum,* MARGARET
and URSULA,] *and* DON JOHN[, BORACHIO *and others.*
Music and dancing begin].

instance) is a 'Deformed creature, on a
filthy swyne, / His belly was up-blowne
with luxury' (*FQ*, 1.4.21.2–3). The
penitent's weak legs would presumably
indicate the feebleness of old age (and
by extension his ward's reluctance to
repent or weakness of spirit), or, alternatively, his propensity for kneeling.
71 **apprehend** perceive
   passing shrewdly very satirically
72 **church** usually the most conspicuous
structure in a town; Beatrice's claim to
the ability to see what is patently obvious
contrasts with imagery elsewhere in the
play in which vision is considered as
a malleable and socially conditioned
quantity, e.g. 2.3.21–2, 'May I be so
converted and see with these eyes?';
3.4.84, 'methinks you look with your
eyes as other women do'; 3.2.107–8, 'If
you dare not trust that you see, confess
not that you know'; 2.1.163–5, 'Let
every eye negotiate for itself, / And
trust no agent; for Beauty is a witch /
Against whose charms faith melteth
into blood.' The phrase could also mean
that she sees a wedding in the near
future (cf. *AYL* 2.7.52).
75 **Make good room** stand aside; clear the

space. Antonio is one of the masquers,
so this provides an opportunity for
him to either step aside and put on a
visor (as the SD indicates), or (as some
editions choose) to exit and re-enter
masked.
75 SD It seems according to the SD and
Renaissance convention that only the
men mask (unless they are already
masked; cf. 5.4), and perhaps only
those (plus Claudio) who participate in
the dance, although most productions
mask both sexes. Leonato, as host,
may remain unmasked (cf. *RJ* 1.5 or
H8 1.4), as well as Don John and his
associates, Don John being professedly
hostile to social amusements. The
dance has often served in productions
as an occasion for great spectacle (Cox,
Shakespeare, 113).
75.2–3 Margaret and Ursula are given
no entry to this scene in Q. Rowe
introduced them at the opening, but
since they have no speaking parts until
the dance they might equally enter
here (particularly to maintain the
pretence that Ursula is meant not to
know Antonio's identity); see Wells,
'Foul-paper', 6.

74 SD] *Oxf¹*   75 SD] *this edn; Exit Antonio. Cam²; Leonato and his company mask. / Capell; He
signals the others to disperse and don masks Oxf¹*   75.1 DON] *Rowe; prince, Pedro Q*   75.2 *masked, with
a Drum*] F (*Maskers with a Drum*)   75.2–3 MARGARET *and* URSULA] *this edn (Wells)*   75.3 *and* DON
JOHN] *Capell (and Don John); or dumb Iohn Q*   BORACHIO] *Capell   and others*] *Rowe*   75.4 *Music
. . . begin*] *Cam² (The dance begins)*

DON PEDRO [*to Hero*]   Lady, will you walk a bout with
   your friend?
HERO   So you walk softly, and look sweetly, and say nothing,
   I am yours for the walk; and especially when I walk away.
DON PEDRO   With me in your company?   80
HERO   I may say so, when I please.
DON PEDRO   And when please you to say so?
HERO   When I like your favour – for God defend the lute
   should be like the case!
DON PEDRO   My visor is Philemon's roof: within the house   85
   is Jove.
HERO   Why then, your visor should be thatched.

76 **a bout** a turn, a portion of the
dance (but the aural sense 'about' also
applies); cf. *RJ* 1.5.17–18: 'Welcome,
gentlemen, ladies that have their toes /
Unplagu'd with corns will walk a bout
with you.' Alan Brissenden suggests
that the dance here is the pavan, 'for
in that elegant perambulation the
couples can be side by side with hands
linked at arm's length and the steps
involve turns back and forth, retreats
and advances, so that it is ideal for
highlighting dramatic conversation'
(Brissenden, 49). It is also possible
that the dialogue between the couples
occurs as they pair off in preparation
for the dance.
77 **friend** partner; lover
78 **So** so long as
79 **walk away** probably a reference to the
movement required by the dance pattern; see 76n.
83 **favour** face, looks
   defend forbid (cf. the French *défendre*)
84 **like the case** This indicates that Don
Pedro wears a grotesque mask (it is
doubtful that Hero toys with the salacious meaning of *case* here, though her
playful speech in this scene indicates

some capacity for the verbal dexterity
of her peers).
85 **visor** mask
   Philemon's roof Don Pedro compares
his ugly visor to the humble cottage
roof ('thatched all with straw and
fennish reed') of Philemon and Baucis,
an elderly and impoverished couple in
Ovid's *Metamorphoses*, who nonetheless
provided unstinting hospitality to the
gods Jove and Mercury disguised as
humble travellers (8.616–735). Don
Pedro's comparison of himself to Jove
hints at his (godlike, or at least well-
born) identity to Hero. The idea of
Jove, king of the gods, in a thatched
cottage was (like Christ in a manger) a
familiar trope of incongruity or paradox;
see *AYL* 3.3.9–10: 'O knowledge ill-
inhabited, worse than Jove in a thatched
house!'
85–8 The couple trade lines here in a
rhyme that shares the 14-syllable verse
line of Arthur Golding's translation
of the *Metamorphoses* (Ovid/Golding,
fol. 113ᵛ, sig. O7ᵛ).
87 **thatched** i.e. like a humble cottage;
whiskered; or Hero's reply could suggest that he is balding.

76+ SP] *Capell (D. Pe)*; *Pedro Q*   76 SD] *Cam¹ (Leading Hero forth)*   a bout] *Cam¹*; about *Q*
78 So you] *F*; So, you *Q*   80 company?] *Rowe³*; company. *Q*   85–6] *Oxf¹ lines* roof. / Jove. / 86
Jove] *(Ioue)*; Loue *F*

DON PEDRO   Speak low if you speak love. [*They move aside; Balthasar and Margaret come forward.*]

BALTHASAR   Well, I would you did like me.

MARGARET   So would not I, for your own sake, for I have   90
many ill qualities.

BALTHASAR   Which is one?

MARGARET   I say my prayers aloud.

BALTHASAR   I love you the better; the hearers may cry
amen!   95

MARGARET   God match me with a good dancer!

BALTHASAR   Amen!

MARGARET   And God keep him out of my sight when the
dance is done! Answer, clerk.

---

88 **Speak low** The instruction suggests a SD for the tone of Hero's voice throughout; it also provides for the invitation to private speech necessary to Don Pedro's proposal, and clears the way for the next pair of dancers.

89, 92, 94 SP *BALTHASAR This edition follows Theobald in assigning these speeches to Balthasar, in keeping with Q's assignment at 97 and 100, and on the grounds of symmetry ('so that every man talks with his woman once round', Furness). By the same logic, some productions partner Margaret with her friend Borachio (using Balthasar as a musician), and yet other editors, and productions, have posited, in keeping with Q's assignments, that Margaret switches partners (i.e. Balthasar cuts in on Benedick at 97). Dyce asked 'is not the effect of the scene considerably weakened if Benedick enters into conversation with any other woman except Beatrice?' (Dyce, *Notes*, 42); however, an exchange between Margaret

and Benedick here could prepare for their flirtatious exchange in 5.2. Capell hypothesized that the women are also masked, and that 'Benedick, who is in search of Beatrice, lights upon Margaret; a sharp one, her voice, suiting her sharpness; this voice (which she raises) betrays her to Benedick, who quits her smartly and hastily, a manner resented slightly by Margaret, who expressed it in her prayer' (Capell, *Notes*, 2.12). Pamela Mason suggests that 'If Benedick is allowed to speak these lines to Margaret it shows a Benedick aware of his attraction to women and following his superior's lead in not respecting established alliances' (Mason, 247). Compositor error or typographical necessity has also been adduced for the change in SPs in the early texts.

93 **aloud** Religious enthusiasts were known for their vocal declamation of prayers.

99 **Answer** i.e. say 'amen'
clerk respondent in a liturgy

88 SD *They move aside*] Capell (*Drawing her aside*)   *Balthasar . . . forward*] Folg² (*Benedick and Margaret move forward*)   89, 92, 94 SP] Theobald; *Bene. Q; Borachio Cam¹*

BALTHASAR   No more words; the clerk is answered. [*They* 100
move aside; Ursula and Antonio come forward.]

URSULA   I know you well enough; you are Signor
Antonio.

ANTONIO   At a word, I am not.

URSULA   I know you by the waggling of your head.

ANTONIO   To tell you true, I counterfeit him.   105

URSULA   You could never do him so ill-well, unless you
were the very man. Here's his dry hand up and down.
You are he, you are he!

ANTONIO   At a word, I am not.

URSULA   Come, come, do you think I do not know you by   110
your excellent wit? Can virtue hide itself? Go to, mum;
you are he; graces will appear, and there's an end. [*They
move aside; Benedick and Beatrice come forward.*]

BEATRICE   Will you not tell me who told you so?

BENEDICK   No, you shall pardon me.

BEATRICE   Nor will you not tell me who you are?   115

BENEDICK   Not now.

BEATRICE   That I was disdainful, and that I had my good
wit out of *The Hundred Merry Tales*! Well, this was
Signor Benedick that said so.

---

100 **the . . . answered** i.e. I get the message
103 **At** in (the word being *not*)
104 **waggling** tremor; like *dry hand* (107), a 'character of age'; *2H4* 1.2.180–2 specifies others: 'Have you not a moist eye, a dry hand, a yellow cheek, a white beard, a decreasing leg, an increasing belly?'
105 **counterfeit** impersonate
106 **do . . . ill-well** imitate him so effectively, by being so doddering, 'represent his imperfection so perfectly' (Brooke)

107 **up and down** exactly, all over; cf. *Tit* 5.2.107: 'up and down she doth resemble thee'.
111 **Go to, mum** go on, hush
112 **graces** good qualities
an end all there is to say
114 **shall** must
118 *Hundred Merry Tales* a collection of comic stories and jokes of not very sophisticated humour, printed by John Rastell in 1526, apparently popular (though only one copy is now extant, in the Royal Library of Göttingen). Its

---

100 SD *Ursula . . . forward*] *Folg²; They move aside* / Kittredge; *parting different ways* / Capell
106 **ill-well**] Theobald; *ill well Q*; *ill Will* Rowe; *ill, well* Pope   112 SD *Benedick . . . forward*] *Folg²*; *They step aside* / Kittredge; *mixing with the company* / Capell   118 *The . . . Tales*] Hanmer; *the hundred mery tales Q*

BENEDICK   What's he?   120
BEATRICE   I am sure you know him well enough.
BENEDICK   Not I, believe me.
BEATRICE   Did he never make you laugh?
BENEDICK   I pray you, what is he?
BEATRICE   Why he is the prince's jester, a very dull fool;   125
only his gift is in devising impossible slanders. None but
libertines delight in him, and the commendation is not
in his wit but in his villainy, for he both pleases men and
angers them, and then they laugh at him and beat him.
I am sure he is in the fleet; I would he had boarded me.   130
BENEDICK   When I know the gentleman, I'll tell him what
you say.
BEATRICE   Do, do. He'll but break a comparison or two on

recitation was rumoured to be a solace of Queen Elizabeth (Furness, citing a letter in the Venetian correspondence of the State Papers Office, 9 March 1603), though Beatrice takes offence at the implication that she owes her verbal prowess to such a hackneyed text (or to any source at all, other than her own imagination).

125 **jester** Beatrice returns the insult by implying that Benedick is a court buffoon, employed to keep royalty entertained (though compare this with her own possible equation with Leonato's fool at 1.1.37).

126 **only his gift** his only skill
impossible slanders incredible or outrageous libels (such as Beatrice getting her wit out of crude jest-books); the play's plot turns on just such a slander.

127 **libertines** persons of loose morals or lightweight intelligence
commendation recommendation, approval

128 **in . . . in** of . . . of
villainy malice; acuity of his slander

128–9 **pleases . . . them** i.e. pleases by his

malice and angers by hitting the mark in his slanders; or, pleases some men by slandering others, and angers those whom he slanders. Neither describes a portrait of a very generous wit.

129 **beat him** a traditional punishment for court fools

130 **in the fleet** i.e. among the dancers
boarded i.e. as one boards a ship, took on, attempted, engaged with (as in a contest of wit, but also with sexual innuendo); cf. *TN* 1.3.55–6, Sir Toby to Sir Andrew: 'You mistake, knight. "Accost" is front her, board her, woo her, assail her.'

133–4 **break . . . me** level (ineffectively) a few slanderous comparisons at me; from the metaphor for tilting, as a knight in a tournament breaks a lance; cf. Lyly, *Campaspe* (1584), 2.1.56–7: '*Psyllus:* Why, you were at mortall iars [i.e. jars = wars]. / *Manus:* In faith no, we brake a bitter iest one vppon another' (*Works*, 2.328). A comparison was an insulting simile; Beatrice implies that the unkind figures of speech with which Benedick will undoubtedly attempt to slander her will fall short of their mark.

128 pleases] pleaseth *F*

186

me, which, peradventure not marked, or not laughed
at, strikes him into melancholy, and then there's a   135
partridge wing saved, for the fool will eat no supper
that night. We must follow the leaders.

BENEDICK In every good thing.

BEATRICE Nay, if they lead to any ill I will leave them at
the next turning.   140

Dance. Exeunt [all but Don John, Borachio and Claudio].

DON JOHN Sure my brother is amorous on Hero and hath
withdrawn her father to break with him about it. The
ladies follow her, and but one visor remains.

BORACHIO *[aside to Don John]* And that is Claudio; I
know him by his bearing.   145

DON JOHN Are not you Signor Benedick?

CLAUDIO You know me well. I am he.

DON JOHN Signor, you are very near my brother in his
love. He is enamoured on Hero. I pray you, dissuade

---

134 **peradventure** perhaps
   marked noticed, commended
136 **partridge wing saved** i.e. the
   valiant trencher-man (1.1.48) will be so
   melancholy that he will refrain from
   eating an entire partridge wing (a bone
   with very little meat). The diminutive
   partridge wing was considered a
   delicacy.
137 **We . . . leaders** i.e. we must keep
   pace with the dance; this could provide
   a SD for their falling out of step whilst
   bickering, and hence needing to regain
   their place in the dance pattern.
140 **turning** parting of roads; a change
   in dance figure
141–3 Whether or not Don John now
   believes that it is Don Pedro who is in
   fact *amorous on Hero*, or whether he is
   even at this point trying to goad Claudio

(which he certainly is by 149), depends
on whether these lines are spoken in
Claudio's hearing or as an aside (i.e. on
how nefariously Don John is played – or,
alternatively, as how he too is subject to
misnoting the evidence of his eyes). If
the former, Borachio's comment at 144–
5 needs to be delivered, and responded
to, as a statement of what is already
obvious to Don John (i.e. Borachio could
be played as being rather slow-witted –
perhaps because drunk?). In either case
the speech is also a signal of the masked
Claudio's identity to the audience.
Garrick's 1777 text clarified the issue by
inserting 'now for a trick of contrivance'
at the beginning of the speech.
148–9 **very . . . love** an intimate friend
   of his
149 **enamoured on** in love with

---

140 SD *Dance. Exeunt] Exeunt.* / *Musicke for the dance.* F *all . . . Claudio.*] *Theobald subst.*
141+ SP] *Capell (D. Jo.); Iohn Q* Sure] *Aside to Borachio.* Sure *Oxf¹* 144 SD] *Oxf¹* 146 Are]
Approaching Claudio. Are *Oxf¹*

him from her; she is no equal for his birth. You may do   150
the part of an honest man in it.

CLAUDIO   How know you he loves her?

DON JOHN   I heard him swear his affection.

BORACHIO   So did I too, and he swore he would marry her
tonight.   155

DON JOHN   Come, let us to the banquet.

                            Exeunt all but Claudio.

CLAUDIO

Thus answer I in name of Benedick,
But hear these ill news with the ears of Claudio.
'Tis certain so; the prince woos for himself.
Friendship is constant in all other things,   160
Save in the office and affairs of love.
Therefore all hearts in love use their own tongues:
Let every eye negotiate for itself,
And trust no agent; for Beauty is a witch

---

150 **no . . . birth** of too low a social
station, for the *too important* Don Pedro
(as Beatrice describes him at 62). (Not,
apparently, something that occurs to
Leonato, Antonio, Claudio or Benedick,
all of whom at some time believe that the
Prince woos on his own behalf.) René
Girard's reading of the play emphasizes
the intended slight here, to argue that 'If
he, Claudio, is really allowed to marry
Hero, it means that the Prince has no
personal interest in her; immediately,
she seems less interesting than when
the opposite appeared to be true.
Cut off from the model whose desire
transfigured her, she looks less attractive
. . . [Claudio] wonders if some secret
disgrace might not account for her
willingness to bind her fate to such a
lowly character as himself' (Girard,
86).

150–1 **do the part** perform the service

151 **honest** loyal; truthful

156 **banquet** a 'course of sweetmeats,
fruit, and wine, served either as a
separate entertainment, or as a
continuation of the principal meal, but
in the latter case usually in a different
room' (*OED sb.*[1] 3). Cf. *TS* 5.2.9–10:
'My banquet is to close our stomachs
up / After our great good cheer.'

158 **news** See 1.2.5n.

160–1 proverbial: 'When love puts in,
friendship is gone' (Dent, L549). Male
rivalry over women is a feature of the
euphuistic plot.

161 **office** functions, business

162 **Therefore** i.e. therefore let

164 **Beauty . . . witch** Claudio attributes
Don Pedro's behaviour to female sorcery rather than male perfidy; the
conversion of faith into the more carnal blood (or passion) recalls Circe's
transformation of Odysseus' men into

156 SD *all but*] *Rowe subst.; manet Q*

Against whose charms faith melteth into blood.   165
This is an accident of hourly proof
Which I mistrusted not. Farewell, therefore, Hero!

Enter BENEDICK.

BENEDICK   Count Claudio.
CLAUDIO   Yea, the same.
BENEDICK   Come, will you go with me?   170
CLAUDIO   Whither?
BENEDICK   Even to the next willow, about your own
business, county. What fashion will you wear the
garland of? About your neck, like an usurer's chain? Or
under your arm, like a lieutenant's scarf? You must   175
wear it one way, for the prince hath got your Hero.
CLAUDIO   I wish him joy of her.
BENEDICK   Why, that's spoken like an honest drover; so
they sell bullocks. But did you think the prince would
have served you thus?   180

swine in Homer's *Odyssey* (10.148–631), as well as Ovidian instances of persons and deities being converted into animal form.

165 **blood** passion, desire
166 **accident** event
    hourly i.e. frequent
167 **mistrusted not** never suspected; should have expected (more likely the latter, given the claim for frequency)
169 **the same** Perhaps Claudio has yet to unmask, though many productions have him do so before his soliloquy.
172 **willow** Willow garlands were the emblem of the forsaken (see *Oth* 4.3.50) or the merely lovelorn.
173 **county** count. This common form of 'count' is 'app[arently] an adoption of AF. *counte*, or OF. and It. *conte*,

with unusual retention of final vowel, confused in form with COUNTY (*OED* county²). 'Shakespeare uses both forms although one may be felt to add a little local colour' (*TxC*, 372).
174 **of** in
    usurer's chain a heavy gold chain worn by a money-lender, a reviled profession
175 **lieutenant's scarf** a sash worn diagonally across the body marking the rank of a lieutenant, that below captain; a lieutenant was empowered to stand in, or take the place (from the French *lieu tenir*) of his superior. Cam¹ glosses 174–5 as 'are you going to make capital out of this by claiming preferment from the Prince in return for your loss, or shall you challenge him to a duel?'
178 **drover** cattle-dealer

173 county] Count *F*   174 of] off *F*   178 drover] *(Drouier)*

CLAUDIO   I pray you leave me.

BENEDICK   Ho, now you strike like the blindman! 'Twas
the boy that stole your meat, and you'll beat the post.

CLAUDIO   If it will not be, I'll leave you.   *Exit.*

BENEDICK   Alas, poor hurt fowl, now will he creep into   185
sedges. But that my Lady Beatrice should know me,
and not know me! The prince's fool – hah! It may be I
go under that title because I am merry. Yea, but so I am
apt to do myself wrong. I am not so reputed; it is the
base, though bitter, disposition of Beatrice that puts the   190
world into her person and so gives me out. Well, I'll be
revenged as I may.

Enter DON PEDRO, HERO [*and*] LEONATO.

DON PEDRO   Now, signor, where's the count? Did you see
him?

182–3 **strike . . . blindman . . . beat
. . . post** i.e. behave irrationally, as in
blind anger
183 **post** pillar; messenger
186 **sedges** reeds, a good hiding place for
a wounded bird. This image inaugu-
rates a chain of like references to the
hunting and trapping of wild animals.
188 **merry** high-spirited (rather than
foolish)
190 **base** mean, low-minded
   though bitter albeit stinging, cutting
190-1 **puts . . . person** claims to speak
for everyone else, represents her own
opinion as the world's
191 **gives me out** portrays me according
to that opinion
192.1 *Q includes Don John, Borachio and
Conrade in this entrance, though it is
clear from 2.2 that Don John has not
been present, and presumably nor have

his henchmen. F has the Prince enter
alone here, and Leonato and Hero with
Claudio and Beatrice at 239. As the
latter choice perhaps indicates, given
that Hero and Leonato have no lines
until 277 (Hero is mute until 346), their
silent presence during the exchange
between Benedick and Don Pedro about
the latter's purloining of Claudio's girl
could be theatrically awkward (though
Benedick is hardly a model of tact);
alternatively, the tone (and sting) of
Benedick's subsequent diatribe can
be conditioned by his playing to the
additional audience of her uncle and
cousin, as well as by the timing of
Beatrice's own entry (some productions
have her enter when Benedick is in mid-
rant, which can produce humour or
embarrassment at the expense of either
party). Benedick's reference to *this young*

187 fool – hah!] *Capell* (fool? Ha!*)*; fool! – ha? *Johnson;* foole! hah, *Q;* foole! Hah? *F*   190 though
bitter] *((though bitter))*; and bitter *Oxf¹ (Craven)*   192.1] *Rowe; Enter the Prince, Hero, Leonato,
Iohn and Borachio, and Conrade. Q; Enter the Prince. F*   193–295+ SP DON PEDRO] *Capell (D. Pe.);
Pedro Q*   193 signor] *(signior)*

BENEDICK   Troth, my lord, I have played the part of Lady   195
Fame. I found him here as melancholy as a lodge in
a warren. I told him, and I think I told him true, that
your grace had got the good will of this young lady, and
I offered him my company to a willow tree, either to
make him a garland, as being forsaken, or to bind him   200
up a rod, as being worthy to be whipped.

DON PEDRO   To be whipped? What's his fault?

BENEDICK   The flat transgression of a schoolboy, who,
being overjoyed with finding a bird's nest, shows it his
companion, and he steals it.   205

DON PEDRO   Wilt thou make a trust a transgression? The
transgression is in the stealer.

BENEDICK   Yet it had not been amiss the rod had been
made, and the garland too; for the garland he might
have worn himself, and the rod he might have bestowed   210
on you, who, as I take it, have stolen his bird's nest.

DON PEDRO   I will but teach them to sing, and restore
them to the owner.

BENEDICK   If their singing answer your saying, by my
faith you say honestly.   215

---

lady at 198 can suggest that Hero is
present; Q's 'this' could, though, be a
misreading of copy 'his'.
195–6 **Lady Fame** a spreader of news;
Virgil's *Fama* (*Aeneid*, 4.181–90) has
many eyes, ears and tongues (much
like Shakespeare's Rumour personified
in *2H4* Prologue), and in this sense
communicates information more generally rather than exclusively connot-
ing notoriety or celebrity.
196–7 **lodge . . . warren** isolated hunting
lodge in a game park
198 **good will** agreement
200 **garland** i.e. of willow
203 **flat** outright

transgression . . . schoolboy i.e.
error of youth and naivety
205 **he** i.e. the companion; the purloining
of a nest belonging to another is in fact
the habit of the cuckoo, from which
the word 'cuckold' derives.
206 **Wilt . . . transgression** i.e. are you
interpreting a trust as a transgression?
Don Pedro questions the logic of
Benedick's metaphor.
212 **them** perhaps a reference to both
Leonato and Hero, both of whom
must be consulted in the transaction;
the 'song' is an agreement to wed.
214 **answer** corroborate
215 **say honestly** speak in good faith

197 think I told] thinke, told *F*   198 good will] *(goodwil)*; will *F*   201 up] *om. F*

DON PEDRO   The Lady Beatrice hath a quarrel to you.
The gentleman that danced with her told her she is
much wronged by you.

BENEDICK   O, she misused me past the endurance of a
block! An oak but with one green leaf on it would have   220
answered her; my very visor began to assume life and
scold with her! She told me, not thinking I had been
myself, that I was the prince's jester, that I was duller
than a great thaw, huddling jest upon jest with such
impossible conveyance upon me that I stood like a man   225
at a mark, with a whole army shooting at me. She
speaks poniards, and every word stabs. If her breath
were as terrible as her terminations there were no living
near her, she would infect to the North Star. I would
not marry her though she were endowed with all that   230
Adam had left him before he transgressed. She would

216 to with
218 **wronged by you** injured by your
slanders
219 **misused** abused
220 **block** insensible object; cf. *JC* 1.1.36:
'You blocks, you stones, you worse
than senseless things!'
with . . . leaf immature; with the
faintest sign of life
222 **scold** argue, but the verb implies
Beatrice's shrewish identity
223–4 **duller . . . thaw** more boring than
the spring rainy season (when roads
were impassable and visiting impossible)
224 **huddling** piling up
225 **impossible conveyance** incredible
dexterity; outrageous expression
226 **mark** target; a man standing near a
target could, albeit perilously, inform
the archers of how close their arrows
were to their object – as in e.g. John
Webster, *The White Devil* (1612),

3.2.24–5: 'I am at the mark, sir: I'll
give aim to you / And tell you how
near you shoot.'
227 **poniards** daggers; cf. Philip
Massinger, *The Duke of Milan* (1623),
2.1.377–8: 'euerie word's a Poynard, /
And reaches to my Heart' (Massinger,
1.244).
228 **terminations** descriptive terms
(Shakespeare's sole use and the *OED*'s
sole citation for this use, solicited perhaps by the tempting alliteration and
rhythm)
229 **she . . . Star** i.e. she would pollute
the entire universe
230 **marry her** Benedick has obviously thought of Beatrice as a marriage
partner, just as she has of him at
10–15.
231 **Adam . . . transgressed** Before dis-
obeying God's instruction to eschew
the fruit of the tree of knowledge of
good and evil, Adam lived in paradise,

223 jester, that] Iester, and that *F*   228 her] *om. F*

have made Hercules have turned spit, yea, and have
cleft his club to make the fire too. Come, talk not of her,
you shall find her the infernal Ate in good apparel. I
would to God some scholar would conjure her, for   235
certainly while she is here a man may live as quiet in
hell as in a sanctuary, and people sin upon purpose
because they would go thither – so indeed all disquiet,
horror and perturbation follows her.

Enter CLAUDIO *and* BEATRICE.

whose benefits included freedom from
death, sin and labour, and, theoreti-
cally, dominion over the rest of creation, including his wife (Genesis,
2.16–17, 3.1–23). Benedick perhaps
wants his audience to recall also that
Adam's wife Eve provoked the fall of
man ('The woman thou gavest to be
with mee, she gave mee of the tree, and
I did eat', Genesis, 3.12).
231–3 **She . . . too** i.e. she would have
    out-henpecked Omphale of classical
    legend; see 29–30n.
232 **have turned** For duplication of the
    perfect tense, see Abbott, 360.
    turned spit Turning the roasting
    spit over the fire was considered the
    most menial of Elizabethan kitchen
    tasks. Hercules' club was a massive
    (and phallic) one, and splitting it into
    firewood would have been an ardu-
    ous as well as emasculating task for
    him to undertake. The misogyny of
    Benedick's caricatures increases as he
    elaborates them.
233 **cleft** split
234 **Ate . . . apparel** the classical goddess
    of discord (pronounced 'ah-tay'), and
    eldest daughter of Zeus, beautiful in
    appearance but usually clad in rags,
    and instigator of the Trojan war; cf.
    JC 3.1.271–3: 'Ate . . . come hot from
    hell, / Shall . . . / Cry havoc'; and *KJ*
    2.1.63: 'An Ate, stirring him to blood

and strife'. *The Lamentable Tragedy of
Locrine* (1595) presents Ate as a chorus,
entering 'with thunder and lightning,
all in black, with a burning torch in
one hand and a bloody sword in the
other', and warning that 'a woman was
the only cause / That civil discord was
then stirred up' (*Locrine*, Epilogue,
200–1). The image of Beatrice here
joins other female figures of dissent
with misleadingly pleasant appearance,
such as Duessa and Ate in Spenser's
Faerie Queene: 'in face / And outward
shewe faire semblance they did beare; /
[though] vnder maske of beautie
and good grace, / Vile treason
and fowle falshood hidden were, /
That mote to none but to the warie
wise appeare' (*FQ*, 4.1.17.5–9); cf.
Claudio's speech to Hero at 4.1.56–9:
'You seem to me as Dian in her orb
. . . / But you are more intemperate in
your blood / Than Venus'.
235 **conjure her** Scholars were thought
    adept at both summoning spirits and
    exorcising them back again to the place
    whence they came.
236 **here** i.e. on earth
237 **sanctuary** religious refuge
238 **thither** i.e. to hell
239.1 The timing of this entrance can
    affect the tenor of Benedick's speech;
    he may, for instance, shift at once into
    a different tone of voice.

239.1 BEATRICE] *Beatrice, Leonato, Hero.* F

DON PEDRO   Look, here she comes.   240
BENEDICK   Will your grace command me any service to
the world's end? I will go on the slightest errand now to
the Antipodes that you can devise to send me on. I will
fetch you a toothpicker now from the furthest inch of
Asia; bring you the length of Prester John's foot; fetch   245
you a hair off the Great Cham's beard; do you any
embassage to the Pygmies, rather than hold three words
conference with this harpy. You have no employment
for me?
DON PEDRO   None, but to desire your good company.   250

243 **Antipodes** region and people on the other side of the earth (and thus the soles of whose feet 'are as it were planted against' our own, *OED* 1); Benedick's desire to undertake far-fetched and exotic journeys of derring-do in order to avoid a woman associated, through Ate, with sorcery recalls the type of the male adventurer Odysseus fleeing Circe for home, or Aeneas fleeing Dido for duty. Both are cited by Ovid in his *Remedies of Love* as examples of how to swear off love (sig. C1ʳ).

244 **toothpicker** i.e. like the objectives he lists, a trivial pursuit for such an arduous errand (but presumably worth it if it allows him to avoid Beatrice). Toothpicks were considered fashion accessories; in *AW* they are outmoded (1.1.158–9); in *KJ* (1.1.190) they are considered the affectation of travellers.

245 **Prester John's foot** Prester John was a figure of medieval legend, a Christian ruler sometimes identified with the king/emperor-priest of Abyssinia (a fabulously rich kingdom in the East). Presumably securing the measurement of his foot, like procuring a beard-hair of the Great Cham, would be a

difficult enterprise. All the exotic locales Benedick speaks of are mentioned in the travel writings of Sir John Mandeville and Marco Polo.

246 **Great Cham** the title of the Mongol emperors (Khan of Tartary), e.g. Khublai or Genghis (who defeated Prester John in battle). Another powerful figure of oriental rule.

247 **Pygmies** The battle of the Pygmies (a race of tiny people) and the Cranes was an ancient Greek folk tale. The Pygmies are mentioned in passing by Homer (*Iliad*, 3.5–7); later Pliny the Elder, in his *Natural History*, set the story in India. The encounters of a traveller with dwarfish peoples was a stock feature of medieval and classical legend.

248 **harpy** a term for a cruel and vicious woman, from the Greek verb 'to seize', and in classical legend a monster with the head and body of a beautiful woman and the wings and claws of an eagle; cf. *haggard* at 3.1.36. Like Ate (234) and her sisters, a duplicitous figure that combines an alluring female appearance with danger. It is a comment which nevertheless notes Beatrice's beauty.

246 off] of *Steevens–Reed*

BENEDICK O God, sir, here's a dish I love not; I cannot
endure my Lady Tongue!   *Exit.*

DON PEDRO Come, lady, come; you have lost the heart of
Signor Benedick.

BEATRICE Indeed, my lord, he lent it me awhile, and I   255
gave him use for it, a double heart for his single one.
Marry, once before he won it of me with false dice;
therefore your grace may well say I have lost it.

DON PEDRO You have put him down, lady, you have put
him down.   260

BEATRICE So I would not he should do me, my lord, lest I
should prove the mother of fools. I have brought Count
Claudio, whom you sent me to seek.

DON PEDRO Why, how now, Count? Wherefore are you
sad?   265

CLAUDIO Not sad, my lord.

DON PEDRO How then? Sick?

252 **Lady Tongue** like the 'good
continuer' Lady Disdain (1.1.136,
112), a figure of female shrewishness and garrulousness; cf. *Lady Fame*,
2.1.195–6.

255–6 **I . . . it** I paid him interest on the
use of his heart (i.e. Beatrice returned
her own heart – *a double heart* – in
addition to, or in exchange for, his).
Along with 1.1.138–9, a suggestion of
a past romantic disappointment (which
would make Benedick and Beatrice's
history analogous to Claudio and
Hero's in consisting of an initial setback
followed by a reaffirmation).

257 **it** i.e. his – or perhaps her own –
heart
false dice dice that have been weigh-
ted so as to permit cheating in a game
of chance. Beatrice implies that at

some point in the past Benedick broke
faith with her despite her own generous terms of 100 per cent interest
(usury was, however, itself a suspect
practice).

259–60 **put him down** defeated or
demeaned him. Beatrice's response
sexualizes the phrase, and, as John
Traugott observes, 'Beatrice is forever
thinking of (or being made to think
of) the ultimate female position in
the congress of the sexes – put down,
overmastered, lying in woolen, dancing
the love dance down into the grave'
(Traugott, 173).

262 **fools** errant humans; additionally, any
children of Benedick's might resemble
their foolish father, the Prince's jester.

265 **sad** solemn, serious; an implied SD
for the actor playing Claudio

252 my Lady Tongue] this Lady tongue *F*   256 his] a *F*

CLAUDIO   Neither, my lord.

BEATRICE   The count is neither sad, nor sick, nor merry,
nor well – but civil count, civil as an orange, and   270
something of that jealous complexion.

DON PEDRO   I'faith, lady, I think your blazon to be true;
though I'll be sworn if he be so his conceit is false. Here,
Claudio, I have wooed in thy name, and fair Hero is won.
I have broke with her father, and his good will obtained.   275
Name the day of marriage, and God give thee joy!

LEONATO   Count, take of me my daughter, and with her
my fortunes. His grace hath made the match, and all
grace say amen to it.

BEATRICE   Speak, Count, 'tis your cue.   280

CLAUDIO   Silence is the perfectest herald of joy; I were
but little happy if I could say how much. Lady, as you

---

270 **civil** grave, with a pun on Seville,
the Spanish town renowned for oranges of a bittersweet flavour (i.e. like
Claudio, neither sweet nor sour); the
words could be and often were spelled
the same in Elizabethan orthography.
Cam[1] cites Nashe, *Strange News, Of
the Intercepting Certain Letters* (1592):
'For the order of my life, it is as civil
as a civil orange' (Nashe, 1.329). In the
contrast between their bitter rind and
sweet fruit, oranges were also a figure
of deception; see 4.1.30n.
271 **jealous complexion** Yellow was
considered the symbol of jealousy
and suspicion, perhaps because of the
melancholy attendant upon jaundice
(the word comes from the Old English
geolo, related to the word for gall). Cf.
Robert Greene's *Quip for an Upstart
Courtier* (1592): 'Amongst the rest
was a yellow daffodil, a flowre fit for
gelous Dottrels, who through the
bewty of their honest wives grow
suspicious' (Greene, *Courtier*, 213);

and see *WT* 2.3.105–7. Seville oranges
also have a greenish tint, which makes
them an apt emblem of the green-eyed
monster.
272 **blazon** a poetic technique (derived
from the term for the heraldic representation of armorial bearings) for
describing the (usually female) person
of the beloved in discrete parts; cf. *TN*
1.5.286–7: 'Thy tongue, thy face, thy
limbs, actions, and spirit / Do give
thee five-fold blazon'.
273 **conceit** idea (i.e. that Hero has been
wooed by the Prince for himself)
Here This could imply a SD for Don
Pedro to hand Hero to Claudio.
275 **broke** broached the matter
278–9 **all grace** God (i.e. the source of
all grace)
279 **say amen** bless; confirm
280 Beatrice's prompt implies a pregnant
pause following Leonato's speech.
281 **herald** announcer, one who blazons
282 **how much** i.e. how happy I am;
Claudio's   reticence   would   have

271 that] a F   275 obtained.] obtained. *Don Pedro signals; enter Leonato with Hero* Oxf[1] (*Jenkins*)

are mine, I am yours. I give away myself for you, and
dote upon the exchange.

BEATRICE   Speak, cousin, or, if you cannot, stop his   285
mouth with a kiss and let not him speak neither.

DON PEDRO   In faith, lady, you have a merry heart.

BEATRICE   Yea, my lord, I thank it, poor fool, it keeps on
the windy side of care. My cousin tells him in his ear
that he is in her heart.   290

CLAUDIO   And so she doth, cousin.

BEATRICE   Good Lord, for alliance! Thus goes everyone
to the world but I, and I am sunburnt. I may sit in a
corner and cry 'Hey-ho for a husband'.

DON PEDRO   Lady Beatrice, I will get you one.   295

BEATRICE   I would rather have one of your father's
getting. Hath your grace ne'er a brother like you? Your

been uncharacteristic of a typical
Renaissance lover, who was thought to
be rendered garrulous by the strength
of his feelings (see 1.1.287n.).

289 **windy side** upwind (a location which
would allow care to be blown away
from one, or from which one could,
by blocking the wind, prevent it from
accelerating care's momentum)
tells . . . ear an indication for Hero's
stage action

292 **alliance** marriage, or the association of families thereby produced (a
response to Claudio's calling her his
cousin)

293 **the world** i.e. the married state of
the majority, worldly and carnal compared with the innocence of celibacy.
Cf. *AW* 1.3.18; and Genesis, 19.31,
where one of Lot's daughters says to
her sister, 'Our father is old, and there
is not man in the earth to come unto us
after the manner of all the world.'
sunburnt (1) unhoused by marriage, and
hence exposed to the elements; (2) unat-

tractively browned by the sun; cf. 5.4.38,
'I'll hold my mind were she an Ethiope',
and *TC* 1.3.282–3, 'The Grecian dames
are sunburnt, and not worth / The
splinter of a lance.' The comment could
also reflect that Beatrice's colouring (like
her *too brown* cousin's, 1.1.164) departs
from the conventional Renaissance norm
of fair beauty.

293–4 **in a corner** the resting place of
wallflowers and spinsters

294 **Hey-ho . . . husband** the proverbial sigh (Dent, H833) of the woman
on the shelf, and the title of a ballad
(subtitled 'or, a willing Maids wants
made known'). Cf. Burton's *Anatomy
of Melancholy*, 3.231): 'Hai-ho for a
husband, cries she, a bad husband, nay
the worst that ever was, is better than
none' (Burton, 3.231).

297 **getting** begetting; cf. *get* at 295.
ne'er . . . you Don Pedro does indeed
have a half-brother (Don John), though
one presumably not so like him as to
inhibit Beatrice's rejoinder.

290 her] my *F*   294 'Hey-ho . . . husband'] *Staunton;* heigh ho . . . husband *Q;* 'heigh-ho' . . .
husband *Theobald*

197

father got excellent husbands, if a maid could come by
them.

DON PEDRO   Will you have me, lady?   300

BEATRICE   No, my lord, unless I might have another for
working days. Your grace is too costly to wear every
day. But I beseech your grace pardon me, I was born to
speak all mirth and no matter.

DON PEDRO   Your silence most offends me, and to be   305
merry best becomes you, for out o'question, you were
born in a merry hour.

BEATRICE   No, sure, my lord, my mother cried; but then
there was a star danced, and under that was I born. [*to
Hero and Claudio*] Cousins, God give you joy!   310

LEONATO   Niece, will you look to those things I told you
of?

BEATRICE   I cry you mercy, uncle. [*to Don Pedro*] By your
grace's pardon.   *Exit.*

298–9 **come by them** acquire one
(implies the rarity of Don Pedro's
kind)
302 **costly** well born; expensive
304 **no matter** nothing of substance or
sense; cf. 1.1.260–1: 'I have almost
matter enough in me for such an
embassage.'
305 **Your . . . me** i.e. I don't want you to
inhibit your speech
307 **merry hour** i.e. both astrologically
and auspiciously
308 **my mother cried** a corrective characteristic of Beatrice's emotional realism – as well as her scriptural sense;
see Genesis, 3.16: 'Unto the woman he
said, I will greatly multiply thy sorrow
and thy conception, in sorrow thou
shalt bring forth children, and thy
desire shall be to thy husband, and he

shall rule over thee.'
309 **a star danced** as the sun was reputed to dance on Easter morning; a
shooting star
under . . . born i.e. born at the time
when a benign astrological sign was
predominant, and hence possessing a
character influenced by that planet. Cf.
1.3.10–11: 'being as thou sayst thou art,
born under Saturn'; 5.2.39–40: 'No, I
was not born under a rhyming planet.'
311–12 Leonato could be saving Beatrice
– or the Prince – from further embarrassment by inventing for her an
excuse to leave.
313–14 Beatrice apologizes to her uncle
and excuses herself from the Prince's
company; the second phrase could also
serve as apology for any offence her
humour may have caused.

300, 305, 315 SP] *Capell (D. Pe.); Rowe (Pedro); Prince Q*   300 me, lady?] *Rowe;* me? lady. *Q*   306
o'] *(a); of F*   309–10 SD] *Oxf¹*   313 SD] *Oxf¹*

DON PEDRO By my troth, a pleasant-spirited lady.   315

LEONATO There's little of the melancholy element in her, my lord. She is never sad but when she sleeps, and not ever sad then; for I have heard my daughter say she hath often dreamt of unhappiness and waked herself with laughing.   320

DON PEDRO She cannot endure to hear tell of a husband.

LEONATO O, by no means. She mocks all her wooers out of suit.

DON PEDRO She were an excellent wife for Benedick.

LEONATO O Lord, my lord, if they were but a week   325
married, they would talk themselves mad.

DON PEDRO County Claudio, when mean you to go to church?

CLAUDIO Tomorrow, my lord. Time goes on crutches till Love have all his rites.   330

LEONATO Not till Monday, my dear son, which is hence a just sennight – and a time too brief, too, to have all things answer my mind.

DON PEDRO Come, you shake the head at so long a

---

316 **melancholy element** one of the four humours, believed to be engendered by black bile (the other three provoked by blood, phlegm and choler), and, like earth, dry and cold. Leonato's diagnosis contradicts Beatrice's own description of her *cold blood* at 1.1.124; here, she is temperamentally the opposite of the saturnine Don John.

317, 318 **sad** serious

318 **ever** always

318–20 **she . . . laughing** i.e. even in her sleep, if she is visited by sad dreams, she recovers her good humour; cf. 2.1.18 and n., another image of Beatrice as possess-ing a mixed emotional constitution.

323 **suit** courtship

329 **on crutches** i.e. slowly and painfully

330 **Love** i.e. Cupid, a god requiring observances
all his rites religious solemnities; sexual consummation, or marital 'rights'. The senses are indistinguishable in performance.

332 **a just sennight** exactly a week

333 **answer my mind** arranged to my liking

334 **shake the head** an indication for Claudio's gesture

---

315 pleasant-spirited] *(pleasant spirited)*, *Theobald*   321 SP] *Capell (D. Pe)*; *Pedro Q*
324+ SP] *Capell (D. Pe)*; *Prince Q*   327 County] *(Countie)*; Counte *F*   332 sennight]
(seuennight)   333 my] *om. F*

breathing, but I warrant thee, Claudio, the time shall   335
not go dully by us. I will, in the interim, undertake one
of Hercules' labours, which is to bring Signor Benedick
and the Lady Beatrice into a mountain of affection
th'one with th'other. I would fain have it a match, and
I doubt not but to fashion it, if you three will but   340
minister such assistance as I shall give you direction.

LEONATO My lord, I am for you, though it cost me ten
nights' watchings.

CLAUDIO And I, my lord.

DON PEDRO And you too, gentle Hero?   345

HERO I will do any modest office, my lord, to help my
cousin to a good husband.

DON PEDRO And Benedick is not the unhopefullest
husband that I know. Thus far can I praise him: he is
of a noble strain, of approved valour and confirmed   350
honesty. I will teach you how to humour your cousin

335–4 **breathing** interval, pause
warrant promise
335–6 **time . . . us** Don Pedro's proposal savours of the kind of courtly pas-
time found in the worlds of Baldasarre
Castiglione's *Il libro del cortegiano* (*The
Courtier*) (1528) or Lyly, *Anatomy*.
337 **Hercules' labours** In classical legend Hercules was sentenced by Apollo
to serve the Argive king Eurystheus
in penance for having slain his own
family; the latter imposed 12 nearly
impossible tasks of strength and skill
upon him, such as cleaning the capa-
cious Augean stables, capturing the
Cretan bull, obtaining the apples of
the Hesperides, etc.
338 **mountain** large quantity
339 **fain** gladly
340 **fashion** engineer. For some
heartless critics, this language of
artifice is proof that the ultimate
union of Beatrice and Benedick is
more indebted to social convention
and machination than voluntary
feeling; e.g. Stephen Greenblatt in

the Norton Shakespeare: 'they are
tricked into marriage against their
hearts . . . [they] constantly tantalize
us with the possibility of an identity
. . . deliberately fashioned to resist the
constant pressure of society. But that
pressure finally prevails. Marriage is a
social conspiracy' (Greenblatt, 1386);
compare, however, the play's contrast
between malicious and beneficent
('honest', 3.1.84) slanders, the latter
sometimes a paradox but in this play
argued to be true.
341 **minister** administer, provide, afford
343 **nights' watchings** wakeful nights;
the term (like *candle-wasters*, 5.1.18)
implies that the task will require much
study as well as observation.
346 **modest office** seemly role
348 **unhopefullest** most unpromising
350 **strain** birth or lineage (*JC* 5.1.57);
temperament (*KL* 5.3.41)
approved proven
351 **honesty** honour
humour put her in such a humour;
indulge so as to persuade; manipulate

that she shall fall in love with Benedick; [*to Claudio and Leonato*] and I, with your two helps, will so practise on Benedick that, in despite of his quick wit and his queasy stomach, he shall fall in love with Beatrice. If we   355
can do this, Cupid is no longer an archer; his glory shall be ours, for we are the only love-gods. Go in with me and I will tell you my drift.   *Exeunt.*

[**2.2**]   *Enter* [DON] JOHN *and* BORACHIO.

DON JOHN   It is so; the Count Claudio shall marry the
daughter of Leonato.
BORACHIO   Yea, my lord, but I can cross it.
DON JOHN   Any bar, any cross, any impediment will be
medicinable to me. I am sick in displeasure to him, and   5
whatsoever comes athwart his affection ranges evenly
with mine. How canst thou cross this marriage?

353–4 **practise on** scheme upon
354 **quick wit** i.e. sharp intelligence, and his intellectual defence against marriage; Draper (262) observes that 'quick wit, though sometimes attributed to the sanguine type and to certain sorts of melancholy, was thought on the authority of Aristotle to be a common effect of choler . . . [albeit] such under the influence of the sun, [which] . . . made men strong, valiant, honest, and loyal' (unlike choleric persons under the influence of Mars, who tended to be brawlers).
355 **queasy stomach** fastidious pride; delicate appetite (for love)
356 **Cupid . . . archer** The cherubic god of love wounded his victims with arrows; Don Pedro suggests they will trump his efforts.

358 **drift** plan, intention
2.2 The location is a space in Leonato's house or its environs.
1–2 Don John's remark could indicate that his entrance overlaps with the exit of the previous scene, and thus is a comment upon what can be observed of Hero and Claudio's behaviour.
3 **cross** prevent, hinder
4 **bar** impediment, obstacle
  cross affliction, trouble
5 **medicinable** salutary, healing
  to with
6 **comes athwart** crosses the path of, impedes or hinders (as of a ship's course)
  affection desire, inclination
  ranges evenly lines up with (*OED* range *v.*[1] II 5b); the metaphor derives from printing practice (*ranges evenly* is a tautology).

352–3 SD] *Kittredge*   358 SD] *Rowe; exit. Q*   2.2] *Capell*   0.1] DON] *Rowe*   1+ SP DON JOHN] *Capell (D. Jo.); Iohn Q*

BORACHIO   Not honestly, my lord, but so covertly that no
dishonesty shall appear in me.

DON JOHN   Show me briefly how.   10

BORACHIO   I think I told your lordship, a year since, how
much I am in the favour of Margaret, the waiting-
gentlewoman to Hero.

DON JOHN   I remember.

BORACHIO   I can, at any unseasonable instant of the night,   15
appoint her to look out at her lady's chamber window.

DON JOHN   What life is in that to be the death of this
marriage?

BORACHIO   The poison of that lies in you to temper. Go
you to the prince your brother; spare not to tell him that   20
he hath wronged his honour in marrying the renowned
Claudio – whose estimation do you mightily hold up
– to a contaminated stale, such a one as Hero.

DON JOHN   What proof shall I make of that?

BORACHIO   Proof enough to misuse the prince, to vex   25
Claudio, to undo Hero and kill Leonato. Look you for
any other issue?

DON JOHN   Only to despite them I will endeavour
anything.

---

15 **unseasonable instant** late hour
16 **appoint** instruct
   chamber bedroom
19 **temper** concoct, mix
22 **estimation** reputation and/or worth
   hold up maintain, affirm
23 **contaminated stale** depraved prostitute; *stale* was the term for a decoy,
   including the prostitute used by
   thieves to lure victims (*OED n.*³ 4).
24 How will I demonstrate that?
25 **misuse** abuse, deceive
   vex injure, distress (stronger than the

modern sense of irritate)
26 **undo** ruin in reputation
   kill Leonato As if to underscore the
   degree to which the assault on Hero's
   honour is an attack on male identity,
   Borachio considers the effects of the
   slander to be more lethal to the aged
   Leonato than to his daughter or the
   others abused.
27 **issue** result
28 **despite** maliciously or contemptuously injure; Shakespeare's only use of the
   word as a verb

12–13 waiting-gentlewoman] *(waiting gentlewoman)*, *Rowe*

BORACHIO   Go, then. Find me a meet hour to draw Don   30
Pedro and the Count Claudio alone. Tell them that you
know that Hero loves me. Intend a kind of zeal both to
the prince and Claudio – as in love of your brother's
honour, who hath made this match, and his friend's
reputation, who is thus like to be cozened with the   35
semblance of a maid – that you have discovered thus.
They will scarcely believe this without trial; offer them
instances, which shall bear no less likelihood than to
see me at her chamber window, hear me call Margaret
'Hero', hear Margaret term me 'Claudio'. And bring   40
them to see this the very night before the intended
wedding (for in the meantime I will so fashion the
matter that Hero shall be absent), and there shall
appear such seeming truth of Hero's disloyalty that

30 **meet hour** convenient time
32 **Intend** pretend
   zeal fervent loyalty
35 **cozened** cheated
36 **semblance** mere appearance
   maid virgin
   discovered revealed
   thus i.e. that Hero consorts with
   Borachio
37 **trial** proof
38 **bear . . . likelihood** seem no less
   convincing
40 **Claudio** Some editors read 'Borachio'
   for Claudio, on the grounds that
   for Claudio to overhear a supposed
   Hero call to Claudio might suggest
   that she were herself deceived;
   but presumably it would be easier
   to convince the socially ambitious
   Margaret ('Why, shall I always keep
   below stairs?', 5.2.9–10) to dress as her
   mistress and play-act with Borachio
   the love affair of Hero and Claudio, in
   a kind of sex game of social class, and

it would also doubly injure Claudio
to watch Hero mock him by calling
her lover by his name. Shakespeare's
sources have the man actually entering
the bedroom window, as opposed
to merely speaking at it, and it is
worth noting here that Shakespeare
renders this scene in report only,
although some productions choose to
stage it, a choice which can either (if
convincingly staged) mitigate Claudio's
rejection of Hero or (if not plausibly
incriminating) make his distrust of her
all the more repellent; Shakespeare
however leaves the audience to judge
his decision to reject her on the basis
of our imagination of the scene, given
aural evidence alone. Like many of
the characters, we too are dependent
on report.
42 **fashion** contrive, arrange; cf. 2.1.339–
   40: 'I would fain have it a match, and I
   doubt not but to fashion it.'
44 **disloyalty** unfaithfulness

30 Don] on *F*   33 – as] (as *Q*   in] in a *F*   34–6 match, . . . maid –] *Capell;* match) . . . maid,
Q   39 Margaret] *(Marg.)*   40 'Hero'] *this edn;* Hero *Q*   'Claudio'] *this edn;* Claudio *Q;* Borachio
Theobald   42 meantime] *(*mean time*)*   44 truth] truths *F*

jealousy shall be called assurance, and all the   45
preparation overthrown.

DON JOHN   Grow this to what adverse issue it can, I will
put it in practice. Be cunning in the working this and
thy fee is a thousand ducats.

BORACHIO   Be you constant in the accusation and my   50
cunning shall not shame me.

DON JOHN   I will presently go learn their day of marriage.

Exeunt.

[**2.3**]   *Enter* BENEDICK *alone.*

BENEDICK   Boy!

[*Enter* Boy.]

BOY   Signor.

BENEDICK   In my chamber window lies a book. Bring it
hither to me in the orchard.

BOY   I am here already, sir.   5

---

45 **jealousy** suspicion
   assurance certainty
46 **preparation** i.e. for the wedding
47 **Grow this** let this grow
   what issue whatever outcome
48 **working this** i.e. working of this
   (Abbott, 93)
49 **ducats** A ducat was a gold or silver coin
   worth about 9s 4d (i.e. about 47p, or a
   modern equivalent of around £20).
51 **cunning** guile, underhanded clever-
   ness
52 **presently** at once, directly
2.3 The location is Leonato's orchard.
   The staging needs to provide for
   Benedick's concealment from the
   gullers (though he must be visible
   to the audience); its elaborateness
   will depend on the nature of the

production (on the Elizabethan stage,
presumably the actor playing Benedick
concealed himself downstage behind
the pillars). Modern production
choices have included shrubbery,
trees, lattice, garden furniture, etc.,
as well as arbours, both imaginary and
actual. Property arbours did exist in
Elizabethan staging practice (one is
featured on the title page of the 1615
edition of Kyd's *Spanish Tragedy*; see
p. 112).
5 **already** i.e. immediately; cf. *AW*
2.2.65: 'I am there before my legs.'
There is no SD for the boy's re-
entry (and Cam[1] suggests that he
exists merely to let Benedick identify
the location in his address to him),
although many productions have

50 you] thou *F*   52 SD] *Rowe; exit. Q*   **2.3**] *Capell*   0.1] *Enter* Benedick *and a boy. / Rowe*
1.1] *Collier*   2+ Signor] *(Signior)*

BENEDICK   I know that, but I would have thee hence and
    here again.   *Exit* [*Boy*].
    I do much wonder that one man, seeing how much
    another man is a fool when he dedicates his behaviours
    to love, will, after he hath laughed at such shallow   10
    follies in others, become the argument of his own
    scorn by falling in love. And such a man is Claudio. I
    have known when there was no music with him but the
    drum and the fife, and now had he rather hear the tabor
    and the pipe. I have known when he would have walked   15
    ten mile afoot to see a good armour, and now will he lie
    ten nights awake carving the fashion of a new doublet.
    He was wont to speak plain and to the purpose, like
    an honest man and a soldier, and now is he turned

successfully had him reappear and attempt to deliver the book to the concealed Benedick while the latter frantically attempts to maintain his concealment.

7 SD Q marks this at 5, perhaps so as to avoid inserting a SD in Benedick's long speech, but if this direction is followed Benedick can address himself to the retreating boy, or to no one in particular (as if he were puzzling over the phrase *here already*).

9–10 **dedicates . . . love** fashions his actions in the habits of a lover. The notion suggests a set of conventional gestures and attitudes appropriate to a lover; see 3.2.38n.

11 **argument** subject

12 **And . . . Claudio** Draper (264) comments that Benedick's reading himself 'a lengthy lecture against marriage' is 'quite a needless task for a truly confirmed bachelor!'

14 **drum . . . fife** i.e. instruments usually reserved for military music

14–15 **tabor . . . pipe** The tabor was a small drum, used principally as an

accompaniment to the whistle, or pipe, i.e. instruments for dances and love songs (and often played by fools). Cf. *R3* 1.1.5–8, 24: 'Now are . . . / chang'd . . . / Our dreadful marches to delightful measures . . . in this weak piping time of peace . . . '; and Lyly, *Campaspe*, 2.2.35–9: 'Is the warlike sou[n]d of drumme and trumpet turned to the soft noyse of lire and lute? The neighing of barbed steeds. . . conuerted to dilicate tunes and amorous glaunces?' (*Works*, 2.330). Claudio's entrance at 34 with musicians bears out Benedick's criticism.

16 **armour** i.e. suit of armour

17 **carving** designing

    doublet upper part of a man's dress, a close-fitting jacket with detachable sleeves

18–19 **like . . . soldier** Shakespeare also associates a soldier's speech with a blunt and unornamented style in *H5* 5.2.148–9: 'I speak to thee plain soldier.'

19–20 **turned ortography** become the very spirit of an over-polished or

7 SD] *Johnson; exit opp. 5 Q; after* that 6 *Collier*

205

ortography; his words are a very fantastical banquet,   20
just so many strange dishes. May I be so converted and
see with these eyes? I cannot tell; I think not. I will not
be sworn but love may transform me to an oyster, but
I'll take my oath on it, till he have made an oyster of me
he shall never make me such a fool. One woman is fair,   25
yet I am well. Another is wise, yet I am well. Another
virtuous, yet I am well. But till all graces be in one
woman, one woman shall not come in my grace. Rich

fastidious style; cf. *LLL* 5.1.19, 'such
rackers of orthography', who 'draweth
out the thread of his verbosity finer
than the staple of his argument' (16–
17). The word *turned*, like *converted*
(21), suggests that Claudio has undergone a metamorphosis of Ovidian
proportions. Editors since Rowe have
emended to 'orthography' (or sometimes 'orthographer') but Q's spelling
could equally be a colloquialism.
20 **fantastical banquet** Benedick's
choice of metaphor suggests the irony
of this silver-tongued man disdaining
verbal prowess.
22–3 **I will . . . may** I cannot promise
that love might not
23–4 **transform...oyster** (1) render me
a mollusc, one of the more ignominious
animals in the divine hierarchy,
and tight-lipped in the manner of a
melancholy lover; (2) split me wide
open: Dent, O116, cites as proverbial
'Undone as you would do an oyster'.
Cf. Lyly, *Anatomy*, 97, where an oyster
represents a man made vulnerable to a
perfidious female appetite: 'Think this
with thyself, that the sweet songs of
Calypso were subtle snares to entice
Ulysses, that the crab which catcheth
the oyster when the sun shineth
. . . that women when they be most
pleasant pretend most treachery.'
The image recalls the anecdote of
Albertus Magnus (1208–80) in his *De*

Animalibus: 'Ambrose relates that a
crab would willingly reach within the
shell of a mollusc to eat its inhabitant,
but out of fear of having its claw
trapped and crushed in the bivalve's
shell, it dares not enter. Consequently,
it watches until the mollusc is relaxed
by the warm rays of the sun, and opens
its shell. Then, using its scissor-like
claw, the crab inserts a stone between
the halves of the shell, preventing
them from closing, and finally eats the
mollusc at leisure' (Albertus, 24.23).
28 **in my grace** into my favour
28–33 **Rich . . . God** Despite his
professed disdain for marriage,
Benedick apparently finds it difficult to
lay the fascinating subject to rest. His
criteria here recall Beatrice's at 2.1.13–
15. They also reflect those of conduct-
book recommendations for the choice
of a spouse (see pp. 38–9) as well as
the terms of the formal controversy
about women; see Tasso, *Of Marriage
and Wiving*: 'Demosthenes, writing
vnto the Tyrant *Corynthus* . . . what
qualities one should seeke to finde in a
woman that he ment to marry withal,
returned him this answere: "First,
shee must be rich, that thou maist
have wherewithall to live in shewe and
carrie a port; next, she must be nobly
borne, that thou maist be honoured
through her bloud; then she must be
yong, that she may content thee; then

24 an] *(and)*, F

she shall be, that's certain; wise, or I'll none; virtuous,
or I'll never cheapen her; fair, or I'll never look on her;   30
mild, or come not near me; noble, or not I for an angel.
Of good discourse, an excellent musician, and her hair
shall be of what colour it please God. Hah! The prince
and Monsieur Love. I will hide me in the arbour.
[*Withdraws.*]

Enter DON PEDRO, LEONATO, CLAUDIO
[*and* BALTHASAR], *with Music.*

DON PEDRO
Come, shall we hear this music?   35
CLAUDIO
Yea, my good lord. How still the evening is,

---

faire, that thou need not to hunt after
other game; and lastly, honest and
vertuous, that thou maiest not take
the paines to provide a spie to watch
her"' (sig. B2ᵛ). No mention is made in
the play of Beatrice's fortune (unlike
Hero's), and she has been played both
as a grand lady of independent means
and as a poor relation.
29 **I'll none** i.e. I'll have nothing to do
with her, have none of her
30 **cheapen** bid or bargain for
31 **noble** well-born; a coin worth one-
third of a sovereign (7s 6d or about
37p)
  angel celestial being; a coin worth
  half of a sovereign, i.e. more than a
  noble (so called because it pictured
  the archangel Michael vanquishing a
  dragon)
32 **Of good discourse** well spoken;
  despite the early modern horror of
  talkative women, the ideal woman was
  nonetheless supposed to be conversa-

tionally adept when called upon (see
1.1.163–5n.).
33 **of . . . God** i.e. an issue of little
matter, that could be left to chance,
although there is perhaps some sense
that the colour should be natural; the
Elizabethan 'Homily on Excess of
Apparel' inveighed 'who can paint her
face, and curl her hair, and change it
into an unnatural colour, but there
doth work reproof to her Maker, who
made her, as though she could make
herself more comely than God hath
appointed the measure of her beauty'
(*Homilies*, 315). Women also wore false
hair (cf. 3.4.12–13: 'I like the new tire
within excellently, if the hair were a
thought browner').
34 **Monsieur Love** Mr Love, i.e. Claudio;
the French implies affectation.
  hide me The actor must conceal himself so that his responses are visible to
the audience.
34.2 *and* BALTHASAR See List of Roles 5n.

31 I] *om. F*   34 SD] *Theobald*   34.1 DON PEDRO] *Rowe; Prince Q*   34.2 *and* BALTHASAR] *Rowe;
after 45 Q (Enter Balthaser with musicke)   with Music*] *and Iacke Wilson F*   35+ SP] *Capell (D.
Pe.); Prince Q*

As hushed on purpose to grace harmony!

DON PEDRO [*aside to Claudio and Leonato*]

See you where Benedick hath hid himself?

CLAUDIO [*aside*]

O, very well, my lord. The music ended,
We'll fit the kid-fox with a pennyworth.   40

DON PEDRO

Come, Balthasar, we'll hear that song again.

BALTHASAR

O good my lord, tax not so bad a voice
To slander music any more than once.

DON PEDRO

It is the witness still of excellency
To put a strange face on his own perfection.   45
I pray thee sing, and let me woo no more.

BALTHASAR

Because you talk of wooing I will sing,
Since many a wooer doth commence his suit

---

37 **grace harmony** favour music
39 **The music ended** once the music is over
40 **fit** get even with
   kid-fox young fox, or cub; the epithet conveys both Benedick's own sense of his cunning, and his naive vulnerability to the charade about to be played upon him. Editors unpersuaded of Benedick's actual youth (and requiring it for the metaphor) have emended this to 'hid fox', based on the evidence of Don Pedro's use of *hid* at 38, Hamlet's line 'hide Fox, and all after' (4.2.29 in the Folio text), and the Elizabethan game of 'Fox i'th' hole', in which children hopped on one leg and pursued one of

their fellows (the fox), who emerged from hiding and ran for home.
   pennyworth a bargain, often a bad one, though here Claudio's meaning is perhaps 'we'll give him what – or more than – he bargained for'. Cf. Lyly, *Anatomy*, 195: 'thou shalt haue repentaunce . . . at suche an vnreasonable rate, that thou wilt curse thy hard penyworth'.
41 **again** This corroborates Benedick's report that Claudio has recently been given over to love songs.
42 **tax** burden, make demands
43–4 A casting-off error in F reprints these two lines at the top of fol. 108.
44–5 The mark of skill is ever to disparage or misrepresent itself.

38, 39 SD] *Capell*   40 kid-fox] hid fox *Warburton;* cade fox *Hanmer*   44 excellency] excellency, / to slander Musicke any more then once. / *Prince.* It is the witnesse still of excellencie, *F*

To her he thinks not worthy, yet he woos,
Yet will he swear he loves.

DON PEDRO   Nay, pray thee, come,   50
Or if thou wilt hold longer argument,
Do it in notes.

BALTHASAR   Note this before my notes:
There's not a note of mine that's worth the noting.

DON PEDRO
Why, these are very crotchets that he speaks.
Note notes forsooth, and nothing!   [*Balthasar plays.*]

BENEDICK   Now, divine air! Now is his soul ravished!   56
Is it not strange that sheep's guts should hale souls out
of men's bodies? Well, a horn for my money, when all's
done.

49 **To . . . worthy** i.e. Don Pedro flatters Balthasar's music much as a lover flatters a lady he doesn't truly believe worthy of his love, but woos nonetheless, out of custom or duplicity; this exchange and the song that follows are marked by an unusual (for this play) recognition of the role of male amatory untrustworthiness in female perfidy.

52 **notes** i.e. musical ones

54 **crotchets** musical notes; nonsense. Like a true euphuist, Don Pedro joins Balthasar in his lame punning even as he scolds him for it.

55 **nothing** In Elizabethan pronunciation, the *o* in 'nothing' was long, and the *th* could be sounded as *t*, so that 'noting' and 'nothing' sounded the same. See Kökeritz, 132; *WT* 4.4.614–15: 'no hearing, no feeling, but my sir's song, and admiring the nothing of it'. Possible puns here (as with the title of this play) include noticing; knowing; commenting; musical notes; nought; female or male genitalia; and virginity: cf. Philip Massinger, *Maid of Honour* (1621), 2.2.9, where the oath 'by my virginity' is described as 'a perlous oath / In a waiting-woman of fifteene, and is indeed a kinde of nothing' (Massinger, 1.139). The brothers Tasso (sig. C3ᵛ) elaborate: 'a woman that hath no being, but onely what is given to her, (as it were of Almes) from the ribbe of Man, shall without doubt fall under this infamous consideration of such a Non ens being nothing, or a thing without substance'.

56 **ravished** i.e. carried away with rapture, though literally raped or robbed, bereft of itself

57 **sheep's guts** i.e. the prosaic material that furnished the strings of a musical instrument
hale drag, haul

58 **horn** a hunting horn, which like the fife and the drum was a masculine instrument (with the usual emasculating innuendo)

55 nothing] noting *Theobald*   SD] *Capell subst.; Malone (Musick.)*

BALTHASAR *(Sings.)*

             Sigh no more, ladies, sigh no more,   60
               Men were deceivers ever;
             One foot in sea, and one on shore,
               To one thing constant never.
             Then sigh not so, but let them go,
               And be you blithe and bonny,   65
             Converting all your sounds of woe
               Into 'Hey, nonny, nonny'.

             Sing no more ditties, sing no more,
               Of dumps so dull and heavy;
             The fraud of men was ever so,   70
               Since summer first was leavy.
             Then sigh not so, but let them go,
               And be you blithe and bonny,
             Converting all your sounds of woe
               Into 'Hey, nonny, nonny'.   75

DON PEDRO   By my troth, a good song.

60–75 The song's theme of male inconstancy would be more portentous for the
play's audience at this point than for the
audience within the play (we are aware
of Don John's intentions), although
it is perhaps worth noting that Don
Pedro and Balthasar consider the song's
subject unremarkable, or innocent, or
fashionable enough for a love song.
W.H. Auden observes that 'the song
is actually about the irresponsibility of
men and the folly of women taking them
seriously, and recommends as an antidote
good humour and common sense. If
one imagines these sentiments being
the expression of a character, the only
character they suit is Beatrice' (Auden,

115). Shakespeare's other betrayed-
maiden songs include Ophelia's (*Ham*
4.5.23–66) and Desdemona's (*Oth*
4.3.39–46).

65 **blithe and bonny** merry and comely
67 **nonny, nonny** i.e. careless nothings;
'a meaningless refrain, formerly often
used to cover indelicate allusions'
(*OED* nonny-nonny)
69 **dumps** sad songs; drooping dances;
melancholic moods
dull melancholic
heavy ponderous; tedious
71 **leavy** full of leaves, i.e. the beginning
of the season of lovemaking
76 **troth** truth, faith (a form of assevera-
tion)

---

60 SP] *Capell* SD] *Capell subst. (The Song.); as heading before 60 Q* 67 'Hey, nonny, nonny'] *this
edn;* hey nony nony *Q* 68 ²more] *F2;* moe *Q* 70 was] *were F* 71 leavy] *leafy / Pope* 72–5]
Brooke; Then sigh not so, &c. *Q*

BALTHASAR   And an ill singer, my lord.

DON PEDRO   Ha? No, no, faith; thou sing'st well enough
for a shift.

BENEDICK [*aside*]   An he had been a dog that should have   80
howled thus, they would have hanged him. And I pray
God his bad voice bode no mischief. I had as lief have
heard the night-raven, come what plague could have
come after it.

DON PEDRO   Yea, marry, – dost thou hear, Balthasar? I   85
pray thee get us some excellent music, for tomorrow
night we would have it at the Lady Hero's chamber
window.

BALTHASAR   The best I can, my lord.

DON PEDRO   Do so. Farewell.   *Exit Balthasar.*

Come hither, Leonato. What was it you told me of   91
today? That your niece Beatrice was in love with Signor
Benedick?

CLAUDIO [*aside*]   O ay, stalk on, stalk on, the fowl sits.
[*Raises his voice.*] I did never think that lady would have   95
loved any man.

LEONATO   No, nor I neither. But most wonderful that she
should so dote on Signor Benedick, whom she hath in
all outward behaviours seemed ever to abhor.

---

79 **a shift** i.e. in a pinch, as a stop-gap

82 **lief** readily

83 **night-raven** a proverbial harbinger of doom. Cf. Dent, R33: 'The croaking raven bodes disaster'; *FQ*, 2.12.36.5: 'The hoars night-rauen, trump of dolefull drere'; and Lyly, *Sappho and Phao*, 3.359–60: 'the owle hath not shrikte at the window, or the night Rauen croked, both being fatall' (*Works*, 2.397).

85 **Yea, marry** addressed to either Claudio or Leonato (whoever has made the suggestion about providing a serenade at Hero's chamber window); the phrase indicates the conversation in progress between the conspirators while Benedick speaks to the audience.

86 **get . . . music** i.e. get us some (more) excellent music, although asking Balthasar to procure (other) excellent music perhaps could corroborate Benedick's estimate of Balthasar's talents

94 **stalk . . . sits** proceed carefully, our prey is waiting to be caught

80 SD] *Johnson*   An] *(and)*   82 lief] *F*; liue *Q*
Capell   94 SD] *after* sits *Johnson subst.*   ay] *(I)*   90 SD] *after 89 Q; Exeunt Balthasar and Music / 95 SD] Oxf¹*

BENEDICK   Is't possible? Sits the wind in that corner?   100
LEONATO   By my troth, my lord, I cannot tell what to
think of it. But that she loves him with an enraged
affection, it is past the infinite of thought.
DON PEDRO   Maybe she doth but counterfeit.
CLAUDIO   Faith, like enough.   105
LEONATO   O God! Counterfeit? There was never
counterfeit of passion came so near the life of passion
as she discovers it.
DON PEDRO   Why, what effects of passion shows she?
CLAUDIO [*aside*]   Bait the hook well, this fish will bite!   110
LEONATO   What effects, my lord? She will sit you – you
heard my daughter tell you how.
CLAUDIO   She did indeed.
DON PEDRO   How, how, I pray you? You amaze me! I
would have thought her spirit had been invincible   115
against all assaults of affection.
LEONATO   I would have sworn it had, my lord; especially
against Benedick.

100 **Sits . . . corner** proverbial (Dent, W419: 'Is the wind in that door?'), e.g. 'Is that the way the wind blows?' The wind was thought to blow from one of the four quarters of the earth (i.e. north, south, east or west).

102 **enraged** i.e. passionate

102–3 *it. But . . . it** Q's light punctuation (see t.n.) allows for two different meanings: (1) 'I cannot avoid thinking that she loves him to distraction'; (2) 'The degree to which she loves him distractedly passes the utmost reach of thought.'

103 **past . . . thought** unthinkable but true

108 **discovers** displays, reveals

109 **effects** signs; love-melancholy was understood to be accompanied by a host of distinctive behaviours, or 'signs diagnosticke' (Ferrand, 106), such as Beatrice is reported to exhibit at 140–2. Cf. 3.2.37–8: 'If he be not in love with some woman there is no believing old signs.'

111 **sit you – you** Q's punctuation (see t.n.) can be read as a use of the Latin ethical dative, which emphasizes the hearer's interest in the answer (Furness); in performance, however, the sense likely to be conveyed is that of Leonato drawing a blank as to how to answer the Prince's question, stuttering, and then attempting to appeal to Claudio (or to the Prince) for reply: 'Sit – you, you'. The use of the future tense (*will sit*) indicates a repeated action in the past (as at 132).

102–3 it. . . . affection,] *Oxf¹ (Pope)*; it, . . . affection, *Q;* it, . . . affection; *Steevens²*   110, 122 SD] *Theobald*   111 sit you – you] *(sit you, you)*

BENEDICK I should think this a gull, but that the
white-bearded fellow speaks it. Knavery cannot, sure, 120
hide himself in such reverence.

CLAUDIO [*aside*] He hath ta'en th'infection; hold it up!

DON PEDRO Hath she made her affection known to
Benedick?

LEONATO No, and swears she never will. That's her 125
torment.

CLAUDIO 'Tis true indeed, so your daughter says. 'Shall
I,' says she, 'that have so oft encountered him with
scorn, write to him that I love him?'

LEONATO This says she now, when she is beginning to 130
write to him; for she'll be up twenty times a night, and
there will she sit in her smock till she have writ a sheet
of paper. My daughter tells us all.

CLAUDIO Now you talk of a sheet of paper, I remember a
pretty jest your daughter told us of. 135

LEONATO O, when she had writ it, and was reading it
over, she found 'Benedick' and 'Beatrice' between the
sheet?

CLAUDIO That.

119 **gull** hoax
120 **white-bearded fellow** i.e. Leonato
    Knavery trickery
121 **himself** itself
    reverence esteemed old age
122 **ta'en th'infection** i.e. swallowed the
    bait; the metaphor connotes the sta-
    tus of love as an illness. Claudio's
    comment indicates some action on
    Benedick's part that would demon-
    strate his having become persuaded
    or further intrigued by what he over-
    hears.
    hold it up keep the jest going

132 **smock** chemise
    have writ has written; in Leonato's
    jest, as in her own behaviour (revealed
    in 5.4), Beatrice demonstrates her love
    by writing to Benedick.
135 **pretty jest** droll incident
136 **she** i.e. Beatrice
    it . . . it i.e. the piece of paper
137–8 **between the sheet** literally,
    between the (folded) sheet of paper, but
    with sexual innuendo, i.e. bedsheets,
    cf. *TGV* 1.2.123–9
139 **That** yes, that one (jest; with perhaps
    an eye-roll at its familiarity)

120 white-bearded] (white bearded), *F*   127–9 'Shall . . . him?'] *Capell subst.*; shall . . . him? *Q*   135
us of] *F*; of vs *Q*   137 'Benedick' . . . 'Beatrice'] *Cam¹*; Benedick . . . Beatrice *Q*

LEONATO   O, she tore the letter into a thousand halfpence,   140
   railed at herself that she should be so immodest to
   write to one that she knew would flout her. 'I measure
   him', says she, 'by my own spirit; for I should flout him,
   if he writ to me – yea, though I loved him I should.'
CLAUDIO   Then down upon her knees she falls, weeps,   145
   sobs, beats her heart, tears her hair, prays, curses, 'O
   sweet Benedick! God give me patience!'
LEONATO   She doth indeed; my daughter says so. And the
   ecstasy hath so much overborne her that my daughter
   is sometime afeard she will do a desperate outrage to   150
   herself. It is very true.
DON PEDRO   It were good that Benedick knew of it by
   some other, if she will not discover it.
CLAUDIO   To what end? He would make but a sport of it
   and torment the poor lady worse.   155
DON PEDRO   An he should, it were an alms to hang him.
   She's an excellent sweet lady, and, out of all suspicion,
   she is virtuous.
CLAUDIO   And she is exceeding wise.
DON PEDRO   In everything but in loving Benedick.   160
LEONATO   O my lord, wisdom and blood combating in so
   tender a body, we have ten proofs to one that blood hath

---

140 **halfpence** i.e. small pieces (pronounced 'hàypense')
141 **railed at** berated
142, 143 **flout** disdain, scorn
149 **ecstasy** transport, frenzy
153 **other** i.e. other persons
   discover reveal
156 **An** if
   alms act of charity
157 **out . . . suspicion** beyond all doubt
158–9 **virtuous . . . wise** The uncanny

way in which these particular attributes
echo Benedick's own criteria at 28ff.
could suggest a staging of this scene in
which the hoaxers had overheard the
latter end of Benedick's description
of his ideal spouse (or that they had
heard him on the same subject at
another time; or that such criteria were
conventional considerations, qualities
that any man would desire in a wife).

161, 162 **blood** passion

142–4 'I . . . should.'] *Capell subst.;* I . . . should. *Q*   144 loved] *Oxf¹ (Wells);* loue *Q*   146–7 'O
. . . patience!'] *Capell subst.;* O . . . patience. *Q*   154 make but] but make *F*   156 An] *(And)*

the victory. I am sorry for her, as I have just cause, being
her uncle and her guardian.

DON PEDRO   I would she had bestowed this dotage on me.   165
I would have doffed all other respects and made her
half myself. I pray you tell Benedick of it and hear what
'a will say.

LEONATO   Were it good, think you?

CLAUDIO   Hero thinks surely she will die, for she says she   170
will die if he love her not, and she will die ere she
make her love known, and she will die if he woo her,
rather than she will bate one breath of her accustomed
crossness.

DON PEDRO   She doth well. If she should make tender of   175
her love 'tis very possible he'll scorn it, for the man, as
you know all, hath a contemptible spirit.

CLAUDIO   He is a very proper man.

DON PEDRO   He hath indeed a good outward happiness.

CLAUDIO   Before God, and in my mind very wise.   180

DON PEDRO   He doth indeed show some sparks that are
like wit.

CLAUDIO   And I take him to be valiant.

DON PEDRO   As Hector, I assure you. And in the
managing of quarrels you may say he is wise, for either   185

---

165 **bestowed this dotage** conferred
this love
166 **doffed** set aside; cf. 5.1.78 and n.
respects considerations (such as difference in rank); Don Pedro has a habit
of imagining himself the lover of his
subordinates' women.
167 **half myself** i.e. my other half
173 **bate** forgo
174 **crossness** intemperance, cussedness,
obstructiveness
175 **tender** offer
177 **contemptible** contemptuous, scornful, but also worthy of contempt (hence

Claudio's defence)
178 **proper** handsome; admirable (although
Don Pedro's reformulation weakens this
sense)
179 **outward happiness** external appearance
181 **sparks** traces (signs of fire)
182 **wit** intelligence
184 **Hector** valiant Trojan leader in
Homer's *Iliad*, slain by Achilles, who
subsequently dragged Hector's corpse
three times around Troy's walls
(22.465ff.)
185 **wise** prudent

166 doffed] *Pope (*doft*); daft Q   168 'a] he *F*   180 Before] 'Fore *F*   183 SP] *Leon. F*

he avoids them with great discretion, or undertakes
them with a most Christian-like fear.

LEONATO   If he do fear God, 'a must necessarily keep
peace; if he break the peace, he ought to enter into a
quarrel with fear and trembling.   190

DON PEDRO   And so will he do, for the man doth fear God,
howsoever it seems not in him by some large jests he
will make. Well, I am sorry for your niece. Shall we go
seek Benedick and tell him of her love?

CLAUDIO   Never tell him, my lord. Let her wear it out   195
with good counsel.

LEONATO   Nay, that's impossible; she may wear her heart
out first.

DON PEDRO   Well, we will hear further of it by your
daughter. Let it cool the while. I love Benedick well,   200
and I could wish he would modestly examine himself to
see how much he is unworthy so good a lady.

LEONATO   My lord, will you walk? Dinner is ready.

CLAUDIO [*to Don Pedro and Leonato*]   If he do not dote on
her upon this, I will never trust my expectation.   205

DON PEDRO [*to Leonato and Claudio*]   Let there be the
same net spread for her, and that must your daughter
and her gentlewomen carry. The sport will be when
they hold one an opinion of another's dotage, and no
such matter. That's the scene that I would see, which   210

---

187 **Christian-like** i.e. with his mind
  duly on his mortal end (with a
  suggestion of cowardice)
192 **by** to judge by
  large broad, indelicate
196 **counsel** advice
200 **it** i.e. love

202 **unworthy** undeserving of
203 **walk** i.e. within doors
205 **expectation** ability to predict
208 **carry** manage
209–10 **they . . . matter** each holds the
  same opinion of the other's being in
  love, and none of it is true

---

187 most] *om. F*   194 seek] see *F*   202 unworthy] vnworthy to haue *F*   204, 206 SD] *Theobald*
208 gentlewomen] gentlewoman *F*   209 one . . . another's] an opinion of one another's *Pope;* one
opinion of the other's *Oxf¹ (Craven)*

will be merely a dumb-show. Let us send her to call him
in to dinner.   [*Exeunt all but Benedick.*]
BENEDICK [*Emerges.*] This can be no trick. The
conference was sadly borne; they have the truth of this
from Hero. They seem to pity the lady. It seems her   215
affections have their full bent. Love me? Why, it must
be requited. I hear how I am censured: they say I will
bear myself proudly if I perceive the love come from
her. They say too that she will rather die than give any
sign of affection. I did never think to marry. I must not   220
seem proud; happy are they that hear their detractions
and can put them to mending. They say the lady is fair
– 'tis a truth, I can bear them witness. And virtuous –
'tis so, I cannot reprove it. And wise, but for loving
me. By my troth, it is no addition to her wit – nor no   225
great argument of her folly, for I will be horribly in
love with her. I may chance have some odd quirks and
remnants of wit broken on me because I have railed so
long against marriage. But doth not the appetite alter?
A man loves the meat in his youth that he cannot   230

---

211 **dumb-show** a mimed dramatic practice used to preview the events of a plot
(as in *Ham* 3.2.137 SD), and by the time
of *MA*'s composition, a device of somewhat archaic reputation (Gurr, 174); i.e.
both notoriously witty parties will be at
an uncharacteristic loss for words, which
is indeed what happens at 4.1.255ff.
214 **sadly borne** seriously conducted
216 **bent** scope (as in a drawn bow)
   Love . . . it Derek Jacobi, in the 1984
RSC production, directed by Terry
Hands, delivered these words as 'Love
me? Why? It'.
217 **censured** judged
218–21 **proudly . . . proud** disdainfully

. . . disdainful
221 **detractions** faults criticized
224 **reprove** disprove
226 **argument** proof, evidence
227 **chance have** happen to have by
chance, perhaps
   quirks quibbles, quips
228 **remnants** dregs, rags; see 1.1.266–
7 for a similar comparison of wit and
clothing: 'The body of your discourse
is sometime guarded with fragments'.
   broken on levelled against; see
5.1.137n.
   railed ranted
230 **meat** with a pun on 'mate', as at
1.1.44, 115

---

212 SD *Exeunt*] *(Exeunt.)* F   *all but Benedick*] *Capell subst.*   213 *Emerges*] *Capell subst.; advances
from the Arbour / Theobald*   216 *their*] *the* F   225 *wit –*] *(wit,)*

endure in his age. Shall quips and sentences and these
paper bullets of the brain awe a man from the career of
his humour? No, the world must be peopled. When I
said I would die a bachelor, I did not think I should live
till I were married.   235

Enter BEATRICE.

Here comes Beatrice. By this day, she's a fair lady! I do
spy some marks of love in her.

BEATRICE   Against my will I am sent to bid you come in
to dinner.

BENEDICK   Fair Beatrice, I thank you for your pains.   240

BEATRICE   I took no more pains for those thanks than you
take pains to thank me. If it had been painful I would
not have come.

BENEDICK   You take pleasure, then, in the message?

BEATRICE   Yea, just so much as you may take upon a   245
knife's point and choke a daw withal. You have no
stomach, signor? Fare you well.   *Exit.*

---

231 **sentences** maxims, Latin *sententiae*
232 **paper bullets** literary clichés; flimsy
weapons
awe dissuade, intimidate
232–3 **career ... humour** (race)course or
path of his desire (*OED* career *sb.* 1b);
cf. 5.1.134–5: 'I shall meet your wit in
the career an you charge it against me.'
233 **peopled** populated; one of the
standard 'causes for which matrimony
was ordained', as noted in the *Book of
Common Prayer*: 'the procreation of
children to be brought up in the fear
and nurture of the Lord, and praise of
God' (*BCP*, 290)
240 Benedick's first lover-like address
to Beatrice is a verse line, perhaps

an involuntary instance; Beatrice
pointedly does not respond in kind.
246 **choke a daw** silence a jackdaw (a
small crow easily taught to imitate
human speech, and a proverbially
stupid bird), i.e. as much pleasure as
you would get from blocking the throat
of a small and gullible bird (very little,
presumably). A daw was a common
term for a foolish person. The image is
of feeding morsels to a tame bird from
the point of a knife.
withal with; the strong form derives
from the awkwardness of the preposition
at the end of the sentence.
246–7 **You . . . stomach** i.e. aren't you
hungry

236 SD] *after 237 Q*   246 choke] not choke *Oxf¹ (Collier MS)*   247 signor] *(signior)*

BENEDICK   Ha! 'Against my will I am sent to bid you come
in to dinner' – there's a double meaning in that. 'I took
no more pains for those thanks than you took pains to   250
thank me' – that's as much as to say, 'Any pains that I
take for you is as easy as thanks.' If I do not take pity of
her I am a villain; if I do not love her I am a Jew. I will
go get her picture.   *Exit.*

[**3.1**]   *Enter* HERO *and two gentlewomen,*
                      MARGARET *and* URSULA.

HERO
  Good Margaret, run thee to the parlour;
  There shalt thou find my cousin Beatrice

248–52 **Against . . . thanks** 'Whereas
we have previously seen that Benedick
does not want to marry, and have been
amused by the specious way in which
he used logic to avoid that issue, now
we see that he does want to marry, and
that the same tools serve his turn . . .
he turns inside out the conventions
of repartee which Shakespeare has so
thoroughly established. For instead of
taking an unflattering second meaning
and returning it with addition, he takes
an insolent surface meaning and then
bends all his wits to discover a hidden
compliment' (Vickers, 185).

253 **a villain** of base character, a scoundrel (from the French *vilein*, serf or
peasant)
  Jew i.e. ungenerous person (from
the Elizabethan caricature of Jews as
rapacious usurers, void of Christian
charity); person of no faith (from a
Christian perspective). Many modern

productions change this word to
another (e.g. villain, fool), or delete it
altogether.

254 **her picture** Aristocratic Elizabethan
lovers were wont to commission
miniature portraits of their beloveds
– one of the *behaviours* dedicated to
love (see 109n.).

3.1 The location is the orchard; as in the
previous scene, some place must exist
for Beatrice to conceal herself, and this
scene can pose a difficulty for actresses
playing Beatrice, who are faced with the
problem of how not to repeat Benedick's
choices. Sometimes her hiding place
has provided an explanation for the
cold Beatrice has contracted as of 3.4
(for instance wet laundry, a pond, or
under plants that are watered by Hero
and Ursula). It is not clear how much
time has passed between this and the
previous scene, in which Benedick was
called in to dinner.

248–51 'Against . . . dinner' . . . 'I . . . me'] *Theobald subst.;* against . . . dinner . . . I . . . me
Q 251–2 'Any . . . thanks.'] *Alexander subst.;* any . . . thanks: *Q* 3.1] *Actus Tertius. F;* scene i *Rowe*
0.1 *gentlewomen*] *Gentlemen F* 0.2 URSULA] *(Vrsley)*

Proposing with the prince and Claudio;
Whisper her ear and tell her I and Ursley
Walk in the orchard, and our whole discourse   5
Is all of her. Say that thou overheard'st us,
And bid her steal into the pleached bower
Where honeysuckles ripened by the sun
Forbid the sun to enter, like favourites
Made proud by princes that advance their pride   10
Against that power that bred it; there will she hide her
To listen our propose. This is thy office,
Bear thee well in it, and leave us alone.

MARGARET   I'll make her come, I warrant you, presently.

                                                    [*Exit.*]

HERO

Now, Ursula, when Beatrice doth come,   15
As we do trace this alley up and down
Our talk must only be of Benedick.
When I do name him, let it be thy part
To praise him more than ever man did merit;

---

3 **Proposing** conversing; along with
propose at 12, Shakespeare's only use
of the term in this sense
4 **Ursley** a familiar pronunciation of
Ursula
7 **pleached bower** pleachèd: see 1.2.8.
A bower is an arbour or alley formed
of intertwined branches, in this case
with honeysuckle vine growing over
it.
9–11 **like . . . it** like privileged courtiers
who seek to challenge the authority of
the ruler who favours them; these lines
are often cut in production. Harry
Berger Jr observes that 'this is dis-
placed analysis of the whole situation
. . . Beatrice is the rebellious favorite
advancing her virgin pride against
the masculine forces that ripen it –

the solar energy of parents, princes,
admirers' (Berger, 306).
11 **her** herself
12 **our** perhaps spoken with an emphasis
to distinguish it from the proposing of
the men in the parlour
propose conversation; F's 'purpose'
is viable (if unmetrical), and this is the
only location in Shakespeare where
propose means conversation, but the
repetition from 3 argues for Q's form.
office duty, charge
13 **Bear . . . it** perform it skilfully
14 **presently** immediately; Q's punctuation (see t.n.) does not indicate
whether the word refers to Margaret's
action or to Beatrice's.
16 **trace** tread, follow the direction of
alley bordered garden path

---

4 Ursley] *Vrsula F*   12 propose] purpose *F*   14 you, presently] you presently *Q*   14 SD] *F2*

My talk to thee must be how Benedick   20
Is sick in love with Beatrice. Of this matter
Is little Cupid's crafty arrow made,
That only wounds by hearsay.

Enter BEATRICE[, *who hides*].

Now begin,
For look where Beatrice like a lapwing runs
Close by the ground to hear our conference.   25
URSULA [*to Hero*]
The pleasant'st angling is to see the fish
Cut with her golden oars the silver stream
And greedily devour the treacherous bait;
So angle we for Beatrice, who even now
Is couched in the woodbine coverture.   30
Fear you not my part of the dialogue.
HERO [*to Ursula*]
Then go we near her, that her ear lose nothing

---

23 **only wounds** wounds only
24 **lapwing** a ground-nesting bird
(plover) noted for its cunning in
drawing intruders away from its nest
by various diversionary tactics, 'who
fearing her young ones to be destroyed
by passengers, flieth with a false cry
far from their nests, making those
that look for them seek where they
are not' (Lyly, *Euphues*, 4); the term
perhaps suggests the erratic nature
of Beatrice's motion across the stage.
The bird was also a figure of a specifically female deceit, as in e.g. *The Court
of Good Counsel* (1607): 'those women
whose minds are not deckt of virtue,
are those which labour aboue all others in decking up their bodies, thinking belike to haue as good luck as the

lapwing, who though but a vile bird,
and liueth most in durty lakes and
desert places, yet at the marriage of
the eagle, she was honourable aboue
all other birds, because of the crowne
on her head, and of her dyed feathers'
(W. B., sig. D3ʳ).
26 **angling** fishing; much as Benedick's
gullers describe him as prey in the previous scene, Beatrice is imagined here
as a fish about to be caught.
27 **oars** i.e. fins
28 **treacherous** because it hides a hook
30 **couched** couchèd: hidden; ensconced
closely
woodbine coverture honeysuckle
covering, canopy
31 i.e. don't worry about my ability to
play my part

23 SD *Enter* BEATRICE] *Oxf¹; after 25 Q; after 23 F   who hides*] *Theobald subst. (running towards the
arbour)   26 SD*] *Foakes   30 woodbine*] *(wood-bine), Theobald   32 SD*] *Foakes*

Of the false sweet bait that we lay for it.
[*They approach Beatrice's hiding place.*]
— No, truly, Ursula, she is too disdainful.
I know her spirits are as coy and wild   35
As haggards of the rock.

URSULA   But are you sure
That Benedick loves Beatrice so entirely?

HERO
So says the prince and my new-trothed lord.

URSULA
And did they bid you tell her of it, madam?

HERO
They did entreat me to acquaint her of it;   40
But I persuaded them, if they loved Benedick,
To wish him wrestle with affection
And never to let Beatrice know of it.

URSULA
Why did you so? Doth not the gentleman
Deserve at full as fortunate a bed   45
As ever Beatrice shall couch upon?

---

35 **coy** evasive
36 **haggards** untamed mature female hawks (as opposed to those raised from nestlings by human hands, in order to hunt), and hence a figure for unruly women of deceptive wiles and feigned reluctance. Cf. *TS* 4.2.39: 'this proud disdainful haggard'; Lyly, *Anatomy*, 219: 'I know not whether it is peculiar to that sex to dissemble with those who they most desire, or whether they haue learned outwardly to loth that which they most loue, yet wisely did she cast this in her head, if she should yeelde at the first assault he woulde thinke hir a lighte huswife, if she should reiect him scornfully a very haggard.' Edmund

Bert's *Treatise of Hawks and Hunting* (1619) notes that 'your haggard is very loving and kinde to her keeper, after he hath brought her by his sweet and kind familiarity to understand him' (Bert, cited in Furness). Beatrice employs similar imagery in her soliloquy at the end of the scene (112).
38 **new-trothed** trothèd; newly pledged or betrothed
42 **affection** his passion
45–6 *****at . . . upon** fully as blessed a marriage bed as Beatrice will inhabit (*OED* full *a.*, *sb.³* and *adv.* B 1); Q's 'as full' may be a compositor's error for 'at full'.

---

33 SD] *Steevens subst. (they advance to the bower); approaching Beatrice's hiding place* Oxf   38 new-trothed] *(new trothed), Theobald*   42 wrestle] *(wrastle)*   45 at full] *this edn; as full Q*

HERO

    O god of love! I know he doth deserve

    As much as may be yielded to a man.

    But Nature never framed a woman's heart

    Of prouder stuff than that of Beatrice.   50

    Disdain and Scorn ride sparkling in her eyes,

    Misprising what they look on, and her wit

    Values itself so highly that to her

    All matter else seems weak. She cannot love,

    Nor take no shape nor project of affection,   55

    She is so self-endeared.

URSULA   Sure, I think so.

    And therefore certainly it were not good

    She knew his love, lest she'll make sport at it.

HERO

    Why, you speak truth. I never yet saw man –

    How wise, how noble, young, how rarely featured –   60

---

48 **yielded** allowed, credited

51 **sparkling** flashing; the metaphor animates Disdain and Scorn (as at 1.1.114, 'Is it possible Disdain should die?').

52 **Misprising** misconstruing, misvaluing, with the connotation of seeing it as worse than it is in fact
they her eyes; Disdain and Scorn

54 **All matter else** anyone else's conversation

55 **take . . . affection** understand the form or nature of love

56 **self-endeared** enamoured of herself

59–68 Such exaggerations and conversions of virtues into defects as Beatrice reputedly performs were described by Lyly as a particularly female form of euphuism: 'Dost thou not know that women deeme none valyaunt, vnlesse he be too venturesome? That they accompte one a dastarde, if he be not desperate, a pinch penny and if he be

not prodigall, if silent a sotte, if ful of wordes a foole'; 'If he be cleanly, then terme they him proude, if meane in apparel, a slouen, if bolde, blunte, if shamefaste, a coward' (Lyly, *Anatomy*, 249, 254). Such conversions were recommended to men by Ovid in his *Remedies of Love Translated and Intituled to the Youth of England* (1600) as a means of avoiding or exorcising love: 'If she be fat, that she is swollen say: / If browne, then tawny like the Affrike Moor / If slender, leane, meger, and worne away / If courtly, wanton, worst of worst before / If modest, strange, as fitteth womanhead, / Say she is rusticke, clownishe, and ill-bred' (Ovid, *Remedies*, sig. D1ʳ, and paraphrased in Lyly, *Anatomy*, 102). Cf. Petruchio's reversal of the convention in *TS* 2.1.171–81, 237–56.

60 **rarely** exceptionally, handsomely

56 self-endeared] (selfe indeared), Rowe   58 she'll] she *F*

But she would spell him backward. If fair-faced,
She would swear the gentleman should be her sister;
If black, why Nature, drawing of an antic,
Made a foul blot; if tall, a lance ill-headed;
If low, an agate very vilely cut;   65
If speaking, why, a vane blown with all winds;
If silent, why, a block moved with none.
So turns she every man the wrong side out,
And never gives to truth and virtue that
Which simpleness and merit purchaseth.   70

URSULA
Sure, sure, such carping is not commendable.

HERO
No, not to be so odd and from all fashions
As Beatrice is cannot be commendable.
But who dare tell her so? If I should speak,
She would mock me into air. O, she would laugh me   75

---

61 **spell him backward** misrepresent his virtues as vices; witches were imagined to conjure devils by praying in reverse.
  fair-faced of light complexion (a stereotypical female virtue); fresh faced
63 **black** of dark colouring
63–4 **Nature . . . blot** Nature, caricaturing a grotesque, or clown, blotted her composition (or created an ugly image); cf. 5.1.96, *Go anticly*.
64 **lance ill-headed** spear with a dull point
65 If short, an ill-fashioned dwarf; an agate was a gemstone often carved with diminutive figures. Cf. *2H4* 1.2.16–17, for Falstaff's description of his page: 'I was never manned with an agate till now'; and *RJ* 1.4.55–6: 'In shape no bigger than an agate stone / On the forefinger of an alderman'.

66 **vane . . . winds** implies verbose but also inconstant or indiscriminate speech; a vane is a weathervane.
67 **block** See 2.1.220n.
  moved movèd
70 **simpleness** straightforward integrity; cf. *MND* 5.1.82–3: 'never anything can be amiss / When simpleness and duty tender it'.
  purchaseth earn, deserve; for the singular verb after two subject nouns see Abbott, 336.
71, 73 **commendable** pronounced with an accent on the first and third syllables
72 **from all fashions** contrary to, eccentrically divergent from, customary compliment and female decorum
75 **mock . . . air** i.e. ridicule me into nothingness
75–6 **laugh . . . myself** i.e. reduce me to silence

---

61 fair-faced] *(faire faced), F4*   63 antic] *F (anticke);* antique *Q*   64 ill-headed] *(ill headed), F2*   65 agate] *(agot)*   vilely] *(vildly)*

Out of myself, press me to death with wit!
Therefore let Benedick, like covered fire,
Consume away in sighs, waste inwardly.
It were a better death than die with mocks,
Which is as bad as die with tickling.   80

URSULA

Yet tell her of it; hear what she will say.

HERO

No, rather I will go to Benedick
And counsel him to fight against his passion.
And truly, I'll devise some honest slanders
To stain my cousin with: one doth not know   85
How much an ill word may empoison liking.

URSULA

O, do not do your cousin such a wrong!
She cannot be so much without true judgement,
Having so swift and excellent a wit

---

76 **press . . . death** a figure based on the
torture of the '*peine forte et dure*' ('strong
and severe punishment'), in which heavy
weights were loaded upon the criminals
who refused to plead. Most figurative
uses referred to the silence of the victim; cf. *R2* 3.4.71–2: 'O, I am pressed
to death / Through want of speaking!';
Son 140.1–2: 'Be wise as thou art cruel,
do not press / My tongue-tied patience
with too much disdain'.

77 **covered fire** either fire that will burn
all the more fiercely for being damped
down (proverbial: 'Fire that's closest
kept burns most of all', Dent, F265), or
fire that will sputter out for want of oxy-
gen. Either case implies that Benedick
must keep his passion concealed.

78 **Consume away** A sigh was thought
to cost the heart a drop of blood.
  sighs i.e. draughts of air (and the
wordless hallmark of the lover). Cf.
1.1.190.

80 **tickling** three syllables

84 **honest slanders** Hero proposes to
defame her cousin, albeit 'honestly',
by concentrating on foibles rather than
sins, much in the same way that Don
John plans to 'stain' her own reputation;
honest slanders were unlikely to attack
chastity (or 'honesty').

86 **empoison** Cf. 2.2.19: 'The poison of
that lies in you to temper.'

89 **so . . . wit** a female virtue, according
to Nicholas Breton in *The Praise of
Virtuous Ladies* (1606): 'Nowadays,
men are so fantastical (I dare not say
foolish) that if a woman be not so
wise as to make a man a fool, she is
no wise woman. No, forsooth, but he
is a very wise man to match with such
a woman. Women have wit naturally;
wisdom must be had by grace; grace
was given to our Lady; then who wiser
than a woman?' (Breton, *Praise*, 61).
Lyly's Fidus concurs: 'of all creatures

79 than] *(then)*; to F

225

As she is prized to have, as to refuse   90
So rare a gentleman as Signor Benedick.

HERO

He is the only man of Italy –
Always excepted my dear Claudio.

URSULA

I pray you, be not angry with me, madam,
Speaking my fancy. Signor Benedick,   95
For shape, for bearing, argument and valour,
Goes foremost in report through Italy.

HERO

Indeed, he hath an excellent good name.

URSULA

His excellence did earn it ere he had it.
When are you married, madam?   100

HERO

Why, every day, tomorrow! Come, go in,
I'll show thee some attires, and have thy counsel
Which is the best to furnish me tomorrow.

URSULA [*to Hero*]

She's limed, I warrant you! We have caught her,
  madam!

---

the woman's wit is the most excellent,
therefore have the poets feigned the
muses to be women, they nymphs,
goddesses, ensaumples of whose rare
wisdomes and sharp capacities would
nothing but make me commit idolatry
of my daughter' (Lyly, *Euphues*, 263).
90 **prized** esteemed; like Benedick's
  gullers, Hero and Ursula solicit the
  intellectual vanity of their prey to the
  cause of loving.
91 **rare** exceptional
92 **only** unrivalled
95 **fancy** conviction

96 **bearing** deportment
  argument reason, discourse
97 **Goes . . . through** i.e. has the best
  reputation in
99 i.e. he came by it through merit
101 **every day, tomorrow** as of tomorrow, forever
102 **attires** clothing
104 **limed** caught (from birdlime, an
  adhesive substance fashioned from the
  bark of holly trees, used to capture
  small birds). Ursula's observation suggests some revealing stage action by
  Beatrice.

91 as Signor Benedick] as Benedick *Pope*   91, 95 Signor] *(signior)*   96 bearing,] *F4;* bearing
Q   101 day, tomorrow!] *Rowe (*Day, to morrow;*);* euerie day to morrow, *Q*   104 SD] *Capell*   limed]
tane *F*   104] *Pope; Q lines* you, / madame. /

HERO [*to Ursula*]

If it prove so, then loving goes by haps;   105
Some Cupid kills with arrows, some with traps.

[*Exeunt all but Beatrice.*]

BEATRICE

What fire is in mine ears? Can this be true?
Stand I condemned for pride and scorn so much?
Contempt, farewell; and maiden pride, adieu;
  No glory lives behind the back of such.   110
And Benedick, love on, I will requite thee,
  Taming my wild heart to thy loving hand.
If thou dost love, my kindness shall incite thee
  To bind our loves up in a holy band.
For others say thou dost deserve, and I   115
Believe it better than reportingly.   *Exit.*

[3.2]   *Enter* DON PEDRO, CLAUDIO,
                         BENEDICK *and* LEONATO.

DON PEDRO   I do but stay till your marriage be
consummate, and then go I toward Aragon.

105 **haps** chance, accident; Cupid's blindfolded marksmanship always involves
some element of chance.
107 Beatrice speaks verse here (an abbreviated sonnet) for the first time in the play
(a rare event for her, though we will see
her capable of composing it in 5.4).
fire . . . ears i.e. Beatrice's ears are
burning, both because she hears herself being spoken of, and because what
she hears hits home.
110 **lives . . . of** attends, follows
such persons possessed of such qualities
112 Beatrice's language picks up on the
imagery of wild birds used by her
gullers, although she herself will be

the one doing the taming, rather than
submitting to another's rule. It was
thought that a hawk could be tamed
only by love; see 36n.
114 **a holy band** i.e. marriage
116 **better than reportingly** i.e. intrinsically, on grounds other than hearsay (an unusual conviction in a play
where so much is construed as a result
of report). Many modern productions
break for intermission at this point.
3.2 The location is Leonato's house or
environs.
2 **consummate** celebrated ritually (but
also in a sexual sense). See also *predes-
tinate*, 1.1.128 and n.

105 SD] *Capell (aside)*   106 SD] *Rowe (Exeunt); Exeunt Hero, and Ursula. Beatrice advances /
Theobald; Exit. F; not in Q*   111 on] *Qc, F; one Qu*   3.2] scene ii *Pope*   0.1 DON PEDRO] *Rowe;
Prince Q*   1+ SP] *Rowe (Pedro.); Capell (D. Pe.); Prince Q*

CLAUDIO   I'll bring you thither, my lord, if you'll
vouchsafe me.

DON PEDRO   Nay, that would be as great a soil in the new   5
gloss of your marriage as to show a child his new coat
and forbid him to wear it. I will only be bold with
Benedick for his company, for from the crown of his
head to the sole of his foot, he is all mirth. He hath
twice or thrice cut Cupid's bowstring, and the little   10
hangman dare not shoot at him. He hath a heart as
sound as a bell, and his tongue is the clapper: for what
his heart thinks, his tongue speaks.

BENEDICK   Gallants, I am not as I have been.

LEONATO   So say I; methinks you are sadder.   15

CLAUDIO   I hope he be in love.

DON PEDRO   Hang him, truant! There's no true drop of
blood in him to be truly touched with love. If he be sad,
he wants money.

BENEDICK   I have the toothache.   20

DON PEDRO   Draw it.

BENEDICK   Hang it!

---

3   **bring you thither** escort, accompany
you thither (i.e. to Aragon, his home)
4   **vouchsafe** allow
5   **soil in** stain on
7   **be bold with** ask
8–9   **from . . . foot** proverbial (Dent,
C864)
9   **all mirth** This comment is given
an ironic edge applied to a Benedick
freshly shaven and complaining of a
toothache to conceal the fact.
11   **hangman** i.e. rascal, rogue; cf. *TGV*
4.4.53–4: 'stolen from me by the hangman's boys'.
11–12   **as . . . bell** proverbial (Dent,
B272)

12–13   **for . . . speaks** proverbial (Dent,
H334); Don Pedro perhaps varies the
proverb 'as the fool thinks, so the bell
chinks'.
15   **sadder** more serious, or, as at 49,
melancholic – a mark of a lover
17   **Hang him, truant** hang him, the
fickle one; Q's punctuation (see t.n.)
also suggests the possibility of 'hang
him for a truant', i.e. as a truant to love
or to his own vow to disdain love.
18   **blood** passion
19   **he wants** it is because he lacks
20   **toothache** See 24–5n.
21   **Draw** extract

17 Hang him, truant!] *Theobald (*hang him, truant,*)*; Hang him truant, *Q*

CLAUDIO   You must hang it first and draw it afterwards.

DON PEDRO   What? Sigh for the toothache?

LEONATO   Where is but a humour or a worm.   25

BENEDICK   Well, everyone can master a grief but he that has it.

CLAUDIO   Yet, say I, he is in love.

DON PEDRO   There is no appearance of fancy in him, unless it be a fancy that he hath to strange disguises: as   30

---

23 Hanging and drawing (disembowelling) was the punishment for traitors. Cf. Middleton, *The Widow* (1652), 4.1.105–6: '*Martino:* I pray, what's good, sir, for a wicked tooth? / *Ricardo:* Hang'd, drawn, and quartering' (Middleton, 5.193). Teeth were also hung in shop windows to indicate that dentistry was performed within.

24–5 **toothache . . . humour . . . worm** Toothaches and love were associated ailments. Cf. Francis Beaumont and John Fletcher, *The False One* (1620), 2.3.109–10: 'You had best be troubled with the tooth-ach too, / For Lovers ever are'; and Massinger, *The Parliament of Love* (1624), 1B.30–2: 'I am troubled / With the tooth ach, or with love, I know not whether: / There is a worme in both' (Massinger, 2.113). Toothache in Elizabethan medical thought was caused by humours descending from the head and/or by worms penetrating the tooth; cf. Bateman, 'Of the teeth', in *Upon Bartholomew*: 'The cause of such aking is humours that come downe from the heade . . . Also sometime teeth be pearced with holes & sometime by worms they be changed into yellow colour, greene, or black' (Bateman, 5.20). If Benedick is truly suffering (as opposed to hiding his newly shorn face in a towel), then his toothache joins Beatrice's cold as a physical sign

of emotional vulnerability. He is either claiming not to be sad because of love, or ostentatiously claiming he bears the marks of true love.

26–7 proverbial: 'All commend patience but none can endure to suffer' (Dent, A124), and 'The healthful man can give counsel to the sick' (M182); cf. 5.1.35–6: 'For there was never yet philosopher / That could endure the toothache patiently'.

29–30 **fancy . . . fancy** love . . . whim; the wordplay is repeated at 34–6.

30 **strange disguises** *strange* = foreign, outlandish. Presumably Benedick's transformation into a lover has been indicated sartorially, by an attempt at excessively fashionable dress; if so, he appears as the commonplace caricature of English gallants, who borrowed with indiscriminate enthusiasm from other countries' styles. Cf. *MV* 1.2.72–3, where Portia guesses that her English suitor 'bought his doublet in Italy, his round hose in France, his bonnet in Germany'; and Dekker's *Seven Deadly Sins*: 'For, an English-mans suite is like a traitors bodie that hath beene hanged, drawne, and quartered, and is set vp in seuerall places: the coller of his Dublet and the belly in Fraunce: the wing and narrow sleeue in Italy . . . thus wee that mocke euerie Nation, for keeping one fashion, yet steale patches

26 can] *Pope;* cannot *Q*

to be a Dutchman today, a Frenchman tomorrow – or
in the shape of two countries at once, as a German from
the waist downward, all slops, and a Spaniard from the
hip upward, no doublet. Unless he have a fancy to this
foolery – as it appears he hath – he is no fool for   35
fancy, as you would have it appear he is.

CLAUDIO   If he be not in love with some woman there is
no believing old signs. 'A brushes his hat o'mornings:
what should that bode?

DON PEDRO   Hath any man seen him at the barber's?   40

CLAUDIO   No, but the barber's man hath been seen with
him, and the old ornament of his cheek hath already
stuffed tennis balls.

LEONATO   Indeed, he looks younger than he did by the
loss of a beard.   45

from euerie one of them, to peece out
our pride, are now laughing stockes
to them, because their cut so scuruily
becomes vs' (Dekker, *Sins*, 60).
31–4 **or . . . doublet** This passage was
omitted from F, perhaps because the
play had been cut for performance
at Court during the wedding festivities of the Princess Elizabeth and the
Elector Palatine in 1613; or perhaps
because, as a Scot, King James was
sensitive to English caricatures of for-
eigners.
33 **slops** large loose breeches
34 **no doublet** i.e. all cloak, the hip-length
Spanish cape, according to Malone,
concealing a doublet (see 2.3.17n.).
A person dressed to this description
would be veritably overflowing in fab-
ric.
34–6 **Unless . . . is** i.e. unless it be the
case that he is given to this kind of
dress, as it appears he is from his attire,
then he is no lover, as you would construe it

38 **old signs** conventional marks; cf.
the 'marks' of love denoted in *AYL*
3.2.364–72: 'A lean cheek . . . a blue
eye and sunken . . . an unquestionable
spirit . . . a beard neglected . . . your
hose should be ungartered, your bonnet unbanded, your sleeve unbut-
toned, your shoe untied, and everything
about you demonstrating a careless
desolation.'
brushes his hat i.e. in order to clean it
(presumably, a mark of fastidiousness
that the soldierly Benedick would have
forgone)
39 **bode** indicate
43 **stuffed tennis balls** an actual practice.
Cf. Dekker, *The Shoemaker's Holiday*
(1600), 5.5.23–4: 'yet I'll shaue [my
beard off] and stuffe tennis balls with it
to please my bully king' (*Works*, 1.84).
Ard² surmises that perhaps Benedick
is aware of Beatrice's preference at
2.1.26–7; Benedick's action anticipates
Borachio's vision of the shaven
Hercules at 3.3.131–2.

31–4 or . . . doublet] *om. F*   36 it] it to *F*   38 o'] *(a)*

DON PEDRO   Nay, 'a rubs himself with civet. Can you
smell him out by that?

CLAUDIO   That's as much as to say the sweet youth's in love.

DON PEDRO   The greatest note of it is his melancholy.

CLAUDIO   And when was he wont to wash his face?   50

DON PEDRO   Yea, or to paint himself? For the which I
hear what they say of him.

CLAUDIO   Nay, but his jesting spirit, which is now crept
into a lute-string and now governed by stops.

---

46 **civet** a foppish perfume obtained from the scent glands of the civet cat; cf. *AYL* 3.2.60–1: 'The courtier's hands are perfumed with civet.'

47 **smell him out** smell his perfume; detect his secret; proverbial (Dent, S558)

50 **wash his face** perhaps with perfume (though not with civet): 'In Shakespeare's time our race had not abandoned itself to that reckless use of water, either for ablution or potation, which has more recently become one of its characteristic traits' (White, cited in Furness). Oxf¹ comments more generously: 'Benedick deserves the benefit of the doubt; he probably washes his face, though possibly more often post-Beatrice.'

51 **paint himself** use cosmetics
the which i.e. his use of cosmetics; according to Burton, the most damning of the love-stricken man's traits: they 'go beyond women, they wear harlot's colours, and do not walk but jet and dance, he-women, she-men, more like players, Butterflies, Baboons, Apes, Antickes, than Men . . . in a short space their whole patrimonies are consumed' (Burton, 3.101).

51–2 **For . . . him** i.e. and I know what rumours *that* is generating

53 **but** but what of

53–4 **now . . . now** at times . . . at other times

54 **lute-string** The plaintive lute was a conventional instrument of the love-lorn; cf. *1H4* 1.2.70–2: 'as melancholy as . . . an old lion, or a lover's lute'.
stops the frets, or points on a lute's neck where the fingers press in order to regulate sounds; or the holes on a pipe (also a favourite of lovers): i.e. Benedick's jesting spirit 'at times conceals itself in a lute string, and at other times permits itself to be played upon (in, by implication, a melancholy fashion) like the finger-holes of a recorder' (Wells, *Re-editing*, 45). Claudio puns on the notion of the pauses that have crept into Benedick's heretofore free-wheeling wit. (The notion that love robs one of one's wit when it doesn't render one garrulous is expressed both by Don Pedro, at 2.3.208–11 – 'The sport will be when they hold one an opinion of another's dotage . . . That's the scene that I would see, which will be merely a dumb-show' – and by Margaret, at 3.4.63, in her reply to Beatrice's 'how long have you professed apprehension?': 'Ever since you left it.') Of course, Don Pedro and Claudio are hardly letting Benedick get a word in edgeways, even if he were in a mood to cross wits with them.

---

49 SP] *F (Prin.); Bene. Q*   51+ SP DON PEDRO] *Rowe (Pedro.); Capell (D. Pe.); Prince Q*   53 now crept] new-crept *Cam¹ (Boas)*   54 now] new *Dyce*

DON PEDRO   Indeed, that tells a heavy tale for him.   55
Conclude, conclude: he is in love.

CLAUDIO   Nay, but I know who loves him.

DON PEDRO   That would I know too; I warrant one that
knows him not.

CLAUDIO   Yes, and his ill conditions, and in despite of all   60
dies for him.

DON PEDRO   She shall be buried with her face upwards.

BENEDICK   Yet is this no charm for the toothache. [*to
Leonato*] Old signor, walk aside with me. I have studied
eight or nine wise words to speak to you which these   65
hobby-horses must not hear.   [*Exeunt Benedick and Leonato.*]

DON PEDRO   For my life, to break with him about
Beatrice!

CLAUDIO   'Tis even so. Hero and Margaret have by this
played their parts with Beatrice, and then the two bears   70
will not bite one another when they meet.

---

55 **heavy** incriminating, conclusive
58–9 **I warrant . . . not** i.e. I swear
it's someone who doesn't know what
a curmudgeonly woman-scorner he
is.
60 **Yes . . . conditions** i.e. You're wrong.
She does know his bad qualities and is
still in love with him.
61 **dies** pines away
62 Don Pedro pursues Claudio's *double
entendre* by implying that she who
loves Benedick will only be buried
while 'dying' under his body in the
sex act. Cf. *WT* 4.4.131–2: 'Not like
a corpse; or if – not to be buried, /
But quick, and in mine arms'. The
innuendo of the passage posed a
problem for eighteenth- and nineteenth-
century editors, who were unwilling or
unable to grant its sexual content, and
hence, after Theobald, often emended

face to 'heels', citing proverbial instances
of the latter.
63 **charm** cure
65–6 **wise . . . hear** Benedick addresses
Leonato on the same subject in our
hearing at 5.4.21, which suggests
either that he loses his nerve here, or,
more likely (since in performance the
repetition generally passes unnoticed),
that Shakespeare must isolate Don
Pedro and Claudio in order to further
Don John's plot.
66 **hobby-horses** buffoons, from the
practice of the morris dance and the
stage, where a performer would don a
wickerwork horse-costume and imitate
the antic movements of a high-spirited
horse
69 **'Tis even so** i.e. you're right
Margaret Actually, Ursula was the
more instrumental agent: either a slip

---

56 conclude] *om. F*   62 face] heels *Theobald*   63 toothache.] *Rowe;* tooth-ake, *Q*   64 signor]
(signior)   66 SD] *Theobald*

Enter [DON] JOHN *the bastard.*

DON JOHN   My lord and brother, God save you!

DON PEDRO   Good e'en, brother.

DON JOHN   If your leisure served, I would speak with you.

DON PEDRO   In private?   75

DON JOHN   If it please you; yet Count Claudio may hear,
for what I would speak of concerns him.

DON PEDRO   What's the matter?

DON JOHN   [*to Claudio*] Means your lordship to be
married tomorrow?   80

DON PEDRO   You know he does.

DON JOHN   I know not that when he knows what I know.

CLAUDIO   If there be any impediment, I pray you discover
it.

DON JOHN   You may think I love you not. Let that appear   85
hereafter, and aim better at me by that I now will
manifest. For my brother – I think he holds you well and
in dearness of heart – hath holp to effect your ensuing
marriage; surely suit ill spent and labour ill bestowed.

DON PEDRO   Why, what's the matter?   90

DON JOHN   I came hither to tell you; and, circumstances

---

by Shakespeare, or evidence of an
original intention subsequently
changed in order to balance the two
waiting gentlewomen's roles; or an
error by a Claudio ignorant of the
details (and assuming that the more
mischievous Margaret would be the
active party to the deception).

73 **Good e'en** [God give you] good
evening (i.e. any time after noon)

76 **yet . . . hear** perhaps an indication

that Claudio moves to excuse himself

83 **discover** disclose, reveal

85 **that** i.e. whether I love you or no

86 **aim better** at judge better of

87 **For** as for
holds you well has a high opinion of
you

88 **dearness of heart** friendship
holp helped

89 **suit** pursuit

91 **circumstances** explanations, details

71.1 DON] *Rowe*   72, 74, 76 SP] *Rowe (John); Bastard Q*   73 e'en] *Oxf;* den *Q*   77 of concerns]
Qu; of, concernes *Qc*   79, 82, 85, 91 SP] *Rowe (John); Bast. Q*   79 SD] *Rowe*   87–8 brother . . .
heart –] brother (I thinke, . . . heart) *Qc;* brother, I think, . . . heart *Rowe;* brother, I thinke, . . . heart,
Qu   88 holp] *Qc (*holpe*);* hope *Qu*

shortened – for she has been too long a-talking of – the
lady is disloyal.

CLAUDIO   Who, Hero?

DON JOHN   Even she: Leonato's Hero, your Hero, every   95
man's Hero.

CLAUDIO   Disloyal?

DON JOHN   The word is too good to paint out her
wickedness; I could say she were worse. Think you of a
worse title, and I will fit her to it. Wonder not till   100
further warrant. Go but with me, tonight you shall see
her chamber window entered, even the night before her
wedding day. If you love her then, tomorrow wed her.
But it would better fit your honour to change your mind.

CLAUDIO   May this be so?   105

DON PEDRO   I will not think it.

DON JOHN   If you dare not trust that you see, confess not
that you know. If you will follow me I will show you
enough, and when you have seen more and heard more,
proceed accordingly.   110

92 **too . . . of** Don John insinuates that
for a woman to be a subject of general conversation was in itself a dubious portent of female reputation.
He echoes an opinion also shared by
Rich in his *Excellency of Good Women*:
'Thucydides will needs approve that
women to be most honest, that is least
knowne, and I think indeed that the
most honest woman is least spoken of,
for they doe please the least in member, and vertue was never graced by
the multitude' (sig. C2ʳ).

93, 97 **disloyal** unfaithful

98 **paint out** depict fully; Don John's verb
suggests the link between female untrustworthiness and the use of cosmetics.

101 **warrant** proof
Go but only go

102 **chamber window entered** This
contrasts with Borachio's plan of 2.2
and the accusation of 4.1.91, that Hero
did merely 'Talk with a ruffian at
her chamber window'. In the sources
Claudio's counterpart does indeed
witness her chamber window entered
(e.g. Bandello: 'he who simulated the
lover climbed up and entered the
house as if he had a mistress within.
When the unhappy Sir Timbreo saw
it, being convinced . . . he felt himself
swooning', Bullough, 117).

104 **honour** reputation

107–8 **If . . . know** a difficult line, to the
effect of 'if you won't believe your
eyes, then you must refuse the knowledge they present'
that . . . that what . . . what

92 – for . . . talking of –] *Qc* ((for . . . .talking of)*); for . . . talking, *Qu*   has] hath *F*   a-talking] *(a
talking)*   95 SP] *Rowe (John.)*; Bastar. *Q*   98, 107 SP] *Rowe (John.)*; Bast. *Q*   101 me, tonight]
Qu; me tonight *Qc*   103 her then,] *Hanmer;* her, then *Q*

CLAUDIO   If I see anything tonight why I should not
marry her, tomorrow in the congregation where I
should wed, there will I shame her.

DON PEDRO   And as I wooed for thee to obtain her, I will
join with thee to disgrace her.   115

DON JOHN   I will disparage her no farther till you are my
witnesses. Bear it coldly but till midnight, and let the
issue show itself.

DON PEDRO   O day untowardly turned!

CLAUDIO   O mischief strangely thwarting!   120

DON JOHN   O plague right well prevented! So will you say
when you have seen the sequel.   [*Exeunt.*]

[**3.3**]   *Enter* DOGBERRY[, *the constable*], *and his compartner*
[VERGES,] *with the* Watch[, *among them*
George SEACOAL *and Hugh Oatcake*].

111 **why** i.e. that would provide a reason
why

112 **in the congregation** Unlike his
precedents in the prose and poetic sources, who communicate their
rejection of Hero by messenger to
the bride's father, Claudio immediately plots a very public repudiation
of Hero. In Ariosto, he withdraws
from the court without a murmur
(*Orlando*, 96.56), is believed a suicide,
and it is his grief-stricken brother
Lurcanio who 'undertakes before them
all, / To give them perfect notice and
instruction, / Who was the cause of
Ariodante's fall' (97.63.3–5).

117 **coldly** calmly; without betraying you
know it

118 **issue** outcome

119 **untowardly turned** unhappily
altered

120 **mischief** evil plight (*OED sb.* 1a),
i.e. Hero's infidelity

strangely thwarting unaccountably
obstructive (*OED* strangely *adv.* 5)

121–2 **So . . . sequel** 'The exit of Don
John with this string of sibilants cannot be accidental' (Craik, 304).

122 This point in the action has often
been the location of an interpolated
scene of Borachio's assignation with
Margaret (Cox, *Shakespeare*, 156). See
p. 87 for discussion of the ramifications of such a production choice.

3.3 The location is a street, with a church
bench in it and a *penthouse* (100), or
overhanging shed or porch roof; see
100n.

0.1 *constable* the chief civil officer of
a parish, nominally holding office
for a year. The post was unpaid and
was meant to rotate amongst citizens,
although some holders (like *MM*'s
Elbow) were persuaded to occupy it
for a price, so as to spare others their
turn. Proverbially witless ('You might

112 her, tomorrow in] *Alexander;* her tomorrow, in *Rowe;* her to morrow in *Q;* her; to morrow, in
Capell congregation] *Qu;* congregation, *Qc*   116, 121 SP] *Rowe (John); Bastard Q*   117 midnight]
night *F*   122 SD] *F2; Exit. F*   3.3] *Capell (SCENE III)*   0.1 the constable] *this edn*   0.2 VERGES]
Rowe   0.2–3 among . . . Oatcake] *this edn*

DOGBERRY   Are you good men and true?

VERGES   Yea, or else it were pity but they should suffer
salvation, body and soul.

DOGBERRY   Nay, that were a punishment too good for
them, if they should have any allegiance in them, being   5
chosen for the prince's watch.

VERGES   Well, give them their charge, neighbour
Dogberry.

DOGBERRY   First, who think you the most desertless man
to be constable?   10

1 WATCHMAN   Hugh Oatcake, sir, or George Seacoal, for
they can write and read.

---

be a constable for your wit', Dent,
C616).

compartner fellow office-bearer; the
only use of this word in Shakespeare's
works

0.2 *the* Watch a neighbourhood citizen
patrol; their number could include at
least four men (Oatcake, Seacoal, the
speaker who distinguishes them, and
perhaps one other from whom they
are distinguished). As Seacoal is the
only speaker whose speeches can be
identified, he is alone in being speci-
fied in the SPs.

3   salvation i.e. damnation. A feature of
Dogberry's unique attempt at an ele-
vated diction is frequent malapropisms
which sound somewhat like the correct
words for the circumstances he intends;
whereas the characters of higher rank
delight in deliberate word-play and
semantic conversions, Dogberry, 'in his
obsessive quest for polysyllables as sym-
bols of status' (Davis, 10), inadvertently says the opposite of what he means.
John Barton's 1976 RSC production of
the play rendered this verbal slippage
by casting the members of the Watch
as a band of colonized Sikhs under the

British Raj, i.e. locals for whom English
was not their first language. The British
(and rural) names of the local constabu-
lary mark them as different in fictional
register from the higher-ranking and
etymologically Latinate Messinese.

5   allegiance Dogberry's error for disloyalty

6   prince's watch Elizabethan society
had no regular police force (or standing army).

7   charge assignment; instructions

9   desertless malapropism for 'deserving'

10 constable deputy leader of the Watch
in the absence of Dogberry

11 SP Q distinguishes between SPs
for individual watchmen only at the
beginning and the ending of the scene:
Watch 1 appears at 11, 157 and 162;
Watch 2 (George Seacoal) at 17, 27, 159
and 165. The remainder are assigned to
the undifferentiated '*Watch*'. Various
assignments of all the lines are possible; many editions assign the lion's
share of the undifferentiated lines (e.g.
the questions to Dogberry) to Watch
2, on the grounds that this character, once designated leader, further

---

11 SP] *(Watch* 1*)*; SECOND WATCHMAN *Oxf*; A WATCHMAN *Oxf¹*   Oatcake] *(Ote-cake)*, *F4*   11, 13
Seacoal] *(Sea-cole)*, *F4*

DOGBERRY Come hither, neighbour Seacoal; [*Seacoal steps forward.*] God hath blest you with a good name. To be a well-favoured man is the gift of fortune, but to   15
write and read comes by nature.

SEACOAL Both which, master constable –

DOGBERRY You have. I knew it would be your answer. Well, for your favour, sir, why, give God thanks, and make no boast of it; and for your writing and reading,   20
let that appear when there is no need of such vanity. You are thought here to be the most senseless and fit man for the constable of the watch, therefore bear

questions Dogberry about his duties, and then, assuming the mantle of authority, orders his men about. Line 121 ('I know that Deformed') generally goes to Watch 1 because 162 ('And one Deformed is one of them') does in Q, and both seem to indicate a personage of some pretensions to criminology (which could be in keeping with Watch 1's being the first to reply to Dogberry at 11, and his initiative at 157); it is not necessary, however, that they be the same person, and there may be greater flexibility for a production if they are left as in Q (so that 162 could be an attempt to assert an authority usurped at 121). Similarly, the assignment of the other speeches exclusively to Watch 2 weights the dialogue heavily in favour of that actor at the expense of awkward silence for whatever other actors are present. Productions more often distribute 37–123 amongst the other actors in the Watch, returning (as here) to Watch 2/Seacoal for the directives at 86–7, 93 and 103. With the exception of these three directives, this edition leaves the undiffer-

entiated assignments as in Q, on the assumption that the indeterminacy (a result of printing practice as well as playing) permits the reader to imagine Dogberry besieged by multiple voices, and frees a director to assign roles according to the resources and talents of the company.

Oatcake The oaten cake was a Scottish food; like Seacoal's name, it identifies its bearer as hailing from northern parts considered provincial by London standards.

14 **a good name** Seacoal was high-grade coal shipped from Newcastle (a city of north-east England), as opposed to the charcoal sold in London by colliers.

15 **well-favoured** handsome
fortune Lady Luck; cf. Lyly, *Euphues*, 15: 'To bee rich is the gift of Fortune, to be wise the grace of God.' Dogberry, however, attributes hereditary features to chance and literacy to heredity.

17 Seacoal's prompt suggests that a mysterious pause may occur after Dogberry's sentence.

19 **favour** appearance

22 **senseless** malapropism for 'sensible'

13–14 SD] *Bevington*   14 name. To] *Qc (*name: to*)*; name, to *Qu*   15 well-favoured] *(*welfauoured*)*,
F   17 SP] *Bevington²*; *Watch* 2 Q; FIRST WATCHMAN *Oxf*; A WATCHMAN *Oxf¹*   constable –] *Rowe;*
Constable. *Q;* Constable *F*

you the lantern. [*Hands Seacoal the lantern.*] This is
your charge: you shall comprehend all vagrom men.   25
You are to bid any man stand, in the prince's name.

SEACOAL   How if 'a will not stand?

DOGBERRY   Why then, take no note of him, but let him
go, and presently call the rest of the watch together, and
thank God you are rid of a knave.   30

VERGES   If he will not stand when he is bidden, he is none
of the prince's subjects.

DOGBERRY   True, and they are to meddle with none but
the prince's subjects. You shall also make no noise in
the streets, for for the watch to babble and to talk is most 35
tolerable, and not to be endured.

WATCHMAN   We will rather sleep than talk; we know what
belongs to a watch.

DOGBERRY   Why, you speak like an ancient and most quiet
watchman. For I cannot see how sleeping should   40
offend. Only have a care that your bills be not stolen.

---

24 **lantern** On the Renaissance stage the
lantern would have indicated that it
was night time.
25 **comprehend** malapropism for 'apprehend'
vagrom malapropism for 'vagrant'
26, 27, 31 **stand** halt
28 **note** notice
29 **presently** immediately
31–2 **none . . . subjects** i.e. not subject to
the Prince's jurisdiction
36 **tolerable** malapropism for 'intolerable'. Cf. *TS* 5.2.94: 'Intolerable, not
to be endur'd!'; Smith notes that 'This
famous phrase at once took root in the
language' (Smith). See also Thomas
Heywood's *Fair Maid of the Exchange*
(1607), 4.3.157–8: ''tis most tolerable,
and not to be indured' (Heywood,

Maid, 140). It may have been suggested
by an expression in John Northbrook's
Treatise against . . . Plays (1577): 'Plays
and Players are not tolerable nor to be
endured' (Northbrooke, 76).
37 **sleep** The comic indolence of watchmen was noted in Thomas Dekker's
Gull's Hornbook (1609): 'If you smell
a watch, and that you may easily do,
for commonly they eat onions to keep
them in sleeping, which they account
a medicine against cold' (Dekker,
Hornbook, 63).
38 **belongs to** becomes, is appropriate
for
39 **ancient** experienced
41 **bills** halberds, long wooden weapons
with a pointed axe head on top
stolen i.e. whilst you are napping

24 SD] *this edn (RP)*   27 SP] *Bevington²; Watch* 2 *Q*; FIRST WATCHMAN *Oxf*; A WATCHMAN *Oxf ¹*
35 for] for, for *Q*   and to] and *F*   37, 44, 48, 53 SP] *(Watch); Watch* 2 / *Rowe;* SEACOAL *Folg²*

Well, you are to call at all the alehouses, and bid those
that are drunk get them to bed.

WATCHMAN   How if they will not?

DOGBERRY   Why then, let them alone till they are sober. If   45
they make you not then the better answer, you may say
they are not the men you took them for.

WATCHMAN   Well, sir.

DOGBERRY   If you meet a thief, you may suspect him, by
virtue of your office, to be no true man. And for such   50
kind of men, the less you meddle or make with them,
why, the more is for your honesty.

WATCHMAN   If we know him to be a thief, shall we not lay
hands on him?

DOGBERRY   Truly, by your office you may; but I think they   55
that touch pitch will be defiled. The most peaceable
way for you, if you do take a thief, is to let him show
himself what he is, and steal out of your company.

VERGES   You have been always called a merciful man,
partner.   60

DOGBERRY   Truly, I would not hang a dog by my will,
much more a man who hath any honesty in him.

VERGES   If you hear a child cry in the night you must call
to the nurse and bid her still it.

---

46 **better** more tractable
47 **for** to be
50 **true** honest
51 **meddle or make** have to do; proverbial (Dent, M852)
52 **more is** better it is
56 **touch . . . defiled** proverbial: 'He that
toucheth pitch shall be defiled' (Dent,
P358, from Ecclesiastes, 13.1)
57–8 **show . . . is** reveal his true nature
61 **hang a dog** Animals were sometimes
subject to legal penalties; cf. 2.3.80–1:
'An he had been a dog that should have

howled thus, they would have hanged
him.'
62 **more** i.e. less
64 **still** quiet (ironic given that the
Watch themselves are calling out); the
expectation for quiet night-time hours
is emphasized in *The Statutes of the
Night* (1595): '22. No man shall blow
any horn in the night, within this citie,
or whistle after the hour of nyne of
the clock in the night, under paine
of imprisonment . . . 30. No man
shall, after the houre of nyne at night,

42 those] them *F*

WATCHMAN   How if the nurse be asleep and will not hear   65
us?

DOGBERRY   Why then, depart in peace, and let the child
wake her with crying; for the ewe that will not hear her
lamb when it baas will never answer a calf when he
bleats.   70

VERGES   'Tis very true.

DOGBERRY   This is the end of the charge. You, constable,
are to present the prince's own person. If you meet the
prince in the night you may stay him.

VERGES   Nay, by'r Lady, that I think 'a cannot.   75

DOGBERRY   Five shillings to one on't with any man that
knows the statutes. He may stay him – marry, not
without the prince be willing, for indeed the watch
ought to offend no man, and it is an offence to stay a
man against his will.   80

VERGES   By'r Lady, I think it be so.

DOGBERRY   Ha, ah ha! Well, masters, good night; an there

keepe any rule, whereby any suche suddaine outcry be made in the still of the night, as making any affray, or beating his wyfe or seruaunt, or singing, or reuyling in his house, to the disturbaunce of his neighbours.'

69 **calf** can mean fool (i.e. the Watchman) (*OED* calf¹ 1c); Dogberry's formulation lends this sentiment the force of a proverb.

73 **present** i.e. represent, take on the authority of

74, 77 **stay** arrest, stop for questioning

75, 81 **by'r Lady** by our Lady

77 **statutes** Acts of Parliament (though the law in question governing apprehension of the Prince belongs to the common law). F's 'Statues' is most likely an error in keeping with Dogberry's own; F2

restores Q's spelling.

79 **offend no man** A watch's efficacy was no doubt compromised by the difficulty, or snobbery, in a hierarchical society of members of a lower status apprehending those of a higher social station (who were themselves exempt from serving as watchmen); on these grounds, Dekker's *Hornbook* recommends that those abroad after curfew who meet a watch call out the name of a nobleman, e.g. '"Sir Giles." It skills not though there be none dubbed in your bunch; the watch will wink at you, only for the love they bear to arms and knighthood' (63).

82 **Ha, ah ha!** most likely a triumphant exultation over Verges' error (e.g. Ha, I told you so!); Smith suggests that the first 'Ha' be interrogative.

65 SP] *(Watch); Watch 2 / Rowe*   77 statutes] Statues F   82 an] *(and)*

be any matter of weight chances, call up me. Keep your
fellows' counsels, and your own, and good night. [*to*
Verges] Come, neighbour. [*Dogberry and Verges begin to*   85
exit.]

SEACOAL Well, masters, we hear our charge. Let us go sit
here upon the church bench till two, and then all to bed.

DOGBERRY [*Returns.*] One word more, honest neighbours. I pray you watch about Signor Leonato's
door, for the wedding being there tomorrow, there is a   90
great coil tonight. Adieu. Be vigitant, I beseech you.

Exeunt [Dogberry and Verges].

Enter BORACHIO *and* CONRADE.

BORACHIO What, Conrade!

SEACOAL [*aside*] Peace, stir not.

BORACHIO Conrade, I say!

CONRADE Here, man, I am at thy elbow.   95

BORACHIO Mass, and my elbow itched; I thought there
would a scab follow!

83 **any . . . weight** anything important
83–4 **Keep . . . own** The oath of a grand-
jury man was 'The King's counsel, your
fellows' and your own you shall observe
and keep secret' (Cam); cf. Dent, C682:
'The counsel thou wouldst have another
keep, first keep thyself.'
91 **coil** hubbub, to-do
vigitant malapropism for 'vigilant'.
In many productions the Watch retire
upstage, or down, or otherwise dispose
themselves inconspicuously, often to
sleep (although on the Renaissance
stage it was a convention that separate
parties could be invisible and inaudible

to each other).
92 **What** hey there
96 **Mass** i.e. by the Mass (for a late
sixteenth-century Protestant English-
man, an outdated oath; Borachio is of
course Italian or Spanish)
my elbow itched An itchy elbow
was an omen presaging unsavoury
company: 'My elbow itched, I must
change my bedfellow' (Tilley, E98).
97 **scab** lesion; parasitic rascal. Cf. *Cor*
1.1.163–5: 'What's the matter, you
dissentious rogues, / That, rubbing
the poor itch of your opinion, / Make
yourself scabs?'

84–5 SD] *Oxf¹*   85 SD] *Folg²*   86 SP] *Bevington²; Watch 2 / Rowe; Watch Q*   88 SD] *this edn*
(RP)   89 Signor] *(signior)*   91 SD *Dogberry and Verges*] *Pope; Exeunt Q*   93 SP] *Capell; Watch Q;*
FIRST WATCHMAN *Oxf*   SD] *Rowe*

CONRADE   I will owe thee an answer for that. And now,
        forward with thy tale.

BORACHIO   Stand thee close, then, under this penthouse,   100
        for it drizzles rain, and I will, like a true drunkard, utter
        all to thee.

SEACOAL [*aside*]   Some treason, masters. Yet stand close.

BORACHIO   Therefore, know I have earned of Don John a
        thousand ducats.   105

CONRADE   Is it possible that any villainy should be so
        dear?

BORACHIO   Thou shouldst rather ask if it were possible
        any villainy should be so rich. For when rich villains
        have need of poor ones, poor ones may make what price   110
        they will.

CONRADE   I wonder at it.

BORACHIO   That shows thou art unconfirmed. Thou
        knowest that the fashion of a doublet, or a hat, or a
        cloak, is nothing to a man.   115

CONRADE   Yes, it is apparel.

---

100 **close** near; hidden
    penthouse overhanging canopy; on
    the unlocalized Renaissance stage,
    the word could establish a location
    for the audience, or perhaps indicate
    that Borachio and Conrade situated
    themselves under the tiring-house
    canopy.
101 **true drunkard** Cf. the Latin prov-
    erb '*in vino veritas*' ('in wine there
    is truth'), and Borachio's own name
    (see List of Roles 7n.). Borachio and
    Conrade are often played as if drunk
    in this scene.
103 **Yet** for now
    close together; nearer; hidden; impli-
    citly another SD
107 **dear** expensive, precious
113 **unconfirmed** ignorant
113–37 **Thou . . . fashion** Borachio's

digression on fashion (usually cut
in performance) seems, as Conrade
suggests, rather far afield from his
story, unless we take it as a meditation
on the fickleness of *all the hot-bloods*
(127–8) when it comes to choice of
either clothing or women; or perhaps
as a reflection on the misleading con-
nections between clothing and identity
(crucial to Margaret's impersonation of
Hero); or, indeed, on the discrepancy
between the conduct and the rank
of apparent gentlemen Don John,
Claudio and Don Pedro.
114 **doublet** See 2.3.17n.
115 **nothing to a man** tells us nothing about a man; does not matter to a
man (another play on the word, which
Conrade's reply compounds); cf. *TS*
3.1.117

103 SP] *Bevington²; 2 Watch / Capell; Watch Q*   SD] *Johnson*   104 Don] *F;* Dun *Q*

BORACHIO I mean the fashion.

CONRADE Yes, the fashion is the fashion.

BORACHIO Tush, I may as well say the fool's the fool. But
seest thou not what a deformed thief this fashion is? 120

WATCHMAN [*aside*] I know that Deformed. 'A has been
a vile thief this seven year; 'a goes up and down like a
gentleman; I remember his name.

BORACHIO Didst thou not hear somebody?

CONRADE No, 'twas the vane on the house. 125

BORACHIO Seest thou not, I say, what a deformed thief
this fashion is, how giddily 'a turns about all the
hot-bloods between fourteen and five-and-thirty,
sometimes fashioning them like Pharaoh's soldiers in
the reechy painting, sometime like god Bel's priests in 130

---

120 **deformed** deforming
122 **seven year** a number denoting an
indefinite term (Furness)
goes ... down walks about
122–3 **like a gentleman** In a culture of
(largely flouted) sumptuary laws (which
decreed that a person's clothing must
indicate his or her social station and
gender) it is possible to impersonate
another status by wearing its designated apparel (much as actors do). The
'Homily on Excess of Apparel' exhorts
that 'every man behold and consider
his own vocation, inasmuch as God
hath appointed every man his degree
and office, within the limits whereof it behoveth him to keep himself.
Therefore all may not look to wear like
apparel, but everyone according to his
degree ... ' (*Homilies*, 310).
124 Borachio's question indicates either
that the Watchman's speech is audible,
or, in productions that cut the passages
on fashion, that the Watch betray their
presence in some other way (often by

dropping a weapon or the lantern).
125 **vane** weathervane
the house may refer both to the fictional setting and to the roof of the
playhouse
129 **Pharaoh's soldiers** soldiers of
Pharaoh, king of Egypt, who were
drowned along with their leader in the
Red Sea while pursuing the escaping
Israelites (Exodus, 14.23–8)
130 **reechy** smoke-begrimed, discol-
oured; Borachio refers here and in the
following lines to visual representations
of biblical and classical subjects
(which would have portrayed ancient
persons in the fashion contemporary
to the painter's own moment, e.g. a be-
codpieced Hercules).
god Bel's priests the priests of Baal,
or the Sumerian god of winds and
agriculture. The reference is to the
apocryphal story 'Bel and the Dragon',
once attached to the Book of Daniel;
the story tells how Daniel overthrew
the priests of Bel by convincing their

---

120 deformed] *Qc;* defermed *Qu*   121 SP] *(Watch); First Watch / Capell; 2 Watch / Bevington;* SEACOAL
Bevington² SD] *Capell* Deformed] *Rowe;* deformed *Q*   122 year] yeares *F* year;] *Qc* (yeere,*); yeere
Qu   123 I] *Qc; not in Qu*   128 five-and-thirty] *(*fiue and thirtie*), Cam*   130 reechy] *(*rechie*)*

the old church window, sometime like the shaven
Hercules in the smirched worm-eaten tapestry, where
his codpiece seems as massy as his club.

CONRADE   All this I see, and I see that the fashion wears
out more apparel than the man. But art not thou thyself   135
giddy with the fashion, too, that thou hast shifted out of
thy tale into telling me of the fashion?

king (Cyrus of Persia) that Bel was
not a deity but a mere image. God
Bel's priests, as idolators, were no
doubt richly clothed (Tudor–Stuart
Protestantism posited a strong connection between idolatry and sartorial
excess, the whore of Babylon, or the
Roman Church, being a chief exem-
plar of the trend).
131 **old church window** The idolatrous
stained-glass window was a hallmark
of Catholic practice.
131–2 **shaven Hercules** likely to be a
confusion with the shorn Samson
(Judges, 16), but perhaps a reference to
Hercules in the house of Omphale (see
2.1.231–3 and 2.1.29–30n.), except that
Hercules in the latter circumstance
is not usually shaven though he is
dressed as a woman (much being made
of the contrast between his beard and
his clothing): 'So in Hercules, painted
with his great beard and furious countenance, in a woman's attire, spinning
at Omphale's commandment, it breed-
eth both delight and laughter' (Sidney,
Defence, 68). Or, as Cam[2] suggests,
Hercules at the crossroads, a popular
representation of the youthful (and
beardless) Hercules poised between
the paths of virtue and vice. The
drunken Borachio may be garbling his
allusions, but the thrust of his comparison seems to point to the image of
an overly preened (clean-shaven, such
as Benedick is in 3.2) and ornately
dressed figure of a man, by contrast

with his bedraggled tapestry.
132 **smirched** besmirched, grimy
133 **codpiece** laced-up attachment to a
man's breeches, covering his genitals. In
Elizabethan fashion (to 1580) codpieces
were often outsized and ornately bejew-
elled in order to draw attention to, and
suggest, the proportions and capacities
of their contents. Cf. Montaigne, 'On
some verses of Virgil': 'what was the
meaning of that ridiculous part of the
breeches worn by our fathers, which
is still seen on our Swiss? What is the
point of the show we make even now
of the shape of our pieces under our
galligaskins, and what is worse, often
by falsehood and imposture beyond
their natural size?' (Montaigne, 653).
Like the *reechy painting* and the
worm-eaten tapestry, the codpiece was
outdated by 1600.
club i.e. prodigious object (Hercules
being known for his strength, and
the corresponding heft of his club).
Borachio here draws a distinction
between actual strength (the club) and
the mere (and often fallacious) representation of it. Borachio's observations contribute to the play's thematic
fascination with what constitutes 'a
man' (see p. 59).
134–5 **wears . . . man** consumes more
clothing than is strictly needed by its
wearer
136 **giddy with** entranced by
shifted out pun on changing one's
shift, or shirt

134 and I] and *F*

BORACHIO   Not so neither. But know that I have tonight
  wooed Margaret, the Lady Hero's gentlewoman, by the
  name of Hero; she leans me out at her mistress'   140
  chamber window, bids me a thousand times goodnight
  – I tell this tale vilely. I should first tell thee how the
  prince, Claudio and my master, planted and placed and
  possessed by my master Don John, saw afar off in the
  orchard this amiable encounter.   145

CONRADE   And thought they Margaret was Hero?

BORACHIO   Two of them did, the prince and Claudio,
  but the devil my master knew she was Margaret. And
  partly by his oaths, which first possessed them, partly
  by the dark night, which did deceive them, but chiefly   150
  by my villainy, which did confirm any slander that Don
  John had made, away went Claudio enraged, swore he
  would meet her as he was appointed next morning at
  the temple, and there, before the whole congregation,
  shame her with what he saw o'ernight, and send her   155
  home again without a husband.

1 WATCHMAN *[Starts out upon them.]*   We charge you in
  the prince's name, stand!

---

140 **leans me out** leans out towards me;
  cf. 1.3.55 and n.
141 **thousand   times   goodnight**
  Borachio and Margaret apparently
  played a conventional lovers' leave-
  taking scene in the tradition of *RJ*
  (2.2).
144 **possessed** primed, or deluded, by
  the (false) story of what they were
  about to see; with possibly a 'sense
  of demoniac possession, inasmuch as
  Borachio refers in his next sentence
  and at 148 to "the devil, my master"'
  (Furness). Borachio's syntax is
  somewhat garbled (with drink or the
  pleasures of alliteration?); *planted and*

placed can refer to all three witnesses,
  though *possessed* only to the Prince and
  Claudio.
  afar off from far off (presumably a
  distance at which the deception of
  Margaret's borrowed garments would
  be plausible)
149 **possessed** prejudiced
150 **dark** Unlike Shakespeare's sources,
  which note the brightness of the scene
  ('the night was not very dark but very
  still', Bullough, 116), Claudio's error
  is mitigated by the tenebrousness of
  the evening.
154 **temple** i.e. the church
158 **stand** i.e. stand forth, don't move;

---

143 prince, Claudio] *Rowe;* prince Claudio *Q*   146 SP] *Qc (Conr.); Con Qu*   they] thy *F*   157, 162
SP] *(Watch 1); 2 Watch Ard²; SEACOAL Cam²*   157 SD] *Capell*

SEACOAL   Call up the right master constable! We have
here recovered the most dangerous piece of lechery that   160
ever was known in the commonwealth!

1 WATCHMAN   And one Deformed is one of them. I know
him, 'a wears a lock.

CONRADE   Masters, masters –

SEACOAL   You'll be made bring Deformed forth, I   165
warrant you.

CONRADE   Masters –

SEACOAL   Never speak, we charge you! Let us obey you
to go with us.

BORACHIO *[to Conrade]*   We are like to prove a goodly   170
commodity, being taken up of these men's bills.

this command follows Dogberry's pre-
scribed formula at 26 ('You are to bid
any man stand, in the prince's name'),
but may derive added humour from
the fact that Conrade and Borachio are
in fact already standing ('Stand thee
close, then, under this penthouse',
100).
159 **right** an honorific intensifier, as in
'right honourable', 'right worshipful'
160 **recovered** malapropism for 'discovered'. Dogberry's malapropisms are
seemingly contagious (as at 168).
Folg² provides an exit for the Second
Watchman at 161 and a re-entrance for
him along with Dogberry and Verges
at 165 (the uncorrected Q in fact prints
the SP at 164 and 167 as *Con.*). See
t.n.
lechery malapropism for 'treachery'
163 **lock** a lock of hair grown longer than
its fellows, and often ornamented with

tokens of the beloved. William Prynne
wrote an entire treatise against the
affectation (*The Unloveliness of Love-
Locks*, 1628); Sidney's Astrophel, on
the other hand, argues in sonnet 54 of
Astrophel and Stella for the originality
of his love despite his lack of tokens:
'Because I breathe not loue to euery
one, / Nor doe not vse set colours for
to wear, / Nor nourish special locks of
vowèd hair . . . '.
164 **Masters** i.e. officers (*OED sb.*[1] III
19a)
168 **obey** malapropism for 'order',
'command'
170–1 **goodly commodity** valuable art-
icle; goods obtained on credit from an
usurer, typically at exorbitant interest
171 **taken up of** under arrest, at the
point of; received on credit for
bills halberds; bonds given as security
for goods

159, 165 SP] *Folg²; Watch 2 Q; First Watch Ard²;* A WATCHMAN *Oxf* 159 constable!] constable!
Second Watchman exits Folg² (Cam²) 163 lock.] lock. *Enter Dogberry, Verges, and Second Watchman
Folg²* 164, 167 SP] *(Conr) Qc; Con. Qu;* DOGBERRY *Folg² (Cam²)* 164 masters –] *Theobald;*
masters. *Q* 167–8 CONRADE . . . Never] *Theobald subst; Conr.* Masters, neuer *Qc; Con.* Masters,
neuer *Qu;* DOGBERRY Masters, never *Folg² (Cam²)* 168 SP] *Bevington²; First Watch / Theobald; Sec.
Watch / Bevington;* A WATCHMAN *Oxf* 170 SD] *Oxf*

CONRADE A commodity in question, I warrant you.
Come, we'll obey you.   *Exeunt.*

[**3.4**]   *Enter* HERO, MARGARET *and* URSULA.

HERO Good Ursula, wake my cousin Beatrice and desire
her to rise.
URSULA I will, lady.
HERO And bid her come hither.
URSULA Well.   [*Exit.*]
MARGARET Troth, I think your other rebato were better.   6
HERO No, pray thee, good Meg, I'll wear this.
MARGARET By my troth, 's not so good, and I warrant
your cousin will say so.
HERO My cousin's a fool, and thou art another. I'll wear   10
none but this.
MARGARET I like the new tire within excellently, if the
hair were a thought browner. And your gown's a most
rare fashion, i'faith. I saw the Duchess of Milan's gown
that they praise so.   15
HERO O, that exceeds, they say.

---

172 **in question** (1) sought after; (2) subject to legal trial or interrogation (cf. *2H4* 1.2.60: 'He that was in question for the robbery'); (3) doubtful

3.4 The location is the interior of Leonato's house, sometimes Hero's chambers (although Ursula's scene-changing command to *withdraw* at the arrival of the menfolk (87) suggests that Hero's preparations take place in a public space).

5 **Well** yes

6 **Troth** in truth (a mild oath)
rebato a stiff collar or ruff; also used to describe the wire architectural support of the lace or linen

7, 10, 16 SP F's '*Bero.*' might suggest setting from an unknown uncorrected state of Q.

12 **tire** complete head-dress, including false hair and ornaments, viewed by some with the same contempt reserved for male affectations such as the lovelock
within i.e. in another room

13 **a thought browner** a bit, slightly more, brunette (i.e. more closely allied to Hero's own colouring)

14 **rare** exceptional

16 **exceeds** i.e. excels, outdoes (all praise)

---

172 SP] *Qc (Conr.)*; *Con Qu*   3.4] *Capell (SCENE IV)*   0.1 HERO,] *Rowe; Hero, and Q*   1 Good]
Qc; God *Qu*   5 SD] *Hanmer*   8, 17 troth, 's] *Capell;* troth's *Q*   7, 10, 16 SP] *Bero. F*

MARGARET   By my troth, 's but a night-gown in respect of
yours – cloth o'gold, and cuts, and laced with silver, set
with pearls, down sleeves, side sleeves and skirts round
underborne with a bluish tinsel. But for a fine, quaint,   20
graceful and excellent fashion, yours is worth ten on't.

HERO   God give me joy to wear it, for my heart is
exceeding heavy.

MARGARET   'Twill be heavier soon by the weight of a
man.   25

HERO   Fie upon thee! Art not ashamed?

MARGARET   Of what, lady? Of speaking honourably? Is
not marriage honourable in a beggar? Is not your lord
honourable without marriage? I think you would have
me say, saving your reverence, 'a husband'. An bad   30
thinking do not wrest true speaking, I'll offend nobody.
Is there any harm in 'the heavier for a husband'? None,

---

17 **'s** it is
    night-gown dressing gown
    in respect of compared with
18 **cuts** slashed openings on the edge or
    in the body of the overdress which
    would have revealed the rich lining
    inlaid beneath
    laced trimmed; embroidered
18–19 **set with pearls** Pearls were often
    sewn into the fabric of ornate gar-
    ments.
19 **down sleeves** tight-fitting sleeves to
    the wrist
    side sleeves ornamental sleeves
    draped away from the shoulders down
    the back
19–20 **round underborne** trimmed all
    the way around underneath; or held
    out by an ornamental petticoat
20 **tinsel** a fine silk tissue laced with silver
    or gold
    quaint elegant

21 **on't** of it
24 **heavier** Margaret's sexual innuendo
    compares with Don Pedro's at 3.2.62
    that the woman who loves Benedick
    will be 'buried with her face upwards'.
26 **Fie** expresses serious offence
    Art not i.e. art thou not
28 **honourable . . . beggar** proverbial
    (Dent, M683). Protestantism encour-
    aged the appropriateness of marriage
    for all people (including priests); the
    Book of Common Prayer proclaims that
    'Matrimony . . . is an honourable estate
    . . . commended of Saint Paul to be hon-
    ourable among all men' (*BCP*, 290).
30 **saving your reverence** a formula for
    excusing the mention of an indelicate
    subject
    a husband i.e. instead of the indeter-
    minate *man* (25)
    An if
31 **wrest** twist the meaning of

---

17 in] *F;* it *Q*   18 o'] *(a)*   30 saving . . . 'a husband'] *Pope;* 'saving . . . a husband' *Cam;* sauing . . .
a husband *Q*   An] *(&)*   32 'the . . . husband'] *Pope;* the . . . husband *Q*

I think, an it be the right husband and the right wife;
otherwise 'tis light and not heavy.

Enter BEATRICE.

Ask my lady Beatrice else; here she comes.   35
HERO   Good morrow, coz.
BEATRICE   Good morrow, sweet Hero.
HERO   Why, how now? Do you speak in the sick tune?
BEATRICE   I am out of all other tune, methinks.
MARGARET   Clap's into 'Light o'love', that goes without   40
a burden. Do you sing it, and I'll dance it.
BEATRICE   Ye light o'love with your heels? Then if your
husband have stables enough, you'll see he shall lack
no barns.

34 **light** i.e. if the husband and wife in
question are not married to one another
35 **else** i.e. if it is otherwise
36 **morrow** morning
38 **how now** i.e. what's the matter
sick tune Beatrice speaks as if she has
a head cold (cf. 58–60). 'Sick, sick' was
the name and refrain of a late sixteenth-
century tune entitled 'Captain Car', cited
in Nashe's *Summer's Last Will* (1600),
852–3: 'Sicke, Sicke, and very sicke / &
sicke and for the time' (Nashe, 3.260, also
see 4.432). Ross Duffin also cites another
song, 'My Heart is Leaned on the Land'
(*c.* 1558), a more plaintive love ballad,
with a 'sick' refrain: 'I so sick; make my
bed, I will die now' (Duffin, 369). A.P.
Rossiter observes that 'It is a notable
point in Shakespeare's contrivance that
he gives both wits their off-day, as soon
as love has disturbed their freedom'
(Rossiter, 48). Many productions account
for the ailment by the choice of Beatrice's
hiding place in 3.1 (see 3.1n.).
40 **Clap's into** let us clap
Light o'love as in *TGV* 1.2.83, a popular dance tune, probably written by

Leonard Gibson *c.* 1570, and apparently a 'light' (i.e. wanton) one, as at 83–5:
'JULIA Best sing it to the tune of "Light
o'love". / LUCETTA It is too heavy for
so light a tune. / JULIA Heavy? Belike it
hath some burden then?' Margaret tells
Beatrice (and Hero) to cheer up.
41 **burden** refrain; bass harmonic under-
song sung by male voices; heavy weight
(like that of a man's body); child in the
womb
42 **Ye . . . heels** are you, or will you be,
light-heeled, i.e. unchaste (the modern 'round-heeled' or 'short-heeled',
i.e. easily tipped backwards). Cf. Henry
Porter, *Two Angry Women of Abingdon*
(1599): 'Light aloue, short heels, mistress
Goursey' (Porter, l. 740); and 5.4.116–
17: 'that we may lighten our own hearts
and our wives' heels'. Beatrice's question
perhaps suggests some capering stage
action on Margaret's part.
light o'love wanton
43 **stables** with punning reference to its
sexual sense of 'erections'
44 **barns** with pun on bairns, the northern (and rustic) word for children

33 an] *(and)*   40 'Light o'love'] *Pope;* Light a loue *Q*   42 o'love] *(aloue)*   heels?] *Capell* (heels!*);*
heels, *Q*   43 see] looke *F*

MARGARET   O illegitimate construction! I scorn that with   45
my heels.

BEATRICE   'Tis almost five o'clock, cousin; 'tis time you
were ready. By my troth, I am exceeding ill. Hey-ho!

MARGARET   For a hawk, a horse, or a husband?

BEATRICE   For the letter that begins them all: H.   50

MARGARET   Well, an you be not turned Turk, there's no
more sailing by the star.

BEATRICE   What means the fool, trow?

MARGARET   Nothing, I, but God send everyone their
heart's desire.   55

HERO   These gloves the count sent me, they are an
excellent perfume.

BEATRICE   I am stuffed, cousin, I cannot smell.

MARGARET   A maid and stuffed! There's goodly catching
of cold.   60

---

45 **illegitimate construction** false interpretation, with pun on bastard birth
45–6 **scorn . . . heels** (1) reject that with
scorn, as one would grind with one's
heel (*OED* heel *sb.*[1] I 3b); (2) outrun (3c),
cf. *MV* 2.2.8–9: 'scorn running with thy
heels'; (3) kick, as does a horse
48 **Hey-ho** a yearning sigh of regret,
with, as Margaret's punning response
suggests, various objects; cf. 2.1.293–4:
'I may sit in a corner and cry "Hey-ho
for a husband"'.
50 **H** Both the letter and the word 'ache'
were pronounced in the same way, as
'aitch'; hence quibbles such as Beatrice's
on her cold, or John Heywood's *A
Dialogue . . . of All the Proverbs in
the English Tongue* (1546): 'H is worst
among the letters in the crosse row,
/ For if thou find him other in thine
elbow, / In thine arm, or leg, in any
degree, / In thy head, or teeth, in thy
toe or knee, / Into what place so euer H,
may like him, / Where euer thou finde
ache, thou shalt not like him.'

51 **turned Turk** i.e. converted to Islam,
changed your faith (i.e. to being in
love, instead of a scorner of men). To
'turn Turk', from a Christian perspective, means to become an infidel; the
phrase was proverbial (Dent, T609).
51–2 **there's . . . star** we cannot any
longer navigate by the North Star, i.e.
there's nothing left that we can rely on
53 **trow** I wonder
57 **perfume** Perfumed gloves were a luxury item; cf. the wares of Autolycus,
WT 4.4.222: 'Gloves as sweet as dam-
ask roses'. Hero is perhaps trying to
divert Margaret from baiting Beatrice
and thus drawing her suspicion to the
hoax.
58–9 **I am stuffed . . . stuffed** i.e. my
nose is stuffed-up; Margaret's rejoinder turns the word to indicate the
condition of pregnancy or its sexual
preamble (cf. *stuffed man*, 1.1.55).
59 **maid** i.e. virgin
59–60 **goodly . . . cold** i.e. that's some
cold you've caught

48 Hey-ho] *(hey ho)*, *Cam*   51 an] *(and)*

250

BEATRICE   O God help me, God help me, how long have
you professed apprehension?

MARGARET   Ever since you left it. Doth not my wit
become me rarely?

BEATRICE   It is not seen enough; you should wear it in   65
your cap. By my troth, I am sick.

MARGARET   Get you some of this distilled *carduus
benedictus*, and lay it to your heart; it is the only thing
for a qualm.

HERO   There thou prick'st her with a thistle.   70

BEATRICE   *Benedictus?* Why *benedictus?* You have some
moral in this *benedictus.*

MARGARET   Moral? No, by my troth, I have no moral
meaning, I meant plain holy-thistle. You may think
perchance that I think you are in love? Nay, by'r Lady, I   75
am not such a fool to think what I list, nor I list not to
think what I can, nor indeed I cannot think, if I would
think my heart out of thinking, that you are in love, or
that you will be in love, or that you can be in love. Yet
Benedick was such another, and now is he become a   80

---

62 **professed apprehension** claimed to
be a wit
63 **left it** gave it up
64 **rarely** infrequently, excellently
65–6 **in your cap** 'i.e., as a fool does his
coxcomb' (Cam¹)
67–8 *carduus benedictus* the thistle plant,
often termed 'holy' or 'blessed' (i.e.
benedictus) for its expansive healing
properties; cf. the herbal of Thomas
Cogan, *Haven of Health* (1574):
'Carduus benedictus or blessed thistle,
so worthily named for the vertues that
it hath, . . . may worthily be called
Benedictus or Omnimorbia, that is, a
salue for euery sore' (cited in Furness).
The plant was particularly well thought
of as a remedy for 'perillous diseases
of the heart' (*Gardener's Labyrinth*,

1594), 'good to be laid upon the biting
of mad dogs, serpents, spiders, or any
venomous beast whatsoever' (Gerard's
Herbal, 1597). Clearly also a pun on
Benedick's name.
68 **lay . . . heart** apply it medicinally;
embrace it passionately
69 **qualm** a feeling of faintness, especially
about the heart (but also produced by
orgasm)
70 i.e. now you've struck home (but presumably also with bawdy meaning of
'prick')
72 **moral** hidden meaning; i.e. an im-
moral (bawdy) one, as Margaret under-
lines in her response.
76 **list . . . list** wish . . . wish
80–1 **become a man** i.e. a man like any
other, vulnerable to affection

74 holy-thistle] *(holy thissel)*, *Rowe*

man. He swore he would never marry, and yet now in despite of his heart he eats his meat without grudging. And how you may be converted I know not, but methinks you look with your eyes as other women do.

BEATRICE   What pace is this that thy tongue keeps?   85
MARGARET   Not a false gallop.

Enter URSULA.

URSULA   Madam, withdraw! The prince, the count, Signor Benedick, Don John and all the gallants of the town are come to fetch you to church.
HERO   Help to dress me, good coz, good Meg, good   90
Ursula.   [*Exeunt.*]

[3.5]   *Enter* LEONATO, [DOGBERRY,] *the constable, and* [VERGES,] *the headborough.*

LEONATO   What would you with me, honest neighbour?
DOGBERRY   Marry, sir, I would have some confidence with you, that discerns you nearly.

81–2 **in . . . heart** in spite of his former determination (not to love)
82 **eats his meat** i.e. acknowledges his normal human appetites
86 **false gallop** (1) a forced burst of speed, cf. Nashe's *Terrors of the Night* (1594): 'I haue rid a false gallop these three or foure pages, now I care not if I breathe mee, and walke soberly and demurely half a dozen turnes, like a graue Citizen going about to take the ayre' (Nashe, 1.368); (2) a canter, a controlled gait as opposed to a full-out gallop. Touchstone's rhymes in *AYL* 3.2 are 'the very false gallop of verses' (110), i.e. an artificially controlled gait;

Margaret's point is that she speaks the truth.
3.5   The location is before Leonato's house.
0.2   *headborough* parish officer, local constable
2   **confidence** malapropism for 'conference' ('talk'). Cf. *RJ* 2.3.126–7: 'I desire some confidence with you'; or *MW* 1.4.147–9: 'I will tell your worship more . . . the next time we have confidence.' Both uses are by persons of low social caste (the nurse; Mistress Quickly), though the term, meaning confidential speech, is technically apt in the circumstance.
3   **discerns** i.e. malapropism for 'concerns'

---

88 Signor] *(signior)*   91 SD] *Rowe*   3.5] scene v *Capell*   0.1 DOGBERRY] *Rowe (Dogb.)*   0.2 VERGES] *Rowe (Verg.)*   2, 6 SP] *Rowe; Const. Dog. Q*

LEONATO   Brief, I pray you, for you see it is a busy time
with me.   5

DOGBERRY   Marry, this it is, sir.

VERGES   Yes, in truth it is, sir.

LEONATO   What is it, my good friends?

DOGBERRY   Goodman Verges, sir, speaks a little off the
matter. An old man, sir, and his wits are not so blunt as,   10
God help, I would desire they were; but, in faith, honest
as the skin between his brows.

VERGES   Yes, I thank God, I am as honest as any man
living, that is an old man and no honester than I.

DOGBERRY   Comparisons are odorous; *palabras*, neighbour   15
Verges.

LEONATO   Neighbours, you are tedious.

DOGBERRY   It pleases your worship to say so, but we are
the poor duke's officers. But truly, for mine own part, if

9   **Goodman** title for a man below the
rank of gentleman; Dogberry is attentive to caste.

10   **blunt** malapropism for 'sharp'

11–12 **honest . . . brows** proverbial
(Dent, S506), explained by another
proverb, 'Everyone's fault is written
in his forehead', presumably because
furrowed by care or conscience
(Foakes); also the site of branding for
some felonies. Brows are an especially
charged site in this play full of jokes
about the cuckold's horns; Thomas
Buoni explains in *Problems of Beauty
and All Human Affections* (1606):
'why is the seat of Shamefastnesse in
the forehead . . . because it is most
visible and apparent to the eye of man'
(Buoni, sig. O5ᵛ).

15   **odorous** malapropism for 'odious';
proverbial (Dent, C576); cf. *Sir Giles
Goosecap* (1606), 4.2.45: '*Goosecappe:*

Be Caparisons odious, sir Cut; what,
like flowers? / *Rudsbie:* O asse they be
odorous' (*Goosecappe*, 65).

palabras i.e. silence, from the popular
Spanish tag '*pocas palabras*' (few
words); cf. *Spanish Tragedy*, 3.14.118:
'*Pocas Palabras*, milde as the lambe'.

17   Constables were notoriously tedious
(perhaps because they think they
are witty: see 3.3.0.1n.). Cf. Jonson,
Cynthia's Revels (1601), 2.3.82–6:
'He is his own promoter in every
place. The wife of the ordinarie
giues him his diet, to maintain her
table in discourse, which (indeede)
is a meere tyrannie ouer her other
guests, for hee will vsurpe all the talke;
ten constables are not so tedious'
(Jonson, 4.73).

19   **poor duke's** i.e. duke's poor; see *MM*
2.1.46 for a similar transposition on
the part of Elbow.

7 SP] *Rowe; Headb.* Q   9 SP] *Rowe; Con. Do.* Q   off] *Steevens–Reed² (Capell);* of Q   13, 27 SP]
Rowe; Head. Q   15+ SP] *Rowe; Const. Dog.* Q

I were as tedious as a king I could find in my heart to   20
bestow it all of your worship.

LEONATO   All thy tediousness on me, ah?

DOGBERRY   Yea, an 'twere a thousand pound more than
'tis, for I hear as good exclamation on your worship as
of any man in the city, and though I be but a poor man,   25
I am glad to hear it.

VERGES   And so am I.

LEONATO   I would fain know what you have to say.

VERGES   Marry, sir, our watch tonight, excepting your
worship's presence, ha' ta'en a couple of as arrant   30
knaves as any in Messina.

DOGBERRY   A good old man, sir, he will be talking. As they
say, 'When the age is in, the wit is out.' God help us, it
is a world to see! Well said, i'faith, neighbour Verges.
Well, God's a good man. An two men ride of a horse,   35
one must ride behind. An honest soul, i'faith, sir,
by my troth, he is, as ever broke bread. But, God is
to be worshipped, all men are not alike. Alas, good
neighbour!

---

20 **tedious** Dogberry thinks tedious means wealthy.

21–2 **of . . . on** See Abbott, 175, for *on* and *of* interchange.

24 **exclamation** i.e. acclamation (*exclamation* means loud complaint; cf. *R3* 4.4.154: 'Thus will I drown your exclamations')

28 **fain** gladly

29 **tonight** last night
excepting malapropism for 'respecting', i.e. if I may be permitted to speak in your presence; despite his own verbal difficulties, Verges at least manages to begin to state the problem.

30 **arrant** unmitigated, extreme

33 **When . . . out** as Dogberry is unabashed to admit, a proverb (although in its original form, 'When the ale is in, the wit is out', Dent, W878)

34 **a . . . see** a sight worth seeing; proverbial (Dent, W878)

35 **Well . . . man** proverbial (Dent, G195), meaning that God's dispositions are providential
An if

35–6 **two . . . behind** proverbial (Dent, T638)

37 **as . . . bread** i.e. as any in the world; proverbial (Dent, M68)

---

22 on me, ah?] me! ah – *Rowe;* me! ah! *Capell*   23 an 'twere] *(and't twere)*   pound] times *F*   30 ha']
haue *F*   32 talking. As] *Capell (*talking; as*);* talking as *Q*   33 'When . . . out.'] *Cam¹;* when . . . out,
Q   34 see!] *Qc (*see:*);* see, *Qu*   35 An] *(and)*   37 he is, as] *Qc;* he is as *Qu*

LEONATO   Indeed, neighbour, he comes too short of you.   40

DOGBERRY   Gifts that God gives.

LEONATO   I must leave you.

DOGBERRY   One word, sir. Our watch, sir, have indeed
comprehended two aspicious persons, and we would
have them this morning examined before your worship.   45

LEONATO   Take their examination yourself, and bring it
me. I am now in great haste, as it may appear unto you.

DOGBERRY   It shall be suffigance.

LEONATO   Drink some wine ere you go. Fare you well!

[*Enter* Messenger.]

MESSENGER   My lord, they stay for you to give your   50
daughter to her husband.

LEONATO   I'll wait upon them; I am ready.

[*Exit with Messenger.*]

DOGBERRY   Go, good partner, go get you to Francis
Seacoal. Bid him bring his pen and inkhorn to the jail;
we are now to examination these men.   55

VERGES   And we must do it wisely.

DOGBERRY   We will spare for no wit, I warrant you. Here's

---

40 **comes too short** i.e. in speech;
Dogberry interprets it as 'doesn't
measure up to'. The joke is usually
brought out by having Verges played
by a smaller actor than Dogberry.

44 **comprehended** malapropism for
'apprehended'
aspicious malapropism for 'suspicious'

48 **suffigance** malapropism for 'sufficient'

50 **stay** are waiting

53–4 **Francis Seacoal** either another
member of the literate Seacoal family,
the sexton of 4.2, or the member of
the Watch whose Christian name was
previously given as George

55 **examination** malapropism for
'examine'

57–8 **Here's that** we have here that which;
some actors point to their heads (i.e.
brains) with this line, though it could
also refer to the assembled Watch.

---

41 SP] *Rowe; Const. Do. Q*   47 it] *om. F*   48 SP] *Rowe; Constable Q*   49 well!] *Rowe;* well. *Q*   49.1]
Rowe   52 SD] *Rowe (Ex. Leonato.); opp.* 49 *Q ((exit))*   55 examination these] examine those *F*

that shall drive some of them to a noncome. Only get
the learned writer to set down our excommunication,   59
and meet me at the jail.   [*Exeunt.*]

[**4.1**]   *Enter* DON PEDRO, [DON JOHN *the*] *bastard,*
          LEONATO, FRIAR [Francis], CLAUDIO, BENEDICK,
          HERO *and* BEATRICE [, *with others*].

LEONATO   Come, Friar Francis, be brief: only to the plain
    form of marriage, and you shall recount their particular
    duties afterwards.
FRIAR   You come hither, my lord, to marry this lady?
CLAUDIO   No.   5
LEONATO   To be married to her, Friar; you come to marry
    her.
FRIAR   Lady, you come hither to be married to this count?
HERO   I do.

---

58 **noncome** error for *non plus* (bewil-
    derment) or *non compos mentis* (of
    unsound mind)
59 **excommunication** malapropism for
    'examination'
4.1 The location is a church.
0.1–3 There is no entrance for Margaret
    or Ursula here, although some pro-
    ductions have them in attendance, and
    hence present a need for some silent
    reaction from Margaret during the alle-
    gations of Hero's nocturnal activities.
1–2 **plain form** simple liturgical form,
    i.e. skip over the preliminaries.
    Leonato's interference here is in
    keeping with his similar impulse in
    5.4; see 5.4.53 SDn.
2–3 **particular duties** specific
    obligations elaborated in the *Book of
    Common Prayer*, prescribed to be read
    by the Minister in the event of there

being no sermon, 'as touching the
duty of husbands toward their wives,
and wives toward their husbands';
these include, for men, loving and
honouring their spouse, and, for
women, submission and reverence,
'so that if any [husbands] obey not
the Word, they may be won without
the Word, by the conversation of the
wives, while they behold your chaste
conversation coupled with fear, whose
apparel let it not be outward, with
broided hair and trimming about with
gold, either in putting on of gorgeous
apparrel, but let the hid man which is
in the heart, be without all corruption
so that the spirit be mild and quiet,
which is a precious thing in the sight
of God . . . as Sarah obeyed Abraham
calling him lord; whose daughters ye
are made' (*BCP*, 297, 298–9).

---

60 SD] *F*   **4.1**] *Actus Quartus. F;* scene i *Rowe*   0.1 DON PEDRO, [DON JOHN *the*] *Rowe; Prince,*
Q   0.2 Francis] *Dyce*   0.3 *with others.*] *Dyce subst.; and Attendants. / White²*   4 SP] *Rowe; Fran.*
Q   lady?] *Rowe³; lady. Q*   6 her, Friar;] *Rowe³; her, Frier, Rowe; her: Frier, Q*

FRIAR   If either of you know any inward impediment why   10
  you should not be conjoined, I charge you on your souls
  to utter it.

CLAUDIO   Know you any, Hero?

HERO   None, my lord.

FRIAR   Know you any, Count?   15

LEONATO   I dare make his answer: none.

CLAUDIO   O, what men dare do! What men may do! What
  men daily do, not knowing what they do!

BENEDICK   How now? Interjections? Why then, some be
  of laughing, as ha, ha, he.   20

CLAUDIO

  Stand thee by, Friar. [*to Leonato*] Father, by your leave:
  Will you with free and unconstrained soul
  Give me this maid, your daughter?

LEONATO

  As freely, son, as God did give her me.

CLAUDIO

  And what have I to give you back whose worth   25
  May counterpoise this rich and precious gift?

---

10 **inward impediment** secret obstacle; the term *impediment* is from the Anglican service, which the Friar begins to follow: 'I require and charge you both, as ye will answer at the dreadful day of judgement . . . that if either of you know any impediment . . . ye do now confess it.'

18 **not . . . do** omitted in F perhaps because the compositor overlooked the fourth phrase ending in *do*

19–20 **Interjections . . . he** Benedick's comment on Claudio's rhetorical display cites William Lyly's *Short Introduction of Latin Grammar* (1538): 'An interiection . . . betokeneth a

sudden passion of the minde . . . Some are of . . . laughing, as Ha ha he' (sig. C8ᵛ). Cf. Lyly's *Endymion* (1591), 3.3.5: 'An interiection, whereof some are of mourning: as eho, vah' (*Works*, 3.42).
be of are to do with

21 **Stand thee by** stand aside
by your leave with your permission. Claudio asks if he may put a question to Leonato, ironically calling him *Father* even as he rejects any connection with him; he shifts into verse for his denunciation.

22 **unconstrained soul** unconstrainèd: clear conscience

26 **counterpoise** balance

18 not . . . do!] *om.* F   20 ha, ha] *F;* ah, ha *Q*   21 SD] *Oxf*¹

DON PEDRO
    Nothing, unless you render her again.
CLAUDIO
    Sweet Prince, you learn me noble thankfulness.
    There, Leonato, take her back again.
    Give not this rotten orange to your friend;   30
    She's but the sign and semblance of her honour.
    Behold how like a maid she blushes here!
    O, what authority and show of truth
    Can cunning sin cover itself withal!
    Comes not that blood as modest evidence   35

27 **render** return
28 **learn me** teach me; transitive use was not at the time considered ungrammatical.
30 **rotten orange** Oranges were associated with prostitutes (perhaps because pocked skin was an effect of venereal disease); they are also a symbol of deception, as one cannot tell from their covering what taste lies within. Cf. Beatrice's comparison of Claudio to a 'civil' orange, that bittersweet fruit, at 2.1.270; or Philip De Mornay, *Work Concerning the Trueness of Christian Religion* (1617): 'The rinde of the Orrendge is hot, and the meate within it is colde' (De Mornay, 10.141). The phrase was considered unsavoury enough to be bowdlerized from most productions from Garrick (1748) to the first decade of the twentieth century, replaced by 'blemished Brilliant' (Cox, *Shakespeare*, 177).
32, 37 **maid** virgin
32 **blushes** Claudio's and the Friar's contrasting readings of Hero's blush (158ff.) reflect its identity as a complex sign in Elizabethan moral physiognomy: index of shame and innocence alike, proof that the blusher was cognizant of (and hence potentially complicit in) the nature of what provoked the blush, though still virtuous enough to

be embarrassed by it. In Dent we find 'Blushing is virtue's colour' (B480), and Erasmus writes in *De Civilitate Morum Puerilium* that a blush should denote 'a natural and wholesome modesty . . . Although even that modesty should be so moderated that it is not construed as insolence, and does not connote . . . shame' (Erasmus, 23.275). Cf. Cesare Ripa's *Iconologia* (1593), fig. 265, which glosses the Roman emblem of Chastity as 'a woman veiled, pointing with the forefinger of her right hand to her face, to signifie that she had no reason to blush'; Rich's *Excellency of Good Women*: 'the blush of a woman's face, is an approbation of chaste and honourable minde, and a manifeste signe, that shee doth not approve any intemperate actions' (sig. D3ʳ); and Lyly's *Euphues*: 'virtuous women are for to bee chosen by the face, not when they blushe for the shame of some sinne committed but for feare she should comitte any' (101). Cf. *Edward III* 2.1.1–21.
33 **authority** power to inspire belief (*OED* 6)
    show impersonation, false representation
34 **withal** with
35 **blood** i.e. blush
    modest evidence evidence of modesty

27 SP] *Rowe (Pedro.); Princn Q*

To witness simple virtue? Would you not swear,
All you that see her, that she were a maid,
By these exterior shows? But she is none;
She knows the heat of a luxurious bed.
Her blush is guiltiness, not modesty.   40

LEONATO
What do you mean, my lord?

CLAUDIO
Not to be married, not to knit my soul
To an approved wanton.

LEONATO
Dear my lord, if you, in your own proof,
Have vanquished the resistance of her youth   45
And made defeat of her virginity –

CLAUDIO
I know what you would say: if I have known her,
You will say she did embrace me as a husband
And so extenuate the forehand sin.
No, Leonato,   50
I never tempted her with word too large,
But as a brother to his sister showed
Bashful sincerity and comely love.

HERO
And seemed I ever otherwise to you?

36 **witness** bear witness to
38 **exterior shows** superficial signs
39 **luxurious** lecherous, lascivious
41 **What . . . mean** What are you saying?
How can that be true? (But Claudio
understands *mean* as 'intend to do'.)
43 **approved wanton** approvèd: proven
slut
44 **in . . . proof** trial; experience
47 **known** i.e. sexually; 'And Adam knew
Heva his wife, who conceiving bare
Cain, saying, 'I have gotten a man of
the Lord' (Genesis, 4.1).
49 **extenuate . . . sin** i.e. their imminent
marriage would excuse the sin of
pre-marital fornication (or anticipating
marriage); as in the case of *MM*'s
Claudio, Elizabethan marriage custom
was divided on the question of whether
pre-marital sex was wrong if both
parties were contracted to marry.
51 **large** broad, lewd (as at 2.3.192, *large
jests*)
53 **comely** proper, decorous

42–3] *Ard²* *(Dyce); Q lines* married, / wanton. /
Q lines Leonato, / large, /   46 virginity –] *Rowe;* virginitie. *Q*   49–51] *Pope;*

CLAUDIO

   Out on thee, seeming! I will write against it: 55
   You seem to me as Dian in her orb,
   As chaste as is the bud ere it be blown;
   But you are more intemperate in your blood
   Than Venus, or those pampered animals
   That rage in savage sensuality.   60

HERO

   Is my lord well that he doth speak so wide?

LEONATO [*to Don Pedro*]

   Sweet Prince, why speak not you?

DON PEDRO   What should I speak?

---

55 'To hell with your pretence (to chastity);
I will bear witness against/denounce
it (your hypocrisy).' The ability of
women to dissemble virtue, and thus
the difficulty of discriminating between
good women and those who were
only pretending to be so, is a common
theme of Renaissance literature, as in
Spenser's *Faerie Queene*, or Alexander
Niccholes's guide to bachelors, *How
to Tell a Good Wife from a Bad* (1615):
'This undertaking is a matter of some
difficulty, for good wives are many
times so like unto bad, that they are
hardly discerned betwixt; they could
not otherwise deceive so many as they
do' (Niccholes, sig. B4ʳ). Alan Craven
conjectures that 'thee' for 'thy' is a
common error of Compositor A, in
which case the line could read 'Out on
thy seeming' (the comma is Collier's)
(Craven, 48).
56 **Dian . . . orb** The Roman goddess of
chastity was associated with the hunt
and the changeable moon, wherein she
was thought to reside (hence her ornament of crescent horns). The flower
of *Agnus Castus*, or 'Dian's buds', was
thought to preserve chastity; cf. *MND*

4.1.72–3: 'Dian's bud o'er Cupid's
flower / Hath such force and blessed
power'.
57 **blown** fully opened
58 **intemperate** ungoverned
   blood passion, lust
59 **Venus** the goddess of love (and mother
of Cupid), notorious adulteress to
her husband Vulcan, with Mars:
'According therefore to the opinion of
the Poets, Venus was taken to be the
goddess of wantonness and amorous
delights as that she inspired into the
minds of men, libidinous desires,
and lustful appetites' (Cartari, sig.
CC2ʳ).
   those pampered animals perhaps
pet monkeys, notoriously randy; see
Oth 3.3.406–7: 'Were they as prime as
goats, as hot as monkeys, / As salt as
wolves in pride'. Well-fed horses are
also a candidate; see *KL* 4.5.120–2, 'The
fitchew, nor the soiled horse, goes to't
with a more riotous appetite. Down
from the waist they are centaurs,
though women all above,' where
soiled = indulgently fed on fresh-cut
grass, and hence high in spirits.
61 **wide** wide of the mark; derangedly

---

55 thee, seeming!] *Collier (Knight);* thee seeming, *Q;* thee! Seeming! *(Seymour);* thy seeming! *Pope;*
the seeming! *Knight*   62 SD] *this edn*   62+ SP2] *Rowe (Pedro.); Prince Q*

I stand dishonoured that have gone about
To link my dear friend to a common stale.

LEONATO

Are these things spoken, or do I but dream? 65

DON JOHN

Sir, they are spoken, and these things are true.

BENEDICK

This looks not like a nuptial.

HERO

True? O God!

CLAUDIO

Leonato, stand I here?
Is this the prince? Is this the prince's brother? 70
Is this face Hero's? Are our eyes our own?

LEONATO

All this is so, but what of this, my lord?

CLAUDIO

Let me but move one question to your daughter,
And by that fatherly and kindly power
That you have in her bid her answer truly. 75

LEONATO

I charge thee do so, as thou art my child.

HERO

O, God defend me, how am I beset!
What kind of catechizing call you this?

---

64 **stale** (1) prostitute of the lowest class
(cf. 2.2.23: 'a contaminated stale, such
a one as Hero'); (2) decoy
69–71 Claudio's questions go to the heart
of the play's concern with the ability to
make judgements based on visual evidence; ironically, Don John is only the
Prince's half-brother, and Claudio has
just finished claiming that Hero's face is
not an adequate index of her identity.
73 **move** put

74 **kindly** natural (of kin)
75 **in** over
76 **as . . . child** i.e. by the truth of my
paternity (a warrant whose credibility
has already been established at 1.1.100)
77 **beset** surrounded, besieged, i.e. by
accusations
78 **catechizing** examination; the
Elizabethan catechism of faith is a
series of questions, beginning with
'What is your name?'

66 SP] *Rowe (John.)*; *Bastard Q* 68 True?] 'True?' *Cam;* True, *Q* 76 so] *om. F*

CLAUDIO

To make you answer truly to your name.

HERO

Is it not Hero? Who can blot that name   80
With any just reproach?

CLAUDIO   Marry, that can Hero;
Hero itself can blot out Hero's virtue.
What man was he talked with you yesternight
Out at your window betwixt twelve and one?
Now, if you are a maid, answer to this.   85

HERO

I talked with no man at that hour, my lord.

DON PEDRO

Why, then are you no maiden. Leonato,
I am sorry you must hear. Upon mine honour,
Myself, my brother and this grieved count
Did see her, hear her, at that hour last night,   90

79 **your name** Hero's name was that of a Greek literary heroine, a priestess of Venus who nonetheless inspired the devoted love of Leander and his arduous swim across the river Hellespont on her behalf; she loyally drowned herself after his own watery demise. Her reputation thus conjoined elements of both fidelity and carnality, and Claudio and Hero's exchange turns on this crux. Claudio's intention to make Hero *answer truly* to her name perhaps recalls his memory of Borachio's calling her name (3.3.139–40). Barbara Lewalski notes that in Chapman's translation of Musaeus' *Hero and Leander* (1616) 'Hero becomes also an emblem of dissimulation in regard to chastity, in that she continues as a priestess despite her love for Leander, and is hence denounced by Venus: "Since Hero had dissembled, and disgrast / Her rites so

much, and every breast infect, / With her deceits; she made her Architect / Of all dissimulation, and since then, / Never was any trust in maides or men"' (Lewalski, 'Namesake', 178). Claudio could mean either that the unchaste Hero shames the constancy of the legendary Hero, or that the famously unchaste Hero blots any virtues this Hero might have.

80 **blot** smudge, delete, so stain, as in writing with pen and ink, a medium of slander; cf. 139–41: 'O, she is fallen / Into a pit of ink that the wide sea / Hath drops too few to wash her clean again'.

81 **just reproach** fair criticism

82 **Hero itself** the very name (by becoming henceforth a name for scandalous rather than loyal behaviour)

83 **yesternight** last night

89 **grieved** grievèd: injured; grief-stricken

86 SP] *Qc; Bero Qu*   87 are you] you are *F*

Talk with a ruffian at her chamber window,
Who hath indeed, most like a liberal villain,
Confessed the vile encounters they have had
A thousand times in secret.

DON JOHN

Fie, fie, they are not to be named, my lord,   95
Not to be spoke of!
There is not chastity enough in language
Without offence to utter them. Thus, pretty lady,
I am sorry for thy much misgovernment.

CLAUDIO

O Hero! What a Hero hadst thou been   100
If half thy outward graces had been placed
About thy thoughts and counsels of thy heart!
But fare thee well, most foul, most fair. Farewell
Thou pure impiety and impious purity.
For thee I'll lock up all the gates of love,   105

92 **liberal** free in speech or behaviour; licentious
93–4 As Beatrice's scorn will illustrate ('Talk with a man out at a window! A proper saying!', 307–8), Don John needed to bolster the evidence of the window scene with Borachio's further corroboration of its meaning.
94 In productions in which Margaret is included in this scene (contrary to the original SDs) she often begins to react to this speech, sometimes even moving to interrupt; and Don John's interjection at 95ff. serves to silence her. It is of course crucial to the development of the plot that verification of Don John's plot be delayed.
97–8 **There . . . them** i.e. there is no language decorous enough to relate them without being indelicate
99 **thy** Don John's adoption of this form could either be contemptuous or express mock pity.

much misgovernment great misconduct.
101 **outward graces** physical qualities. The relation of inner and outer properties is a chief concern of conduct books; see *Court of Good Counsel*: 'I deny not but by the lookes of a woman, a man may gather somewhat of her disposition: but seeing God hath commanded vs not to judge altogether by the face of the woman, we must yet vse a more certain and commodious way' (W. B., sig. B1ᵛ).
102 **thy thoughts** Craven (48) conjectures (as did Rowe) that Compositor A committed his trademark error of substituting 'thy' for 'the' here.
counsels promptings
103 **foul, most fair** Dent, F29, gives as proverbial 'Fair without but foul within'.
105 **gates of love** the senses, especially the eyes, which will be closed to love

95 SP] *Capell; Iohn Q*   95–6] *Q; Hanmer lines* are / of! /   96 spoke] spoken *F*   102 thy thoughts] the thoughts *(Craven)*

263

And on my eyelids shall conjecture hang
To turn all beauty into thoughts of harm,
And never shall it more be gracious.

LEONATO

Hath no man's dagger here a point for me?

[*Hero falls.*]

BEATRICE

Why, how now, cousin! Wherefore sink you down?   110

DON JOHN

Come, let us go; these things come thus to light
Smother her spirits up.

[*Exeunt Don Pedro, Claudio and Don John.*]

BENEDICK

How doth the lady?

BEATRICE   Dead, I think. Help, uncle!
Hero! Why Hero! Uncle, Signor Benedick, Friar!

LEONATO

O Fate, take not away thy heavy hand!   115
Death is the fairest cover for her shame
That may be wished for.

BEATRICE   How now, cousin Hero?

[*Hero stirs.*]

FRIAR   Have comfort, lady.

LEONATO

Dost thou look up?

FRIAR   Yea, wherefore should she not?

---

106 **conjecture** suspicion
109 SD Hero's swoon (indicated by Beatrice's reaction at 110) follows upon her father's turning against her.
112 **spirits** vital powers
113 **Help, uncle!** This appeal can indicate Leonato's stage distance from Hero.
114 **Signor Benedick** '[Benedick] makes

an important decision when he does not leave the church with Claudio, Don Pedro, and the Bastard, as might be expected' (*Riv*, 329).
119 **look up** The ability to look (i.e. show one's face) towards the heavens was a sign of innocence; cf. *Ham* 3.3.50–1: 'Then I'll look up. / My fault is past'.

109 SD] *Hanmer (*Hero *swoons)   111 SP] *Capell; Bastard Q   112 SD] *Rowe (Exe. D. Pedro, D. John and Claudio)   114+ Signor] *(signior)   117 SD] *this edn (Collier MS (reviving))*

LEONATO

Wherefore? Why, doth not every earthly thing   120
Cry shame upon her? Could she here deny
The story that is printed in her blood?
Do not live, Hero; do not ope thine eyes!
For did I think thou wouldst not quickly die,
Thought I thy spirits were stronger than thy shames,   125
Myself would on the rearward of reproaches
Strike at thy life. Grieved I, I had but one?
Chid I for that at frugal Nature's frame?
O, one too much by thee! Why had I one?
Why ever wast thou lovely in my eyes?   130
Why had I not with charitable hand
Took up a beggar's issue at my gates,
Who smirched thus, and mired with infamy,
I might have said: 'No part of it is mine;
This shame derives itself from unknown loins.'   135

120–43 Cox reports that many productions from the eighteenth to the early twentieth centuries cut this speech so as to 'dignify and idealise Leonato in this scene . . . softening his resentment and self-pity and making him a more sympathetic figure than in the full text' (Cox, *Shakespeare*, 181). Unlike his prototype in the Bandello source, who 'never having found his daughter anything but honest, thought that the knight had been seized with disdain at their poverty and present lack of worldly success' (Bullough, 118–19), Leonato has no such economic explanation to fall back upon.

122 **printed . . . blood** (1) shown by her blood: 'The story which her blushes discover to be true' (Johnson); as at 55, 80 and 140, the metaphor is bibliographical; (2) the innate weakness of women

123 **ope** open
125 **spirits** vital forces, as at 112
126 **on the rearward** (1) as a rearguard action following her disgrace (a military metaphor); (2) after reproaching. The sense is that if Hero's shames do not kill her, Leonato will.
127 **Strike** This can serve as a cue for Leonato's action.
   but one i.e. only one child
128 **Chid . . . that** did I complain about that; did I reproach because of that
   frugal i.e. for allowing him only one child
   Nature's frame i.e. the goddess's scheme of things
129 **by** in
132 **issue** offspring
133 **smirched** smirchèd: being so soiled
   mired soiled, defiled; a mire = a muddy bog

120 Why, doth] *Theobald;* why doth *Q*   126 rearward] *(rereward);* reward *F;* hazard *Collier MS*
133 smirched] smeered *F*   134–5 'No . . . loins.'] *Capell subst.;* no . . . loynes, *Q*

But mine, and mine I loved, and mine I praised,
And mine that I was proud on – mine so much
That I myself was to myself not mine
Valuing of her. Why she – O, she is fallen
Into a pit of ink that the wide sea   140
Hath drops too few to wash her clean again,
And salt too little which may season give
To her foul-tainted flesh.
BENEDICK   Sir, sir, be patient.
For my part, I am so attired in wonder
I know not what to say.   145
BEATRICE
O, on my soul, my cousin is belied!
BENEDICK
Lady, were you her bedfellow last night?
BEATRICE
No, truly, not – although until last night
I have this twelvemonth been her bedfellow.

---

138 **to . . . mine** i.e. that I was worth
nothing in my own eyes, compared
with the value I placed upon her
142 **season give** preserve from decay;
render palatable
143 ***foul-tainted** befouled; Dyce (see
t.n.) hyphenated Q's 'foule tainted' on
the grounds that 'foule' was the intensifier of 'tainted' rather than the other
way round.
143–5 **Sir . . . say** Q prints these lines
as prose, and the irregularity of their
rhythm (and the idea of Benedick's
prosaic interjection interrupting the
flow of Leonato's aria) argue for the
same. However, a similar prosifying
at 155–8 suggests that Q's compositor
seems to have found himself with more
text than expected to fit on this page
(the foot of sig. G1ʳ), perhaps as a result
of faulty casting off of copy (although
Newcomer suggested compositorial

eye-skip between the 'I have' of 156
and that of 158). Sig G1ᵛ, being part
of the inner forme, was already printed
off. Hence the compositor made the
fit by rendering these two passages
as prose (compressing seven lines of
verse into five lines), and extending his
page by two lines; he may indeed have
been forced to omit some of the MS
text, rendering the passage difficult
to explain. F's compositor followed
Q's lining.
144 **attired in wonder** filled with amazement; cf. *Mac* 1.7.35–6: 'Was the hope
drunk, / Wherein you dress'd yourself?'
146 **belied** slandered
149 **this twelvemonth** Beatrice is concerned here to respond to the charge
that Borachio confessed to multiple
vile encounters (93). The point is lost
on Leonato.

143 foul-tainted] *Dyce (Walker);* foule tainted *Q;* soul-tainted *(Collier)*   143–5 Sir . . . say] *Pope;*
prose *Q*   148 truly, not –] *Rowe (*truly, not;*);* truly, not *Q;* truly: not *F*

LEONATO

Confirmed, confirmed! O, that is stronger made   150
Which was before barred up with ribs of iron.
Would the two princes lie, and Claudio lie
Who loved her so, that speaking of her foulness
Washed it with tears? Hence from her, let her die.

FRIAR

Hear me a little: 155
For I have only been silent so long,
And given way unto this course of fortune,
By noting of the lady. I have marked
A thousand blushing apparitions
To start into her face, a thousand innocent shames   160
In angel whiteness beat away those blushes;
And in her eye there hath appeared a fire
To burn the errors that these princes hold
Against her maiden truth. Call me a fool,
Trust not my reading nor my observations,   165

150 **that** i.e. the accusation
151 **before** already
   barred up reinforced
154 **Washed it** See Abbott, 399, for the omitted nominative. The lines provide a retrospective SD for the actor playing Claudio.
155–8 These lines are set as prose in Q at the foot of the page (sig. G1ʳ); see 143–5n. The half line at 155 gives a pause in which the other actors can quiet themselves (Leonatos have an opportunity to engage in violent stage action with *Hence from her* at 154, and thus the Friar's words are an order as well as a request).
156–8 **For . . . lady** i.e. for my silence and passivity up to this point are due only to my having observed Hero's behaviour
157 **given . . . fortune** allowed matters to proceed thus far
159–161 **apparitions . . . blushes** The

Friar's *noting* of Hero's physiognomy interprets her blushes as potentially incriminating signs, but he also adduces the alternating paleness of her skin as a countervailing mark of innocence. See 32n.
160 **start** rush
   innocent shames i.e. as opposed to blushes occasioned by sin; see 32n.
162–3 **fire . . . errors** The metaphor is from the burning of heretics or their books; cf. 1.1.217–18: 'the opinion that fire cannot melt out of me'. The observation suggests that Hero's response includes an element of indignation as well as devastation.
164 **maiden truth** i.e. innocence, truth of her maidenhood
165–7 **Trust . . . book** i.e. I have good intuition and lots of experience, both of which confirm my book learning/interpretation of Hero's appearance

152 two] *om. F*   155–8] *Pope; prose Q*   156 been silent] silent been *White²*   158 lady.] *Pope;* lady, *Q*   161 beat] beare *F*

Which with experimental seal doth warrant
The tenor of my book; trust not my age,
My reverence, calling nor divinity,
If this sweet lady lie not guiltless here
Under some biting error.

LEONATO   Friar, it cannot be.   170
Thou seest that all the grace that she hath left
Is that she will not add to her damnation
A sin of perjury. She not denies it.
Why seek'st thou then to cover with excuse
That which appears in proper nakedness?   175

FRIAR
Lady, what man is he you are accused of?

HERO
They know that do accuse me. I know none.
If I know more of any man alive
Than that which maiden modesty doth warrant,
Let all my sins lack mercy! – O my father,   180
Prove you that any man with me conversed

166 **experimental seal** the validation of
experience
167 **tenor . . . book** teachings of my
education
168 i.e. my solemnity, my position, nor
theology
170 **biting** stinging, bitter
171 **grace** virtue, but also (with *damna-*
tion and *sin* a theological term) invok-
ing a notion of salvation; Leonato
responds in theological terms to the
Friar's warrant of his own *divinity*.
173 **not denies** does not deny; see Abbott,
305, on this construction.
175 **proper nakedness** truthful exposure
176 The Friar's question is designed to
trick Hero into revealing the truth,
should it be incriminating. 'He was
all the while at the accusation, and
heard no names mentioned . . . had

Hero been guilty, it was very probable
that, in that hurry and confusion of
spirits, into which the terrible insult
of her lover had thrown her, she
could barely have observed that the
man's name was not mentioned, and
so, on this question, have betrayed
herself by naming the person she was
conscious of having an affair with'
(Warburton).
177 **I know none** Hero echoes Claudio's
use of the verb at 47.
179 **that . . . warrant** i.e. the acquaint-
ance which is appropriate to maiden
innocence
180 **my father** This appeal could be
directed to either the Friar or Leonato,
but by 184 Hero is talking to Leonato
alone.
181 **Prove** if you can prove

167 tenor] *(tenure)*   180 mercy!] *F (*mercy.*);* mercy, *Q*

At hours unmeet, or that I yesternight
Maintained the change of words with any creature,
Refuse me, hate me, torture me to death!

FRIAR

There is some strange misprision in the princes.   185

BENEDICK

Two of them have the very bent of honour.
And if their wisdoms be misled in this,
The practice of it lives in John the bastard,
Whose spirits toil in frame of villainies.

LEONATO

I know not. If they speak but truth of her,   190
These hands shall tear her; if they wrong her honour,
The proudest of them shall well hear of it.
Time hath not yet so dried this blood of mine,
Nor age so eat up my invention,
Nor fortune made such havoc of my means,   195
Nor my bad life reft me so much of friends
But they shall find awaked in such a kind

182 **unmeet** inappropriate
183 **change** exchange
184 **Refuse** disown
185 **misprision** error, misunderstanding
the princes technically, only Don
Pedro and Don John, though Benedick's
response includes Claudio in royalty
186 **have . . . of** are wholly inclined to,
given to; the metaphor is from archery,
of a bow drawn to its full extent.
188 **practice** deceitful contrivance
John the bastard This is the first
explicit mention to the audience of
Don John's illegitimacy (noted in SDs
and SPs), though signs of melancholy
and envy could have suggested it (in
the Renaissance, signified by black
clothing).
189 i.e. who devotes himself to contriving
villainous plots

191–2 **if . . . it** As does the defender of
the slandered princess in Shakespeare's
Ariostan source, Leonato (whose
softening occurs only after Benedick's
entertainment of the possibility of a
mistake) now turns to the postures
of chivalry, 'that will in armes defend
his daughter dear, / And prove her
innocent in open fight' (*Orlando*,
5.68.3–4).
194 **eat** past tense, pronounced 'et'
invention mental powers, 'policy of
mind', as at 198; four syllables
195 **means** resources, perhaps financial
196 **reft** i.e. bereft, deprived
friends includes kindred, such as his
brother Antonio (who is not, however,
given an entrance in this scene in Q)
197 **they** i.e. the princes
kind manner

190 not.] *F (*not:*); not, Q*

Both strength of limb and policy of mind,
Ability in means and choice of friends
To quit me of them throughly.

FRIAR   Pause awhile,   200
And let my counsel sway you in this case.
Your daughter here the princes left for dead.
Let her awhile be secretly kept in,
And publish it that she is dead indeed.
Maintain a mourning ostentation,   205
And on your family's old monument
Hang mournful epitaphs, and do all rites
That appertain unto a burial.

LEONATO

What shall become of this? What will this do?

FRIAR

Marry, this well carried shall on her behalf   210

---

198 **policy of mind** See 194n.
199 **choice of friends** i.e. to act as his seconds in a duel
200 **quit . . . throughly** thoroughly revenge myself upon them
   Pause awhile The Friar's words (as at 155) can provide a SD for Leonato's behaviour.
202 ***princes** Q's 'princesse' makes a certain grammatical, but not social, sense.
205 **mourning ostentation** formal, public show of mourning; the Friar's plan to deceive Claudio into a recognition of true feeling resembles Don Pedro's plan to gull Beatrice and Benedick into love.
206 **monument** tomb
207 **mournful epitaphs** The writing and affixing of epitaphs to the hearse or tomb was a mourning practice. Cf. Jonson's *Epitaph of the Countess of Pembroke*: 'Underneath this sable hearse / Lies the subject of all verse

. . . ' (Jonson, 8.433); and the opening SD of Middleton's *A Chaste Maid in Cheapside* (1613), 5.4: '*enter . . . the coffin of the virgin . . . with a garland of flowers, with epitaphs pinned upon it*' (Middleton, 5.109). Leonato will instruct Claudio to so hang an epitaph upon Hero's sepulchre.
209 **become of** result from
210–22 Jonathan Bate notes a resemblance to the Greek myth of Alcestis, who volunteers to die in place of her husband Admetus; Hercules discovers her sacrifice and returns her to her husband, who, guilt-stricken, recognizes her true worth: 'if Hero is an Alcestis, Claudio is an Admetus who repents of and learns from earlier unfair conduct . . . the mock death must make Claudio see Hero's virtues, must make him into a nobler lover' (Bate, 'Dying', 83).
210 **well carried** i.e. well carried off, well managed

202 princes . . . dead] *Theobald;* princesse (left for dead) *Q*

Change slander to remorse; that is some good.
But not for that dream I on this strange course,
But on this travail look for greater birth:
She, dying, as it must be so maintained,
Upon the instant that she was accused,   215
Shall be lamented, pitied and excused
Of every hearer. For it so falls out
That what we have we prize not to the worth
Whiles we enjoy it, but being lacked and lost,
Why, then we rack the value, then we find   220
The virtue that possession would not show us
Whiles it was ours. So will it fare with Claudio:
When he shall hear she died upon his words,
Th'idea of her life shall sweetly creep
Into his study of imagination,   225
And every lovely organ of her life
Shall come apparelled in more precious habit,
More moving, delicate and full of life,
Into the eye and prospect of his soul
Than when she lived indeed. Then shall he mourn –   230

213 **on this travail** as a result of this
effort, with a play both on travail/
travel (not distinguished in early
modern orthography), generated by
course (212), and *travail*, as labour-
pains; cf. *birth* (213).
217 **Of** by
218 **to the worth** for what it is worth; a
proverbial idea, cf. Dent, W924: 'The
worth of a thing is best known by the
want.'
220 **rack** stretch to the utmost (from the
torture device)
223 **upon** at the sound of, as a result of
225 **study of imagination** imaginative

reflection; memory
226 **organ . . . life** living feature (with
some sense of actual body parts, but
the more abstract sense as well)
227 **in . . . habit** more richly adorned;
the Friar seems to suggest that news
of Hero's death will make Claudio
remember her as even more glorious
than she had been in his actual
experience of her. In the Bandello
source, the intention is merely to
make the Claudio figure confess his
true motive in slandering her, i.e.
his second thoughts about her social
station (Bullough, 118).

221 show] (shew)   224 idea] (Idæa)   228 moving, delicate] *F2;* moouing delicate *Q;* moving-
delicate *Capell*

271

If ever love had interest in his liver –
And wish he had not so accused her;
No, though he thought his accusation true.
Let this be so, and doubt not but success
Will fashion the event in better shape   235
Than I can lay it down in likelihood.
But if all aim but this be levelled false,
The supposition of the lady's death
Will quench the wonder of her infamy.
And if it sort not well, you may conceal her,   240
As best befits her wounded reputation,
In some reclusive and religious life,
Out of all eyes, tongues, minds and injuries.

BENEDICK

Signor Leonato, let the friar advise you,
And though you know my inwardness and love   245
Is very much unto the prince and Claudio,
Yet, by mine honour, I will deal in this
As secretly and justly as your soul

---

231 **interest in** claim upon
  liver Elizabethans often imagined the liver as much a seat of love as the heart (the brains and the genitals were also contenders), though the liver has perhaps more comical connotations than the latter. Cf. *TN* 2.4.98–9: 'their love may be call'd appetite, / No motion of the liver, but the palate'; *MW* 2.1.105: 'FORD Love my wife? / PISTOL With liver burning hot'; *LLL* 4.3.73–4: 'This is the liver vein, which makes flesh a deity, / A green goose a goddess.' The liver was thought to play a key role in producing signs of love such as pallor, weight loss, hollow eyes and sleeplessness: 'because of the distraction of spirits the liver doth not performe his part, nor turns the aliment into blood as it ought, and for that cause the members are weake for want of sustenance' (Burton, 3.139).

232 **accused** accusèd
234–6 Follow this plan and doubt not that its accomplishment will produce a better outcome than I can predict.
237–9 i.e. but at the very least, if the plan doesn't wholly succeed, her supposed death will silence discussion about her shame
237 **all aim but** every outcome except
  be levelled false fail to come to fruition
239 **wonder of** wondering at, speculation about
240 **sort** turn out
242 **reclusive . . . life** i.e. in a convent
243 **Out of** out of the reach of, beyond
245 **inwardness** intimacy; Shakespeare's only such use. Cf. *MM* 3.2.127: 'Sir, I was an inward of his.'
246 **Is** Abbott, 336, illustrates singular verbs after two or more singular nouns as subjects.

Should with your body.

LEONATO   Being that I flow in grief,
The smallest twine may lead me.   250

FRIAR
'Tis well consented. Presently away,
For to strange sores strangely they strain the cure.
Come, lady, die to live. This wedding day
Perhaps is but prolonged. Have patience and endure.
                              Exeunt [all but Beatrice and Benedick].

BENEDICK   Lady Beatrice, have you wept all this while?   255

BEATRICE   Yea, and I will weep awhile longer.

BENEDICK   I will not desire that.

BEATRICE   You have no reason; I do it freely.

BENEDICK   Surely I do believe your fair cousin is
wronged.   260

BEATRICE   Ah, how much might the man deserve of me
that would right her!

BENEDICK   Is there any way to show such friendship?

BEATRICE   A very even way, but no such friend.

BENEDICK   May a man do it?   265

BEATRICE   It is a man's office, but not yours.

---

249 **flow in** am overcome by, am swept
away by (as by a current, perhaps of
tears)
251–4 The Friar closes the verse with a
quatrain, with the last line an alex-
andrine.
251 **Presently** immediately
252 **to . . . cure** Shakespeare's alliterative
rendition of the proverbial phrase 'a
desperate disease must have a desperate remedy' (Dent, D357)
254 **prolonged** postponed
258 **freely** of my own accord
262 **right** i.e. avenge (following from
wronged, 260)
264 **even** straightforward, direct
266 **office** duty

but not yours i.e. because Hero
should properly be revenged by a male
member of her own family, or because
Benedick is friends with Claudio and
the Prince – or because Beatrice does
not feel she has the right, given their
history, to ask Benedick to do this.
Cox reports that some nineteenth-
century actresses delivered this phrase
sarcastically, up until the performance
of Ellen Terry, who delivered it as
'the afterthought of a woman . . .
unwilling to expose her love to the
dangers of a duel, even at the risk
of his manhood being compromised'
(Cox, *Shakespeare*, 189). Benedick's
acceptance of her charge is tantamount

254 SD] *Rowe (Exeunt manent Benedick and Beatrice.); exit. Q*

273

BENEDICK   I do love nothing in the world so well as you.
    Is not that strange?
BEATRICE   As strange as the thing I know not. It were as
    possible for me to say I loved nothing so well as you.   270
    But believe me not – and yet I lie not. I confess nothing,
    nor I deny nothing. I am sorry for my cousin.
BENEDICK   By my sword, Beatrice, thou lovest me.
BEATRICE   Do not swear and eat it.
BENEDICK   I will swear by it that you love me, and I will   275
    make him eat it that says I love not you.
BEATRICE   Will you not eat your word?
BENEDICK   With no sauce that can be devised to it. I
    protest I love thee.
BEATRICE   Why then, God forgive me.   280

to acceptance of kinship ('Good Lord, for alliance!', 2.1.292). Rich notes in *The Excellency of Good Women* that 'I have seldom seene an honest woman . . . to haue many freendes to vndertake for her, that will quarrel for her, that will fight for her, or that will be at any great costes and charge by any means to support her, vnless it be a father, a brother a kinsman or some such like. But Thucydides will needes approve that woman to be most honest, that is least knowne, and I think indeed that the most honest woman is least spoken of, for they doe please the least in number and vertue was never graced by the multitude' (sig. C1ᵛ–2ʳ).
269 **As . . . not** i.e. as strange as anything unknown could imaginably be. Both speakers continue to quibble (significantly, on *nothing* and knowing) in their first admissions of love, as if to leave an escape clause in their declarations. 'They manage by a deft indirectness to put nothing into a syntax where the other person can

choose either its negative or its positive meaning' (Jorgensen, 30).
273 **By my sword** a mild oath, derived from the function of a sword as a guarantor of a gentleman's honour and status (as well as its cross-shape formed by the handguard, useful for swearing upon). Beatrice's reply (don't eat – or renege on – your oath/word) may pun on the more serious oath, 'God's word', which contracts to 'sword, as in *H5* 2.1.98–101: 'BARDOLPH By this sword, he that makes the first thrust, I'll kill him. By this sword, I will. / PISTOL Sword is an oath, and oaths must have their course.' Cf. Dent, W825: 'To eat one's words'.
278 **to** for
279, 283 **protest** solemnly affirm
280 **God forgive me** either for 'infringing the convention that the woman takes no initiative in love' (Ard²), or, given her reference to a *happy hour* (282), for thinking of love in the midst of her cousin's tragedy

274 swear] *Q;* sweare by it *F*

BENEDICK   What offence, sweet Beatrice?

BEATRICE   You have stayed me in a happy hour; I was
about to protest I loved you.

BENEDICK   And do it, with all thy heart.

BEATRICE   I love you with so much of my heart that none   285
is left to protest.

BENEDICK   Come, bid me do anything for thee.

BEATRICE   Kill Claudio.

BENEDICK   Ha, not for the wide world.

BEATRICE   You kill me to deny it. Farewell. [*Moves as if to*   290
leave.]

BENEDICK   Tarry, sweet Beatrice. [*Stays her.*]

BEATRICE   I am gone, though I am here. There is no love
in you; nay, I pray you, let me go.

BENEDICK   Beatrice –

BEATRICE   In faith, I will go.   295

BENEDICK   We'll be friends first.

BEATRICE   You dare easier be friends with me than fight
with mine enemy.

BENEDICK   Is Claudio thine enemy?

BEATRICE   Is 'a not approved in the height a villain, that   300
hath slandered, scorned, dishonoured my kinswoman?
O, that I were a man! What, bear her in hand until they

282 **stayed me** stopped me (perhaps
physically, as at 291, or by interrupting her with his query at 281); caught
me, found me
happy hour lucky moment
286 **protest** quibble on the meaning at
279, 283
288 **Kill Claudio** This line, its delivery
and its reception, by both Benedick
and the audience (laughter? shocked
silence?) is one of the indices of a
production's tenor. See Cox, 'Stage'.
290 **deny it** refuse my request

292 ¹**I . . . here** I have left in spirit,
even though you are forcibly retaining
me.
300 **approved . . . height** proved to the
utmost extreme
302 **a man!** i.e. able to avenge Hero in
a duel
bear . . . hand lead her on, delude
her; cf. Jonson, *Volpone*, 1.1.88–90:
'still bearing them in hand, / Letting
the cherry knock against their lips, /
And draw it, by their mouths, and back
againe' (Jonson, 5.27).

290 it] *om. F*   SD] *this edn*   291 SD] *Oxf¹ (Barring her way)*   294 Beatrice –] *Theobald;* Beatrice. *Q*

come to take hands, and then with public accusation,
uncovered slander, unmitigated rancour? O God, that I
were a man! I would eat his heart in the marketplace.   305

BENEDICK   Hear me, Beatrice –

BEATRICE   Talk with a man out at a window! A proper
saying!

BENEDICK   Nay, but Beatrice –

BEATRICE   Sweet Hero! She is wronged, she is slandered,   310
she is undone.

BENEDICK   Beat –

BEATRICE   Princes and counties! Surely a princely
testimony, a goodly count! Count Comfit, a sweet
gallant surely. O that I were a man for his sake! Or   315
that I had any friend would be a man for my sake!
But manhood is melted into curtsies, valour into

303 **take hands** i.e. be wedded
304 **uncovered** barefaced; suddenly
revealed
307–8 **A proper saying** a likely story;
given that Beatrice knows herself to
have *this twelvemonth* been Hero's
bedfellow (149), and thus clear of the
charge of having had 'vile encounters
. . . A thousand times in secret' with
Borachio (93–4) (during night-time
hours, anyhow).
311 **undone** ruined (in her reputation
and her future marital prospects)
313 **counties** mocking term for multiple
countships
314 **a goodly count** a fine excuse for
a nobleman; a fine story (account);
a likely accusation (cf. *testimony*).
Beatrice's rage seems only to hone her
quibbling power.

Count Comfit Count Sweetmeat,
'i.e. a specious nobleman made out of
sugar' (Steevens), with the sense of
insubstantial concoction – *conte confect*,
French for invented tale (White, cited
in Furness); Beatrice apparently found
Claudio's loverly demeanour as cloying
as Benedick once did. Cf. Sir Thomas
Overbury's Theophrastian character
of an Amorist: 'his fashion exceeds
the worth of his weight. He is never
without verses, and muske comfects,
and sighs to the hazard of his buttons'
(Overbury, 10–11).
317 **curtsies** Q's 'cursies' can be read
either as 'curtsies' (a subservient and/
or scraping bow, as at 2.1.46–7: 'it is
my cousin's duty to make curtsy');
or 'courtesies': fancy manners (which
might include curtseying).

304 rancour?] rancour – *Rowe*   306, 309 Beatrice –] *Collier;* Beatrice. *Q*   307 window!] *Malone;*
window? *Hanmer;* window – *Rowe;* window, *Q*   312 Beat –] *Theobald;* Beat? *Q*   314 count! Count]
*Q (*Counte, Counte*);* Count, *F*   317 curtsies] *(*cursies*);* curtesies *F3*

compliment, and men are only turned into tongue, and trim ones, too. He is now as valiant as Hercules that only tells a lie and swears it. I cannot be a man   320
with wishing, therefore I will die a woman with grieving.

BENEDICK   Tarry, good Beatrice. By this hand, I love thee.

BEATRICE   Use it for my love some other way than swearing by it.

BENEDICK   Think you in your soul the Count Claudio   325
hath wronged Hero?

BEATRICE   Yea, as sure as I have a thought or a soul.

BENEDICK   Enough, I am engaged. I will challenge him. I will kiss your hand, and so I leave you. By this hand, Claudio shall render me a dear account. As you hear of   330
me, so think of me. Go comfort your cousin. I must say she is dead, and so farewell.   [*Exeunt by different doors.*]

318 **compliment** insubstantial flattery (such as Benedick's offer to 'do anything for thee', 287)
are . . . tongue have become words only
319 **trim** fine, glib
321 **with** by
322 **By this hand** either hers, which he has taken, or his own, which he holds up as proof of his sincerity
327 a solemn oath, and a relatively novel possibility for a woman in this period, when the female possession of souls was still, for some, a matter of at least mock debate. See, for instance, John Donne, *Certain Problems* (1623): 'Why hath the Common Opinion afforded Women Soules? Wee deny soules to others equall to them in all but in speech . . . Haue they so many aduantages and meanes to hurt vs that we dare not displease them,

but giue them what they will . . . doe we somewhat (in this dignifying of them) flatter Princes and great personages that are so much gouerned by them? Or do wee in that easinesse and prodigality wherein we daily lose our owne soules to wee care not whom, so labour to perswade ourselues, that sith a woman hath a soule, a soule is no great matter?' (sig. G2ᵛ–3ʳ). Women do have souls in the King James Bible, e.g. Genesis, 35.18.
328 **engaged** committed, i.e. contracted to fight on her behalf. This crucial switch of allegiance from the word of his male companions to a woman's belief is a defining moment for Benedick.
330 **dear account** costly payment (with perhaps some pun, similar to Beatrice's at 314, on *count*)

329 I] *om.* F   331 cousin] (coosin)   332 SD] *F2 (Exeunt.)*   by different doors] *this edn*

[4.2]   *Enter the constables*[, DOGBERRY *and* VERGES],
   and the [Sexton *as*] *town clerk, in gowns,* [*with the* Watch,]
            BORACHIO [*and* CONRADE].

DOGBERRY   Is our whole dissembly appeared?

VERGES   O, a stool and a cushion for the sexton.

SEXTON [*Sits.*]   Which be the malefactors?

DOGBERRY   Marry, that am I, and my partner.

VERGES   Nay, that's certain; we have the exhibition to   5
examine.

SEXTON   But which are the offenders that are to be
examined? [*to Dogberry*] Let them come before, master
constable.

4.2 The location is a prison.

0.2 *the **Sexton** This term was inserted by Capell (following the SP at 3ff.). A sexton was a minor church official in charge of church property; here, presumably, being the *learned writer* named at 3.5.59, he also moonlights as the town clerk.

in gowns Black gowns were the official robes of Elizabethan constables.

1+ SP *The original SPs throughout this scene, which denote actors' (or intended actors') names, betray the marks of the play's composition, and perhaps that the copy-text that served as the basis for Q was a promptbook used in the theatre (and hence puzzled over by a compositor). Dogberry's part is rendered variously as '*Kemp*' (or '*Keeper*', '*Ke.*', '*Kem.*') or '*Andrew*', for the actor Will Kemp, who often took the parts of the clown (or the 'Merry Andrew') in the company of the Lord Chamberlain's Men (until 1599; see pp. 25, 128). Verges, similarly, is assigned to '*Cowley*' or '*Couley*', for

the actor Richard Cowley, or '*Const.*' (at 53). The speeches of the Watch are assigned to '*Watch 1*', '*Watch 2*' and '*Watch*', which may or may not correspond to the assignments of 3.3 (e.g. some editions assign Watch 1 here to Seacoal, given his promotion in the earlier scene to head of the Watch).

1 **dissembly** malapropism for 'assembly'

2 From this line it appears that Verges is in charge of arranging the examination room (this directive may serve to finesse the scene change, if the moving of stage furniture is involved).

4 **that am I** It is not entirely clear what misunderstanding of *malefactor* leads Dogberry and Verges to come forward here, although it probably relies on the meaning of 'factor' as steward (Cam[2]).

5 **exhibition** i.e. commission (given to them by Leonato in 3.5)

8 ***before**, i.e. to the fore; the punctuation (or enunciation) of this line to include a pause after *before* (and so to render it an instruction to Dogberry

---

4.2] *Capell (SCENE II)*   **0.1** DOGBERRY *and* VERGES] *Rowe subst.*   **0.2–3** *and . . .* BORACHIO] *Capell subst.; Borachio, and the Towne clearke in gownes. Q; Borachio, Conrade, the Town Clerke and Sexton in gowns / Rowe*   **0.3** *and* CONRADE] *Rowe*   **1** SP] *Capell; Keeper Q; To. Cl. / Rowe*   **2, 5** SP] *Capell; Cowley Q; Dog. / Rowe*   **3** SD] *Oxf*   **4** SP] *Capell; Andrew Q; Verg. / Rowe*   **8** before, master] *this edn;* before maister *Q*   SD] *this edn*

DOGBERRY   Yea, marry, let them come before me. [*Watch*   10
lead Borachio and Conrade forward, then step back.]
[*to Borachio*] What is your name, friend?

BORACHIO   Borachio.

DOGBERRY [*to the Sexton*]   Pray write down 'Borachio'. [*to
Conrade*] Yours, sirrah?

CONRADE   I am a gentleman, sir, and my name is   15
Conrade.

DOGBERRY   Write down 'master gentleman Conrade'.
Masters, do you serve God?

CONRADE, BORACHIO   Yea, sir, we hope.

DOGBERRY   Write down, that they hope they serve God;   20
and write God first, for God defend but God should
go before such villains. Masters, it is proved already
that you are little better than false knaves, and it will go
near to be thought so shortly. How answer you for
yourselves?   25

CONRADE   Marry, sir, we say we are none.

DOGBERRY   A marvellous witty fellow, I assure you. But I
will go a bout with him. [*to Borachio*] Come you hither,

to let the malefactors come forward)
makes his interpretation at 10 yet
another instance of construing the
Sexton's commands as a comment on
his own self-importance.
14 **sirrah** fellow (a term of contempt,
which Conrade's insistence on his status seeks to rebuff)
19–22 **Yea . . . villains** omitted in F,
presumably to comply with the 1606

statute against profanity and the taking
of God's name in vain in plays
21 **defend** forbid (cf. 2.1.83)
22 **Masters** a term of deference, hence
perhaps comically inappropriate
28 **a bout** a round (as in sparring, or
dancing – cf. 2.1.76); heard as '(go)
about' = deal with, outmanoeuvre
him i.e. Borachio (unless *a bout* =
'about', in which case *him* = Conrade)

10 SP] *Capell; Kemp Q; To. Cl. / Rowe*   10–11 *Watch . . . forward*] *Folg² (Conrade and Borachio are
brought forward)*   11 *then step back*] *this edn*   12 SD] *this edn*   13 SP] *Capell; Ke. Q; Kem. F; To.
Cl. / Rowe*   SD] *Oxf* 'Borachio'] *Capell subst;* Borachio *Q*   13–14 SD] *Oxf*   17 SP] *Capell; Ke.
Q; Kee. F; To. Cl. / Rowe* 'master gentleman Conrade'] *Capell subst.;* master gentleman Conrade
Q   19–22 CONRADE *. . .* villains.] *om.* F   19 SP] *Q (Both);* Con., Bor. / *Capell*   20 SP] *Capell; Kem.
Q; To. Cl. / Theobald*   27 SP] *Capell; Kemp Q; To. Cl. / Rowe*   28 SD] *this edn*

sirrah. A word in your ear. Sir, I say to you, it is thought
you are false knaves.   30

BORACHIO   Sir, I say to you, we are none.

DOGBERRY   Well, stand aside. 'Fore God, they are both
in a tale. [*to the Sexton*] Have you writ down, that they
are none?

SEXTON   Master constable, you go not the way to   35
examine. You must call forth the watch that are their
accusers.

DOGBERRY   Yea, marry, that's the eftest way. Let the
watch come forth. [*Watch come forward.*] Masters, I
charge you in the prince's name, accuse these men.   40

1 WATCHMAN   [*Indicates Borachio.*] This man said, sir,
that Don John the prince's brother was a villain.

DOGBERRY   Write down 'Prince John a villain'. Why, this
is flat perjury, to call a prince's brother villain!

BORACHIO   Master constable –   45

DOGBERRY   Pray thee, fellow, peace! I do not like thy look,
I promise thee.

SEXTON   What heard you him say else?

2 WATCHMAN   Marry, that he had received a thousand
ducats of Don John for accusing the Lady Hero   50
wrongfully.

DOGBERRY   Flat burglary as ever was committed!

VERGES   Yea, by mass, that it is.

SEXTON   What else, fellow?

---

29 **in your ear** Dogberry hopes to extort
a confession by interrogating the malefactors separately, despite the fact that
Borachio has just heard the exchange
with Conrade.

33 **in a tale** in collusion

35 **go . . . way** i.e. do not go about the
proper way

38 **eftest** a nonsense word; he seems to
mean 'most expedient', or some combination of 'deftest' and 'easiest'.

---

29 ear. Sir] *Cam subst.;* eare sir, *Q*   32, 38, 43, 46, 52, 58 SP] *Capell; Kemp Q; To. Cl. / Rowe*   33
SP] *this edn*   38 eftest] easiest *Rowe;* deftest *(Theobald)*   39 SD] *this edn*   41 SP] *(Watch* 1)   SD]
this edn   43 'Prince . . . villain'.] *Capell subst.;* prince . . . villaine: *Q*   45 constable –] *Capell*
(Constable, –); Constable. *Q*   49 SP] *(Watch* 2); SEACOAL *Folg²*   52 SP] *Capell; Const. Q; Dog. /*
Rowe   by mass] by th'masse *F*

1 WATCHMAN   And that Count Claudio did mean, upon   55
his words, to disgrace Hero before the whole assembly,
and not marry her.

DOGBERRY   O villain! Thou wilt be condemned into
everlasting redemption for this.

SEXTON   What else?   60

WATCH   This is all.

SEXTON   And this is more, masters, than you can deny.
Prince John is this morning secretly stolen away;
Hero was in this manner accused, in this very manner
refused and, upon the grief of this, suddenly died.   65
Master constable, let these men be bound and brought
to Leonato's. I will go before and show him their
examination.   *[Exit.]*

DOGBERRY   Come, let them be opinioned.

VERGES   Let them be in the hands – *[Watch move to bind*   70
them.]

CONRADE   Off, coxcomb!

DOGBERRY   God's my life, where's the sexton? Let him
write down the prince's officer coxcomb! Come, bind

55–6 **upon his words** on the strength of
his words
59 **redemption** malapropism for 'perdi-
tion' or 'damnation'
65 **refused** disowned (both by Claudio
and by her father)
69 **opinioned** malapropism for 'pinioned'
70–1 *Q gives both these lines, as one
sentence (see t.n.), to 'Couley' (Verges);
F gives them to 'Sex.', and Theobald to
'Conrade' (on the grounds that neither
Verges nor the Sexton would refer to

a watchman as a coxcomb). Malone
redistributed the text as here (following
Warburton, who gave 'Let them be in
hand' to the Sexton, and 'Off, Coxcomb'
to Conrade). Cam[1] suggests that the
compositor perhaps found 'Cou.' and
'Con.' on successive lines and took
the speakers to be the same. Equally
Borachio might speak 71 (although
the gentleman Conrade seems more
disposed to stand on ceremony).
72 **God's my life** God save my life

55 SP] SEACOAL *Folg*[2]   67 Leonato's] *Leonato F*   68 SD] *Theobald*   69 SP] *Rowe; Constable Q*
70 SP VERGES] *Capell; Couley Q; Sex. F; Conrade / Theobald*   SD] *this edn; Watchmen seize Conrade*
and Borachio Oxf[1]*; he offers to bind Conrade Cam*[1] *(Brae)*   70–1 in . . . coxcomb!] *Malone; Warburton*
(*in hand. Exit. / Conr. Off Coxcomb!); in the hands of Coxcombe. Q; in bands. Con. Off, coxcomb!*
Capell; be bound; in the – / Con. Hands off! coxcomb! (Lloyd (Kinnear)); in the hands of – Con.
Coxcomb! Staunton; – in the hands. Conrade. Off, coxcomb! Cam[1] *(Brae)*   72, 76 SP] *Rowe; Kemp Q*

them. [*to Conrade, who resists*] Thou naughty varlet!
CONRADE   Away! You are an ass, you are an ass!   75
DOGBERRY   Dost thou not suspect my place? Dost thou
not suspect my years? O, that he were here to write me
down an ass! But masters, remember that I am an ass;
though it be not written down, yet forget not that I am
an ass. No, thou villain, thou art full of piety, as shall be   80
proved upon thee by good witness. I am a wise fellow,
and which is more, an officer, and which is more, a
householder, and which is more, as pretty a piece of
flesh as any is in Messina, and one that knows the law
– go to! – and a rich fellow enough – go to! – and a   85
fellow that hath had losses, and one that hath two
gowns, and everything handsome about him. – Bring
him away. – O, that I had been writ down an ass!   *Exeunt.*

[5.1]   *Enter* LEONATO *and his brother* [ANTONIO].

ANTONIO
If you go on thus you will kill yourself,
And 'tis not wisdom thus to second grief

---

74 **naughty varlet** worthless knave, rascal
76, 77 **suspect** malapropism for 'respect'
77 **years** age, but perhaps an unwitting
pun, if *years* is heard as 'ears'. Craik
(309) cites *Misogonus* (1570), 1.2.63–4:
'nothinge greues me but my yeares be
so longe / my master will take me for
balames asse'.
80 **piety** malapropism for 'impiety'
83 **householder** person qualified to vote
by the ownership of property
83–4 **as . . . flesh** i.e. impressive, in
appearance but also in social reputation; there is a stage tradition of playing Dogberry as corpulent; there could

also be an (unwitting?) sexual innuendo, on *flesh* as penis, cf. *RJ* 1.1.29:
'Me they shall feel while I am able to
stand; and 'tis known I am a pretty
piece of flesh.'
85 **go to!** an intensifying exclamation; a
command to move forward
86 **hath had losses** i.e. has been wealthy
enough to afford to lose money, and
still have *two gowns*
5.1 The location is before Leonato's
house. The action takes place on the
evening of the wedding day.
2 **second** reinforce; act as a second to (as
in a duel)

---

74 them. Thou] *F3* (them; thou*); them, thou *Q*; them thou *F*   SD] *Oxf¹*   75 SP] *Rowe; Couley
Q*   84 is] *om. F*   88 SD] *Pope; exit. Q*   5.1] *Actus Quintus. F*; scene i *Rowe*   0.1 ANTONIO]
Rowe   1+ SP ANTONIO] *Rowe; Brother Q*; LEONATO'S BROTHER *Folg²*

Against yourself.

LEONATO   I pray thee cease thy counsel,
Which falls into mine ears as profitless
As water in a sieve. Give not me counsel,   5
Nor let no comforter delight mine ear
But such a one whose wrongs do suit with mine.
Bring me a father that so loved his child,
Whose joy of her is overwhelmed like mine,
And bid him speak of patience.   10
Measure his woe the length and breadth of mine,
And let it answer every strain for strain,
As thus for thus, and such a grief for such,
In every lineament, branch, shape and form.
If such a one will smile, and stroke his beard   15
And sorrow; wag, cry 'hem', when he should groan,

7   **suit** compare
9   **overwhelmed** drowned (in tears)
11   **Measure** measure against
12   **strain for strain** The word *strain*
     has three possible meanings here: (1)
     burst, pang; (2) stretch, stress; (3) per-
     haps with musical connotation, one
     phrase answering another
14   **lineament** contour
15–16 **stroke . . . 'hem'** To stroke the
     beard and cry 'hem' (or 'ahem') in
     order to clear the throat were regard-
     ed as overtures to dull or platitudinous
     speech; cf. *TC* 1.3.165–6: 'Now play me
     Nestor; hem, and stroke thy beard, / As
     he being dressed to some oration.'
16   **sorrow** grieve; this passage was
     first deemed a crux by Capell, who
     changed it to 'Bid sorrow, wag; cry
     hem!' (i.e. 'drive grief away by croaking
     platitudes', Ard²), an emendation which
     initiated a history of similar efforts,

though his version is generally adopted.
The wording of Q was followed only by
Johnson, whose punctuation rendered
it as 'And, Sorrow wag! cry; hem,
when'. Another possibility (RP) is that
'sorry wag' = miserable joker; as 'sorry'
was often spelt 'sor[r]ie' the mistaken
setting of 'sorrow' in its place would
not be impossible. This edition retains
Q's wording on the grounds of its
intelligibility, emotional descriptiveness,
and rhythm (i.e. in the two three-
part syntactic units generated by the
enjambment of 15–16, and the caesura
of 16, Leonato refines and condenses
his sentiment through repetition).
wag play the wag, or mischievous prank-
ster, i.e. pretend to be light-hearted
cry 'hem' i.e. clear away or disguise
with a cough; cf. *AYL* 1.3.16–18:
'ROSALIND . . . these burrs are in my
heart. / CELIA Hem them away.'

6 comforter] comfort *F*   7 do] doth *F*   16 And . . . 'hem',] *Cam²;* And sorrow, wagge, crie hem, *Q;*
And hallow, wag, cry hem *F3;* And Hollow, wag, cry hem, *F4;* And Sorrow wage; cry, hem! *Theobald;*
And sorrow waive, cry hem, *Hanmer;* And sorrowing, cry 'hem' *Halliwell (Heath);* And, Sorrow wag!
cry; hem, *Johnson;* In sorrow wag; cry hem, *Steevens–Reed;* In sorrow wag; cry hem, *Malone;* Cry
– sorrow, wag! and hem, *Steevens-Reed² (Johnson);* And sorrow, wag! cry hem, *Collier;* Bid sorrow,
wag; cry hem! *Capell;* And sorrow raze *(Craven)*   'hem'] *Cam;* hem *Q*

Patch grief with proverbs, make misfortune drunk
With candle-wasters, bring him yet to me,
And I of him will gather patience.
But there is no such man. For, brother, men   20
Can counsel and speak comfort to that grief
Which they themselves not feel. But tasting it,
Their counsel turns to passion which before
Would give preceptial medicine to rage,
Fetter strong madness in a silken thread,   25
Charm ache with air and agony with words.
No, no, 'tis all men's office to speak patience
To those that wring under the load of sorrow,
But no man's virtue nor sufficiency
To be so moral when he shall endure   30
The like himself. Therefore give me no counsel;
My griefs cry louder than advertisement.

ANTONIO

Therein do men from children nothing differ.

LEONATO

I pray thee peace; I will be flesh and blood.
For there was never yet philosopher   35

17 **Patch ... proverbs** attempt to assuage sorrow with clichés

17–18 **make ... candle-wasters** inundate grief with philosophical precepts, *candle-wasters* being a term used to express contempt for scholars; cf. Jonson, *Cynthia's Revels*, 3.2.2–3: 'a whoreson booke-worme, a candle-waster ... Foh, he smells all lamp-oil with studying by candlelight' (Jonson, 4.84).

18 **yet** then; even now

19 **patience** three syllables

22 **not feel** For the omission of the auxiliary verb 'do' before 'not' see Abbott, 305, and *Tem* 5.1.38: 'Whereof the ewe not bites'.

24 **preceptial medicine** balms composed of moral precepts, the *moral medicine* disdained by Don John at 1.3.12

25 **Fetter** chain

26 **air** breath, i.e. talk, words

27 **office** duty

27–31 **No ... himself** Cf. Dent, A124: 'All commend patience, but none can endure to suffer.'

28 **wring** suffer

29 **sufficiency** ability, capacity

30 **moral** glibly comforting with moral precepts
   shall must

32 **advertisement** precept (*OED* 2); good advice. Pronounced (as in British English) with the stress on the second syllable.

35–6 i.e. even philosophers, with all their wisdom, cannot avoid feeling pain; cf. 3.2.26–7: 'Well, everyone can master a grief but he that has it.'

That could endure the toothache patiently,
However they have writ the style of gods
And made a push at chance and sufferance.

ANTONIO

Yet bend not all the harm upon yourself;
Make those that do offend you suffer too.   40

LEONATO

There thou speak'st reason. Nay, I will do so:
My soul doth tell me Hero is belied,
And that shall Claudio know, so shall the prince
And all of them that thus dishonour her.

Enter DON PEDRO *and* CLAUDIO.

ANTONIO

Here comes the prince and Claudio hastily.   45

DON PEDRO

Good e'en, good e'en.

CLAUDIO   Good day to both of you.

LEONATO

Hear you, my lords?

DON PEDRO   We have some haste, Leonato.

LEONATO

Some haste, my lord! Well, fare you well, my lord.

---

37 **writ . . . of** claimed the title of (*OED* style *sb.* 18a) by claiming a divine indifference to misfortune (a trait of the Stoic philosophers)

38 **made . . . at** defied, scoffed
chance and sufferance accident and predestination; the line is about philosophers who, while they might, remarkably, have attempted to solve the puzzles of free will and divine prescience, are still unable to endure a simple toothache.

39 **bend** direct, aim; the metaphor is from archery

45 **comes** For singular verbs preceding plural subjects see Abbott, 335. See also 5.4.7: 'I am glad that all things sorts so well'; and 5.4.52: 'Here comes other reckonings.'

46 **Good e'en** [God give you] good even[ing] (i.e. any time after noon)

47 **Hear you** will you hear me

38 push] pish *Oxf* 44.1 DON PEDRO] *Rowe (Pedro); Prince Q* 46+ SP] *Pedro / Rowe; Prince Q* e'en . . . e'en] *Oxf;* den . . . den *Q* 47 lords?] Lords! *Rowe;* lords, – *Capell*

285

Are you so hasty now? Well, all is one.

DON PEDRO

Nay, do not quarrel with us, good old man.   50

ANTONIO

If he could right himself with quarrelling,
Some of us would lie low.

CLAUDIO   Who wrongs him?

LEONATO

Marry, thou dost wrong me, thou dissembler, thou!
Nay, never lay thy hand upon thy sword;
I fear thee not.

CLAUDIO   Marry, beshrew my hand   55

If it should give your age such cause of fear.
In faith, my hand meant nothing to my sword.

LEONATO

Tush, tush, man, never fleer and jest at me!
I speak not like a dotard nor a fool,
As under privilege of age to brag   60
What I have done being young, or what would do
Were I not old. Know, Claudio, to thy head,
Thou hast so wronged mine innocent child and me
That I am forced to lay my reverence by,
And with grey hairs and bruise of many days   65

---

49 **all is one** it makes no difference
52 **lie low** i.e. in death, perhaps with a pun on 'base lying'. It is not clear whether Antonio knows that Hero's death is feigned, as the entry SD at 4.1 does not include him in the wedding party (though he is often present in productions).
53 **thou** Leonato uses the more familiar pronoun to address Claudio (reserving the respectful *you* for the Prince).
54 an indication for Claudio's stage action, and perhaps for a threatening

gesture on Leonato's part
55 **beshrew** curse
57 **my . . . sword** my hand intended nothing in moving toward my sword
58 **Tush** a contemptuous exclamation
fleer sneer, mock
59 **dotard** senile person
60 **under . . . age** excused by senility, or the reverence due to an elderly person
62 **to thy head** to your face; cf. *MND* 1.1.106: 'I'll avouch it to his head'.
64 **lay . . . by** set my age aside
65 **bruise** injuries, wear and tear

52–3 him? / Marry] him? Marry? *Malone*   63 mine] my *F*

Do challenge thee to trial of a man.
I say thou hast belied mine innocent child.
Thy slander hath gone through and through her heart,
And she lies buried with her ancestors –
O, in a tomb where never scandal slept,   70
Save this of hers, framed by thy villainy.

CLAUDIO
My villainy?

LEONATO   Thine, Claudio; thine, I say.

DON PEDRO
You say not right, old man.

LEONATO   My lord, my lord,
I'll prove it on his body, if he dare,
Despite his nice fence and his active practice,   75
His May of youth and bloom of lustihood.

CLAUDIO
Away! I will not have to do with you.

LEONATO
Canst thou so doff me? Thou hast killed my child;
If thou kill'st me, boy, thou shalt kill a man.

ANTONIO
He shall kill two of us, and men indeed.   80
But that's no matter, let him kill one first.
Win me and wear me! Let him answer me.

---

66 **trial . . . man** a duel. Leonato's chivalric gesture is modelled after that of
Genevra's defender in Shakespeare's
Ariostan source (see 4.1.191–2n.); it
is often accompanied in production by
some action signifying a challenge (the
drawing of Leonato's sword, his fling-
ing of a glove at Claudio's feet, etc.).
71 **framed** plotted, engineered
74 **prove it** Trial by combat was considered a method of judicial inquiry, the
victory being decided by God.

75 **nice fence** fancy fencing skill
76 **May . . . lustihood** prime of life and
peak of vigour
78 **doff me** put me off, brush me aside;
cf. *Oth* 4.2.177: 'Every day thou doff'st
me with some device'. Cf. 2.3.166
and n.
82 **Win . . . me!** a challenge: i.e. if you
subdue me, then you may do with me
as you wish; proverbial (Dent, W408).
Let . . . me i.e. let him fight me in a
duel; or perhaps a directive to Leonato

78 doff] *(daffe)*

287

Come, follow me, boy. Come, sir boy, come, follow me,
Sir boy! I'll whip you from your foining fence!
Nay, as I am a gentleman, I will.   85

LEONATO

Brother –

ANTONIO

Content yourself. God knows, I loved my niece,
And she is dead, slandered to death by villains
That dare as well answer a man indeed
As I dare take a serpent by the tongue.   90
Boys, apes, braggarts, jacks, milksops!

LEONATO   Brother Anthony –

ANTONIO

Hold you content. What, man? I know them, yea,
And what they weigh, even to the utmost scruple.
Scambling, outfacing, fashion-monging boys,
That lie, and cog, and flout, deprave and slander,   95
Go anticly and show outward hideousness,
And speak off half a dozen dangerous words

---

to refrain from restraining Antonio
(*Let* him answer me). Antonio's enthusiasm for the fight (so at odds with his
earlier counsel of patience) risks paro-
dying Leonato's own challenge; some
productions have underscored the
humour of his indignation by portray-
ing him as literally deaf to Leonato's
pleas.

84 **foining fence** thrusting sword-play,
as in fencing (as opposed to striking in
earnest, and putting himself at risk)

89 **answer . . . indeed** fight a real man

91 **apes** imitations of real men
jacks rascals
milksops cowards

93 **scruple** a small apothecary's weight
(20 grains)

94 **Scambling, outfacing, fashion-
monging** contentious, brazen, dandi-
fied

95 **cog** cheat
flout jeer
deprave defame

96 **Go anticly** go about in grotesque
manner or dress; cf. 3.3.127–33: 'how
giddily 'a turns about all the hot-
bloods between fourteen and five-and-
thirty . . .'.
outward hideousness appearance of
ferocity. Rowe's addition of 'an' serves
to smooth the metre; 'an' could have
been omitted by haplography or eye-
skip (an/ou).

97 **speak off** casually throw out
dangerous threatening

85 gentleman, I] *F;* gentleman I, *Q*   86 Brother –] *Theobald (*Brother, –*);* Brother. *Q*   91 Anthony –]
Theobald; Anthony. *Q*   94 Scambling] Scrambling *Craig*   96 anticly] *(*antiquely*), Rowe*   outward]
an outward *Rowe*   97 off] *Theobald;* of *Q*   dangerous] *(*dang'rous*)*

How they might hurt their enemies, if they durst –
And this is all.

LEONATO

But brother Anthony –

ANTONIO   Come, 'tis no matter.   100
Do not you meddle; let me deal in this.

DON PEDRO

Gentlemen both, we will not wake your patience.
My heart is sorry for your daughter's death,
But on my honour she was charged with nothing
But what was true and very full of proof.   105

LEONATO

My lord, my lord –

DON PEDRO   I will not hear you.

LEONATO   No?
– Come, brother, away. I will be heard.

ANTONIO

And shall, or some of us will smart for it.

Exeunt Leonato and Antonio.

Enter BENEDICK.

DON PEDRO   See, see: here comes the man we went to
    seek.   110

CLAUDIO   Now, signor, what news?

BENEDICK [*to Don Pedro*]   Good day, my lord.

DON PEDRO   Welcome, signor. You are almost come to
    part almost a fray.

---

98 **durst** dared
99 **And . . . all** i.e. they are nothing but
    words
102 **wake** disturb

112 **my lord** Benedick's address to Don
    Pedro ignores Claudio's greeting.
113–14 **You . . . fray** You are nearly in
    time to part what was almost a fight.

100 Anthony –] *Theobald;* Anthonie. *Q*   SP2] *F (Ant.); Brother Q*   106 lord –] *Pope;* Lord.
Q   106–7 No? . . . heard] *one line Q (*No come brother, away, I wil be heard*)   108 SD] *opp. 107 Q*
(Exeunt amb.); after 107 F (Exeunt ambo.)   111, 113 signor] *(signior)*   112 SD] *Oxf*

289

CLAUDIO We had liked to have had our two noses   115
snapped off with two old men without teeth.

DON PEDRO Leonato and his brother. What think'st
thou? Had we fought, I doubt we should have been too
young for them.

BENEDICK In a false quarrel there is no true valour. I   120
came to seek you both.

CLAUDIO We have been up and down to seek thee, for
we are high-proof melancholy and would fain have it
beaten away. Wilt thou use thy wit?

BENEDICK It is in my scabbard. Shall I draw it?   125

DON PEDRO Dost thou wear thy wit by thy side?

CLAUDIO Never any did so, though very many have
been beside their wit. I will bid thee draw as we do the
minstrels – draw to pleasure us.

DON PEDRO As I am an honest man, he looks pale. Art   130
thou sick, or angry?

CLAUDIO What, courage, man! What though care killed a
cat, thou hast mettle enough in thee to kill care.

BENEDICK Sir, I shall meet your wit in the career an you
charge it against me. I pray you choose another subject.   130

---

115 **We had liked** i.e. we were in danger of having
116 **with** by
118 **I doubt** I'm afraid
123 **high-proof** in the highest degree
fain gladly
126–8 **wit . . . wit** Don Pedro attempts a sally on the notion of being 'besides one's wits' (i.e. at the end of one's wits with frustration), which Claudio turns into the notion of being separated from one's wit (i.e. foolish). Claudio here assumes that Benedick's role is indeed that of 'the prince's jester' (2.1.223).
128–9 **as . . . minstrels** i.e. as we bid the

minstrels draw their bows across the strings. Claudio deflects the menacing meaning of Benedick's *draw* at 125.
129 **pleasure** entertain
132–3 **What though . . . cat** proverbial (Dent, C84). Claudio perhaps jests about what he thinks is Benedick's lovelorn condition, although the main drift of this sequence is that he cannot believe Benedick is in earnest.
134 **in the career** galloping at full speed; the metaphor is from jousting.
135 **charge** level, aim; urge it on
another subject i.e. other than Beatrice, or love

115 liked] *(likt); like F2*   123 high-proof] *(high proofe), Theobald*   134 an] *(and)*

CLAUDIO   Nay, then, give him another staff; this last was
broke cross.

DON PEDRO   By this light, he changes more and more. I
think he be angry indeed.

CLAUDIO   If he be, he knows how to turn his girdle.   140

BENEDICK   Shall I speak a word in your ear?

CLAUDIO   God bless me from a challenge.

BENEDICK [*aside to Claudio*]   You are a villain. I jest not.
I will make it good how you dare, with what you dare
and when you dare. Do me right, or I will protest   145
your cowardice. You have killed a sweet lady, and
her death shall fall heavy on you. Let me hear from
you.

CLAUDIO   Well, I will meet you, so I may have good cheer.

DON PEDRO   What, a feast, a feast?   150

CLAUDIO   I'faith, I thank him, he hath bid me to a calf's

---

136 **staff** lance-shaft
137 **broke cross** broken across, as in a
failed attempt at the tilt in a joust, such
that the spear is broken across the body
of an opponent rather than by the push
of the point (Claudio still believes they
are having a combat of wits); cf. *AYL*
3.4.37–41: 'He . . . swears brave oaths,
and breaks them bravely, quite traverse,
athwart the heart of his lover; as a puis-
ny tilter that spurs his horse but on one
side breaks his staff.'
140 **turn his girdle** indicate his
unwillingness to fight. The proverbial
expression (Dent, B698) is of uncertain
origin, and could possibly mean either
to rotate a belt in order to bring the
dagger or scabbard (usually worn
behind) within range of the grasp, or,
more likely, to turn a belt so that the
buckle was behind the body to signify
that one had decided to bear with a
provocation rather than contest it.
143 SD *added by Cam on the strength

of Benedick's request to speak a word
in your ear, and Don Pedro's query at
150 (although it is clear at 192 that
Don Pedro had gathered what passed
between the two)
144 **make it good** i.e. make good my
word, prove that Claudio is a villain by
fighting and defeating him
with . . . dare i.e. offering Claudio his
choice of weapon
145 **Do me right** i.e. meet my challenge
protest proclaim; denounce
149 **so** provided, on condition that
good cheer entertainment (make it
worth my while)
151–4 **calf's head . . . capon . . . woodcock** types of likely feasting food, but
also insults: a calf's head is a fool (a
calf being a type of immaturity); a
capon (a castrated rooster) is a figure
for cowardice; the woodcock, for stu-
pidity, as it is a bird easily captured (cf.
the ironic proverb 'As wise as a woodcock', Dent, W746).

143 SD] *Cam*   151 him,] *F*; him *Q*

head and a capon, the which if I do not carve most
curiously, say my knife's naught. Shall I not find a
woodcock too?

BENEDICK   Sir, your wit ambles well; it goes easily.   155

DON PEDRO   I'll tell thee how Beatrice praised thy wit the
other day. I said thou hadst a fine wit. 'True,' said she,
'a fine little one.' 'No,' said I, 'a great wit.' 'Right,' says
she, 'a great gross one.' 'Nay,' said I, 'a good wit.' 'Just,'
said she, 'it hurts nobody.' 'Nay,' said I, 'the gentleman   160
is wise.' 'Certain,' said she, 'a wise gentleman.' 'Nay,'
said I, 'he hath the tongues.' 'That I believe,' said she,
'for he swore a thing to me on Monday night, which
he forswore on Tuesday morning. There's a double
tongue; there's two tongues.' Thus did she an hour   165
together trans-shape thy particular virtues. Yet at last
she concluded, with a sigh, thou wast the properest
man in Italy.

CLAUDIO   For the which she wept heartily and said she
cared not.   170

DON PEDRO   Yea, that she did, but yet for all that, an if
she did not hate him deadly, she would love him dearly.

---

153 **curiously** cleverly
   naught useless, blunt
155 **ambles** moves (as in – ironic – praise
   for a horse's gait)
   goes easily doesn't exert itself; goes
   away quickly, i.e. is of no import
157 **fine** excellent; diminutive
159 **Just** just so
161 **a wise gentleman** Johnson suggests
   that 'perhaps "wise gentleman" was
   in that age used ironically, and always
   stood for silly fellow'.
162 **hath the tongues** speaks various
   languages; cf. *TGV* 4.1.33–5: '2
   OUTLAW Have you the tongues? /
   VALENTINE My youthful travel therein

made me happy, / Or else I often had
been miserable.'
164–5 **a double tongue** *double* = deceitful. Beatrice's alleged comment
   paraphrases her own account of
   her personal history with Benedick,
   delivered to the Prince at 2.1.255–6.
166 **trans-shape** metamorphose (as Hero
   claims she does at 3.1.59–70)
167 **properest** most handsome, finest
171–2 **an ... dearly** proverbial: 'A woman
   either loves or hates to extremes'
   (Dent, W651); cf. Lyly, *Anatomy*, 238:
   'I haue heard that women eyther loue
   entirely or hate deadly.'
171 **an if** if

---

157 said she] saies she *F*   157–65 'True . . . tongues.'] *Capell subst.;* True . . . tongues *Q*   171 an] *(and)*

The old man's daughter told us all.

CLAUDIO   All, all. And moreover, God saw him when he
was hid in the garden.   175

DON PEDRO   But when shall we set the savage bull's horns
on the sensible Benedick's head?

CLAUDIO   Yea, and text underneath: 'Here dwells Benedick
the married man.'

BENEDICK   Fare you well. Boy, you know my mind. I will   180
leave you now to your gossip-like humour. You break
jests as braggarts do their blades, which, God be
thanked, hurt not. My lord, for your many courtesies,
I thank you. I must discontinue your company. Your
brother the bastard is fled from Messina; you have   185
among you killed a sweet and innocent lady. For my
Lord Lack-beard there, he and I shall meet, and till
then peace be with him.   [*Exit.*]

DON PEDRO   He is in earnest.

CLAUDIO   In most profound earnest. And, I'll warrant   190
you, for the love of Beatrice.

DON PEDRO   And hath challenged thee?

CLAUDIO   Most sincerely.

---

173 **old man's daughter** i.e. Hero
174–5 **God . . . garden** The allusion in
Claudio's hint about Benedick's eavesdropping in 2.3 is to Genesis, 3.8, when
God discovers Adam and Eve in a state
of post-lapsarian shame in the wake of
eating from the tree of the knowledge
of good and evil: they 'heard the voice
of the Lord walking in the garden in the
cool of the day: and . . . hid themselves
from the presence of the Lord God
amongst the trees of the garden'.
181 **gossip-like humour** talkative wom-
en's mood
181–2 **break jests** crack jokes

182 **as . . . blades** as cowardly boasters
break their swords in order to give the
impression they've been fighting; cf.
1H4 2.4.296–8, where Falstaff 'hacked
[his sword] with his dagger, and said
he would swear truth out of England
but he would make you believe it was
done in fight'.
184 **discontinue   your   company**
Benedick is resigning from his service
to the Prince.
187 **Lord Lack-beard** i.e. Claudio, a reference to his youth and/or his lack of
manliness
meet in a duel

177 on] *(one)*   178–9 'Here . . . man.'] *Capell subst.;* here . . . man. *Q*   180 well.] *this edn (RP);* wel,
Q   187 Lack-beard there,] *F;* Lacke-beard, there *Q*   188 SD] *Rowe*

293

DON PEDRO   What a pretty thing man is when he goes in
his doublet and hose, and leaves off his wit!   195
CLAUDIO   He is then a giant to an ape; but then is an ape
a doctor to such a man.
DON PEDRO   But soft you, let me be. Pluck up, my heart,
and be sad – did he not say my brother was fled?

Enter Constables [DOGBERRY *and* VERGES, *with the*
Watch], CONRADE *and* BORACHIO.

DOGBERRY   Come you, sir. If justice cannot tame you, she   200
shall ne'er weigh more reasons in her balance. Nay, an
you be a cursing hypocrite once, you must be looked to.
DON PEDRO   How now? Two of my brother's men bound?
Borachio one.
CLAUDIO   Hearken after their offence, my lord.   205
DON PEDRO   Officers, what offence have these men done?
DOGBERRY   Marry, sir, they have committed false report.
Moreover they have spoken untruths, secondarily they

194 **goes in** i.e. goes about only in
195 **leaves . . . wit** forgets to wear his
intelligence (like a cape covering his
other clothing, which a person would
remove in preparation to fight)
196–7 **is then . . . man** i.e. seems
heroic to a fool (*ape*), but the fool is
a scholar compared with such a man.
The ape could also be a literal one,
cf. *Ham* 4.2.15–18: 'such officers do
the King best service in the end: he
keeps them, like an ape, in the corner
of his jaw – first mouthed, to be last
swallowed'; and *MM* 2.2.121–3: 'His
glassy essence – like an angry ape /
Plays such fantastic tricks before high
heaven / As makes the angels weep.'
198 **soft you** wait a moment
198–9 **Pluck . . . sad** rouse yourself, my
mind, and be serious
201 **reasons** In Elizabethan pronunciation this word would have sounded the
same as 'raisins', and so there is perhaps
an inadvertent joke in the image of the
icon of Justice – a blindfolded woman
holding a set of scales – weighing
reasons much as a shopkeeper weighs
fruit; cf. *1H4* 2.4.232–3: 'If reasons
were as plentiful as blackberries . . . '.
See Cercignani, 243. Dogberry's
meaning seems to be that if Justice
cannot punish the scoundrel in
question (whether he means Conrade
or Borachio is not clear), she should
hang up her scales.
201–2 **an . . . to** if you are a 'lying impost-
er' (Kittredge), in a word (Abbott, 57),
you must be punished
205 **Hearken** enquire
208 **secondarily** Dogberry attempts to
enumerate his claims in the manner of
a logical proposition.

198 up,] *Steevens*; vp *Q*   199.1–2] *after 195 Q*   DOGBERRY . . . Watch] *Rowe subst. (Enter Dogberry,
Verges, Conrade and Borachio, guarded.)*   200, 207 SP] *Rowe; Const. Q*   201 an] (and)

294

are slanders, sixth and lastly, they have belied a lady, thirdly they have verified unjust things, and, to 210 conclude, they are lying knaves.

DON PEDRO First I ask thee what they have done, thirdly I ask thee what's their offence, sixth and lastly why they are committed, and, to conclude, what you lay to their charge? 215

CLAUDIO Rightly reasoned and in his own division; and, by my troth, there's one meaning well suited.

DON PEDRO Who have you offended, masters, that you are thus bound to your answer? This learned constable is too cunning to be understood. What's your offence? 220

BORACHIO Sweet Prince, let me go no farther to mine answer. Do you hear me, and let this count kill me. I have deceived even your very eyes. What your wisdoms could not discover, these shallow fools have brought to light, who in the night overheard me confessing to this 225 man how Don John your brother incensed me to slander the lady Hero; how you were brought into the orchard and saw me court Margaret in Hero's garments; how you disgraced her when you should marry her. My villainy they have upon record, which I 230 had rather seal with my death than repeat over to my shame. The lady is dead upon mine and my master's

209 **slanders** malapropism for 'slanderers'
210 **verified** Dogberry's error for 'sworn to'
214 **committed** i.e. to custody
216 **in . . . division** according to his own rhetorical enumeration
217 **well suited** neatly set out (by various phrasings)
219 **bound . . . answer** required to respond; tied up in preparation for your trial
220 **cunning** clever, ingenious
221–2 **go . . . answer** reply without preamble; travel no further (especially

in Dogberry's company?) to my punishment
226 **incensed** provoked, as in *MW* 1.3.95–6, 'I will incense Ford to deal with poison', and *KL* 2.2.499, 'what they may incense him to'
228–9 **in Hero's garments** 'This important touch is added for the first time in this, the last account of the midnight episode' (Smith); it is never explained why Margaret would do this.
231 **seal** i.e. prove, pay for; the metaphor is from sealing wax.
232 **upon** in consequence of

false accusation, and, briefly, I desire nothing but the
reward of a villain.

DON PEDRO

Runs not this speech like iron through your blood?   235

CLAUDIO

I have drunk poison whiles he uttered it.

DON PEDRO

But did my brother set thee on to this?

BORACHIO

Yea, and paid me richly for the practice of it.

DON PEDRO

He is composed and framed of treachery,
And fled he is upon this villainy.   240

CLAUDIO

Sweet Hero! Now thy image doth appear
In the rare semblance that I loved it first.

DOGBERRY   Come, bring away the plaintiffs. By this
time our sexton hath reformed Signor Leonato of the
matter. And masters, do not forget to specify, when   245
time and place shall serve, that I am an ass.

VERGES   Here, here comes master Signor Leonato, and
the sexton too.

Enter LEONATO, *his brother* [ANTONIO] *and the* Sexton.

LEONATO

Which is the villain? Let me see his eyes,
That when I note another man like him   250
I may avoid him. Which of these is he?

---

235 **like iron** i.e. as a sword; Don Pedro
  shifts into verse here.
238 **practice** accomplishment
239 **framed of** shaped by (*OED v.* 5)
242 **rare semblance** exceptional, or

exceptionally lovely, likeness
that in which; see Abbott, 394, and
5.2.45.
243 **plaintiffs** for 'defendants'
244 **reformed** malapropism for 'informed'

244, 247 Signor] *(signior)*   247 SP] *Rowe; Con.2 Q*   248.1 *his . . .* Sexton] *om. F*   ANTONIO] *Rowe*

BORACHIO

If you would know your wronger, look on me.

LEONATO

Art thou the slave that with thy breath hast killed
Mine innocent child?

BORACHIO   Yea, even I alone.

LEONATO

No, not so, villain, thou beliest thyself.   255
Here stand a pair of honourable men;
A third is fled that had a hand in it.
I thank you, princes, for my daughter's death;
Record it with your high and worthy deeds.
'Twas bravely done, if you bethink you of it.   260

CLAUDIO

I know not how to pray your patience.
Yet I must speak. Choose your revenge yourself.
Impose me to what penance your invention
Can lay upon my sin. Yet sinned I not
But in mistaking.

DON PEDRO   By my soul, nor I.   265
And yet to satisfy this good old man
I would bend under any heavy weight
That he'll enjoin me to.

LEONATO

I cannot bid you bid my daughter live –
That were impossible. But I pray you both,   270
Possess the people in Messina here
How innocent she died. [*to Claudio*] And if
    your love

---

256 **honourable men** presumably a sarcastic reference to Don Pedro and
Claudio; cf. *JC* 3.2.83–4: 'For Brutus
is an honourable man, / So are they
all, all honourable men.'

261 **patience** three syllables
263 **Impose** subject
    invention imagination
271 **Possess** inform

253–4 Art . . . child] *prose F*   255 thou] thou thou *F*   272 SD] *this edn*

Can labour aught in sad invention,
Hang her an epitaph upon her tomb
And sing it to her bones. Sing it tonight.   275
Tomorrow morning come you to my house,
And since you could not be my son-in-law,
Be yet my nephew. My brother hath a daughter,
Almost the copy of my child that's dead,
And she alone is heir to both of us.   280
Give her the right you should have given her cousin,
And so dies my revenge.

CLAUDIO   O noble sir!
Your over-kindness doth wring tears from me.
I do embrace your offer, and dispose
For henceforth of poor Claudio.   285

LEONATO

Tomorrow, then, I will expect your coming;
Tonight I take my leave. This naughty man
Shall face to face be brought to Margaret,
Who I believe was packed in all this wrong,
Hired to it by your brother.

BORACHIO   No, by my soul she was not,   290
Nor knew not what she did when she spoke to me,
But always hath been just and virtuous
In anything that I do know by her.

---

273 **labour . . . invention** bestir itself
at all in serious creation; *invention* has
four syllables.
274 **an epitaph** as suggested by the Friar;
see 4.1.207 and n.
280 **alone . . . us** Antonio's son, mentioned at 1.2.1–2, is quite forgotten; see
pp. 138–9.
281 **right** just treatment, with pun on rite
(of marriage)
284 **dispose** you may dispose
285 The metre of this line is irregular. It is
possible that *dispose* (284) belongs at the

beginning of this line, and something
has been dropped from the end of 284.
287 **leave** Don Pedro and Claudio often
exit here (in which case 316–18 are
brought forward to this point or cut).
naughty wicked
289 **packed** in league, an accomplice; cf.
CE 5.1.219–20: 'That goldsmith there,
were he not pack'd with her, / Could
witness it'. See 2.2.40n. and 5.4.4n. for
speculation about Margaret's awareness of her role in the plot.
293 **by** of

281 given] *(giu'n)*   283 over-kindness] *(ouer kindnesse)*, *Rowe*

DOGBERRY   Moreover, sir, which indeed is not under
white and black, this plaintiff here, the offender, did   295
call me ass. I beseech you let it be remembered in his
punishment. And also the watch heard them talk of one
Deformed; they say he wears a key in his ear and a lock
hanging by it, and borrows money in God's name, the
which he hath used so long, and never paid, that   300
now men grow hard-hearted and will lend nothing for
God's sake. Pray you examine him upon that point.

LEONATO
I thank thee for thy care and honest pains.

DOGBERRY   Your worship speaks like a most thankful and
reverent youth, and I praise God for you.   305

LEONATO [*Gives him money.*]   There's for thy pains.

DOGBERRY   God save the foundation!

LEONATO   Go, I discharge thee of thy prisoner, and I
thank thee.

DOGBERRY   I leave an arrant knave with your worship,   310
which I beseech your worship to correct yourself, for
the example of others. God keep your worship! I wish
your worship well! God restore you to health! I humbly
give you leave to depart, and if a merry meeting may be
wished, God prohibit it! Come, neighbour.   315

[*Exeunt Dogberry and Verges.*]

LEONATO
Until tomorrow morning, lords, farewell.

294–5 **under . . . black** i.e. written down
298 **a key** In Dogberry's garbled apprehension, Deformed's love-lock has acquired
   a key, and the man himself the financial
   habits of a borrower who invokes God's
   name like a beggar.
299–300 **the which** i.e. the trick of persuading men to lend for God's sake
300 **paid** repaid

305 **reverent** malapropism for 'reverend'
   youth malapropism for 'elder'
307 the usual thanks given by recipients
   of charity, especially at the entrances
   to convents or monasteries
310 **arrant** (1) thorough; (2) perhaps a
   mistake for 'errant'
314 **give** malapropism for 'ask'
315 **prohibit** malapropism for 'permit'

294 SP] *Rowe (Dog.); Const.* Q   301 hard-hearted] *(*hard hearted*), F*   305 reverent] reuerend
F   306 SD] *Oxf*   315 SD] *F (Exeunt.) after 316*

299

ANTONIO
    Farewell, my lords. We look for you tomorrow.
DON PEDRO
    We will not fail.
CLAUDIO   Tonight I'll mourn with Hero.
LEONATO [*to the Watch*]
    Bring you these fellows on. We'll talk with Margaret,   319
    How her acquaintance grew with this lewd fellow.   *Exeunt.*

[5.2]   *Enter* BENEDICK *and* MARGARET.

BENEDICK   Pray thee, sweet mistress Margaret, deserve
    well at my hands by helping me to the speech of
    Beatrice.
MARGARET   Will you then write me a sonnet in praise of
    my beauty?   5
BENEDICK   In so high a style, Margaret, that no man
    living shall come over it; for in most comely truth thou
    deservest it.
MARGARET   To have no man come over me? Why, shall I
    always keep below stairs?   10

320 **lewd** worthless, wicked, rascally, as
in e.g. Acts, 17.5: 'the Jews . . . took
unto them certain lewd fellows of the
baser sort'
5.2 The location is the vicinity of
Leonato's house.
0.1 Capell's addition (see t.n.) interposes
a separation between Benedick and
Margaret, although their dialogue (e.g.
Margaret's knowledge of Benedick's
literary efforts) could equally suggest
the possibility that they are in mid-
conversation upon entry; or that she
observes him in the act of composition.
1–2 **deserve . . . hands** i.e. earn a reward
from me
2   **to . . . of** to speak with

6   **style** with pun on 'stile' (a step for
climbing over a fence); cf. Chaucer,
The Squire's Tale, 97–8: 'Al be it that
I can nat sowne his style, / Ne can nat
clymen over so high a style.'
7   **come over** surpass; climb over
    comely pleasant
9   **come over me** cover me in the act of
    intercourse
10 **keep below stairs** remain a servant
    (rather than, according to the con-
    vention of sonnets, become a mistress
    to a servant-lover); Margaret perhaps
    also suggests that she would like to
    improve her social rank via marriage
    to someone in possession of a house,
    stairs and servants.

319 SD] *Cam*   319–20] *Pope; prose Q*   **5.2]** *Capell (SCENE II)*   0.1] *meeting / Capell*   9 me?
Why] *Rowe;* me, why *Q*

BENEDICK   Thy wit is as quick as the greyhound's mouth, it catches.

MARGARET   And yours as blunt as the fencer's foils, which hit, but hurt not.

BENEDICK   A most manly wit, Margaret, it will not hurt a   15
woman. And so, I pray thee, call Beatrice. I give thee the bucklers.

MARGARET   Give us the swords; we have bucklers of our own.

BENEDICK   If you use them, Margaret, you must put in   20
the pikes with a vice, and they are dangerous weapons for maids.

MARGARET   Well, I will call Beatrice to you, who I think
hath legs.   *Exit.*

BENEDICK   And therefore will come.   25
    [*Sings.*]

The God of love
That sits above,
And knows me, and knows me,
How pitiful I deserve –

---

11 **greyhound's mouth** Greyhounds were used as hunting dogs.

12 **catches** seizes swiftly

13 **foils** blunted rapiers used in fencing practice

16–17 **I give . . . bucklers** I concede (to your superior wit). A buckler was a small shield with a detachable spike screwed (sexual pun intended) into the centre; 'to give the bucklers is to yield, or to lay by all thought of defence' (Johnson).

18 **swords** innuendo for penises
bucklers innuendo for hymens or vulvas, or thighs, protecting the vulva

21 **pikes** spikes
vice (1) screw (with sexual innuendo); (2) clamp used to screw an item into place; (3) sin; (4) thighs closed in inter-

course as the screw of a vice compresses its jaws

24 **hath legs** can move

25 **come** come when called; yield, be favourably moved (*OED v.* II 16)

26–9 the first stanza of a popular song by William Elderton, printed in 1562, of a melancholy lover praying for grace from his disdainful mistress. Duffin (175) writes that 'the melody survives under "The Gods of love" and other names, including "Turkeylony", which may be a corruption of the Italian "Tordiglione" . . . The mismatch of the plural subject with the singular verb of the first line in the original poem ("the gods off love yt sytts a bove") along with the orthography of

---

13 yours] *(your's)*   24 SD] *(Exit Margarite.)*   25 SD] *Pope*   26–9] *Capell; prose Q*

301

I mean in singing; but in loving, Leander the good   30
swimmer, Troilus the first employer of pandars and
a whole bookful of these quondam carpet-mongers,
whose names yet run smoothly in the even road of a
blank verse, why, they were never so truly turned over
and over as my poor self in love. Marry, I cannot show   35
it in rhyme. I have tried; I can find out no rhyme to
'lady' but 'baby' – an innocent rhyme; for 'scorn', 'horn'
– a hard rhyme; for 'school', 'fool', a babbling rhyme:
very ominous endings. No, I was not born under a
rhyming planet nor I cannot woo in festival terms.   40

"Gods" in some sources (i.e. "Godes," "Goddes"), may suggest that the song originally began, "The Goddess of love . . .".'

30 **Leander** a famously and tragically loyal lover, who contrary to Benedick's (ironic?) estimate of his athletic prowess drowned while swimming the Hellespont. See 4.1.79n. Marlowe's poem *Hero and Leander*, was published in 1598, although echoes of the poem in *MND* suggest that Shakespeare knew it in manuscript.

31 **Troilus** another hapless hero of faithful love, loved and left by Criseyde, after he was assisted to her bed by her go-between uncle Pandarus; their story was celebrated by Chaucer in his poem *Troilus and Cresyde* and by Shakespeare himself in his play of 1601–2.

32 **quondam** erstwhile, bygone
carpet-mongers literally, carpet salesmen, but Benedick seems to mean something along the lines of 'pretend lovers' (in the senses of fictional, literary and lightweight), or the twentieth-century 'bedroom warriors'; from the term 'carpet-knight', a lover as opposed to a fighter, one awarded a knighthood for service not in battle but at court, 'on carpet consideration' (*TN* 3.4.235)

34 **verse** Benedick's examples are literary ones. The versifying effects of love are noted elsewhere in Shakespeare's works, e.g. Berowne in *LLL* 4.3.13–14: 'By heaven, I do love, and it hath taught me to rhyme, and to be melancholy'; and *Ham* 2.2.119–20: '*I am ill at these numbers. I have not art to reckon my groans.*'

37 **innocent** childish (but perhaps ominously so, as suggesting the consequences of loving ladies)
horn cuckold's horn; erect penis

38 **hard** (1) harsh, in sound, in import (because the horn was the mark of a cuckold), and in material substance, and hence (2) erect
fool (1) speaker of nonsense, or babble (*babbling* comes from the term for the speech of infants); (2) a cuckolded father of bastards

39 **ominous endings** incompetent rhymes; inauspicious ends (to be brought to by love)

40 **rhyming planet** astrological sign conducive to verse-making; cf. 1.3.10–11: 'being as thou sayst thou art, born under Saturn'; and 2.1.306–9.
festival terms (1) lighthearted, holiday language, cf. *1H4* 1.3.46–7: 'With many holiday and lady terms / He questioned me'; (2) conventionally

37–8 'lady' . . . 'fool'] *quotation marks as Pope; none in Q*   40 nor] for *F*

Enter BEATRICE.

Sweet Beatrice, wouldst thou come when I called thee?

BEATRICE   Yea, signor, and depart when you bid me.

BENEDICK   O, stay but till then.

BEATRICE   'Then' is spoken; fare you well now. And yet,
ere I go, let me go with that I came for, which is, with   45
knowing what hath passed between you and Claudio.

BENEDICK   Only foul words – and thereupon I will kiss
thee.

BEATRICE   Foul words is but foul wind, and foul wind is
but foul breath, and foul breath is noisome, therefore I   50
will depart unkissed.

BENEDICK   Thou hast frighted the word out of his right
sense, so forcible is thy wit. But I must tell thee plainly:
Claudio undergoes my challenge, and either I must
shortly hear from him, or I will subscribe him a coward.   55
And I pray thee now tell me, for which of my bad parts
didst thou first fall in love with me?

BEATRICE   For them all together, which maintained so
politic a state of evil that they will not admit any good
part to intermingle with them. But for which of my   60
good parts did you first suffer love for me?

---

sentimental love poetry – like another
soldier of professed incompetence at
love language, Henry V (*H5* 5.2.132–3):
'Marry, if you would put me to verses,
or to dance for your sake, Kate, why,
you undid me.' Benedick nonetheless
does manage to produce a sonnet in
5.4.
44 **fare you well** This often serves
as a cue for Beatrice to move as if to
exit.
45 **that** what; see 5.1.242n. on *that*.
49 **Foul . . . but foul wind** Cf. Job, 6.26:

'Do you imagine to reprove words, that
the talke of the afflicted should be as
the winde?'; Dent, W833.
50 **noisome** offensive
52 **his** its
54 **undergoes** has received
55 **subscribe** publish, publicly proclaim
over a signature
59 **politic**   well-governed;   canny.
Beatrice's metaphor invokes that of
the body politic.
61 **suffer** undergo, but with (as Benedick
glosses) a sense of resistance

40.1] *F; after 41 Q*   42+ signor] *(signior)*   44 'Then'] *Malone;* Then, *Q*   45 came for] *Rowe³;*
came *Q*

BENEDICK   'Suffer love'! A good epithet. I do suffer love
indeed, for I love thee against my will.

BEATRICE   In spite of your heart, I think. Alas, poor heart!
If you spite it for my sake, I will spite it for yours, for I   65
will never love that which my friend hates.

BENEDICK   Thou and I are too wise to woo peaceably.

BEATRICE   It appears not in this confession: there's not
one wise man among twenty that will praise himself.

BENEDICK   An old, an old instance, Beatrice, that lived in   70
the time of good neighbours. If a man do not erect in
this age his own tomb ere he dies, he shall live no longer
in monument than the bell rings and the widow weeps.

BEATRICE   And how long is that, think you?

BENEDICK   Question: why, an hour in clamour and a   75
quarter in rheum. Therefore is it most expedient for
the wise, if Don Worm – his conscience – find no

65–6 **If . . . hates** 'If you love me in spite
of your desire, then I will spite your
heart for your sake, for I would never
love something (a heart) which my
lover spites.'

67 **too wise** i.e. because their wit
prevents them from taking statements
unequivocally or conventionally (although the statement could also be
taken as an acknowledgement of the
risks and vulnerabilities involved in
loving)

68 **in** by

69–71 **praise himself . . . neighbours**
Dent, N117, gives as proverbial 'He
has ill neighbours that is fain to praise
himself.'

70 **instance** precept

72–3 **live . . . monument** be no longer
remembered or memorialized

73 **bell** i.e. the funeral bell, or the 'passing bell', rung as a person lay dying
(nine times for a man plus one peal for

every year of his age) in order to signify to the community and the person in
question that the end is near (Gittings,
133)

75 **Question** i.e. good question
in clamour noise of the funeral bell,
here three-quarters of an hour longer than the weeping of the widow; in
popular literature, widows were notorious for the rapidity of their recover-
ies and remarriages. A ballad of the
period entitled 'How to Wyve Well'
includes the verse 'But when she heres
thee deade / She shifteth thee to grave
/ and for she cannot weepe / With
clothe she hides her face / And shakes
her head as though / She weepte for
thee apace.'

76 **rheum** tears

77 **Don . . . conscience** The image
of one's conscience as a gnawing
worm derives from Mark, 9.46:
'Their worm dieth not, and the fire

---

62 'Suffer love'!] *Capell subst.;* Suffer loue! *Q*   73 monument] monuments *F*   bell rings] Bels ring *F*

impediment to the contrary, to be the trumpet of his
own virtues, as I am to myself. So much for praising
myself, who I myself will bear witness is praiseworthy. 80
And now tell me, how doth your cousin?

BEATRICE Very ill.

BENEDICK And how do you?

BEATRICE Very ill too.

BENEDICK Serve God, love me and mend. There will I 85
leave you too, for here comes one in haste.

Enter URSULA.

URSULA Madam, you must come to your uncle. Yonder's
old coil at home. It is proved my lady Hero hath
been falsely accused, the prince and Claudio mightily
abused, and Don John is the author of all, who is fled 90
and gone. Will you come presently?

BEATRICE Will you go hear this news, signor?

BENEDICK I will live in thy heart, die in thy lap, and be
buried in thy eyes – and moreover, I will go with thee 94
to thy uncle's.   *Exeunt.*

is not quenched'; cf. *R3* 1.3.222: 'The
worm of conscience still begnaw thy
soul.' *Don* is a term of mock-respect,
although, as Mason (258) argues, 'In a
play with characters called Don Pedro
and Don John the introduction at this
late stage of Don Worm can be read
strongly; Benedick has severed both
bonds of allegiance and friendship
with Don Pedro . . . his "new sworn
brother" (1.1.68) is Don Worm, his
conscience.'
85 **mend** feel better

There i.e. with that
88 **old coil** a fine uproar
90 **abused** deceived
91 **presently** immediately
93 **die** achieve orgasm
    lap front portion of a seated body
    from waist to knees; vagina (*OED sb.*[1]
    2b)
93–4 **be . . . eyes** a conventional trope of
    love poetry; Benedick seems to have
    mastered some *festival terms*, despite
    his earlier disavowal, but takes care to
    deflate them with an anticlimax.

79 myself. So] *Rowe subst.*; my self so *Q*   86.1] *after 84 F*   95 SD] *F; exit. Q*

[5.3]   *Enter* CLAUDIO, DON PEDRO, *and three or four*
       [*Attendants, including a* Lord *and* Musicians,] *with tapers.*

CLAUDIO   Is this the monument of Leonato?
LORD   It is, my lord. [*Reads the*] *epitaph.*

5.3 The location is a churchyard, including the tomb of Leonato's family. This scene was frequently cut in productions from Garrick to the early twentieth century, thus removing the performance of Claudio's penance; or, given the allocation of SPs (see 2 SPn.), removing the problem of his penitence not seeming sincere enough. In more recent productions it has often been witnessed by a concealed Hero, presumably to provide her with proof of Claudio's remorse.

0.1–2 According to line 30, the company is dressed in mourning costume.

0.2 *including a* Lord See 2 SPn.

and Musicians Q does not include musicians, though they are clearly of the party at line 11; many editions include Balthasar here, given his habitual association with Claudio and Don Pedro and his affiliation with music, but since he was asked to procure *excellent* music in the wake of his rendition of 'Sigh no more' in 2.3, it may be that his skills are not up to the more reverent task here. F's '*Iacke Wilson*' at 2.3.34.1–2 (see List of Roles 5n.) presumes a good singer here (if one artfully bad in 2.3).

tapers On the Renaissance stage, these would signify that it was night time. While this ceremony is not strictly speaking a funeral, night-time funerals (particularly for women) were coming into aristocratic vogue in the early seventeenth century (Gittings, 188).

1 **monument** family burial vault; 'the inclusion of a tomb in Henslowe's 1598 inventory of stage properties

for the Rose Theatre (Henslowe, 179) raises the possibility that a property monument may also have been used in Renaissance theatres where *Much Ado* was performed' (Cox, *Shakespeare*, 225). Alternatively, Claudio's very question helps to locate the scene verbally, obviating the need for such a visual cue.

2 SP *Q assigns the epitaph and 22–3 to the attendant Lord; or, as Capell decided, and most editors agree, fails to provide a SP before the epitaph for Claudio (who in Q speaks again at 11). Following Capell, productions usually assign the epitaph to Claudio, given that Leonato had explicitly instructed him to 'Hang her an epitaph upon her tomb / And sing it to her bones' (5.1.274–5). (However, Leonato's instruction notwithstanding, in Q he instructs others to sing to her bones.) The assumption is that 'we must assign the epitaph to the character whose importance merits the speech and who is an appropriate choice to speak it' (Myers, 415). This edition leaves the scene as in Q, agreeing in part with Cam[2] that 'it does not seem out of character for Claudio to do his grieving by proxy, as he did his wooing', but also on the grounds that it need not appear cold-hearted for a delegate lord to read the epitaph on Claudio's behalf, and the collective behalf of the male community that has slandered Hero. On the contrary, given the highly formal, public and ritual nature of this act, it might be equally possible that the '"I" of the unnamed lord functions as the liturgical "I" of a ritualized,

5.3] *Capell (SCENE III)*   0.1 DON PEDRO] *Rowe; Prince Q*   0.2 *Attendants*] *Rowe   including a Lord*] *this edn   and* Musicians] *this edn (Wells); Capell subst. (and Musick); Balthasar and musicians Cam[1]*   2 SP] *Q; Cla. / Capell*   SD] *Cam[2] subst.; Epitaph Q*

306

> *Done to death by slanderous tongues*
> *Was the Hero that here lies;*
> *Death, in guerdon of her wrongs,*   5
> *Gives her fame which never dies;*
> *So the life that died with shame,*
> *Lives in death with glorious fame.*

[*Hangs scroll.*]

Hang thou there upon the tomb,
Praising her when I am dumb.   10

CLAUDIO
Now music sound, and sing your solemn hymn.   [*Music*]

ONE OR MORE SINGERS [*Sing.*]

Pardon, goddess of the night,
Those that slew thy virgin knight,

---

corporate, performative, gendered identity' (PG). The collective voice of the song ('Pardon . . . Those . . . assist our moan . . . Help us') supports the corporate nature of this act. Another reason for Claudio's silence could be that he's too upset to read the epitaph or sing himself. So too it can be argued that following the Q SP means that here (and only here) does Claudio initiate and control the action, becoming in effect director or stage manager of the scene, whereas heretofore he has been content to be directed by Don Pedro; this role lends him a new theatrical authority and weight.

5 *guerdon* recompense, reward
7 *with* as a consequence of
12–21 There is no contemporary setting extant for this song, in effect a pagan ritual of exorcism; Collier cites a reference in *Laugh and Lie Down* (1605) to a ballad sung to the tune of 'Heavily, heavily', and Duffin (302) proposes the conjectural setting of the tune 'Robin Goodfellow', 'which seems like a good

match for the structure of the poem as well as for the invocation of nocturnal spirits'.

12 SP Q does not specify a singer, despite the fact that Claudio calls for one in the previous line. Balthasar seems a plausible choice, since the actor playing him (see 0.2n. on *and* Musicians) has been responsible for singing and playing throughout; or, given the line 'Help *us* to sigh', it could be sung as a chorus by all present.

12 **goddess . . . night** Diana or Artemis, the huntress goddess of the moon and chastity (as at 4.1.56, 'You seem to me as Dian in her orb'). The image returns Hero to virgin status, and is an attempt to mollify the goddess whose anger resulted in Actaeon (the model of the cuckold) acquiring antlers (Ovid, *Met.*, 3.138–249).

13 **virgin knight** votary, follower. A frequent image of the chaste woman, like Diana the huntress, was one safely clad in male garb; cf. Spenser's armed Britomart in Book 3 of *The Faerie*

---

8 SD] *Capell (affixing it)*   10 dumb] *F (dombe); dead Q*   11 SP] *om. Capell*   SD] *Oxf¹*   12 SP] *this edn (Wells); Song Q*

> For the which with songs of woe
> Round about her tomb they go.   15
>   Midnight, assist our moan,
>   Help us to sigh and groan,
>   Heavily, heavily.
> Graves yawn and yield your dead,
>   Till death be uttered,   20
>   Heavily, heavily.

LORD

> Now unto thy bones good night;
> Yearly will I do this rite.

DON PEDRO

Good morrow, masters. Put your torches out.
The wolves have preyed, and look, the gentle day,   25
Before the wheels of Phoebus, round about
Dapples the drowsy east with spots of grey.
Thanks to you all, and leave us. Fare you well.

CLAUDIO

Good morrow, masters; each his several way.

Queene, or the lady of Milton's *Comus*, 420–3: 'She that has [chastity], is clad in complete steel, / And like a quiver'd Nymph with Arrows keen / May trace huge Forests and unharbor'd Heaths, / Infamous Hills and sandy perilous wilds' (Milton, *Poems and Prose*, 100).

15 **Round about** Clockwise circling was the traditional way of averting evil.

19–21 **Graves . . . heavily** The meaning of these lines is perplexing; there is perhaps a hint of resurrection (depending on the second meaning of *uttered*; see 20n.), in which case F's '*Heauenly, heauenly*' at 21 is attractive. However, the more likely sense

is that death's utterance, or expression, is on a par with the sighing and groaning of 17; the title of the ballad cited by Collier (see 12–21n.) supports the latter.

20 **uttered** utterèd: expressed, commemorated; driven out

25 **gentle day** i.e. dawn, in which case the *Midnight* of 16 is figurative; this phrase may suggest that the ceremony (and the monument) are located out of doors.

26 **Phoebus** the Roman sun-god, who drives a chariot pulled by the horses of the sun

29 **each . . . way** let each man go his own way

17–18] F3; *one line* Q   21] *Heauenly, heauenly* F   22 SP] Q *(Lo.); Claudio /* Rowe   22–3] Pope; *one line* Q   23 rite] *Pope;* right Q   24, 30 SP] *Rowe; Prince* Q

DON PEDRO

    Come, let us hence and put on other weeds,   30
    And then to Leonato's we will go.

CLAUDIO

    And Hymen now with luckier issue speed's
    Than this for whom we rendered up this woe.   *Exeunt.*

[5.4]   *Enter* LEONATO, BENEDICK, MARGARET,
        URSULA, ANTONIO, FRIAR [Francis],
        HERO [*and* BEATRICE].

FRIAR

    Did I not tell you she was innocent?

LEONATO

    So are the prince and Claudio who accused her,
    Upon the error that you heard debated.
    But Margaret was in some fault for this,
    Although against her will, as it appears   5
    In the true course of all the question.

ANTONIO

    Well, I am glad that all things sorts so well.

---

30 **other weeds** more festive garments (a suggestion for costuming in this scene and in 5.4)
32 **Hymen** Roman god of marriage
issue outcome; result
speed's speed us, i.e. favour us. The distinction between the verb 'speeds' (i.e. comes quickly) and the contraction is generally lost in performance.
5.4 The location is Leonato's house.
0.3 Beatrice is absent from the SDs in Q, which may indicate the need for time for a change of costume from 5.2; on the other hand, Leonato refers to *gentlewomen all* at 10, in giving the

women their instructions to return veiled. If Beatrice is absent until an entry at 51, a production could generate further speculation about her whereabouts and intentions towards Benedick.
3 **Upon** because of (Abbott, 191)
4 **some fault** presumably the fault of borrowing her mistress's clothing, if we are to take Borachio at his word at 5.1.291 that she 'knew not what she did when she spoke to me'
5 **against her will** unintentionally
6 **question** investigation (three syllables)
7 **sorts** turn out; see 5.1.45n.

32 speed's] *Theobald (Thirlby);* speeds *Q* **5.4**] *Capell (SCENE IV)* 0.2 ANTONIO] *Rowe; old man Q; Leonato's Brother / Folg²* Francis] *Rowe* 0.3 *and* BEATRICE] *Rowe* 5 will, as] *Capell;* will as *Q* 7, 17 SP] *Rowe; Old Q; Leonato's Brother / Folg²* 7 sorts] sort *F*

BENEDICK

> And so am I, being else by faith enforced
> To call young Claudio to a reckoning for it.

LEONATO

> Well, daughter, and you gentlewomen all,   10
> Withdraw into a chamber by yourselves,
> And when I send for you, come hither masked.
> The prince and Claudio promised by this hour
> To visit me. You know your office, brother:
> You must be father to your brother's daughter   15
> And give her to young Claudio.   *Exeunt Ladies.*

ANTONIO

> Which I will do with confirmed countenance.

BENEDICK

> Friar, I must entreat your pains, I think.

FRIAR

> To do what, signor?

BENEDICK

> To bind me, or undo me, one of them.   20
> Signor Leonato – truth it is, good signor,
> Your niece regards me with an eye of favour.

LEONATO

> That eye my daughter lent her? 'Tis most true.

---

8 **by faith** by a promise
9 **young** As at 16, there is a renewed
   emphasis on Claudio's youth.
   reckoning i.e. duel
17 **confirmed countenance** a straight
   face; due propriety
18 **entreat your pains** ask for your
   assistance
20 **bind . . . me** i.e. tie me up (in the knot
   of marriage) or finish me off (by marrying me to a wife); cf. 3.1.114: 'bind

   our loves up in a holy band'.
22 **eye of favour** a favourable regard;
   as elsewhere, the sense is that different kinds of vision render their
   objects differently. Cf. 4.1.106–7: 'on
   my eyelids shall conjecture hang /
   To turn all beauty into thoughts of
   harm'.
23 **That . . . her** i.e. my daughter helped
   her to see Benedick in a favourable
   light

16 SD] *after 12 Cam*   19, 21 signor] *(Signior)*   23 her?] *this edn (RP);* her, *Q*

BENEDICK

And I do with an eye of love requite her.

LEONATO

The sight whereof I think you had from me, 25
From Claudio and the prince. But what's your will?

BENEDICK

Your answer, sir, is enigmatical.
But for my will, my will is your good will
May stand with ours this day to be conjoined
In the estate of honourable marriage; 30
In which, good Friar, I shall desire your help.

LEONATO

My heart is with your liking.

FRIAR   And my help.
Here comes the prince and Claudio.

Enter DON PEDRO *and* CLAUDIO, *with Attendants.*

DON PEDRO

Good morrow to this fair assembly.

LEONATO

Good morrow, Prince, good morrow, Claudio. 35
We here attend you. Are you yet determined

24 **eye of love** an eye which sees with love; see also 22 and n.

28 **is your** is that your

29 **stand** join

33 This line is missing from F (sig. L1ʳ), due to a casting-off error. Other space-saving stratagems on this final page include the absence of space around entry directions; the abbreviation of names in SDs; the alteration of Q's 'two or three other' (33.1) to 'with attendants'; the shortening of SPs to avoid turnovers in verse lines (52, 55); the setting of verse as prose (75–6);

the omission of *that* in 80 and 81 and *such* at 82 in order to avoid turnovers in verse lines; the treatment of an entry direction as if it were an exit (122.1); the use of tildes and abbreviations in tightly set lines (110–13); and the setting of '*FINIS*' in the direction line, usually reserved for the signature and/ or catchword. F's cumulative saving is of 17 lines.

33.1 *Attendants* possibly including the Lord of 5.3

34 **assembly** four syllables

36 **yet** still

30 estate] *Johnson;* state *Q*   33] *om. F*   33.1 DON PEDRO] *Rowe; Prince Q*   *with Attendants*] *F; and two or three other Q*   34 SP] *Rowe; Prince Q*

311

Today to marry with my brother's daughter?

CLAUDIO

I'll hold my mind were she an Ethiope.

LEONATO

Call her forth, brother. Here's the friar ready. [*Exit Antonio.*]

DON PEDRO

Good morrow, Benedick. Why, what's the matter   40
That you have such a February face,
So full of frost, of storm and cloudiness?

CLAUDIO

I think he thinks upon the savage bull.
Tush, fear not, man: we'll tip thy horns with gold,
And all Europa shall rejoice at thee,   45
As once Europa did at lusty Jove
When he would play the noble beast in love.

BENEDICK

Bull Jove, sir, had an amiable low,
And some such strange bull leaped your father's cow

---

38 **Ethiope** i.e. an Ethiopian, foreign in both nation and race; therefore unattractive. The *OED* (Ethiop) lists a possible derivation from the Greek for 'to burn' + 'face' = burnt-face, 'later sunburnt'. Cf. 2.1.292–3: 'Thus goes everyone to the world but I, and I am sunburnt.'

41 **February face** wintry (forbidding) aspect; Benedick is either still angry with Claudio or unusually serious-looking.

44 **tip** gild; cf. 121–2.

45 **Europa** Europe the continent, but in the next line Europa is a Phoenician princess whose beauty inspired Jove to transform himself into an alluring bull in order to capture her and carry her across the sea to Crete (Ovid, *Met.*, 2.833–75). Claudio's jest attempts to mock the prospect of being horned

(or cuckolded) by promising that Benedick, like the golden calf, will become the glorious idol of a sacrilegious and widespread cult.

49 **leaped** mounted sexually; Benedick answers Claudio's jest by calling him, albeit politely, a bastard, and son of an unfaithful mother. The tone of these jests (as always) depends on their delivery in performance; the men could be portrayed as happily returning to their banter as if nothing untoward had happened, or using word-play to continue the aggression of 5.1. In either case, the recent events have done nothing to deflect the terms of their taunting away from jokes about marital infidelity, which fly thick and fast through to the end of this scene. These lines are often cut in productions eager to end on a more seemly note.

---

39 SD] *Theobald*   40 SP] *Rowe (Pedro); P. Q* Benedick.] *(Bened.)*

And got a calf in that same noble feat   50
Much like to you, for you have just his bleat.

Enter ANTONIO, HERO, BEATRICE, MARGARET
[*and*] URSULA[*, the women masked*].

CLAUDIO
For this I owe you. Here comes other reckonings.
Which is the lady I must seize upon?
[*Antonio leads Hero forward.*]

LEONATO
This same is she, and I do give you her.

CLAUDIO
Why then she's mine. [*to Hero*] Sweet, let me see your
face.   55

LEONATO
No, that you shall not till you take her hand
Before this friar and swear to marry her.

CLAUDIO
Give me your hand before this holy friar.

---

50 **calf** with play on 'fool'; see 5.1.151–
4n.
51.2 Leonato's directive to the women
at 10–12 ('you gentlewomen all, /
Withdraw into a chamber by
yourselves, / And when I send for
you, come hither masked') suggests
that all four women mask, as is often
the case in production, although
Theobald's SD (see t.n.) leaves open
the possibility that only Hero and
Beatrice do so (which could render
Benedick's question at 72, *Which is
Beatrice?*, especially droll). If all four
mask, a director must decide when
and if Margaret and Ursula unmask;
likely moments include when Beatrice
does, or at 78, when they are referred

to by Beatrice.
52 **reckonings** accountings (for his
debts); the plural refers to the number
of veiled figures.
53 **seize upon** take possession of
SD *This edition's SD preserves both
the content of Leonato's directive to
Antonio at 15–16 ('You must be father
to your brother's daughter / And give
her to young Claudio') and Q's SP at
54. Most editions substitute Antonio
for Leonato in the latter SP (and also
at 56), but retaining the original text's
assignments provides for a Leonato
who jumps in to direct matters despite
his earlier directive, an action in
keeping with his stage-managing
presence at the original wedding.

50 And] A *F*   51.1 ANTONIO] *Theobald; brother Q*   51.2 *the women masked*] *this edn; the ladies masked /
Theobald*   52 reckonings] *(recknings)*   53 SD] *this edn*   54 SP] *Antonio / Theobald*   55 SD] *Oxf¹*

I am your husband, if you like of me.

HERO [*Unmasks.*]

And when I lived I was your other wife;   60

And when you loved, you were my other husband.

CLAUDIO

Another Hero!

HERO   Nothing certainer.

One Hero died defiled, but I do live,

And surely as I live, I am a maid.

DON PEDRO

The former Hero! Hero that is dead!   65

LEONATO

She died, my lord, but whiles her slander lived.

FRIAR

All this amazement can I qualify,

When after that the holy rites are ended,

I'll tell you largely of fair Hero's death.

Meantime, let wonder seem familiar,   70

And to the chapel let us presently.

BENEDICK

Soft and fair, Friar. [*to Antonio*] Which is Beatrice?

---

59 Claudio does here offer his unknown
bride the right of refusal.
like of For 'of' following 'like' see
Abbott, 177.
63 defiled slandered
67 qualify mitigate, render more intelligible
67–9 Q's punctuation (retained here)
leaves a choice as to whether 68 modifies the line before it or the succeeding
one (i.e. 'after the rites I will explain all
this amazement' or 'after the rites I'll
tell you all about Hero's death').
69 largely in full
70 let . . . familiar treat these surprises
as if they were natural matters

71 presently immediately
72 Soft and fair wait a moment, not so
fast (*OED* soft *adv.* I 8a); the command
suggests some herding or exiting stage
action prompted by the Friar's previous lines.
*fair, Friar See 72 SDn. on the significance of the added comma. *Friar* here
is bisyllabic.
72 SD *The question is not necessarily
directed to Antonio; the actor playing
Benedick has a wide range of options,
including addressing Leonato, Hero,
the ladies in general, the lady he can
already identify (by some other token)
as Beatrice – anyone, in fact, except

---

60 SD] *Rowe*   65 SP] *Rowe (Pedro); Prince Q*   72 fair, Friar.] faire Frier, *Q*   SD] *this edn (RP)*

BEATRICE [*Unmasks.*]

    I answer to that name. What is your will?

BENEDICK

    Do not you love me?

BEATRICE   Why no, no more than reason.

BENEDICK

    Why then your uncle and the prince and Claudio   75

    Have been deceived – they swore you did.

BEATRICE

    Do not you love me?

BENEDICK   Troth no, no more than reason.

BEATRICE

    Why then my cousin, Margaret and Ursula

    Are much deceived, for they did swear you did.

BENEDICK

    They swore that you were almost sick for me.   80

BEATRICE

    They swore that you were well-nigh dead for me.

BENEDICK

    'Tis no such matter. Then you do not love me?

BEATRICE

    No truly, but in friendly recompense.

LEONATO

    Come, cousin, I am sure you love the gentleman.

---

the Friar, Don Pedro or Claudio. His purpose is to add his own wedding to that of Claudio, so he must first delay the general move towards the chapel, and then identify Beatrice. Q's punctuation ('Soft and faire Frier, which . . .') could suggest that Benedick addresses the question to the Friar; however, since it is Antonio,

not the Friar, who has brought the masked ladies on stage, and who knows which is Hero, presumably he is best equipped to identify them.

75–6 F lines these as prose, which keeps Benedick and Beatrice prose speakers.

83 **but . . . recompense** but only reciprocally as a friend (which you have proved yourself by challenging Claudio)

73 SD] *Capell* 75–6] *prose F* 80, 81 that] *om. F* 81 well-nigh] *(welnigh), F (*wel-nye*)* 82 such] *om. F* me?] *F;* me. *Q*

CLAUDIO

And I'll be sworn upon't that he loves her,   85
For here's a paper written in his hand,
A halting sonnet of his own pure brain
Fashioned to Beatrice.

HERO   And here's another,
Writ in my cousin's hand, stolen from her pocket,
Containing her affection unto Benedick.   90

BENEDICK   A miracle! Here's our own hands against our
hearts. Come, I will have thee, but by this light I take
thee for pity.

BEATRICE   I would not deny you, but by this good day I
yield upon great persuasion – and partly to save your   95
life, for I was told you were in a consumption.

LEONATO   Peace! [*to Beatrice*] I will stop your mouth.
[*Hands her to Benedick.*]

---

87 **halting** irregular in rhythm
   his . . . brain his original composition
88–92 Many productions stage Benedick
   and Beatrice attempting to snatch
   these papers from Claudio's and Hero's
   hands; either in order to retrieve their
   own from view, or to secure that of
   the other. In the latter case, they often
   pause to read the poems.
91 **against** writing contrary to; pressed
   against (as if to swear by them)
92 **by this light** a familiar oath, i.e.
   by the morning sun (which, like the
   dancing star under which Beatrice was
   born, or the daylight by which she can
   see a church, draws a contrast with the
   night time in which much of the play's
   action has taken place)
97 **SP** Q's assignment of this speech to
   Leonato (rather than to Benedick, as
   in most editions after Theobald) is in
   keeping with his characteristic attempts
   to stage-manage this scene, and his role

as Beatrice's guardian; it also provides
for a more egalitarian accommodation
between the lovers than would
Benedick's own declaration of intent
to silence Beatrice, an egalitarianism
which seems in keeping with the tenor
of their relationship throughout.
(*Peace* could in fact be delivered to
both of them.) As a directive delivered
by a third party to a couple, it has the
precedent of Beatrice's command to
Hero at 2.1.285–6, to 'Speak, cousin,
or, if you cannot, stop his mouth
with a kisses and let not him speak
neither.' Leonato's statement (and
accompanying gesture indicated in
this edition's SD2) need not imply
that Benedick kisses Beatrice (though
most editions signal as such), but
merely that in handing Beatrice over to
Benedick (as Leonato is entitled to do,
being both her uncle and guardian) he
will silence her merely by getting her a
husband.

---

94 not] *yet Theobald*   97 SP] *Benedick / Theobald*   SD1] *this edn*   SD2] *this edn; kissing her /*
Theobald

DON PEDRO
How dost thou, Benedick, the married man?

BENEDICK   I'll tell thee what, Prince; a college of wit-
crackers cannot flout me out of my humour. Dost thou   100
think I care for a satire or an epigram? No, if a man will
be beaten with brains, 'a shall wear nothing handsome
about him. In brief, since I do purpose to marry, I will
think nothing to any purpose that the world can say
against it; and therefore never flout at me for what I   105
have said against it. For man is a giddy thing, and this
is my conclusion. For thy part, Claudio, I did think
to have beaten thee, but in that thou art like to be my
kinsman, live unbruised and love my cousin.

CLAUDIO   I had well hoped thou wouldst have denied   110
Beatrice, that I might have cudgelled thee out of thy
single life, to make thee a double-dealer – which out
of question thou wilt be, if my cousin do not look
exceeding narrowly to thee.

BENEDICK   Come, come, we are friends. Let's have a   115
dance ere we are married, that we may lighten our own
hearts and our wives' heels.

LEONATO   We'll have dancing afterward.

BENEDICK   First, of my word! Therefore play, music!
Prince, thou art sad – get thee a wife, get thee a wife!   120

99–100 **college of wit-crackers** assembly of jokers
102 **brains** i.e. products of the brain, such as epigrams and satires
shall ... handsome must give up all pretensions to fashionable clothes
106–7 **this ... conclusion** (1) this is how I've ended (in marriage); (2) so I conclude (that man is a giddy thing)
108 **in that** since
112 **double-dealer** married man (i.e.

no longer single); unfaithful husband. The image also recalls Beatrice's claim that she gave Benedick a double heart for his single one at 2.1.256.
114 **narrowly** closely
117 **wives' heels** another innuendo about female sexual licence, although here in the legitimate sexuality of marriage; cf. 3.4.42: 'Ye light o'love with your heels?'
119 **of** by

98 SP] *Rowe (Pedro); Prince Q* 105 what] *om. F* 112 double-dealer] *(double dealer), Cam* 119 play,] *Pope;* plaie *Q*

There is no staff more reverend than one tipped with horn.

Enter Messenger.

MESSENGER

My lord, your brother John is ta'en in flight
And brought with armed men back to Messina.
BENEDICK   Think not on him till tomorrow; I'll devise   125
thee brave punishments for him. Strike up, pipers!

Dance. [Exeunt.]

FINIS

---

121 **staff** walking stick of an elderly person; sceptre-like sign of rule; wife, who is meant as a support for her husband
121–2 **tipped with horn** the obvious cuckolding pun, exacerbated by the fact that 'tip' is a variant of 'tup', a sheep-breeder's term for the male animal and its sexual act, as well as for the act of furnishing with horns like a ram (*OED* tup *v.* 3); as with the other horn jokes, this line is often cut in productions seeking for a more decorous finale. Cf. 44n.
124 **armed** armèd
126 **brave** worthy, excellent (*OED adj.* 3b); the word carries a certain jaunty aspect.
126 SD *Dance* This is the only play of Shakespeare's explicitly to end with a dance for the general company (a clown's jig was the more usual finale, taking place as a discrete entertainment

after the close of the play). J.R. Mulryne observes that the harmonies of dance served as a 'symbol of order . . . every [actor's] movements allied to his fellows' movements and the whole governed by music', much akin to the institution of marriage itself, 'society's divinely-sanctioned means of controlling and directing sexual relations' (Mulryne, 24). This ascribes perhaps a more decorous purpose to dancing than is Benedick's (to 'lighten our . . . wives' heels', 116–17), and, of course, the type of dance selected by a production (pavane or tango?), as well as the extent of its inclusiveness, determines just what kind and degree of social order is being represented. In the Elizabethan theatre, a jig may well have followed this dance, as Will Kemp (the actor who initially played Dogberry) was famous for his jigs, which were short, comic song-and-dance sketches.

121 reverend] *F;* reuerent *Q*   126 SD *Exeunt.*] *Rowe*

APPENDIX

CASTING CHART

This is a chart of a possible casting of this edition's text of the play. There are fifteen adult speaking parts, not counting the Watch (see 3.3.0.2n. for a discussion of the Watch numbers). These can be played by thirteen players, although a further economy could be achieved by having the mute Balthasar of 1.1 play the Messenger in 1.1 (instead of entering, as in the Quarto SD, with the soldiers at 90.1) and 5.4, as well as the Lord of 5.3 (a production relying on this actor's musical skills would be likely to have him present in 5.3 in any case).

The four female roles would have been played by boys in the Elizabethan theatre, one of whom could have also served as the boy who speaks briefly to Benedick at the beginning of 2.3. I have not assigned the parts of the Attendants or Watchmen, on the assumption that these minor roles could have been acted by members of the company; it is plausible that the players of the Watch could also serve as the Attendants.

In the Elizabethan theatre doubling no doubt took place, probably more aggressively when on tour than in London; the factors conditioning the practice would have included whether or not players of bigger parts also played minor parts, whether men played women's parts, and how much time was necessary to change costume. This chart represents only the roles noted in the Quarto, either in entry SDs or in SPs, and included in this edition (i.e. excluding the 'ghost' roles of Leonato's wife Innogen in 1.1 and 2.1 and the 'kinsman' in 2.1); however, a given production might well choose to include non-listed roles in a scene without compromising resources (Margaret, Ursula and Antonio, for instance, might or might not appear in 1.1 or 4.1, or Conrade and Borachio in 1.1, as part of the general throngs).

For an alternative version, see T. King, 193.

Actor	1.1	1.2	1.3	2.1	2.2	2.3	3.1	3.2	3.3
1	Benedick			Benedick		Benedick		Benedick	
2	Leonato	Leonato		Leonato		Leonato		Leonato	
3	Don Pedro			Don Pedro		Don Pedro		Don Pedro	
4	Claudio			Claudio		Claudio		Claudio	
5									Dogberry
6			Borachio	Borachio	Borachio				Borachio
7	Don John		Don John	Don John	Don John			Don John	
8			Conrade						Conrade
9	Balthasar*			Balthasar		Balthasar			
10		Antonio		Antonio					
11									
12									Verges
13	Messenger								
14	Beatrice			Beatrice		Beatrice	Beatrice		
15	Hero			Hero			Hero		
16				Margaret			Margaret		
17				Ursula			Ursula		
misc.						Boy			
misc.		Attendants*		Attendants*					
misc.									Watchmen

320

Actor	3.4	3.5	4.1	4.2	5.1	5.2	5.3	5.4
1			Benedick		Benedick	Benedick		Benedick
2		Leonato	Leonato		Leonato			Leonato
3			Don Pedro		Don Pedro		Don Pedro	Don Pedro
4			Claudio		Claudio		Claudio	Claudio
5		Dogberry		Dogberry	Dogberry			
6				Borachio	Borachio			
7			Don John					
8				Conrade	Conrade			
9				Sexton	Sexton*		(Balthasar)	
10					Antonio			Antonio
11			Friar					Friar
12		Verges		Verges	Verges			
13		Messenger					Lord	Messenger
14	Beatrice		Beatrice			Beatrice		Beatrice
15	Hero		Hero					Hero
16	Margaret					Margaret		Margaret*
17	Ursula					Ursula		Ursula*
misc.				Watchmen	Watchmen*			
misc.								
misc.							Attendants	Attendants*

* mute
( ) optional

ABBREVIATIONS AND REFERENCES

Quotations and references to works by Shakespeare other than *Much Ado About Nothing* are keyed to the most recently published Arden editions: for *1H4*, *3H6*, *Per*, *R2* and *TGV*, the individual Arden 3 volumes; for all others, *The Arden Shakespeare: Complete Works*, gen. eds Richard Proudfoot, Ann Thompson and David Scott Kastan (revised edn, 2001). Biblical citations are from the Bishops' Bible (*The Holy Bible . . . authorized and appointed to be read in Churches*, 1588) unless otherwise indicated. Place of publication is London unless otherwise indicated.

ABBREVIATIONS

ABBREVIATIONS USED IN NOTES

*	precedes commentary notes involving readings altered from the text on which this edition is based
c	corrected state
n.	(in cross-references) commentary note
n.d.	no date
n.s	new series
SD	stage direction
SP	speech prefix
subst.	substantially
this edn	a reading adopted for the first time in this edition
t.n.	textual note
u	uncorrected state

WORKS BY AND PARTLY BY SHAKESPEARE

AC	*Antony and Cleopatra*
AW	*All's Well That Ends Well*
AYL	*As You Like It*
CE	*The Comedy of Errors*
Cor	*Coriolanus*
Cym	*Cymbeline*

E3	*King Edward III*
Ham	*Hamlet*
1H4	*King Henry IV, Part 1*
2H4	*King Henry IV, Part 2*
H5	*King Henry V*
1H6	*King Henry VI, Part 1*
2H6	*King Henry VI, Part 2*
3H6	*King Henry VI, Part 3*
H8	*King Henry VIII*
JC	*Julius Caesar*
KJ	*King John*
KL	*King Lear*
LC	*A Lover's Complaint*
LLL	*Love's Labour's Lost*
Luc	*The Rape of Lucrece*
MA	*Much Ado About Nothing*
Mac	*Macbeth*
MM	*Measure for Measure*
MND	*A Midsummer Night's Dream*
MV	*The Merchant of Venice*
MW	*The Merry Wives of Windsor*
Oth	*Othello*
Per	*Pericles*
PP	*The Passionate Pilgrim*
PT	*The Phoenix and Turtle*
R2	*King Richard II*
R3	*King Richard III*
RJ	*Romeo and Juliet*
Son	*Sonnets*
STM	*Sir Thomas More*
TC	*Troilus and Cressida*
Tem	*The Tempest*
TGV	*The Two Gentlemen of Verona*
Tim	*Timon of Athens*
Tit	*Titus Andronicus*
TN	*Twelfth Night*
TNK	*The Two Noble Kinsmen*
TS	*The Taming of the Shrew*
VA	*Venus and Adonis*
WT	*The Winter's Tale*

323

REFERENCES

EDITIONS OF SHAKESPEARE COLLATED OR REFERRED TO

Alexander	*William Shakespeare: The Complete Works*, ed. Peter Alexander (1951)
Ard[1]	*Much Ado About Nothing*, ed. Grace Trenery, Arden Shakespeare (1924)
Ard[2]	*Much Ado About Nothing*, ed. A.R. Humphreys, Arden Shakespeare (1981)
Bell	*Bell's Edition of Shakespeare's Plays, as they are performed at the Theatres Royal in London*, 9 vols (1773–4)
Bevington	*Works*, ed. David Bevington (Glenview, Ill., 1980)
Bevington[2]	*Much Ado About Nothing*, ed. David Bevington, Bantam Shakespeare (New York, 1988)
Boas	*Much Ado About Nothing*, ed. F.S. Boas (Oxford, 1916)
Brooke	*Much Ado About Nothing*, ed. C.F. Tucker Brooke (New Haven, Conn., 1917)
Cam	*Works*, ed. William George Clark, John Glover and William Aldis Wright, 9 vols (Cambridge, 1863–6)
Cam[1]	*Much Ado About Nothing*, ed. J. Dover Wilson, New Shakespeare (Cambridge, 1923)
Cam[2]	*Much Ado About Nothing*, ed. F.H. Mares, New Cambridge Shakespeare (Cambridge, 1988)
Capell	*Comedies, Histories, and Tragedies*, ed. Edward Capell, 10 vols (1767–8)
Collier	*Works*, ed. J.P. Collier, 8 vols (1842–4)
Collier[2]	*Plays*, ed. J.P. Collier, 8 vols (1853–65)
Collier MS	MS annotations once thought to be by an 'Old Corrector' but probably by J.P. Collier, in his copy (the Perkins–Collier–Devonshire copy) of F2 in the Huntington Library, and entered by Collier in his own copy of the first of his editions, now in the Folger Shakespeare Library
Craig	*Works*, ed. W.J. Craig (Oxford, 1892)
Deighton	*Much Ado About Nothing*, ed. K. Deighton (1888)
Dyce	*Works*, ed. Alexander Dyce, 6 vols (1857)
F	*Comedies, Histories, and Tragedies*, The First Folio (1623)
F2	*Comedies, Histories, and Tragedies*, The Second Folio (1632)
F3	*Comedies, Histories, and Tragedies*, The Third Folio (1663)
F4	*Comedies, Histories, and Tragedies*, The Fourth Folio (1685)

Foakes	*Much Ado About Nothing*, ed. R.A. Foakes, New Penguin Shakespeare (1968)
Folg²	*Much Ado About Nothing*, ed. Barbara A. Mowat and Paul Werstine, New Folger Library Shakespeare (New York, 1995)
Furness	*Much Ado About Nothing*, ed. Horace Howard Furness, New Variorum Edition (1899, repr. New York, 1964)
Furnivall	F.J. Furnivall, *The Leopold Shakespeare* (1877)
Halliwell	*Works*, ed. James O. Halliwell, 16 vols (1853–65)
Hanmer	*Works*, ed. Thomas Hanmer, 6 vols (1743–4)
Hinman	*Much Ado About Nothing*, ed. Charlton Hinman, Shakespeare Quarto Facsimiles no. 15 (Oxford, 1971)
Johnson	*Plays*, ed. Samuel Johnson, 8 vols (1765)
Kittredge	*Works*, ed. George Lyman Kittredge (Boston, 1936)
Knight	*Works*, ed. Charles Knight, 8 vols (1839–42)
Malone	*Plays and Poems*, ed. Edmund Malone, 10 vols (1790)
Newcomer	*Much Ado About Nothing*, ed. A.G. Newcomer (1929)
Oxf	*Works*, ed. Stanley Wells and Gary Taylor, with John Jowett and William Montgomery (Oxford, 1986)
Oxf¹	*Much Ado About Nothing*, ed. Sheldon P. Zitner (Oxford, 1993)
Pope	*Works*, ed. Alexander Pope, 6 vols (1723–5)
Pope²	*Works*, ed. Alexander Pope, 6 vols (1728)
Q	*Much Ado About Nothing*, The Quarto (1600)
Riv	*The Riverside Shakespeare*, ed. G. Blakemore Evans (Boston, 1974)
Rowe	*Works*, ed. Nicholas Rowe, 6 vols (1709)
Rowe²	*Works*, ed. Nicholas Rowe, 2nd edn, 6 vols (1709)
Rowe³	*Works*, ed. Nicholas Rowe, 3rd edn, 8 vols (1714)
Smith	*Much Ado About Nothing*, ed. J.C. Smith (Boston, 1902)
Staunton	*Plays*, ed. Howard Staunton, 3 vols (1858–60)
Steevens	*Plays*, ed. Samuel Johnson and George Steevens, 2nd edn, 10 vols (1778)
Steevens–Reed	*Plays*, ed. Samuel Johnson, George Steevens and Isaac Reed, 3rd edn, 10 vols (1785)
Steevens–Reed²	*Plays*, with notes by Samuel Johnson and George Steevens, ed. Isaac Reed, 4th edn, 10 vols (1793)
Stevenson	*Much Ado About Nothing*, ed. David L. Stevenson, Signet Classic Shakespeare (New York, 1964)
Theobald	*Works*, ed. Lewis Theobald, 7 vols (1733)
Warburton	*Works*, ed. William Warburton, 8 vols (1747)
Waters-Bennett	*Much Ado About Nothing*, ed. Josephine Waters Bennett, in *The Complete Works*, gen. ed. A. Harbage, revised Complete Pelican Shakespeare (Baltimore, 1969)
White	*Works*, ed. R.G. White, 12 vols (Boston, 1857–66)

White[2]   *Works*, ed. R.G. White, 2nd edn, 6 vols (Boston, 1883)
Wilson, J.D.   See Cam[2]
Wright   *Works*, ed. William Aldis Wright and George Clark (1924)

OTHER WORKS CITED

Abbott   E.A. Abbott, *A Shakespearian Grammar*, 3rd edn (1870)
Acts   *Acts of the Privy Council, A.D. 1599–1600*, n.s., 30, 1905
Aeneid   Virgil, *The Aeneid*, trans. Robert Fitzgerald (New York, 1983)
Albertus   Albertus Magnus, *De Animalibus*, in *On Animals: A Medieval Summa Zoologica*, trans. and annotated by Kenneth F. Kitchell Jr and Irven Michael Resnick (Baltimore, 1999)
Allen   John A. Allen, 'Dogberry', *SQ*, 24 (1972), 90–112
Altick   Richard D. Altick, *Paintings from Books: Art and Literature in Britain 1760–1900* (Columbus, Ohio, 1985)
Altman   Joel Altman, *The Tudor Play of Mind: Rhetorical Inquiry and the Development of Elizabethan Drama* (Berkeley, Calif., 1978)
Anger   Jane Anger, *Her Protection for Women* (1589)
Arber   *A Transcript of the Registers of the Company of Stationers of London, 1554–1640 AD*, ed. Edward Arber, 5 vols (1876)
Aubrey   John Aubrey, *Brief Lives*, ed. O.L. Dick (London, 1949)
Auden   W.H. Auden, *Lectures on Shakespeare*, ed. Arthur Kirsch (Princeton, NJ, 2000)
Bacon   Francis Bacon, 'Of Envy', in *The Essays and Counsels Civil and Moral of Francis Bacon Lord Verulam*, ed. Oliphant Smeaton (1906)
Baker   David Baker, 'Surprise with all': rereading character in *Much Ado About Nothing*', in David Galef (ed.), *Second Thoughts: A Focus on Rereading* (Detroit, 1980), 228–45
Baldwin   Thomas Whitfield Baldwin, *'Loves Labor's Won': New Evidence from the Account Books of an Elizabethan Bookseller* (Carbondale, Ill., 1957)
Bandello   Matteo Bandello, *La Prima Parte de le Novelle* (1554), novella 22
Barber   C.L. Barber, *Shakespeare's Festive Comedy: A Study of Dramatic Form and Its Relation to Social Custom* (Princeton, NJ, 1959)
Barish   Jonas Barish, 'Pattern and purpose in the prose of *Much Ado About Nothing*', Rice University Studies, 60 (1974), 19–30
Bate, 'Dying'   Jonathan Bate, 'Dying to live in *Much Ado About Nothing*', in Yasunari Takada (ed.), *Surprised by Scenes: Essays in*

	Honour of Professor Yasunari Takahashi (Tokyo, 1994), 69–85
Bate & Jackson	Jonathan Bate and Russell Jackson, *Shakespeare: An Illustrated Stage History* (Oxford, 1996)
Bateman	Stephen Bateman, *Batman upon Bartholomew* (1582)
BCP	*The Book of Common Prayer* (1559), ed. John E. Booty (Washington, DC, 1976)
Beaumont & Fletcher	Francis Beaumont and John Fletcher, *Comedies and Tragedies* (1647)
Becon	T. Becon, *Principles of Christian Religion* (1552)
Belleforest	François de Belleforest, *Histoires Tragiques* (1569)
Berger	Harry Berger Jr, 'Against the sink-a-pace: sexual and family politics in *Much Ado About Nothing*', *SQ*, 33 (1982), 302–13
Berry	Ralph Berry, 'Problems of knowing', in *Shakespeare's Comedies: Explorations in Form* (Princeton, NJ, 1972), 154–74
Bert	Edmund Bert, *Treatise of Hawks and Hunting* (1619)
Blayney	Peter W.M. Blayney, 'The publication of playbooks', in John D. Cox and David Scott Kastan (eds), *A New History of Early English Drama* (New York, 1997), 383–422
Blazon	Benedetto Varchi, *The Blazon of Jealousy*, trans. R.T. (1615)
Breton, *Cornucopiae*	Nicholas Breton, *Cornucopiae, Pasquil's Night-Cap, or Anti-dote for the Headache* (1612)
Breton, *Praise*	Nicholas Breton, *Praise of Virtuous Ladies* (1606)
Brewer	*Brewer's Dictionary of Phrase and Fable*, 15th edn, revised Adrian Broom (1996)
Bright	Timothy Bright, *A Treatise of Melancholie* (1586)
Brissenden	Alan Brissenden, *Shakespeare and the Dance* (1981)
Bruster	Douglas Bruster, 'The horn of plenty: cuckoldry and capital in the drama of the age of Shakespeare', *SEL*, 30 (1990), 197–215
Bullinger	Heinrich Bullinger, *Christian State of Matrimony* (1541)
Bullough	Geoffrey Bullough, *Narrative and Dramatic Sources of Shakespeare*, 8 vols (New York, 1957–75), vol. 2
Buoni	Thomas Buoni, *Problems of Beauty and All Human Affections* (1606)
Burton	Robert Burton, *The Anatomy of Melancholy*, ed. Thomas C. Faulkner, Nicholas K. Kiessling and Rhonda L. Blair, 8 vols (Oxford, 1989)
Campbell	Thomas Campbell, *Dramatic Works of Shakespeare* (1838)
Capell, *Notes*	Edward Capell, *Notes and Various Readings to Shakespeare*, 3 vols (1779)
Cartari	Vincenzo Cartari, *The Fountain of Ancient Fiction* (1599)

Castiglione	Baldasarre Castiglione, *Il libro del cortegiano* (*The Courtier*), trans. George Bull (Harmondsworth, England, 1967)
Cerasano	S.P. Cerasano, 'Half a dozen dangerous words', in *Gloriana's Face, Women, Public and Private, in the English Renaissance* (Detroit, 1992), 167–83
Cercignani	Fausto Cercignani, *Shakespeare's Works and Elizabethan Pronunciation* (Oxford, 1981)
Chambers	E.K. Chambers, *William Shakespeare: A Study of Facts and Problems*, 2 vols (1930)
Chaucer	*The Riverside Chaucer*, ed. Larry D. Benson, 3rd edn (Oxford, 1987)
Child	F.J. Child (ed.), *English and Scottish Ballads*, 8 vols (1860)
Cogan	Thomas Cogan, *Haven of Health* (1574)
Coleridge	Hartley Coleridge, *Essays and Marginalia*, 2 vols (1851)
Cook, C.	Carol Cook, 'The sign and semblance of her honor: reading gender difference in *Much Ado About Nothing*', *PMLA*, 101 (1988), 186–202
Cook, D.	David Cook, 'The very temple of delight: the twin plots of *Much Ado About Nothing*', in Antony Coleman and Antony Hammond (eds), *Poetry and Drama 1570–1700: Essays in Honour of Harold F. Brooks* (1981), 32–46
Coryat	Thomas Coryat, *Coryat's Crudities* (1611)
Cotgrave	Randle Cotgrave, *A Dictionary of the French and English Tongues* (1611)
Cox, *Shakespeare*	John D. Cox, *Shakespeare in Production: Much Ado About Nothing* (Cambridge, 1997)
Cox, 'Stage'	John D. Cox, 'The stage representation of the "Kill Claudio" sequence in *Much Ado About Nothing*', *SS 32* (1979), 27–36
Craik	T.W. Craik, '*Much Ado About Nothing*', *Scrutiny*, 19 (1953), 297–316
Crane, M.	Milton Crane, *Shakespeare's Prose* (Chicago, 1951)
Crane, W.	William G. Crane, *Wit and Rhetoric in the Renaissance* (Gloucester, Mass., 1937, reprinted 1964)
Craven	Alan E. Craven, 'Compositor analysis to edited text: some suggested readings in *Richard II* and *Much Ado About Nothing*', *PBSA*, 26 (1982), 43–62
Croll	Morris W. Croll, *Attic and Baroque Prose Style: The Anti-Ciceronian Movement* (Princeton, NJ, 1966)
Davies	Thomas Davies, *Memoirs of the Life of David Garrick*, 2 vols (1780), vol. 1
Davis	Walter Davis, Introduction to *Twentieth Century Interpretations of 'Much Ado About Nothing'* (Englewood Cliffs, NJ, 1969)
Dawson	Anthony Dawson, 'Much ado about signifying', *SEL*, 22 (1982), 211–21

Dekker, *Hornbook*	Thomas Dekker, *Gull's Hornbook* (1609)
Dekker, *Sins*	Thomas Dekker, *Seven Deadly Sins of London*, in *The Non-Dramatic Works of Thomas Dekker*, ed. Rev. Alexander B. Grosart, 5 vols (1884–6), vol. 2
Dekker, *Works*	Thomas Dekker, *The Dramatic Works of Thomas Dekker*, ed. Fredson Bowers, 4 vols (Cambridge, 1953–61)
De Mornay	Philip de Mornay, *Work Concerning the Trueness of Christian Religion . . .*, trans. Arthur Golding (1617)
Dent	R.W. Dent, *Shakespeare's Proverbial Language: An Index* (Berkeley, Los Angeles and London, 1981)
Dobranski	Stephen P. Dobranski, 'Children of the mind: miscarried narratives in *Much Ado About Nothing*', *SEL*, 38 (1998), 233–50
Dobson	Michael Dobson, 'Improving on the original: actresses and adaptations', in Bate & Jackson, 45–68
Donne, 'Indifferent'	John Donne, 'The Indifferent', in *Selected Poetry*, ed. John Carey (Oxford, 1996)
Donne, *Problems*	John Donne, *Certain Problems* (1623)
Drakakis	John Drakakis, 'Trust and transgression: the discursive practices of *Much Ado About Nothing*', in Richard Machin and Christopher Norris (eds), *Post-Structuralist Readings of English Poetry* (Cambridge, 1987)
Draper	John Draper, *Stratford to Dogberry: Studies in Shakespeare's Earlier Plays* (Pittsburgh, 1961)
Duffin	Ross W. Duffin, *Shakespeare's Songbook* (New York, 2004)
Dyce, *Notes*	Alexander Dyce, *A Few Notes on Shakespeare* (1853)
EC	*Essays in Criticism*
Erasmus	Desiderius Erasmus, *De Civilitate Morum Puerilium*, ed. J.K. Sowards, in *Works*, gen. ed. R.J. Schoek, 84 vols (Toronto, 1974–2003), vol. 23
Erne	Lukas Erne, *Shakespeare as Literary Dramatist* (Cambridge, 2003)
Evans, B.	Bertrand Evans, *Shakespeare's Comedies* (Oxford, 1960)
Evans, H.	Hugh C. Evans, 'Comic constables: fictional and historical', *SQ*, 20 (1969), 422–33
Evans, J.	John X. Evans, 'The villainy of one deformed: the complex word fashion in *Much Ado About Nothing*', in John H. Dorencamp (ed.), *Literary Studies: Essays in Memory of Francis A. Drumm* (Wetteren, Belgium, 1973), 91–114
Everett, 'Much Ado'	Barbara Everett, 'Much Ado About Nothing', *Critical Quarterly*, 3 (1961), 319–35
Everett, 'Unsociable'	Barbara Everett, '*Much Ado About Nothing*: the unsociable comedy', in Michael Cordner, Peter Holland and John Kerrigan (eds), *English Comedy* (Cambridge, 1994), 68–84

Faucit	Helena Faucit, *On Some of Shakespeare's Female Characters* (Edinburgh, 1891)
Fedele	Luigi Pasaqualigo, *Il Fedele* (1576), trans. Anthony Munday as *Fedele and Fortunio, the Two Italian Gentlemen* (1585)
Fergusson	Francis Fergusson, '*The Comedy of Errors* and *Much Ado About Nothing*', *Sewanee Review*, 61 (1954), 24–37
Ferrand	Jacques Ferrand, *Erotomania* (1640)
FQ	Edmund Spenser, *The Faerie Queene* (1590/1596)
Friedman, 'Hush'd'	Michael Friedman, 'Hush'd on purpose to grace harmony: wives and silence in *Much Ado About Nothing*', *Theater Journal*, vol. 42, no. 3 (1990), 350–63
Friedman, 'Man'	Michael Friedman, '"For Man is a giddy thing, and this is my conclusion": fashion and *Much Ado About Nothing*', *Text and Performance Quarterly*, vol. 13, no. 3 (1993), 267–82
Frye	Northrop Frye, *A Natural Perspective: The Development of Shakespearean Comedy and Romance* (New York, 1967)
Gardener's	*The Gardener's Labyrinth* (1594)
Gargantua	François Rabelais, *Gargantua and Pantagruel*, trans. Thomas Urquhart and Peter Le Motteux, 3 vols (1934)
Garrick	*Much Ado About Nothing . . . as it is Acted at the Theatres Royal in Drury Lane and Covent Garden* (1778)
Geneva Bible	*The Bible and Holy Scriptures Contained in the Old and New Testaments* (1560)
Gerard	John Gerard, *The Herbal, or General History of Plants* (1597)
Gibson	Anthony Gibson, *A Woman's Worth, defended against all the men in the world* (1599)
Gielgud	John Gielgud, *An Actor and His Time* (New York, 1997)
Gildon	Charles Gildon, 'Remarks', in Rowe (additional vol. 7), 304
Girard	René Girard, 'Love by hearsay: mimetic strategies in *Much Ado About Nothing*', in *A Theater of Envy* (Oxford, 1991), 80–91
Gittings	Clare Gittings, *Death, Burial and the Individual in Early Modern England* (1984)
Gollancz	Israel Gollancz, Introduction to *Much Ado About Nothing*, in *The Works of William Shakespeare*, 5 vols (New York, 1909), vol. 5
Goosecappe	*Sir Gyles Goosecappe*, in A.H. Bullen (ed.), *A Collection of Old English Plays*, 4 vols (1882–5), vol. 3
Greenblatt	Stephen Greenblatt, Introduction to *Much Ado About Nothing*, Norton Shakespeare (New York, 1997)
Greene, *Courtier*	Robert Greene, *A Quip for an Upstart Courtier*, in *The Life and Complete Works in Verse and Prose of Robert Greene*, ed. Rev. Alexander B. Grosart, 15 vols (1881–6), vol. 11

Greene, *Mirror*   Robert Greene, *Mirror of Modesty*, in John Payne Collier (ed.), *Illustrations of English Literature*, 3 vols (1866), vol. 3

Greg   W.W. Greg, *A Bibliography of English Printed Drama to the Restoration*, 2 vols (1962)

Gurr   Andrew Gurr, *The Shakespearean Stage, 1574–1642* (Cambridge, 1982)

Harbage   Alfred Harbage, *As They Liked It* (1947)

Hayne   Victoria Hayne, 'Measuring *Much Ado*: Davenant's *Law Against Lovers*', paper presented to the conference 'Much Ado About Nothing: A Play in History', University of California at Los Angeles, 1998

Hazlitt   William Hazlitt, *Characters of Shakespeare's Plays* (1817)

Hemming   Sarah Hemming, review of Doran production, *Financial Times*, 8 August 2002

Henslowe   *Henslowe's Diary*, ed. R.A. Foakes and R.T. Rickert (Cambridge, 1961)

Henze   Richard Henze, 'Deception in *Much Ado About Nothing*', *SEL*, 11 (1971), 187–201

Heywood, *Maid*   Thomas Heywood, *Fair Maid of the Exchange*, ed. Karl E. Snyder (New York, 1980)

Heywood, *Man*   Thomas Heywood, *How a Man May Choose a Good Wife from a Bad* (1602)

Heywood, *Proverbs*   John Heywood, *A Dialogue . . . of All the Proverbs in the English Tongue . . .* (1546)

Hogan   Charles Beecher Hogan, *Shakespeare in the Theatre, 1701–1800: A Record of Performances in London*, 2 vols (Oxford, 1952–7)

Holland   Peter Holland, *English Shakespeares* (Cambridge, 1997)

Homilies   *The First Book of Homilies* (1547), ed. John Griffiths (Oxford, 1859)

Howard   Jean E. Howard, 'Renaissance anti-theatricality and the politics of gender and rank in *Much Ado About Nothing*', in Jean E. Howard and Marion F. O'Connor, *Shakespeare Reproduced: The Text in History and Ideology* (1987), 163–87

Hunt   Maurice Hunt, 'The reclamation of language in *Much Ado About Nothing*', *SP*, 97 (2000), 165–91

Iliad   Homer, *The Iliad*, trans. Robert Fagles (New York, 1990)

Jameson   Mrs Jameson, *Characteristics of Women*, 2nd edn, 2 vols (1833)

Jenkins   Harold Jenkins, *Structural Problems in Shakespeare: Lectures and Essays by Harold Jenkins*, ed. Ernst Honigmann (2001)

Johnson on Shakespeare   *Samuel Johnson on Shakespeare*, ed. H.R. Woudhuysen (1989)

Jonson   *Ben Jonson*, ed. C.H. Herford, P. Simpson and E. Simpson, 11 vols (Oxford, 1925–52)

Jorgensen	P.A. Jorgensen, 'Much Ado About Nothing', in *Redeeming Shakespeare's Words* (1962), 22–42
Kaplan, *Culture*	M. Lindsey Kaplan, *The Culture of Slander in Early Modern England* (Cambridge, 1997)
Kaplan, 'Slander'	M. Lindsey Kaplan, 'Sexual slander and the politics of the erotic in Garter's *Susanna*', in Ellen Spolsky (ed.), *The Judgement of Susanna: Authority and Witness* (Atlanta, Ga., 1996), 73–85
Kemble	*Much Ado About Nothing . . . revised by J.P. Kemble . . . as it is performed at the Theatres Royal* (1815)
King, T.	T.J. King, *Casting Shakespeare's Plays: London Actors and Their Roles, 1590–1642* (Cambridge, 1992)
King, W.	Walter N. King, 'Much Ado About Something', *SQ*, 15 (1954), 143–55
King James Bible	*The Holy Bible . . . with the former translations diligently compared and revised, by His Majesty's special command* (the Authorized Version) (1611)
Kökeritz	H. Kökeritz, *Shakespeare's Pronunciation* (1953)
Kreiger	Elliot Kreiger, 'Social relations and the social order in *Much Ado About Nothing*', *SS 32* (1979), 49–61
Lambarde	William Lambarde, *Duties of Constables, Borsholders, and Tithing Men* (1583)
Lewalski, 'Love'	Barbara Lewalski, 'Love, appearance, reality: Much Ado About Something', *SEL*, 8 (1968), 235–51
Lewalski, 'Namesake'	Barbara Lewalski, 'Hero's name – and namesake – in *Much Ado About Nothing*', *English Language Notes*, 7 (1970), 175–9
Lindop	Grevel Lindop, review of Kaut-Howson production, *Times Literary Supplement*, 3 October 1997
Locrine	*The Lamentable Tragedy of Locrine* (1595), ed. Jane Lytton Gooch (New York, 1981)
Lodge	Thomas Lodge, Reply to Stephen Gosson's *School of Abuse* in *Defence of Poetry, Music and Stage Plays*, in *Complete Works of Thomas Lodge*, ed. E. Gosse, 4 vols (1883), vol. 1
Logan	Brian Logan, review of Donnellan production, *Observer*, 14 June 1998
Lyly, *Anatomy*	John Lyly, *Euphues: The Anatomy of Wit*, in Lyly, *Works*, vol. 1
Lyly, *Euphues*	John Lyly, *Euphues and His England*, in Lyly, *Works*, vol. 2
Lyly, *Grammar*	William Lyly, *Short Introduction of Latin Grammar* (1538)
Lyly, *Works*	John Lyly, *The Complete Works of John Lyly*, ed. R. Warwick Bond, 3 vols (Oxford, 1902)
McCollum	William G. McCollum, 'The role of wit in *Much Ado About Nothing*', *SQ*, 19 (1968), 165–74

McEachern, 'Blush'	Claire McEachern, 'A whore at the first blush seemeth only a woman: John Bale's *Image of Both Churches* and the terms of religious difference in the early English Reformation', *Journal of Medieval and Renaissance Studies*, vol. 25, no. 2 (1995), 245–69
McEachern, 'Fathering'	Claire McEachern, 'Fathering herself: a source study of Shakespeare's feminism', *SQ*, 39 (1988), 269–90
Magnusson	Lynne Magnusson, 'The pragmatics of repair in *King Lear* and *Much Ado About Nothing*', in *Shakespeare and Social Dialogue: Dramatic Language and Elizabethan Letters* (Cambridge, 1999), 141–62
Mahoney	Elisabeth Mahoney, review of Harvey production, *Guardian*, 4 June 2004
Marlowe, *Hero*	Christopher Marlowe, *Hero and Leander* (completed by George Chapman) (1598)
Marlowe, *Works*	*The Complete Works of Christopher Marlowe*, ed. Alexander Dyce, 3 vols (1850)
Marmion	Patrick Marmion, review of Doran production, *Mail on Sunday*, 4 August 2002
Mason	Pamela Mason, 'Don Pedro, Don John, and Don . . . who? – noting a stranger in Much Adoodle-do', in Edward J. Esche (ed.), *Shakespeare and His Contemporaries* (Aldershot, England, 2000), 241–60
Massinger	Philip Massinger, *The Poems and Plays of Philip Massinger*, ed. Philip Edwards and Colin Gibson, 5 vols (Oxford, 1976)
Middleton	Thomas Middleton, *The Works of Thomas Middleton*, ed. A.H. Bullen, 8 vols (New York, 1964)
Milton, *Poems and Prose*	John Milton, *Complete Poems and Major Prose*, ed. Merritt Hughes (New York, 1985)
Milton, *Religion*	John Milton, *Of True Religion*, in *The Prose Writings of John Milton*, ed. K.M. Burton (1958)
Misogonus	*Misogonus* (1570)
Montaigne	Michel de Montaigne, 'On some verses of Virgil', in *Essays*, trans. Donald M. Frame (Stanford, Calif., 1958)
Mueller	Martin Mueller, 'Shakespeare's sleeping beauties: the sources of *Much Ado About Nothing* and the play of their repetitions', *Modern Philology*, vol. 1, no. 3 (1994), 288–311
Mulryne	J.R. Mulryne (ed.), *Shakespeare: Much Ado About Nothing* (1965)
Musaeus, *Hero*	Musaeus, *Hero and Leander*, trans. George Chapman (1616)
Myers	Jeffrey Rayner Myers, 'An emended *Much Ado About Nothing* Act V Scene 3', *PBSA*, vol. 84, no. 4 (1990), 413–18

Myhill	Nova Myhill, 'Spectatorship in/of *Much Ado About Nothing*', *SEL*, vol. 39, no. 2 (1999), 291–311
Nashe	Thomas Nashe, *The Works of Thomas Nashe*, ed. R.B. McKerrow, 5 vols (Oxford, 1904–10)
Neely	Carol Neely, *Broken Nuptials in Shakespeare's Plays* (New Haven, Conn., 1985)
Neill	Kirby Neill, 'More ado about Claudio: an acquittal for a slandered groom', *SQ*, 3 (1952), 91–107
Niccholes	Alexander Niccholes, *A Discourse of Marriage and Wiving* (1615)
Northbrooke	John Northbrooke, *A Treatise against Dicing, Dancing, Plays, and Interludes, with other Idle Pastimes* (1577)
Odyssey	Homer, *The Odyssey*, trans. Robert Fagles (New York, 1996)
OED	*Oxford English Dictionary*, 2nd edn, prepared by J.A. Simpson and E.S.C. Weiner (Oxford, 1989)
Orlando	Ludovico Ariosto, *Orlando Furioso*, trans. Sir John Harington as *Orlando Furioso in English Heroical Verse* (1591)
Ormerod	David Ormerod, 'Faith and fashion in *Much Ado About Nothing*', *SS 25* (1972), 93–105
Osbourne	Laurie E. Osbourne, 'Dramatic play in *Much Ado About Nothing*: wedding the Italian novella and English comedy', *PQ*, 2 (1990), 167–88
Overbury	Sir Thomas Overbury, *Characters*, ed. Donald Beecher (Ottawa, 2000)
Ovid, *Ars Amatoria*	*Thomas Heywood's Art of Love: The First Complete English Translation of Ovid's Ars Amatoria*, ed. M.L. Stapleton (Ann Arbor, Mich., 2000)
Ovid, *Fasti*	Ovid, *Fasti*, trans. and ed. with an introduction and notes by A.J. Boyle and R.D. Woodard (2000)
Ovid/Golding	Ovid, *The XV Books of Ovidius Naso Intituled Metamorphosis*, trans. Arthur Golding (1567)
Ovid, *Heroides*	*Ovid's Heroines: A Verse Translation of the Heroides*, Daryl Hine (New Haven, Conn., 1991)
Ovid, *Met.*	Ovid, *Metamorphoses*, trans. Rolfe Humphries (Bloomington, Ind., 1957)
Ovid, *Remedies*	Ovid, *Remedies of Love Translated and Intituled to the Youth of England*, trans. F. L. (1600)
Ovid, *Tristia*	Ovid, *Tristia*, trans. A.D. Melville (Oxford, 1992)
Page	Nadine Page, 'The public repudiation of Hero', *PMLA*, 50 (1935), 739–44
Painter	William Painter, *The Palace of Pleasure*, ed. Joseph Jacobs, 3 vols (Hildesheim, Germany, 1968)
Partridge	Eric Partridge, *Shakespeare's Bawdy* (1990)

PBSA	*Publications of the Bibliographical Society of America*
Peele	George Peele, *The Arraignment of Paris*, ed. R.M. Benbow, in *The Life and Works of George Peele*, gen. ed. Charles Tyler Prouty, 3 vols (New Haven, Conn., 1952–70), vol. 3
PG	Phyllis Gorfain, personal communication
PMLA	*Publications of the Modern Language Association*
Porter	Henry Porter, *The Pleasant History of the Two Angry Women of Abingdon* (1599)
PQ	*Philological Quarterly*
Prouty	Charles Prouty, *The Sources of Much Ado About Nothing* (New Haven, Conn., 1950)
Provenzano	Tom Provenzano, review of Plane production, *Theatre Journal*, vol. 52, no. 1 (2000), 118
Prynne	William Prynne, *The Unloveliness of Love-Locks* (1628)
Puttenham	George Puttenham, *The Art of English Poesy*, ed. Edward Arber (1906, reprinted Kent, Ohio, 1970)
R.C.	R[obert].C[leaver]., *A Godly Form of Household Government: For the Ordering of Private Families, According to the Direction of God's Word* (1612)
Rich	Barnaby Rich, *The Excellency of Good Women* (1613)
Ridley	M.R. Ridley, *Shakespeare's Plays: A Commentary* (1936)
Rimbault	E.F. Rimbault, 'Who was Jack Wilson?' (1846)
Ripa	Cesare Ripa, *Iconologia* (1593)
Rose	Steven Rose, 'Love and self love in *Much Ado About Nothing*', *EC*, 20 (1970), 143–50
Rossiter	A.P. Rossiter, 'Much Ado About Nothing', in *Angel with Horns* (1961), reprinted in *Shakespeare: The Comedies*, ed. Kenneth Muir (Englewood Cliffs, NJ, 1965), 47–57
RP	Richard Proudfoot, private communication
Schmidgall	Gary Schmidgall, *Shakespeare and Opera* (New York, 1990)
Scott	Mary Augusta Scott, 'The Book of the Courtyer: a possible source of Benedick and Beatrice', *PMLA*, 16 (1901), 476
SEL	*Studies in English Literature 1500–1900*
Sexton	Joyce Hengerer Sexton, 'The theme of slander in *Much Ado About Nothing* and Garter's *Susannah*', *PQ*, 54 (1975), 419–33
Sharpe	J.A. Sharpe, *Defamation and Sexual Slander in Early Modern England* (York, 1980)
Shattuck	Charles Shattuck, *The Shakespeare Promptbooks* (1965)
Shaw	*Shaw on Shakespeare*, ed. Edwin Wilson (New York, 1968)
Sidney, *Astrophel*	Sir Philip Sidney, *Astrophel and Stella* (1591)

Sidney, *Defence*	Sir Philip Sidney, *A Defence of Poetry*, ed. J.A. Van Dorsten (Oxford, 1966)
Smallwood	Robert Smallwood, 'Directors' Shakespeare', in Bate & Jackson, 176–96
Smith, 'Quarto'	John Hazel Smith, 'The composition of the Quarto of *Much Ado About Nothing*', Studies in Bibliography 16 (1963), 9–26
Snawsel	Robert Snawsel, *A Looking Glass for Married Folks* (1610)
SP	*Studies in Philology*
Spanish Tragedy	Thomas Kyd, *The Spanish Tragedy*, in *Works of Thomas Kyd*, ed. Frederick S. Boas (Oxford, 1901)
Spinrad	Phoebe Spinrad, 'Dogberry hero: Shakespeare's comic constables in their communal context', *SP*, vol. 89, no. 2 (1992), 161–78
SQ	*Shakespeare Quarterly*
SS	*Shakespeare Survey*
Statutes	*The Statutes of the Night* (1595)
Steed	Maggie Steed, 'Beatrice in *Much Ado About Nothing*', in Russell Jackson and Robert Smallwood (eds), *Players of Shakespeare: Further Essays in Shakespearean Performance* (Cambridge, 1993), 42–51
Straznicky	Marta Straznicky, 'Shakespeare and the government of comedy: *Much Ado About Nothing*', *SS 22* (1994), 141–71
Swinburne	A.C. Swinburne, *A Study of Shakespeare* (1880)
Tasso	Torquato and Ercole Tasso, *Of Marriage and Wiving: An excellent, pleasant, and philosophical controversy between the two Tassi*, trans. R.T. (1599)
Taylor, 'Introduction'	Gary Taylor, 'General introduction', in *TxC*
Taylor, M.	Michael Taylor, '*Much Ado About Nothing*: the individual in society', *EC*, 23 (1973), 146–53
Taylor, 'Proximities'	Gary Taylor, 'Theatrical proximities: the Stratford Festival 1998', *SQ*, 50 (1999), 334–54
Terry	Ellen Terry, *The Story of My Life* (1908)
Thompson & Thompson	Ann Thompson and John O. Thompson, *Shakespeare: Meaning and Metaphor* (Brighton, England, 1987)
Tilley	M.P. Tilley, *A Dictionary of the Proverbs in England in the Sixteenth and Seventeenth Centuries* (Ann Arbor, Mich., 1950)
Traugott	John Traugott, 'Creating a rational Rinaldo: a study in the mixture of the genres of comedy and romance in *Much Ado About Nothing*', *Genre*, vol. 15, no. 2–3 (1982), 157–81
TxC	Stanley Wells and Gary Taylor, with John Jowett and William Montgomery, *William Shakespeare: A Textual Companion* (Oxford, 1987)

Vickers   Brian Vickers, *The Artistry of Shakespeare's Prose* (1969)
Watson   Thomas Watson, *Ecatompathia* (1582)
W.B.   W.B., *The Court of Good Counsel, Wherein is set down the true rules, how as man should choose a good wife from a bad, and a woman a good husband* (1607)
Webbe   William Webbe, *A Discourse of English Poetry*, ed. Edward Arber (1871)
Weil   Herbert Weil, '"Be vigitant, I beseech you": a fantasia on Dogberry and doubling in *Much Ado About Nothing*', *Ben Jonson Journal*, 6 (1999), 307–17
Wells, 'Crux'   Stanley Wells, 'A crux in *Much Ado About Nothing*', *SQ*, 31 (1985), 85–6
Wells, 'Foul-paper' Stanley Wells, 'Editorial treatment of foul-paper texts: *Much Ado About Nothing* as test case', *Review of English Studies*, n.s. 31 (1980), 1–16
Wells, *Re-editing* Stanley Wells, *Re-editing Shakespeare for the Modern Reader* (Oxford, 1984)
What You Will   John Marston, *What You Will*, in *The Works of John Marston*, ed. A.H. Bullen, 3 vols (1887), vol. 2
White Devil   John Webster, *The White Devil*, in *Three Plays*, ed. D.C. Gunby (New York, 1972)
Wiles   David Wiles, *Shakespeare's Clown: Actor and Text in the Elizabethan Playhouse* (Cambridge, 1987)
Williams   Mary C. Williams, 'Much ado about chastity in *Much Ado About Nothing*', *Renaissance Papers* (1984), 37–45
Wilson   F.P. Wilson, *Shakespeare and the New Bibliography*, revised and ed. Helen Gardner (Oxford, 1970)
Woodbridge   Linda Woodbridge, *Women and the English Renaissance: Literature and the Nature of Womankind, 1540–1620* (Urbana and Chicago, 1984)
Wright   Louis B. Wright, *Middle-Class Culture in Elizabethan England* (Chapel Hill, NC, 1935)

MODERN STAGE, FILM AND TELEVISION PRODUCTIONS CITED

Alexander   RSC, Royal Shakespeare Theatre, Stratford-upon-Avon, directed by Bill Alexander, 1990
Barton   RSC, Royal Shakespeare Theatre, Stratford-upon-Avon, directed by John Barton, 1976
Boyd   RSC, Royal Shakespeare Theatre, Stratford-upon-Avon, directed by Michael Boyd, 1996
Branagh   Renaissance Films/Samuel Goldwyn Production, directed by Kenneth Branagh, 1993

Craig	Imperial Theatre, London, directed by Edward Gordon Craig, 1903–4
Dench	Renaissance Theatre Company, touring production, directed by Judi Dench, 1988
Donnellan	Cheek by Jowl, Playhouse Theatre, London, directed by Declan Donnellan, 1998
Doran	RSC, Royal Shakespeare Theatre, Stratford-upon-Avon, directed by Gregory Doran, 2002
Hands	RSC, Royal Shakespeare Theatre, Stratford-upon-Avon, directed by Terry Hands, 1982–5
Harvey	Shakespeare's Globe, London, directed by Tamara Harvey, 2004
Irving	Lyceum Theatre, London, and North American tour, directed by Henry Irving, 1884–5
Kaut-Howson	Royal Exchange, Manchester, directed by Helena Kaut-Howson, 1997
Monette	Stratford Festival Theatre, Stratford, Ontario, directed by Richard Monette, 1988
O'Brien	Old Globe, San Diego, California, directed by Jack O'Brien, 1995
Plane	East Los Angeles Classic Theatre, directed by Tony Plane, 1999
Scheie	Sinsheimer-Stanley Festival Glen, Shakespeare Santa Cruz festival, California, directed by Danny Scheie, 1988
Seer	Sinsheimer-Stanley Festival Glen, Shakespeare Santa Cruz festival, California, directed by Richard Seer, 1998
Tree	His Majesty's Theatre, London, directed by Herbert Beerbohm Tree, 1905
Trevis	RSC, Royal Shakespeare Theatre, Stratford-upon-Avon, directed by Di Trevis, 1988
Zeffirelli	BBC Television Production, directed by Franco Zeffirelli, 1967

INDEX